THE PRIORITY *of the* PERSON

THE BEGINNING AND THE BEYOND OF POLITICS

Series editors: James R. Stoner and David Walsh

The series is in continuity with the grand tradition of political philosophy that was revitalized by the scholars who, after the Second World War, taught us to return to the past as a means of understanding the present. We are convinced that legal and constitutional issues cannot be addressed without acknowledging the metaphysical dimensions that underpin them. Questions of order arise within a cosmos that invites us to wonder about its beginning and its end, while drawing out the consequences for the way we order our lives together. God and man, world and society are the abiding partners within the community of being in which we find ourselves. Without limiting authors to any particular framework we welcome all who wish to investigate politics in the widest possible horizon.

THE PRIORITY
of the PERSON

Political, Philosophical, and Historical Discoveries

DAVID WALSH

University of Notre Dame Press
Notre Dame, Indiana

Copyright © 2020 by the University of Notre Dame
Notre Dame, Indiana 46556
www.undpress.nd.edu

All Rights Reserved

Published in the United States of America

Library of Congress Cataloging-in-Publication Data

Names: Walsh, David, 1950- author.
Title: The priority of the person : political, philosophical, and historical discoveries / David Walsh.
Description: Notre Dame, Indiana : University of Notre Dame Press, 2020. | Series: The beginning and the beyond of politics | Includes bibliographical references and index.
Identifiers: LCCN 2020018430 (print) | LCCN 2020018431 (ebook) | ISBN 9780268107376 (hardback) | ISBN 9780268107383 (paperback) | ISBN 9780268107406 (adobe pdf) | ISBN 9780268107390 (epub)
Subjects: LCSH: Philosophical anthropology. | Persons.
Classification: LCC BD450 .W23755 2020 (print) | LCC BD450 (ebook) | DDC 126—dc23
LC record available at https://lccn.loc.gov/2020018430
LC ebook record available at https://lccn.loc.gov/2020018431

To my beautiful sisters,

Joan, Betty, Terry, Pat, and Maureen,

and to my irrepressible brother,

Bob, the best gift our parents left us.

CONTENTS

Preface ix

ONE   The Priority of the Person as the Modern
       Differentiation   1

       PART 1 The Political Discovery

TWO   Are Freedom and Dignity Enough?
       A Reflection on Liberal Abbreviations   29

THREE The Unattainability of What We Live Within:
       Liberal Democracy   53

FOUR   The Person and the Common Good:
       Toward a Language of Paradox   79

FIVE   John Rawls's Personalist Faith   103

SIX   Dignity as an Eschatological Concept   123

       PART 2 The Philosophical Discovery

SEVEN Voegelin's Path from Philosophy of
       Consciousness to Philosophy of the Person   139

EIGHT	The Turn toward Existence as Existence in the Turn	155
NINE	The Indispensability of Modern Philosophy	181
TEN	The Turn to the Subject as the Turn to the Person	195
ELEVEN	Why Kierkegaard Is the Culminating Figure of the Modern Philosophical Revolution	215

PART 3 The Historical Discovery

TWELVE	Epic as the Saving Truth of History: Solzhenitsyn's *Red Wheel*	237
THIRTEEN	Art and History in Solzhenitsyn's *Red Wheel*	257
FOURTEEN	The Person as the Opening to the Secular World: Benedict and Francis	269
FIFTEEN	Science Is Not Scientific	291
SIXTEEN	Hope Does Not Disappoint	303
	Notes	325
	Index	349

PREFACE

The title of the present work expresses its central assertion that the person, each person, is prior to all else that is. There is nothing higher in the universe or of greater worth. The person is the pivot around whom everything revolves. All that is meaningful in our lives flows from the persons we know and love. They are the ones without whom we cannot go on. Each is an inexhaustible depth in the whole of reality. We know it only because we glimpse the extent to which persons we know exceed all that we know about them. Words fail us when we try to define them, for they overflow all that even they can say or do. Each is a mystery in him- or herself, and just as unfathomable to themselves as to us. But this means that the language we use in our mastery of a world of things is defeated in the encounter with persons who unmaster us. The Thou who addresses me is a Who and not a What. How then are we to navigate the transition from someone to something, the most consequential negotiation of our lives? Somehow we must find a way to acknowledge the moral priority of the other over all the inclinations that might obscure that responsibility. To sustain our most crucial conviction we must find a way of articulating the metaphysical difference that establishes the radical priority of the person in being. As the missing category within the history of thought, the person who thinks is a decided latecomer to his or her own self-understanding. What we need to preserve the inexpressible dignity of persons is most impressed upon us as what we most need.

The project is formidable, and most of what is included under the rubric of *personalism* is merely an aspiration rather than an attainment of the goal. I am under no illusions concerning the challenge entailed in developing an account of the person that is adequate to the unique inwardness of each. Our linguistic reference to third parties must be displaced to accommodate the imperative of a second-person address. Some sense of the radical character of the project can be gained from my more systematic attempt in David Walsh, *Politics of the Person as the Politics of Being* (University of Notre Dame Press, 2016). When I completed it I was aware of the daunting nature of the task that readers had before them. They would have to follow the conceptual and linguistic overhaul I had attempted and then sprang upon unsuspecting readers. It struck me that there might be an easier and more accessible way, for the structure of *Politics of the Person* had not emerged fully born. Instead it had gestated over a number of years, and during that time I had been invited or drawn into other studies along the way. Naturally they were never divorced from the large theoretical goal of a philosophy of the person on which I had embarked. It was simply that they provided me with opportunities to think about what it means to be a person in a variety of more concrete contexts and in relation to other issues. As a result there was a series of personalist essays that had emerged in parallel with the theoretical statement and, in turn, contributed to the latter while also illuminating it in significant ways. In short, this book may present a more accessible inquiry into what it means to be a person because it is unfolded in dialogue with texts and controversies that are more specific. Some of the essays came from a time before I had decided to focus on the person, and some followed the conclusion of the major study. Looking back over them, I see that the intuition remained the same and that invitations to address questions of liberalism, the common good, and the work of Eric Voegelin, or to reflect on Solzhenitsyn, Benedict XVI, or the financial crisis of 2008 all provided an invaluable opportunity to broaden my thought beyond the boundaries I would otherwise have set for it. This book is, in other words, tangible proof that thinking is not and cannot be done alone, for it is ever and always in the company of others.

Among the others I would like to thank for making the book possible are the many friends who invited me to present my thoughts on the various occasions that provoked the chapters included here: Robert Kraynak, Glenn Tinder, Jude Daugherty, Chris McCrudden, Patrick Riordan, George Panichas, Barry Cooper, Thomas Heilke, John von Heyking,

Anton Rauscher, Fran O'Rourke, Charles Embry, Steve McGuire, R. J. Snell, Peter Haworth, Ralph Hancock, Dan Mahoney, Nathalia Solzhenitsyn, Ludmila Saraskina, Brendan Leahy, Rafa Garcia Perez, Martin Palous, and William Frank. They along with my other conversation partners in the Eric Voegelin Society, including but not limited to Ellis Sandoz, Chip Hughes, James Greenaway, Tilo Schabert, Wolfgang Leidhold, Lee Trepanier, James Stoner, Henrik Syse, Paul Caringella, Steve Ealy, Bruce Fingerhut, and others, have made it possible for me to think out loud, as we must, if we want to think at all. In addition, there are the more localized conversation partners, in Dublin and Washington, who have provided more regular opportunities for the mutuality of thought, including Brendan Purcell, Joe McCarroll, Brad Lewis, Claes Ryn, Dennis Coyle, Cyril O'Regan, John McNerney, Herb Hartmann, the late James Schall, and many others. They, along with my students, have been important in ways that in the moment none of us fully understands. More tangible and much appreciated financial support has been provided at various stages by the Earhart Foundation. I am grateful to Steve Wrinn, director of the University of Notre Dame Press, for his encouragement of the series, and also to the staff of UNDP, including Rachel Kindler and Matt Dowd, and to copyeditor Scott Barker. To my wife, Gail, I offer again my thanks for her love and constancy as we journey together along the way. With her I share the joy of our own flashes of transcendence, Katie, Brendan, and Patrick—and the glad sunbursts of grandchildren.

Permission to republish earlier versions of many of the essays included here is gratefully acknowledged. The following are the locations where they first appeared:

> "Are Freedom and Dignity Enough? A Reflection on Liberal Abbreviations." In *In Defense of Human Dignity*, edited by Robert Kraynak and Glenn Tinder, 165–91. Notre Dame, IN: University of Notre Dame Press, 2003.
>
> "The Turn toward Existence as Existence in the Turn." In *Philosophy, Literature, and Politics: Essays Honoring Ellis Sandoz*, edited by Charles R. Embry and Barry Cooper, 3–27. Columbia: University of Missouri Press, 2005.
>
> "The Unattainability of What We Live Within: Liberal Democracy." In *Die fragile Demokratie (The Fragility of Democracy)*, edited by Anton Rauscher, 133–56. Berlin: Duncker & Humblot, 2007.
>
> "Voegelin's Place in Modern Philosophy." *Modern Age* 49 (2007): 12–23.

"The Person and the Common Good: Toward a Language of Paradox." In *Human Destinies: Philosophical Essays in Memory of Gerald Hanratty*, edited by Fran O'Rourke, 618–46. Notre Dame, IN: University of Notre Dame Press, 2012.

"Art and History in Solzhenitsyn's *Red Wheel*." In *Life and Work of Aleksandr Solzhenitsyn: The Way to "The Red Wheel,"* edited by Ludmila Saraskina, 40–51. Moscow: Russian Literature Abroad Press, 2013.

"Dignity as an Eschatological Concept." In *Understanding Human Dignity*, edited by Christopher McCrudden, 245–58. Oxford: Oxford University Press, 2013.

"Epic as the Saving Truth of History: Solzhenitsyn's *Red Wheel*." In *The Human Voyage of Self-Discovery: Essays in Honour of Brendan Purcell*, edited by Brendan Leahy and David Walsh, 264–83. Dublin: Veritas, 2013.

"Hope Does Not Disappoint." In *Hunting and Weaving: Essays on Empiricism and Political Philosophy Honoring Barry Cooper*, edited by Thomas Heilke and John von Heyking, 252–71. South Bend, IN: St. Augustine's Press, 2013.

"Science Is Not Scientific." In *Faith and The Marvelous Progress of Science*, edited by Brendan Leahy, 107–20. Hyde Park, NY: New City Press, 2014.

"The Turn to the Subject as the Turn to the Person." In *Subjectivity: Ancient and Modern*, edited by R. J. Snell and Steven McGuire, 149–67. Lanham, MD: Lexington, 2016.

"Why Kierkegaard Is the Culmination of the Modern Philosophical Revolution." In *Christian Wisdom Meets Modernity*, edited by Kenneth Oakes, 1–20. London: Bloomsbury, 2016.

"The Person as the Heart of Benedict's New Evangelization." In *Religion und Politik in der freiheitlichen Demokratie*, edited by Klaus Stüwe, 19–37. Berlin: Duncker und Humblot, 2018.

CHAPTER ONE

The Priority of the Person as the Modern Differentiation

It may seem strange to suggest that there is a distinctly modern advance in human self-understanding. Our primary concern has been the exploration and exploitation of the external world, not interior self-deepening. We are most aptly captured in Walker Percy's inimitable phrase "lost in the cosmos." It suggests that in knowing more and more about the vastness of the universe we know less and less about the mystery each of us is. Yet even in that bursting of our bubble there is a heightened awareness of what has been lost. Perhaps this is why the modern world is so continually characterized by the search for the self who remains both present and absent throughout the search. Self-discovery narratives are our default discourse. We are so familiar with the ubiquitous self in search of itself that we tend to overlook the condition that sustains its possibility. That is, not the fleeting awareness of the self but the substantive reality of the person. Could it be that it is this metaphysical underpinning that has eluded the preoccupation with the self that has driven so much of modern thought? If it is, then the characterization of our world must appear quite differently. The turn to the interior murmurings of the self must then be viewed, not as a futile quest for a permanence never reached, but as the first glimpse of what escapes our fleeting awareness. Beyond the self is the person that is its reality. The endless journeying toward what continually recedes as we approach is only possible for what already contains the end and the beginning. The person is the whole.

That may not be a universally acknowledged understanding of the modern preoccupation, but it is the one toward which it inexorably points. The self that is lost in the cosmos may suffer disorientation, but it is already transparent for what is lost. Loss of self is only a possibility for a person who cannot ultimately be lost. In the language of the person, we know that it is only those who lose themselves that are found, just as those who die to themselves are raised to life. Transcendence is the medium in which the person is, for a person is transcendence. It is toward that realization that the inchoate stirrings of the modern philosophical revolution strain.[1] Before reaching such a glimpse of the person, the provisional attempts may appear hopelessly incoherent, for they can hardly declare what it is toward which they strive. The inquiry recognizes its goal only in the attainment. But that is what the self-transparence of history entails. There is no ready-made phenomenon available for investigation before the observer comes on the scene. The investigator is engaged in the investigation of him- or herself. History is not the history of some other entity of remote and tenuous connection with the present. It is the very meaning of what is present that is at issue. The person as the culminating reality of the whole is nowhere evident but in the moment of self-recognition that underpins the entire movement. It is thus not surprising that the obscure intuitions cannot easily be grasped before they have reached the disclosure of what underpins them in every phase. If history is the apocalypse of the person, then modernity is the moment of its realization. This is why, although the perspective of the person emerges in the preceding two centuries, its connection with the long preparation for it still remains to be clarified. We are often unsure whether to regard the discovery of the person as the culmination or renunciation of the premodern intimations that precede it.

Politics as a Response to the Discovery of Mind

Those intimations begin with the Greek discovery of mind. They are the ones who specify it as reason (*nous*), but a wider awareness of the individual is emergent in all of the Axial Age breakthroughs to the transcendent.[2]

Each human being is open to a divinity that is universally available. It is no longer one's position in the political hierarchy but one's inner capacity for reflection that is the decisive factor.[3] Greek thought, in particular, underlines this shift of authority from a publicly authorized claim to one that depends on the unique self-responsibility of the individual. Neither anointments nor appointments can supersede independent judgment and truth. Socrates stands as the great challenge to the collective authority of the city. He outweighs the whole. Something similar occurs with the Hebrew prophets, the Confucian sages, and the enlightened bodhisattvas. The rise of the individual is unmistakable, and becomes the point from which the modern elevation of the individual traces its beginning. Whenever we defer to the one who knows we acknowledge the priority of such singularity. Even the Greek for "person," *prosōpon*, originates within this setting in which the publicly enacted drama is taken as representative of the whole. The one stands for the many. The actor carries the mask that simultaneously reveals and conceals his identity. The region of the person has been opened. Previously, heroes had undertaken singular feats that were dimly sensed to be momentous for the whole community, but in Homer's depiction that invariably required a divine intervention. Now the self-determining individual has emerged in history with full responsibility for his or her action. This was a watershed event from which regression was largely unthinkable. Having discovered mind, the core of the person, we were unlikely to yield it up again.

At the same time it was difficult to find a place for mind, for the person, within the visible reality of politics. Rule would still be exercised in an externally organized mode as government disseminated order from the center to the periphery. It would be a long time before the last would be affirmed as first. Christianity would eventually find a way of making that recognition endure, but it too would struggle with its institutional realization. We might say that the history of the Church is defined by the tension between its hierarchical structure and its charismatic overflow. Recessive tendencies both in the Church and polity should not, however, be entirely attributed to the inertial forces that resist any historical opening. A large part of the difficulty can be attributed to the intellectual and linguistic overhaul that is required to make sense of the priority of the person within the whole. It is difficult to break with the instinctive subordination of the individual to the whole. That language of parts and wholes is very much on display in Aristotle's analysis of the beginning of the *polis*. "Individuals," he assures us, "are so many parts all equally depending on the whole," which is thus prior by nature.[4] Yet, almost immediately, Aristotle's unease with this designation of the individual as a part of a whole begins to manifest itself. Not only does the *polis* aim at the excellence of the individual, but even the possibility of an individual living outside the *polis*, either because of a lack or an excess of the requisite virtue, is contemplated. Such a one, Aristotle memorably remarks, is "either a beast or a god." By nature human beings are inclined to come together in a *polis* because they are not self-sufficient in themselves. Even then, however, when the natural status of the political association has been asserted, Aristotle posits a founding that is not within the same immanent realm. For "the man who first *constructed* such an association was nonetheless the greatest of benefactors."[5] In the end, it would appear that the individual contains the whole, as the Socratic founding of the city in speech of the *Republic* also attests. The difficulty is that there is no language adequate to this recognition of a part that is itself the whole in the most decisive respect of being able to conceive it.

It would be some time before even the character of the difficulty was admitted. St. Thomas Aquinas with a more avowedly transcendent perspective on the person could at least acknowledge the issue, even though he did not have a politically adequate means of articulating it. He still employed Aristotle's framework of parts and wholes while simultaneously noting the limits of its application. The individual cannot be subsumed to the role that he or she plays within the political whole because "the rationality of a part is contrary to the rationality of a person."[6] Eventually he declares more affirmatively that "man is not ordered to the body politic according to all that he is and has."[7] The person exceeds the whole of which he or she is a part because each is destined for union with God beyond all worldly associations. That may clarify the core principle that even in the classical thinkers had begun to emerge, but it does not advance a political conception congruent with it. At what point would the polity itself reach the recognition that each of its members is an inexhaustible center of meaning and value? That conviction would arise only in the difficult struggles through which a line of demarcation was drawn between the individual and the whole. There were certain things the individual could not be required to surrender to the realm and its ruler, no matter the imputed justifications. The "rights of man" or "natural rights" was not terminology employed by the schoolmen, but it was implicit in the right of conscience they customarily invoked. Frictions between the powerful and the powerless would have to progress much further before the imperative of rights that cannot be alienated would arise. Even in the hands of Hobbes and Locke, however, this was never rooted in mere subjective assertion. It arose from the common order that bound sovereign and subject and was, in essence, the mode by which its breach was resisted. The fruit of that historical rather than theoretical development was a clarification by which the person became the moral boundary of power. No individual could be treated merely as a means toward the collective advancement, for a whole that regarded its members as disposable would cease to be a whole of persons. Eventually Jacques Maritain would give it the paradoxical formulation that the political association is "a whole of wholes."[8]

The political union is one in which the part, the member, takes priority over the whole because each member means the whole to every other. We do not wish to belong if it means the loss or diminution of any one. Only an association that recognized the validity of the claim of each on the whole would be adequate to the responsibility persons place on us. As ends-in-themselves they supersede any other end of the whole. The challenge was to find a model that would clarify the relationship in which each subordinates him- or herself to the whole and yet is assured that each outweighs the interest of the whole. Mutual recognition of inalienable rights was the minimum invocation. To perceive its unfolding it would be necessary to enter into the reciprocal relationship by which alone persons enter into community with one another. Hegel delineated the first stage of this concretely ethical life as the family in which it is feeling that embraces each as an indivisible member of the whole.[9] But to articulate the mutuality at work it would be necessary to identify the rights of each that would eventually become the responsibility of everyone to uphold and preserve. Beyond the freedom and equality of civil society, the system of needs individually pursued, there would have to emerge the state that defined and guaranteed their reciprocity. A system of rights, it turned out, is not a recipe for atomistic individualism, but the summit of mutual respect by which persons hold and behold one another. A community of persons has no other purpose than the preservation of the persons that compose it. That does not ensure that individual self-sacrifice will never be necessary, but it does ensure that the community serves the persons it is pledged to preserve. Only the defense of the imprescriptible (inalienable) rights of others justifies the surrender of one's own, and redemption of that pledge is to be made only when everything has been done to minimize and avoid it. The sacrifice of the part for the whole must always be undertaken in such a way that it maximizes the reverence owed for that transcendent gift. The members outweigh the whole because each is a center of self-transcendence.

Rights and responsibilities may not so easily capture the depth of mutuality from which they derive, but that does not make their intuition any the less powerful. Indeed, terminological brevity may say more than a discursive unfolding could express. Its rightness seems to arise before any full consideration of its cogency. Practice seems to be in advance of theoretical underpinnings, a situation that is not so remarkable when one considers that reflection is always directed by what preexists it. The peculiar constraint under which theory labors may not be as fully apprehended as it might be, but it does work its inexorable effect. Theory cannot overstep the condition of its own possibility. It cannot provide an account of dignity and respect that fails to uphold the dignity and respect at which it aims. Truth and goodness cannot be defended without doing so truthfully and well. We are already committed to them, and take our stand within them, before we have taken a single step toward them. It is for this reason that the wisdom of politics is in advance of the theoretical apprehension of it, and any elaboration always contains less than the encompassing intimation from which it derives. It is therefore not so surprising that the political valuation of the person should precede the theoretical reflection on it. Through the struggles of common life the central notion of mutuality, as it is abbreviated in the language of rights, is glimpsed long before there is a theoretical framework adequate to its intuition. The long failure of the philosophical justification of liberal political principles, which does nothing to dislodge the conviction of their validity, is just what one would expect when theory also begins with the presuppositions of practice.[10] Reflection does not provide principles but discovers them as the imperatives to which it too must submit. When we live within the mutuality of respect that characterizes a community of persons, it takes a long time for the parameters of our life together to reach the clarity of the realization that persons are the horizon of our thought. Intuitively we know, however, that any account that begins from anything less than the priority of the person has already lost the thread by which it was held.

The primacy of the person is what we live by. To have rendered that conviction unmistakable is a singular moral advance, even if the philosophical rationale is limping far behind. Liberal politics is often disparaged as a house of cards incapable of mounting a coherent defense of its foundations.[11] Indeed, it is often touted as a nonfoundational enterprise. But what if this is not just an instance but the preeminent instance of the priority of practice to theory? Our intimations are ahead of our conceptualizations. The authoritative force of the liberal prioritization of the person over any collective purpose is so conclusive that it is no longer possible to suggest any scheme of subordination. No hint of superiority, by which one is to count less than another, can be allowed to stand. Recognition of inviolable dignity and respect provides a glimpse of the inexhaustibility that each human being is.[12] It is by living in relation to the imperative that we behold more fully the source of its moral hold on us. Even in an age when we lack the capacity to name the transcendence that marks the unfathomability of the person we are still compelled to concede that no human being ever reaches the limit of his or her worth.[13] In a world of unending calculation, the one thing that is incalculable is the person. The wealth of persons exceeds any digital summation.[14] Nowhere is that more authoritatively recognized than in the acknowledgment of imprescriptible rights. There alone we seem to affirm what remains contested in every other mode of discourse. It may no longer be possible to talk about the immortal soul of each person, the image of God within, but we continue to attest to the unconditional responsibility we owe one another. None can be regarded as replaceable or interchangeable, for each is an inexhaustible center of meaning and value. That is what we affirm when we accord limitless respect for rights and dignity that guard the unfathomability of each one. Jeremy Bentham may have hit the theoretical weak point of the practice when he declared natural rights to be "nonsense upon stilts," but he did not dislodge the impervious conviction that such a perspective is the only appropriate way to regard one another.[15] Anything less than infinite respect would eventually measure persons on the finite scale of commodities, replaceable and disposable. The practical distillation of human rights jurisprudence is the great moral achievement of our world. It is the way by which what would otherwise be invisible, the infinity of the person, is rendered visible.

The Person as Self-Transcendence

To be persuaded of the priority of the person as the distinctly modern differentiation, however, requires more than acknowledgment of its practical emergence. Conviction remains uncertain so long as it is shrouded in theoretical confusion. This has been the bane of the human rights regime because, as in the case of the UN Universal Declaration of Human Rights (1948), it deliberately avoids any appeal to foundations. It is for this reason that the language of rights has long been dismissed as nonsense, abstractions, and "rights-talk" utterly lacking coherence. Even the appeal to natural law seems to hold more promise than the bare enumeration of rights. It was only when rights became the basis for concrete movements of resistance that their abbreviated invocation was once again filled with the deeper resonances that ground community. Such was the case in the great crisis of slavery and later in the civil rights movement, as well as in the recurrent testaments of opposition and dissidence by which the powerless sought to resist the powerful.[16] Far from brittle shards of self-assertion, rights became the basis for the recovery of moral truth in a post-totalitarian world. The elasticity of the abbreviations, it turned out, could unfold a formidable spiritual arc. But those episodic disclosures of depth still did not amount to the theoretical elaboration that would ground the underlying conviction. For that a far more extended philosophical shift would have to take place. The individual, whose atomistic assertion of rights seemed to dominate, would have to withdraw. In its place would emerge the person who has no existence on his or her own but whose whole being is bound up with relationship to the other. Emmanuel Levinas's formulation that the other is closer to me than I am to myself would have to replace the Cartesian ego affirming itself. We would have to become convinced that there is no isolated self, no pure moment of the I without responsibility toward anyone else, for we carry the other within before we contain ourselves. When every I–Thou has signaled the displacement of the I, we realize that we are in a different conceptual horizon. The I strictly speaking does not exist. It only becomes aware of itself as it vanishes in the transcendence of itself. Metaphysics that seemed to favor the substance of the person must undergo a modulation to include the one who gives his or her substance away. When Kierkegaard, in *Either/Or*, depicts Judge William, with his ceaseless labor of caring for family and society, as the model, while the Seducer has irrevocably lost all that makes him a person, we realize that the notion of substance or core is not at all adequate to what a person is.[17] Could it be that the narrative of self-absorption by which modernity is conventionally viewed is largely mistaken? Would it not be the greatest irony if it was rather through the loss of self that the self has ultimately been regained? Only the example of Christ fully affirms the deepest secret of the suggestion.

That resonance may provide a thread that is all the more precious for its very invisibility in the long modern wandering that sets out from medieval nominalism. The loss of self seems to have already occurred in the nominalist turn away from reason as the link between man and God. Through successive ruptures, medieval wholeness arrives at the atomistic self that is pictured in Hobbes's *Leviathan*. Driven by passion and severed from a common moral order, the inhabitants of the state of nature can only recover reason through the fear of violent death that mutual suspicion evokes. They become rational because it is the only option that remains when life is reduced to a condition that is "solitary, poor, nasty, brutish and short." The pattern of Hobbes's construction is one that recurs over the succeeding centuries in which the collapse of a moral consensus is repeatedly confronted. Metaphysics has vanished in uncertainty and the unity of faith has been shattered. Whatever order is created must be one that can be sustained on the bare minimum of moral agreement. That is the goal of much of the modern philosophical unfolding.[18] It sets out to discover the inextinguishable core that remains when, as with Descartes, all that can be doubted has been doubted. Miraculously it appears there is such an immovable conviction in the human soul. It is Hobbes's reformulation of the Golden Rule that we ought *not* to do to others what we would *not* want done to us.[19] Life demands such an imperative by which we lay down our unlimited right to everything when others are so willing to renounce it too. We are willing to abide by a rule of law laid out by the sovereign to whom we have equally submitted. This is often misconstrued as the imposition of order by a sovereign power who possesses an unlimited capacity for violence. But that is a misreading of Hobbes's central point, that it is our mutual covenant with one another that withdraws us from the state of nature. Even in regard to the sovereign, it is not his power that gives him authority over us but our free submission to him.[20] The sovereign state for all of its supremacy has no other source than the acknowledgment of the obligation of the citizens to support it. Indeed, what other power is there but that which derives from consent? The power of coercion lasts only so long as coercion is applied. The Hobbesian state for all of its unaccountability does not escape the moment of accountability from which it begins. Its sovereignty is distinctly conditioned even if Hobbes has done everything possible to render the condition irreversible.

In doing so he has called attention to the extent to which human beings can bind themselves by a covenant that transcends their lives. Hobbes's anthropology may have demolished metaphysics and discredited faith, but his politics has restored them in the form of a commitment that attests to both. The kind of persons who can enter into an irrevocable covenant, one that, he emphasizes, is not a contract of convenience, are individuals who are capable of transcending themselves. They live in relation to obligations that exceed all interests and limits. The state, like every political community, could not even exist in the absence of the willingness of some to die so that all may not die. By virtue of their membership in this partnership they have abandoned the prerogative of questioning the wisdom of those who must order such a sacrifice. There is something harsh about the starkness of Hobbes's depiction of political necessity, but it is difficult to argue against its accuracy. It may derive from an extreme condition, but that is precisely what illuminates the essential. What redeems it is that Hobbes eventually goes beyond the mechanics of the negotiation by which we authorize a sovereign to decide upon the unavoidable and, indeed, to determine when it is unavoidable. Hobbes then takes the additional step of showing that this brings about a real unity of the citizens. In giving their individual consent they have become more than individuals. Now they are members of the whole, represented by one person of whose actions they have all become the authors. In a remarkable passage, Hobbes elevates the notion of a person as the only appropriate framework for this real unity. The nominalist who could not tolerate universals now regards the union of citizens as a real unity, not a purely notional one. He links this up with the very idea of the person, *prosōpon*, as the face or *persona* by which a person is represented, whether by himself or another: "A Multitude of men, are made *One* Person, when they are by one man, or one Person, Represented; so that it be done with the consent of every one of that Multitude in particular."[21]

A similar identification of the person as the pivot of political reality is provided by Hobbes's great liberal successor, John Locke. Here the personalist case may be even harder to make, given the charge of skepticism persistently lodged against Locke and his reputed installation of self-interest at the heart of the social contract. Neither accusation turns out to be true on closer inspection. It is notable that whatever skeptical implications might have been drawn from the *Essay Concerning Human Understanding*, they failed to trouble its author in the slightest. Despite his erosion of our notions of substance, immortality, and the moral law, Locke maintained his steadfast conviction in their ultimate truth.[22] His failure to demonstrate their validity did not in the slightest diminish his regard for the imperative of justice within which we live. He had no difficulty in erecting a political compact on the basis of the mutual recognition of rights that is obligatory on all human beings in the state of nature. Far from an anarchic pursuit of self-interest, his state of nature was marked by the sense of community derived from what we already owe to God on behalf of ourselves and one another. We are God's property, as Locke phrased it, and are answerable to him for the preservation of ourselves and of others. By contrast, it is those who violate the moral law that set themselves outside the bounds of the community that is the mark of humanity. Throughout, it is Locke's revulsion at those who would abrogate the life and liberty of others that is the principal provocation of his thought. We might say that in Locke the inviolability of liberty becomes the most crucial dimension of human life. Without the freedom to govern themselves, persons lose what cannot be lost. Whether he is inveighing against Filmer's *Patriarcha* or extolling the centrality of freedom in his own *Thoughts on Education*, Locke is determined to underline the core that marks the dignity of a human being. For a thinker who seemed to have jettisoned any notion of substance a very substantive reality seems to be always at stake. Locke's thought turns on the idea of the person even if his philosophy has not caught up to it.

The closest convergence occurs in Locke's *Letter Concerning Toleration*.[23] There the prospect of coercion in a realm so profoundly interior to the person provokes his sharpest assertion of the personalist mandate. The argument is interwoven through several layers in which the difference between a church and a commonwealth form a preliminary approach. But then in a central passage he suddenly drops the whole apparatus he had been developing to declare "the principal consideration" that decides the question for him. It has nothing to do with the different membership circles to which we may belong, but simply and solely with the nature of faith itself. Faith, he insists, is an inner movement of assent that can only occur if it is entirely uncoerced. Even if the magistrate were to point me in a truly evangelical way, "if I be not thoroughly persuaded thereof in my own mind, there will be no safety for me in following it." Above all the uncertainties of religion there is one point of certainty, "that no religion which I believe not to be true can be either true or profitable unto me." Beyond all the differences of opinion and conviction between human beings, we recognize, Locke insists, the unassailable independence of each person. The right of conscience has long been regarded as a part of Christian dogma, but it had not itself become a dogma until then. Even today we can be taken aback by the blunt declaration that religious liberty is the fount of all other liberties, one to which the Church itself is committed even before it is committed to its own principle of divine authority.[24] Locke had proclaimed, in the opening statement of the epistle, that "tolerance is the mark of the true Church," a remark that is still shocking in its novelty. Such is the transposition of the meaning of "toleration" that the text accomplishes. Where previously it had the negative connotation of what is tolerated as a grudging concession, now it has assumed the positive tonality of what is higher than any content. The person precedes all that he or she may hold. The entire moral authority of Locke's principle derives from our realization that the person is prior to all that separates us. In recognizing the person, we are already committed to the integral freedom by which each determines his or her own existence. Even God, indeed God most of all, affirms the inviolability of the response. He acknowledges the person who transcends all that is done or said. That is the nature of the friendship that Jean Bodin was able to affirm a century earlier, in a letter to a friend, separated from him by the bitterly contested differences of the French wars of religion.[25]

The language of rights has in such cases been surpassed by the language of the person. We recognize in the other, not a holder of rights whom we must accommodate, but the other who simply *is* beyond the differences between us. We are united by what divides us because the divisions have been surmounted by the mutuality of persons who are, in that instant, friends. A plurality of perspectives has compelled us to confront the mutuality of persons beyond them. When almost nothing is shared there is still the other in otherness for whom I too am an other. The transcendence of the person comes into view, and we recognize it as the basis of all community. Notions of rights and reciprocity are a limping acknowledgment of that realization even if they do not provide their own condition of possibility. That remains the interpersonal reality that is, not so much a mystical unity behind all saying, as Eric Voegelin suggested, but the precondition of all saying.[26] We know one another apart from all that is said, and we would scarcely be able to grasp what is said without that awareness. Persons know one another as persons because they are known in themselves. Nothing can contain the person but the person him- or herself. To be present to the other is to be present to what transcends all presence. That elusiveness of the person may challenge our linguistic ability, but it is not for all of that mysterious. It is the common experience of everyone we know. Each, we recognize, is more than what can be said by or about him or her. The person in every instance has no identity but in him- or herself, for any putative identification would fall short of who they are. The reality of the person is irreducible, for it cannot be known in terms of anything but itself. It is the ground of being that is beyond being. Each is a new beginning and each matters as if he or she were the whole world, as indeed they are, when seen through the eyes of love.[27]

What is striking is that, when language has reached its limits, the abbreviations of politics succeed in saying what cannot be said. Each human being, as an inexhaustible center of the universe, is incommensurate with every measure. It is the intuition of the priority of the person that sustains the tension that continues to unfold between our fragmentary anthropologies and the humanist faith of our philosophy and our politics. The pattern, exemplified by Locke, of the simultaneity of psychological atomization and political reaffirmation is widely repeated. This is why David Hume can be regarded as a conservative skeptic, one who does everything to undermine the integrity of the human soul and yet upholds it within the sustaining horizon of tradition.[28] Perhaps the limit is reached in Adam Smith, who reflects so successfully without reference to an interior self that he shows how seeing ourselves through the eyes of others is sufficient to sustain the human community. He has reached what Thomas Pfau calls "sentiment without agency."[29] The effort to find in sentiment the rationality of a self that can nowhere be found within it, and thus to ground a common moral order within the episodic setting of consciousness, had reached its limit. Yet it would be hard to conclude that Smith perceived his project in such hopeless terms. On the contrary, he, as did Locke and Hume, preserved his faith in the integrity of the person that had become all but invisible. When everything we human beings do had been reduced to a role in the great theatrical spectacle of society, there ceased even to be anyone left to contemplate it. To exercise judgment would, after all, be to stand apart from the mutual display. There would have to remain that undisplayed self, preserved within itself. Perhaps it was Smith alone who stood within the transcendent perspective, contemplating it under the aspect of eternity that is the condition of all knowledge. But then we realize that all of the social actors carry the same capacity within them. To put themselves on display there must be a self who is not on display. The mask must be carried by one who is not the mask. In acting they put themselves in place of the other, seeing themselves as others see them, and in the process they demonstrate a capacity to go beyond all that can be seen. When I put myself in place of the other I transcend myself. Surely the problem for Smith is not that he had lost the notion of the self, but that he had never fully realized the impossibility of attaining what we live within. The self can never be known. It can only be glimpsed.

The Person as the Horizon of Thought

To unravel that paradox would require theoretical resources beyond the limits of a faculty psychology. The spectator viewpoint of British empiricism would have to be left behind in order to take on board the insight that became the basis for Kant's great reflection and for the stream of German idealism that flows out of him.[30] That is, the realization that the observer cannot observe himself. Kant understood more clearly than any of his predecessors that reason cannot ground itself without presupposing itself. There is thus no way for it to validate its knowledge of reality as if it could stand apart from itself. Certainly, it could not compare its account of the world with any independently existing state of affairs. All that it could do is recognize this peculiar condition of self-limitation, become aware or critical of itself, and thereby avoid the more massive illusions to which it is prone. It could declare that its knowledge was confined only to appearances, never to things-in-themselves. Once again that seemed to suggest a skeptical outcome, especially once it is realized that all knowledge is confined to the realm of appearances within space and time. What lies beyond our immediate experience, all that was previously designated by metaphysics, cannot be known at all. Only the suspicion that the knowledge of such limits is already a presentiment of what lies beyond them injected a more expansive possibility into Kant's thought. Although he never fully capitalized on that intuition in his theoretical reflections, he did considerably enlarge its reach within his practical philosophy.[31] The self that could not be known beyond phenomenal presentation would become the bearer of a moral imperative that transcended all else in the universe. Duty became imprescriptible because any lesser notion of obligation could hardly be obligatory. When the only unqualified good in the universe is a good will, we have an unqualified obligation to uphold it. The categorical imperative that imposes itself upon us before we have had a chance to weigh the hypothetical goals that might be served, and certainly prior to any consideration of our own fulfillment or happiness, is the pure distillation of duty. It can hardly even be duty if it is not perceived as binding for its own sake. In this reflection we are not too far away from the realization that the obligation that reaches us before we have had a chance to weigh our interests points toward the self that is prior to the self. A categorical imperative implies a person who can be grasped by a primordial obligation. Before there is a self, the self has transcended itself. Of course, Kant did not articulate those deeper intimations of his thought that lead toward the metaphysical status of the person as beyond being. But he did acknowledge such metaphysical ramifications in the course of his moral reasoning. He recognized that the self that could initiate such utterly selfless action was marked by an opening of freedom prior to all determining causality. It could weigh its actions in relation to an immortal perspective that reached its culmination in a transcendent

God. These were his famous postulates of God, immortality and freedom, that, despite our inability to ground them in theoretical reflection, turned out to be indispensable in delineating the interior of our practical life. Only a person who transcended all finite existence could respond to the unconditional call of morality.

That was the implication taken up by Kant's idealist successors, even if they did not embrace the centrality of the person as such. They tended rather to employ correlative terms, such as "ego" or "spirit" or "process," that remained susceptible to interpretation in nonpersonalist language. But their intention was to capture the fluid dynamic within which the person moves and for that reason cannot be adequately apprehended. It is well known that the term "personalism," coined by Schleiermacher, originates within these circles and from there reaches into the broader streams of the Romantics and transcendentalists.[32] Hegel might not have employed the language of the person in any extended way, but he did elaborate on the movement that is the essence of the person. As one who ever transcends himself, as one who is ever beyond what he or she has said, the person is marked by transcendence. The person can know itself only as the movement that is never available, even to itself, for contemplation and analysis. This is why Hegel inaugurates such a different philosophical syntax. No longer discoursing about static entities, he emphasizes that truth is to be grasped in the movement, for truth itself is the movement toward truth.[33] What a person is, therefore, is disclosed most faithfully in the going beyond itself by which it aims at truth. Contrary to the misconception that this represents either the dissolution of the self into the movement or its incorporation within the closed dynamic of the system, Hegel's construction can more accurately be seen as a faithful unfolding of the person within a whole that it perceives and yet never fully reaches. The end of history is not a moment in time but the very possibility of time. It is the still point that the person occupies and yet does not occupy. This is the strange paradox by which, in going beyond ourselves, we begin in a particular place while knowing that that is not our place. The person contains the whole and is contained by it. That is the possibility of its life. It is perhaps not so surprising that the very last topic on which Hegel labored before his death was the challenge of the so-called ontological proof. That is, he was meditating on the horizon of God as the horizon of his own thought.[34]

It was a consummate portrayal of the possibility of the person who is not only part of a whole but the part that grasps its own openness to the whole. A new kind of philosophical language would be required to say what could not be said directly, but only shown in the movement of thought itself. Schelling's "Aphorisms" became a widely emulated model. Throughout, they emphasize their radical departure from the Cartesian "I think" that seems to place the thinker at the center of the universe.[35] The dead end reached by the Enlightenment, of the thinker who could no longer comprehend himself from this starting point, had become widely recognized. Kant had raised that realization to the breaking point without himself fully grasping the consequence. In Goethe's perceptive observation, Kant "resolutely limits himself to a certain circle, and constantly points ironically beyond it."[36] A philosophical revolution was required, or was already underway, by which thought would no longer assert its own separation from being but acknowledge its continuity with being. The meaning of Parmenides's most famous fragment, itself an aphorism, was becoming apparent: "To think and to be are one and the same."[37] But it was also becoming clear that both thinking and being are inseparable from the person disclosed within them. Revelation could not entail anything other than the person who reveals. The notion of revelation is interchangeable with the notion of the person. No longer would the Parmenidean designation of being be adequate to what had always been glimpsed as beyond being. Schelling was the one who in his late lectures, which are still insufficiently absorbed by our conventional narrative, transformed the history of mythology into the process of disclosure that culminates in the divine self-revelation: "In the creation he shows, in particular, the power of his Spirit; in Salvation, the power of his heart. This is what I meant when I said that Revelation—or the deed which is the content of Revelation—is his personal act."[38] The only relationship we can have with God is a personal one, for it is impossible to know a person in any other way.[39]

In that realization we are so clearly in the region of Kierkegaard that we scarcely need to be reminded of his attendance at those lectures. He had come to Berlin to learn about the new opening of philosophy by Schelling, but he left disappointed that it had not gone far enough. From that point on, the impossibility of philosophizing apart from the personal horizon had become apparent. *Either/Or*, the magnum opus by which Kierkegaard burst on the literary scene, establishes a new genre of philosophic discourse. It turns resolutely away from the framework of conceptual distance to insist that nothing could have meaning unless it had meaning for me. The personal horizon had become the ineluctable modality of thought. Concepts were only of relevance if they were related to how I am actually going to live. The either/or was the inescapable locus of it all. Kant's prioritization of practical reason over theoretical had reached its denouement in the prioritization of the person, in his or her concrete existence, over all other considerations. Nothing could come before it. Kierkegaard's dramatization of the shift was so powerful that it shaped the overarching philosophic movement of the twentieth century. We know it most commonly under the label "existentialism," however ill-fitting that rubric was regarded by many of those associated with it. They understood that "existence" was too conventional a term to indicate the novelty of what was envisaged. Heidegger and Jaspers played with its hyphenation as "ek-sistenz" to suggest that it went far beyond mere actuality. It betokened the capacity to hold and behold actuality, the very movement by which in acting we go beyond what we are. The philosophic tradition lacked an available term for the kind of entity that is not really an entity. Heidegger employed the German word "Dasein" to denote that which is not simply a being because it can hold itself apart from being. What he meant by it is what we ordinarily know as the person, the one who in him- or herself we know as outside of all that they say and do. The convergence with the liberal elevation of the person, as the inexhaustible pivot of all things, was virtually complete.

All that was missing was recognition of the conjunction that had taken place. Certainly Heidegger did not acknowledge his affinity with the liberal veneration of the rights and dignity of the individual. Nor did the liberal political tradition evince much awareness of its own genesis within the opening of the person unfolded in modern philosophy. Yet there were voices that mooted such a realization. This was particularly the case among those who understood themselves as personalists, even if they did not consistently invoke that term. Thomas Pfau has demonstrated that Coleridge, a crucial British link with the idealists, was such a figure. In his poetry and reflections, Pfau has shown, we find the genesis of the radical decentering of self that was later initiated by Martin Buber's "I and Thou" and culminated in Levinas's affirmation of the other as having taken all precedence over me. The idea of the person as relational, with all of the implications of a primordial openness to others, was in the process of formation. What Kant understood as the movement of reason's self-critique, Coleridge designated as the ontological reality of the person, of the one for whom confession of falling short is both a possibility and a necessity. It would be unthinkable outside of the relationship to the other to whom it is owed, as suggested in the *Rime of the Ancient Mariner*. Pfau states, "The language of the witness—unreservedly oriented toward *and* met by its addressee—establishes a *communion* whose very possibility hinges on the joint presence of the three theological virtues identified by Aquinas: faith, hope, and charity."[40] The distinction between a person and a thing that had formed so central a theme in Coleridge was taken up by a wide variety of figures, from John Henry Newman to Walt Whitman. The banner of "personalism" flowed into the well-known figures of the twentieth century for whom it eventually became, in the hands of Karol Wojtyla, the principal philosophic basis for an account of human dignity. Even John Rawls began his intellectual odyssey within the framework of a personalist-relational account of human society.[41] The only thing that separates him from a more contemporary personalist, such as Robert Spaemann, is that the latter is convinced that the distinction "between someone and something" is a more reliable foundation to dignity and respect than the more formalized agreements Rawls came to favor.[42] Without surveying the multiple strands that weave the personalist garment, we may concede that they meet in the realization that the person exceeds the whole by virtue of the capacity to transcend itself on behalf of the whole. Rights and dignity are accorded to persons who are ends-in-themselves beyond the whole.

That is the conviction that guided the liberal invocation of rights as inalienable and indivisible. The rights of one cannot be abrogated without jeopardizing the rights of all. In that realization we behold the outline of the personalist affirmation of community. Far from being individual claimants, we are already implicated in responsibility for the rights of others. What had always been lacking in such a liberal exposition was an acknowledgment of the ontological condition of its possibility—the person as one who, in claiming for him- or herself claims for all others, had yet to be perceived as a movement of transcendence that opens mutuality. A personalist elaboration was so strongly intuited that its aspiration was often taken as its attainment. Confusion of wish and fulfillment came to so characterize what was called "personalism" that it often failed to acknowledge the extensive linguistic overhaul that would be required. If we were to talk, not *about* the person, but *out* of the person, then we would have to abandon the usual mode of discourse about things. It would no longer do to acknowledge the necessity of treating persons differently and then continue to speak about them in the language of things. This is especially problematic when our theoretical-analytic language has been developed precisely to sustain the objectivity of the I–It relationship. A significant readjustment is required to acknowledge that when we discourse about persons, the possibility of mastery has become impossible. It is not we who master persons, but persons who master us.

Without this admission we wander into the quagmire into which discussions of the definition of the person have led us. The one realization never reached is the recognition that we do not define others but that others define us. In relation to persons, the priority on which science launches us has been overturned. The person is prior and exceeds all definition. We know this in our ordinary relationships with persons, for we know each one as unique, irreplaceable, and incommunicable, knowable only in him- or herself and not in anything else. A personalist account of persons would have to take seriously its beginning in the moral precedence we acknowledge. Just as we cannot talk about truth or goodness without remaining faithful to them, so we cannot talk about persons apart from the responsibility we already bear toward them. The person is prior in every sense.

The Person as Beyond Being

When the person has become the horizon within which our thinking occurs, then we cannot think about the person as a thing. The other is never an object for me. I cannot survey and master the reality of the other, but I find myself unmastered in the encounter. The observer status has been displaced when I am being observed. It is quite unlike the dominance that marks our knowledge in all other areas, for we are known before we know. Where usually I can place myself at the center of the gaze I turn toward the world, now I have lost my primacy to find myself in an eccentric viewpoint. The displacement is radical and irrevocable. Our only chance of regaining equilibrium is to submit to the gaze of the other, greeting it with the maximum empathy of which I am capable. Something like this is what accounts for the amazing social photography of Sebastião Salgado.[43] It is the deep sympathy of the photographer for those whose image he captures that transforms objectification into an opening of mutuality. All artists know that they can only enter into the characters they create by discovering what is lovable about them. It is only with the heart that one sees rightly, as the Little Prince observed.[44] Even when the other is wholly created it is not simply a form of self-expression, for what renders the character worthy of thought is the extent to which it is other than the creator. James Joyce surely loved Leopold Bloom, and Aleksandr Solzhenitsyn was similarly drawn to Ivan Denisovich. Through his prioritization of the other the author could manage to give so much of himself, more even than he thought he possessed, to one who is merely a creature of imagination. Sympathy is the bond that opens knowledge of the other. In art we bear responsibility toward the purely imaginary other, and thereby create an other that is not purely imaginary. This is why Don Quixote is so real. If he has not been loved into existence, he has certainly been loved into reality.

Love is generative in all respects, not simply sexual. It is what affirms the priority of the other to whom I have yielded place. To the extent that responsibility structures our relationship to the other it reorients our relationship to reality as a whole. I am no longer at the center. I have been displaced. Even the question of how I know this must be gingerly approached, for we do not seek to reverse the precedence in a new bid for comprehension that will again place me at the center. Instead we must take on board the profound consequences of a personalist philosophy which consists not so much of invoking the centrality of the person as of living it out. Our thinking too must accept its responsibility in prioritizing the other. The revision is more far-reaching than anticipated, and the difficulty of relinquishing accustomed patterns of thought is formidable. It is no wonder that personalism slipped so frequently into the reifying patterns it abhorred. To avoid such backsliding we must be armed with more than good intentions. We must be ready to acknowledge the profound readjustment required. Knowledge must abandon its monopoly of authority when it recognizes its own emergence from a knowledge that precedes it. More ancient than consciousness, and certainly than self-consciousness, is the obligation that is present before it. Whether an idea, a transcendental, or an a priori, our knowledge proceeds by virtue of that within which its thinking is possible. But this entails a consequence that our whole tradition has intimated without ever fully confronting, namely, that our knowledge cannot include knowledge of the condition of its own possibility. We are, of course, not ignorant of such adumbrations, for their identification as ideas or transcendentals is an attempt at comprehension. It is that the attempt ultimately falls short of its target and that this is not in any sense a defeat. It is the condition of that which derives its possibility from beyond itself and in that finds its supreme foundation. The unmastery that the other effects on my thinking is not in any sense a defect or a weakness but the point of maximum clarity. It is precisely in yielding place to the other that I transcend myself most completely and live most fully in attunement with the transcendent horizon that frames me. There is good reason to suggest that along with the prioritization of the good, the true, and the beautiful, we should add the person as the ultimate priority beyond them.

Just as knowledge consists in putting ourselves in the place of what we want to understand, so its highest form is reached in the most total forgetting of self. Even in regard to the nonhuman we can ask what it is like to be a bat, in Thomas Nagel's famous example.[45] Nagel sought to underline the distance that exists, but it is hard not to argue that, even in raising the question, he had begun to shorten it. We know a little better what it is like to be a bat even if we cannot become a bat. Only by putting ourselves in place of the bat do we know how different the bat is. The one thing we know less about is what it is like to be Thomas Nagel. Yet in a strange way we know all about him. We know that he is capable of reaching out toward all other beings precisely because he is capable of setting himself aside. We know him as a person. But neither he nor we could claim that we have thereby reached any definitive or exhaustive understanding of who he is. The person whom we know and the person who knows remain at the periphery of our knowing. This is not because the person is peripheral but because each one is the container within which all thinking about persons occurs. Knowing each, apart from all that is said or done, they are known only in their unique irreducible personhood. Rather than constituting a species, each is a species whose membership is limited to one.[46] We are in a realm where that which includes all cannot be included within it, much as with the problems to which Aristotle adverted in assimilating being with genus. The person who can contemplate being is similarly beyond being. Such is the awesome capacity of the person to set itself aside that there is nothing in being it may not come to know. A more compelling instantiation of the transcendence of being can hardly be adduced. It is so powerful that we might be inclined to wonder how we come to know persons at all. The reason this is not such an obstacle is that it is persons and persons alone who know persons as such. To be a person is to know what it means to be a person, more clearly in others than in ourselves. We do not ask "What is it like to be a person?" because that is the very beginning of all our questioning. But for that very reason we cannot say what it is like to be a person.

The blind spot, of which our whole intellectual tradition has been persistently aware, is that it cannot assume mastery of the very categories indispensable to its own operation. To the extent to which we have placed ourselves at the center of things we have failed to grasp the extent to which the center has eluded us. We cannot apprehend what is central. The best we can do is follow Hölderlin's advocacy of the "eccentric path" by which we glimpse that wherein we are held. We do not behold what it means to be a person, but we do glimpse it in passing as we live out the primordial responsibility placed upon us. This is why it is in the face of the other, to use Levinas's formulation, that we see most clearly who we are. What we cannot view from outside we know with certainty from within. That does not translate into an account of the person, even of the kind that would form the basis for a philosophical anthropology, but it does provide the bedrock for all serious insight into what the person is. We know more than we can say, and this arises, not from a shortage of data, but from a superabundance of it. The inexhaustibility of the person remains, no matter how exhaustive the inventory. And resort to the universal categories that any intellectual discipline must follow is found to be redundant in light of the uniqueness that each person is. When dealing with a species that defeats the idea of a species we are better served by adhering to the singularity that in every instant remains. Kierkegaard in hewing closely to the imperative of living comes closest to the formulation when he declared, in relation to Abraham, that "the individual exceeds the universal." Not even the universals of ethics could in the final resort apply when the judgment must be made in the unique instance. The person who responds to the call of the person is more than can be said. It may well be that every ethical order will confront the limit of its application, but the decision about it cannot be included within its rules. Only the person who stands outside of all norms can determine the point at which they must be exceeded or overturned. The rupture of all that is routine and expected is inseparable from the idea of the person. Each is a new beginning, a flash of transcendence from outside of time.

The challenge has always been to find the means of retaining awareness of the unrepeatable that constitutes each person. In the Greek discovery of mind, of *nous*, the person as the unique source of authority had emerged, but it was quickly repressed as the universality of a faculty. Even though it had a beginning in a unique person, Socrates, whose refusal to write attests to the impossibility of one person thinking for another, the results were nevertheless handed on as if they could be externally received. This was the subject of more than a few jokes in which Socrates plays along with the illusion that by sitting close to Agathon he could become wiser.[47] Mind, the equal independent rationality of each individual, had been discovered, but it had been promptly forgotten as a personal reality. The possession of a rational nature was touted without adverting to the challenge of actually exercising it. Plato's dialogues still retain awareness of the impossibility of communicating without the personal grasp of what is entailed. Mere repetition, the bane of institutional education, could so easily masquerade for the reality. Even today we have difficulty recognizing that science exists nowhere, not in institutes, or proceedings or prizes, but only in minds capable of grasping it. Aristotle exemplifies a mind in operation, but the challenge of transmitting it is either no longer of interest or is eclipsed by interest in the problems themselves. Mind had begun the long march of self-forgetfulness that is occasionally disturbed by the suspicion of being lost in the cosmos. The slide is only interrupted when the imperative of a personal response is again prompted by the advent of Christ. As Socrates did not, Jesus too did not write anything, thereby placing all of his emphasis on the question he poses to the apostles: "Who do you say that I am?" After Peter confesses him to be Christ, the Son of the living God, Jesus observes that it is not flesh and blood that has revealed it to him but "my Father who is in heaven" (Matt. 16:13–20). The recognition turns on the same openness to the transcendent as is present in Christ. Only a person can glimpse what cannot be seen.

Yet even the great opening to interiority in Christianity could not forestall its eventual occlusion in the specification of dogma. St. Paul exposed the inner conflict between what he wills and what he fails to will, and St. Augustine narrated the interior turning around that is the event of his conversion. But that was not enough to hold onto the idea of the person as a relation of inwardness. Despite the formidable effort of Augustine to articulate the mutual self-giving that is the life of the Trinity, with all of its enormous implications for our understanding of what a person is, he was aware that even there the language of the person was already slipping away. *Prosōpon* had been replaced by *hypostasis*, or "substance," in the dogmatic formulations.[48] The opening of interiority in the *Confessions* would remain as a towering example, but it could no longer be integrated within a personalist horizon. Truth, especially in its definitional form, had overtaken the experiential arrival at it. Of course, devotional life would continue to be sustained by the indispensability of prayer, an inescapably personal event, but it would be only remotely connected with the articulation of its meaning. The Scholastics did not lack an interior life, but they could not readily connect it with the form of disputation their thinking had assumed. The flowering of late medieval mysticism would signal the rupture of experience from theology, a development with enduring consequences. Persons, with their transcendent longings, remain, and, though some are able to find their home within the institutional home of religion, many wander in search of a spiritual fulfillment they are hard-pressed to locate. Out of this arises radical Islam of today, just as the millenarian mystical anarchists did, and apocalyptic revolutionaries of all stripes. The readiness of persons to transcend themselves is turned toward the implacable destruction of persons. Absent is any awareness that those who are killed are persons too. All military killing requires such dehumanization of the enemy, but ideology and religion elevate it to another level.

The lethality of human beings without a concept of the person is on full display. This is why the recovery of the person as the horizon of all of our thinking and acting is of such significance. But neither classical nor traditional models can be so easily adopted to the purpose, given their modulation away from the inwardness in which the other is encountered. This was the inspiration that lead to the rise of personalism, including the term itself, in the nineteenth century. The clear distinction between I–Thou and I–It relationships is an important step in the process, but it should not be taken as its culmination. For one thing it still operates with the pseudo-objectivity that holds both relations at a distance, as if we could master the distinction itself. A far deeper journey must be undertaken if we are to gain the philosophical perspective that is required to confess that the person takes priority over all of existence. We must be prepared to follow the implication that the person is beyond being. To say such a thing seems contrary to all of the established conventions of our metaphysics. How can we discourse about that which is known only by transcendence? Presence must be replaced by absence as the abiding tonality. We begin to see the stretching of philosophical boundaries as more extensive than we thought, as it is in Levinas's insistence that ethics is prior to ontology. What is to become of an ontology that is thus a latecomer to the scene? But rather than despair of rendering a post-Heideggerian account coherent, we should recall that the problems are not of purely recent vintage. The re-elaboration of a personalist account of persons long predates the emergence of the term. Even Descartes, with his incoherent attempt to anchor the I in the I, is nevertheless instructive. In that way we might reread the history of modern philosophy, and all of the return to the Greek and Christian beginnings, as an attempt to develop what Kierkegaard finally acknowledged as a language of paradox.[49] When we must talk about that which cannot be talked about, then we must adopt a syntax that promptly overturns itself. The person who exceeds everything in the universe also exceeds all that can be said about him or her. Only God can adequately pronounce the name of the other.

The chapters that follow are an attempt to acknowledge the priority of the person that not only affirms the principle but continually submits to its imperative. All talk about persons must be within the arc of reverence owed to persons. It is the exact contrary movement to Thomas

Nagel's *Mind and Cosmos*, which cannot find a place for mind precisely because it begins with the dominance of materiality. Nagel is a sufficiently sensitive thinker to be able to note the contradiction that a materialist account can find no place for the mind that grasps it. A vague intimation of spirit is hardly enough to dispel the massively physical. Only the priority of the person, not as an abstraction but as the flesh-and-blood reality that is not simply flesh and blood, is sufficiently weighty to dislodge the sense that even thought is epiphenomenal.[50] The challenge of calling forth an alternative worldview to reductionistic materialism is more formidable than we are inclined to admit. Nagel is a fine example of one who feels the imperative but is powerless to respond. He is of course a useful ally, but he can provide no tangible assistance without acknowledging that the awareness of the other is prior to all awareness we have. What we owe to persons precedes all that we can say about them. The person is the horizon to science and also reflection on it. Nagel exemplifies this insight but he cannot grasp it. A particularly significant resource that he neglects is the liberal political tradition that, as we have suggested, arises precisely out of the recognition that the person, and the respect that it is owed, is prior to all that separates us. This is all the more striking, not only because Nagel was a student of John Rawls but also in light of the role he played in disclosing the personalist beginnings of Rawls. The problem is, of course, that even Rawls sought to erect his principles on the basis of a minimalist account of the person. To do more would have required taking a fuller measure of the philosophical trajectory that heads toward the acknowledgment of the person as the encompassing horizon. An indispensable resource in that philosophical project is the growth of historical experience, especially as it is transmuted in the most memorable artistic creations. In the raid on the inarticulate that arises from the infinity of the person, we can no more afford to omit the authority of art than we can disregard philosophy and revelation.

In some respects, art possesses a unique advantage, for it does not have to establish its bona fides on the basis of a divinity or an order beyond itself. Art speaks, not in the name of an extraneous authority, but with the truth from which it emanates. In a world from which spirit has been expelled, art proves its inextinguishability. The person who cannot be found in the realm of matter steps forward as the creator of what exceeds all expectations. Increasingly this becomes the theme of art itself. It becomes aware of its own authoritative role and takes up the responsibility thrust upon it. Art cannot turn its back on the world that is lost without it. This explains the motivation that compelled Václav Havel, the great Czech playwright, to also become the leader of the dissident movement of Charter 77 and eventually the first president of his newly liberated country. This does not mean that an artist such as Havel can explain the source of the obligation that he finds to be prior to himself, but he does intuit his way toward an intimation of what cannot be evoked in purely material terms. Each of us, he declares, leaves a trace on the memory of being and thus bears an irreplaceable mission.[51] The composer Paul Hindemith made this intersection of art and responsibility a central theme. His opera *Mathis der Maler* is about the great painter Mathias Grünewald, whose Isenheim Altarpiece is a pivotal work in the Renaissance humanization of Christ. But he could only embark on it when he had made peace with the concurrent responsibility he felt toward the suffering peasants and the woman who had pledged her love for him. Art functions within the web of mutual responsibility that is the life of persons. Even more profoundly, Hindemith carried this meditation to its limit in the song cycle *Das Marienleben*. It was a turning point in his own life when he discovered that the story of Mary, narrated in Rainer Maria Rilke's poems, could not be comprehended without entering into the first-person perspective of the young Virgin herself. But far from a purely interior event separated from the world, the disclosure that was to open the possibility of the Incarnation could only be apprehended when Mary glimpsed it through another. The angel is the one who opens up and invites Mary to what she senses she is already called. It is a call only when it comes from another person. Nothing is private or wholly inward when it entails our vulnerability to the God whose call has rendered us, too, vulnerable. Revelation occurs only when it is glimpsed through the self-revelation of the other. The person who can give the response of yes is the epiphany of what a person is.

PART 1

The Political Discovery

CHAPTER TWO

Are Freedom and Dignity Enough?

A Reflection on Liberal Abbreviations

Political language, Michael Oakeshott has taught us, consists of a set of abbreviations for a far more concretely extended knowledge.[1] This is why politics cannot simply be taught or reduced to a science. It must be picked up in all of its embedded complexity as befits a branch of practical wisdom. Nowhere is this characterization more apt than in the liberal language of rights, which appears to have carried the principle of compression to its limit. "Rights-talk" has become so elliptic that the shorthand is in danger of losing its connection with any sustaining political order. We all know that respect for individual rights is meaningful only in the context of a political order that is capable of preserving them. Yet somehow the core liberal vocabulary of individual rights seems not to invite that wider recognition. As a consequence, liberal politics tends to teeter perpetually on the brink of incoherence and collapse.

The pattern generates an unavoidable anxiety, reflected by a multitude of conferences and anthologies, in which the participants are provoked to wonder if this narrow liberal evocation is capable of surviving.

It is a question most eloquently provoked by Glenn Tinder's *Against Fate*, in which the underlying tensions are brought to light. Are liberal abbreviations enough? Or do they necessarily lead to ever-shriller demands of a political order that ever fewer are willing to work to preserve? Is the liberal construction an invitation to self-destruction? Or are there deeper resources within this seemingly fragile arrangement that might yet rescue us from the threat of disintegration? Are there depths within the liberal soul of which liberals themselves are scarcely aware? Such are undoubtedly the questions that press on any observer of our contemporary political scene in which friction and fracture seem to shake liberal democracies to their very roots.

Traditionalists have increasingly concluded that the situation is hopeless. The very defenders of the classical liberal ideal, in which individual liberty is preserved in a constitutional political order, have in many instances lost faith in the project. Not only have liberal democratic polities taken a wrong turn, as conservative voices have argued for half a century, but that misstep was already implanted in the eighteenth-century foundation itself. A pluralist political order was a misconception in principle. Any scheme erected on the principle of transferring conflict from the public to the private realm would inevitably proceed apace until the public arena had been thoroughly evacuated of all substance. At that point the superstructure could no longer endure and the house of cards would collapse of its own weight. A critique that began with a questioning of the welfare state has been radicalized to cast suspicion on the entire constitutional enterprise. Within the United States this means that even the revered founders are declining in conservative estimation. How, after all, can they point us toward a deeper wisdom when it is their foundation that has led to the dead end of liberal disintegration?[2]

The assessment hardly fares better when we turn to the contemporary standard-bearers of the liberal impulse—the progressive liberals. They too have moved in the space of fifty years from confidence in the liberal enlargement of autonomy to a state of profound uncertainty concerning its defensibility. Following World War II and its challenge to liberal democratic regimes, a concerted series of attempts to provide a philosophical articulation of liberal principles culminated in the impressive achievement of John Rawls's *A Theory of Justice* (1971). Within that work Rawls was able to provide a neo-Kantian justification for the core principles of liberty and equality within a constitutional order that respected social differences. His demonstration that "the right is prior to the good" seemed to have furnished the definitive foundation to the neutral state. But the success was short-lived. Closer scrutiny in the years that followed compelled liberal intellectuals, including Rawls, to concede that the achievement had been overstated. There is no way to articulate a conception of right that utterly avoids taking a position on the good. As a consequence, the project of finding an unassailable defense of rights was exposed as a failure. Incoherence returned to the liberal evocations, and Rawls pleaded for an acknowledgment of a politically, if no longer rationally, grounded liberalism. A blunter admission by Richard Rorty insisted on the priority of democracy to philosophy and appealed for solidarity despite the manifest contingency of all our liberal convictions. The collapse of liberal faith was transparent.[3]

The burden of this book is to suggest that both of these perceptions are mistaken. Neither the traditionalist despair nor the postmodern incoherence adequately reflects the enduring and undeniable viability of the liberal political tradition. In the first place, both assessments fly in the face of the evident historical durability of liberal polities. Liberal constitutions have emerged from the competition of modern political forms to outlast and surpass all rivals. Not only did they supersede monarchical and aristocratic forms to establish commercial republics, but they have overcome the far more formidable challenges posed by collectivist and authoritarian rivals in the last and present centuries. Despite their weakness and unpreparedness, liberal democracies found within themselves the resources necessary to defeat fascism and persevere through the long confrontation with communism. Now they stand as the exemplars not only of economic and political success but as the model of moral legitimacy the world over, even as they are challenged by the lingering assertion of authoritarian models. No higher aspiration prevails in the contemporary world than to create a political order that is derived from and ordered toward the preservation of individual dignity and respect. The moral and political authority of liberal democratic forms may be ironic, given their own inner self-doubt, but it can hardly be denied as a global reality.

A political form does not demonstrate that kind of world historic persistence without evoking a substantive reality far deeper than the critics' misgivings. Why then the failure to perceive the hidden liberal strength? The reason lies in the misunderstanding of the genre of liberal abbreviations. It is generally erroneous to take the self-articulation of any political order as a theoretical account of its inner spiritual vitality, but this is doubly problematic in the case of liberal regimes that have been fashioned to be as abbreviated as possible. Not only are their principles merely summative of a larger philosophy of existence, but they have been developed to function without explicit reference to that sustaining moral universe. As a consequence, liberal political formulations appeal to their self-evidence or, in its absence, seek to function as if the question of foundations did not exist. One of the results of such a strategy is that they suggest the nonexistence of any broader philosophic or spiritual orientation by which their coherence and conviction are sustained. The superficiality of the pronouncements almost invites the impression that nothing further is entailed. Few observers are prepared to contemplate the possibility that the surface manifestations may conceal a larger underlying reality, from which crises and confrontations can draw forth reserves of virtue that surprise even the practitioners themselves. To appreciate this possibility we must examine the structure of liberal political thought.

Minimum Consensus

The first characteristic of a liberal regime is that it is based on a minimal political agreement. Consensus has been narrowed to those principles judged indispensable to the preservation of a common public order. The nature of that judgment may vary over time as elements previously viewed as indispensable are regarded as less momentous. Agreement can continue in the absence of many dimensions previously judged crucial. The most obvious example is the early modern struggle over religious or confessional differences. If human beings cannot agree on such fundamental questions as the proper mode of worship or of obedience to the divine will, how could agreement be trusted on any lesser matters? Much blood was spilt in the sixteenth and seventeenth centuries in the effort to compel conformity, before the futility of the exercise became apparent. The turning point was formulated in Locke's *Letter on Toleration*, which recognized the inappropriateness of state attempts to resolve religious differences. Civil society existed for the sake of the political good and could confine itself to the agreement necessary to secure that intermediate end.

The pattern of narrowing the base of consensus had been established. Locke's amplitude of agreement was considerably broader than we would deem necessary, since it excluded atheists and Catholics as unreliable, but it was clearly more limited than what had preceded it. In the centuries that followed, other challenges reduced the consensus further, in line with increasing social pluralism. At each stage it has turned out that agreement on the principles of public order can be maintained with a more limited set of background presuppositions. The pattern of increasing social diversification of all types has indeed made the liberal restriction of agreement almost a necessity. It would be difficult to see how a common political order could be maintained in any other way, short of the unlikely possibilities of coercion or persuasion to resolve differences. Far better to focus on those elements of agreement that are indispensable to the maintenance of political society. In our own day the contraction of consensus has perhaps gone so far that many suspect we may have reached the vanishing point. Whether we have is the question to be tested, but, before hazarding a conclusion, we should make sure we understand more clearly what is entailed in the concept of a limited consensus.

The impression exists that the principles drawn into such a compression are closed and unrelated. It is almost as if the bald formulations of rights are taken at face value. Overlooked is the extent to which such declarations are a selection of the most evocative principles prevailing in the social environment. The liberal invocations of rights, summarizing the necessity of self-determination both individually and collectively, are reflective of the deepest reverence for human dignity. Natural or human rights constitute a recognition of the transcendent worth of each individual, which we are never justified in setting aside in the name of some particular social good. A liberal framework of rights, with all of its constitutional prerequisites, cannot exist in the absence of that underlying resonance. It is not, therefore, that the principles first exist and then find their connection with some more pervasive understanding of humanity and its place in the order of things. Rather, the liberal invocations emerge with authority only because they are regarded as expressive of the most powerful moral sentiments of a society. They function in this sense, not as self-contained principles of the political order, but as visionary maxims redolent with the deepest and most authoritative intimations of an age. A deliberately restricted statement of consensus, in the form of mutual guarantees of rights, is therefore not so precarious a foundation as it is often taken to be. On the contrary, it may evince considerable stability as the best expression of the evocative resonances that remain within a context of disagreement and uncertainty. To the extent that the statement of principle represents the authoritative present, it can be the means of arresting further disintegration. A new stage of stability has been reached in which the moving intimations of truth and goodness have found uncontestable expression. Whatever the debates about the broader philosophical framework, this much at least is certain, that human beings deserve to be treated in such a way and that political society must be organized on the basis of that recognition. During the sixteenth century it was expressed by Jean Bodin as the realization that friendship between human beings transcended their theological differences; such a recognition of their common humanity was sufficient to provide the substance for a community inclusive of differences.[4] The difficult circumstances of increasing animosity and mistrust can be surmounted, in the acknowledgment of mutual humanity, to yield a fairly durable consensus concerning basic obligations despite limited theological explication. Sentiments that had previously sustained a far more elaborate philosophical and theological unfolding now find expression in vaguer but, for that reason, less challenged intellectual expression.

Liberal principles emerge in this way as the residue of resonances that remain of the Christian evocation of the transcendent finality of the person. At the heart of the liberal construct is the recognition of the person as an inexhaustible center of value. When we inquire into the source of this conviction, we recognize that it has its most powerful affirmation in the Christian openness of the soul toward God. Through Christ the invitation to participate in the transcendent Being of God is extended to every human being. From this we derive a sense of the unique unfathomability of every single one. To the extent that each is invited personally to union with God who is the center of all, each human being is already another divine center within the whole order of things. There is no such thing as the good of the whole outweighing the good of the parts when we are dealing with human beings.[5] Each of us is a whole, open to God who is all and in all, and therefore partakers of that transcendent dignity. The liberal language of rights that makes it possible for the good of a single human being to outweigh larger social and historical goods is a reflection of that compelling realization. To the extent that the articulation takes place outside of an explicitly Christian context, it represents a secularization of the Christian revelation, but it is not for that reason any the less durable as an acknowledgment of our common self-understanding.

Indeed, the very stability of the liberal formulation arises from the residue of Christian resonances that remain within a social setting from which explicit theological reference has largely withdrawn. The rightness of a moral and political language in which the inexhaustible worth of the person is placed at the center still lives from a sense of the movement of participation in the life of God. Discovery of the infinite worth of each human being may take place in this theological framework, but its recognition can endure outside of it. The reason for this is that Christianity has awakened us to a permanent dimension of human nature, which, once differentiated, cannot simply be erased. For anyone with a modicum of spiritual sensitivity the rightness of that perspective remains unarguable. What can be more valuable than a human being? How could we conceive of a social and political good outweighing the rights of a person without undermining the very purpose we seek to serve? If the polity does not reverence the fundamental worth of its members, what else can it serve? These are in a sense Christian sentiments that have migrated to a secular context in which they continue to demonstrate their authoritative truth. Conversely, the secular setting may be viewed as replete with a transcendent orientation on which its very coherence now depends. The lowering of the bar of theological reference by the liberal abbreviated consensus may, but it need not, unfold toward religious indifference or hostility. It may also be a way of preserving spiritual openness with a less substantive theology.

Heightening of Dignity of Person

What makes a secularized spirituality more likely to prevail is explained by the second characteristic feature of the liberal construction. Beyond the formation of consensus on implicitly transcendent principles, there is also a distinct heightening of certain aspects of individual dignity. To the extent that all of the weight is placed on the inviolable dignity of the person, there is a corresponding tendency to make that the overarching criterion of moral and political judgment. "Autonomy" becomes the watchword almost as if its promotion constituted the purpose of the moral universe. Anything that obstructs or fetters its unfolding must be removed as anathema to the central conception of what a human being is. It is as free rational beings that we are self-determining and therefore can claim the right to be treated with absolute dignity and respect. No one else can presume to run our lives, not even when they claim to be doing it in our interest. The essence of our humanity requires unimpeachable recognition of our right to make our own decisions. Anything less would be a denial of the dignity of beings that are not only intelligible but also intelligent. It is surely one of the most significant achievements of the liberal philosophical tradition that it has made this recognition a centerpiece of our universe of discourse.

By taking the dignity and respect owed autonomous beings as the focus, a heightening of awareness of its centrality and undeniability has taken place. Liberal moral language marks out the equal dignity and respect owed every human being with dramatic emphasis. A clarity about the criteria for our treatment of one another has been reached through the intensity of emphasis on the autonomy of the person. It may not provide a fully articulated account of the moral life, and it clearly stops short of a developed notion of the life of virtue or excellence as the proper fulfillment of a human being, but an unmistakable clarity has been reached concerning the core integrity of the person. Anything that diminishes respect for the inviolability of the person is on its face irreconcilable with the most fundamental understanding of what a human being is. Good action is, by contrast, what enhances the emergence of a community of persons mutually aware of one another as ends-in-themselves. As Kant formulated it, a rational being must never be regarded as a means but always as determining its own end.[6] This heightened sensitivity to the mistreatment of human beings, which is in many ways the fruit of the liberal concentration on the dignity of the person, has become a significant factor in the movements of social reform that liberal democracies have undertaken in the past two hundred years.

The greater awareness of this central line of emphasis on the person has also been one of the most overlooked sources of its strength. Contrary to the widespread misperception of liberal principles as an inconsequential house of cards, these principles turn out to have considerable resilience precisely because they are rooted in the sense of constituting a moral advance. The focus on the person as an inexhaustible center of value is hardly unique to liberal regimes, since it clearly derives from the Christian opening of the soul, but the single-minded emphasis imparted to it within the liberal framework has generated its own consequences. Not the least is that it has enabled liberals to mount a critique of the Christian and traditional moralities that had hitherto exercised an authoritative role. In part the success of the liberal analysis is derived from its greater strength as a mode of critique than as a comprehensive account of the moral life; neglect of the more intractable dimensions of human fallenness and the need for reconciliation are nowhere developed. In part, too, it must be acknowledged, the liberal critique is convincing within a social environment in which Christian sensitivity to the suffering of the neighbor has often not lived up to its own rigorous demands. But most of all it is because the liberal highlighting of the dignity and respect owed every human being casts a light of searching intensity. Its power as a moral language derives from its identification of what is in fact the core perspective in which the weighing of private and public actions must be judged. Do they retard or advance the unfolding of our humanity?

The abbreviated character of liberal discourse can be tolerated more readily when it is accompanied by this sense of incontrovertible moral authority. It has been able to establish itself as the primary moral framework, despite its inarticulateness, because it has derived its central conviction from the preceding traditions of philosophy and Christianity. Without the Christian illumination of the transcendent worth of each human being, it would be impossible to conceive the inexhaustible dignity of each individual. Nothing in the world of mundane calculation can explain why human beings alone should escape the logic of instrumentalization.[7] In many ways the exclusivity of the liberal focus on the dignity of self-determination is both its weakness and its strength. Liberal critiques are capable of a searing excoriation of injustice precisely because they deliberately neglect the complexity of context and the ambiguity of motive that continue to define the concrete reality of our lives. The Burkean objection to the abstractness of rights has validity, but it overlooks the powerful critical momentum generated by this perspective.[8] Simplification of moral discourse to our essential self-responsibility, though it stands in need of more concrete elaboration, has the inestimable advantage of making the parameters of the human condition inescapably clear. Liberal abbreviations set up an inexorable pressure for reform in line with their elemental sense of right.

Liberal Dependence on Spiritual Traditions

If it is to lead toward substantive enactments and not dissipate the impulse in vacuous idealism, the focus on human rights must still draw upon the richer background of spiritual communities and traditions. A militantly secular liberalism can scarcely be sustained. This broader dependence on the differentiated religious traditions, especially Christianity, is the third essential characteristic. The relationship may be indirect, but it is nevertheless crucial. To the extent that the liberal construction represents a secular derivation of the central Christian opening toward transcendent divinity, it is inextricably involved in the relationship with revelation. However, the expression of that relationship can run a wide gamut from the explicitly Christian acknowledgment of human dignity to an almost mystical silence before the unfathomability of the person. What is clear is that the transcendent demand for respect cannot be derived from the bald statement of rights. Something more is required as a sustaining force if bills of rights are to be more than "parchment barriers" to the perpetration of injustice. The proclivity toward the exploitation of others is so persistent that only a correspondingly powerful countermovement can sustain fidelity to the best impulses of our nature. Liberal imperatives may have separated from religious language, but their expression in concrete individual and political existence can hardly dispense with the more robust spiritual traditions. Without the fund of spiritual capital represented by religion, both in its capacity to evoke the summits of self-sacrifice and to surmount the recurrent experiences of human failure and evil, liberal assertions are prone to shatter under the force of their own shrillness. The transcendent dignity of the person can only be preserved in its relationship to that which is itself transcendent.

The problem is that this dependence is impenetrable from the secular liberal perspective. Convinced of its own rhetoric of independence and endowed with the confidence of its moral superiority, the liberal construction is all too inclined to believe the myth of its own self-sufficiency. As a consequence, the relationship of the liberal movement to the spiritual tradition whence it received its birth, and on whose sustaining depths it still depends for its resonances, is one of great ambivalence. On the one hand, liberal convictions are imbued with confidence in their evocation of the incontrovertible consensus they have reached. The intensity of the focus on autonomous human dignity further emboldens the liberal mind to contemplate its superiority to all other traditions, including the Christian origins from which it has come. Almost simultaneously, however, liberal reflection becomes aware of its own vulnerability to questions. Without any clear relationship to transcendent Being or any developed account of the human trajectory, one has difficulty sustaining the rationale for treating each human being as the only inexhaustible center of value in the universe. In a world defined by instrumental rationality, why should man alone escape the iron law of efficiency? The precariousness of the liberal intimations are less an intrinsic feature of the construction than a result of the peculiar myopia within which it tends to operate.

Fragments of Coherence

It is the combination of these three features that together account for the abiding pattern of liberal theory and practice. The liberal political tradition is marked simultaneously by its stability and its instability. The former is evident from its capacity to successfully articulate the bedrock consensus of rightness or fairness in a social context of pluralism and fragmentation. Whatever the issues that divide us, some things remain incontestable. We agree on how we should regard the differences between us because concrete human beings transcend the limits of all their particularities. Beyond the differences, we recognize a deeper unity in the common humanity that remains inextinguishable at its core. Whatever the features or attainments of an individual, there is always something more to the person, as is the case whenever self-determination takes place. The one who does the governing has already gone beyond any stage of self-disclosure and self-enactment he or she has reached. An inescapable dimension of the infinite attaches to every human being and makes each a center of value outweighing the whole world. To the extent that a liberal order of rights gives voice to that ineliminable sense of right, it has attained a bedrock consensus impervious to further movement. But once the insubstantial basis for these convictions is noticed, the sentiment turns quickly to one of greater uncertainty, especially concerning the possibilities for their justification and communication.

Instability then becomes the permanent obverse to liberal stability. It is a pattern that reaches all the way back to the first creators of the liberal abbreviations, most famously John Locke, and bursts forth with renewed anxiety in virtually every generation up to the present.[9] All of the great liberal thinkers from Rousseau to Rawls sensed the vulnerabilities of convictions whose source had deliberately been submerged and which now sought to survive on the basis of their appeal to self-evidence. It was only a matter of time before their justifiability was put in question. How would we respond when someone objected that it was far from self-evident that all men are created equal? Or how would we be able to sustain the conviction that they are endowed with inalienable rights? Would it not make more sense to acknowledge that men and women are, like everything else in reality, inescapably finite? Do they not reach a point where their rights can be alienated once their value to themselves and everyone else has been expended? Why should man be different from every other entity under the sun? These are unsettling reflections from a liberal perspective, and apprehension of their threat has been at the source of the repeated attempts by liberal theorists over the centuries to construct a larger philosophical defense, and to find their way home to some broader religious intuitions. Such a deeper re-evocation of the liberal abbreviations would not only endow it with a more effective intellectual defense but would also provide it with a means of sustaining the virtues on which its survival depends. Intellectual and moral vulnerabilities unsettle the liberal sense of invincibility and propel its most perceptive advocates to the search for more transparent expositions.

Instability and dissatisfaction with the prevailing defenses become therefore permanent features of the liberal consensus. But anxiety must not be taken as an exclusive or even dominant mood. Equally significant is the equanimity with which the succession of theoretical failures is accepted. The fact that none of the philosophical elaborations has succeeded in establishing its unquestioned primacy is surely indicative of the dimensions of the challenge. But just as impressive is that the theoretical misadventures have not unhinged the underlying certainty of convictions that remain, confident that their rightness has simply not found its most perspicuous elaboration. We may have today reached the limit of such insouciance in the acknowledgment by many liberal intellectuals that the entire quest for philosophical justification has been an exercise in futility. What is most remarkable about this admission is that it is followed immediately by the recommendation that we carry on with our most cherished convictions without adverting in the slightest to their insubstantiality: "To realize the relative validity of one's convictions and yet stand for them unflinchingly, is what distinguishes a civilized man from a barbarian."[10] Despite the intellectual mendacity of the position, it is difficult to deny the cogency of the assertion. To the extent that liberal sentiments have never really lived off a theoretical justification, there is no reason to expect that even the radical collapse of the latter project will overturn the appeal of the former. It is a serious category mistake, Oakeshott has shown, to search among political abbreviations for the source of political convictions. We should rather recognize that the abbreviations are themselves derivative from the practice in which the sentiments that sustain them are activated. This pattern is even more the case with liberal principles that have carried the process of abbreviation virtually to the limits. There would not in fact be the long history of the liberal philosophical quest for transparency if there was not an underlying continuity of sentiments that sustained the search and accepted the limitations of the proposed evocations. The greatest liberal thinkers, such as Tocqueville or Mill, are marked by the inconclusiveness of their reflections, yet their influence is unaffected by the provisionality of their explications.

What then does the quest for foundations accomplish if it is recurrently frustrated in its goal? Its most enduring achievement is surely that it sustains the awareness of the unencompassable depth of conviction from which the liberal formulations arise. There would be no unending search for foundations if there was not already an awareness of that which provides the foundations. The mere fact of our inability to adequately capture them, within the abbreviated language that liberalism imposes on itself, does not gainsay the profound presence of such intimations. This is, after all, the living assurance that supports the indifference to its own theoretical failure. But such failures are never a sheer waste of effort. They are the indispensable paths of reflection by which we approach the inarticulate depths from which the convictions spring. Through the quest for foundations we keep the awareness of foundations alive, and we activate our participation in them most profoundly. Even the embrace of a nonfoundational liberalism, such as we appear to have reached, is not fatal so long as it is not misinterpreted as a sign that foundations are nonexistent. The latter is the mistake of Richard Rorty, who counsels us, albeit philosophically, to give up philosophy. Oakeshott, in contrast, represents a more nuanced response that recognizes the failure of philosophical articulation as implying nothing about the presence or absence of animating sentiments. The latter are sufficiently attested both by the continuing practice of liberal politics and by the conviction that guides the search for re-evocation.

Only this recognition of the peculiarly stable instability of the liberal political tradition adequately accounts for the extraordinary profile it exhibits. Its durability and resilience in overcoming the challenges posed against it through a long historical experience have already been noted. What has not been sufficiently noted is the extent to which even its most persuasive advocates have often taken the role of friendly critics. It is a tradition, or perhaps a nontradition, that seems perpetually in need of being rescued from the dangers harbored within it. Tocqueville is among the most eminent practitioners of this art, because he sifted the American experience to find not only the shape of the future but the means by which it might be saved from itself. "Thus it is," he observed of the extensive associational life of America, "by the enjoyment of a dangerous freedom that the Americans learn the art of rendering the dangers of freedom less formidable."[11] It is no wonder that Tocqueville has become the most admired liberal critic through his harrowing penetration of liberalism's flaws, yet he neither hints at an alternative nor even wistfully sighs for what cannot be. The same is fundamentally true of the contemporary critics whose standpoint is more firmly rooted in classical and medieval political thought. For all of the enlargement of horizons that has taken place as political theory rediscovered the great fount of wisdom in the past, it has hardly taken on the task of surpassing the liberal conception of order. The best for which it can hope is some injection of substance into the incoherence of liberal self-understanding. Even Alasdair MacIntyre, who is among the most disdainful critics of liberalism, still retains the hope of reshaping it within a more robust Aristotelian tradition.[12]

The stability of fragmented liberal politics is perhaps best exemplified by the overarching influence of John Stuart Mill. After Locke, he is undoubtedly the figure who most stamps the construction, and it is in his evocation that the shape of liberal self-understanding remains all the way up to the present. Indeed, the paucity of major theoretical expositions is striking. With the possible exceptions of Oakeshott and Hayek, there are no intermediate figures of stature between Mill and Rawls. With the latter the re-evocation has become so rarefied philosophically that it has ceased to refer to the full range of political reality and not surprisingly reveals its narrowness in the space of a generation. As a result, we still live within the Millian formulation of liberal political society. This is most evident in the principle of liberty of *On Liberty*, which strikes us as identifying the appropriate line to justify public intervention in the exercise of individual autonomy, that is, only when it is likely to lead to direct harm to others. But in addition we still struggle with the full range of related issues that Mill adumbrated in his most prominent texts. *On Utilitarianism* is remarkably close to the principled utilitarian morality around which our public consciousness revolves. The *Principles of Political Economy* proclaims the central struggle between the need for government intervention and the importance of preserving the spirit of private enterprise. We still tinker with the reform of our electoral institutions in order to obviate the problems of mass democracy, that Mill began to address in *On Representative Government*. Even our confused search for a diffuse humanitarian spirituality is not far away from Mill's late musings on religion. The overarching continuity, however, is that these dimensions of the liberal evocation coexist as unintegrated fragments in more or less the way they coexisted for Mill.[13] Just as he could only deal with them in separate books, so we too lack any integrating framework by which a comprehensive liberal philosophy might be constructed. The evocative abbreviations continue their quest for a perspicuous framework.

The question that remains for both the defenders and the critics of the liberal configuration is whether the incoherence of its fragments can be relied upon. Are they sufficient to sustain a public order that enhances rather than erodes our fundamental humanity? The question is itself a quintessentially liberal concern. Oscillating between stability and instability, the liberal outlook feeds the suspicion that the abbreviations are not enough. Disconnected from their place within a whole, the abbreviations are inclined to generate ever-more abstract demands that progressively erode the common basis of consensus. Rights-talk becomes the instrument by which an order of rights is cumulatively undermined. Can we therefore place any confidence in a moral and political framework that hardly even seems to be a framework? Does the single-minded focus on autonomy not eventually displace all other conceptions of the good, leading eventually to the evacuation of all substance within the exercise of autonomy itself? If there is nothing worth choosing for its intrinsic goodness, then freedom of choice loses its value.

Such are certainly the tough questions confronting the liberal tradition when the layers of self-assurance are stripped away. But we must not lose sight of the fact that they are posed from within the same tradition, thereby giving evidence of a perspective that goes beyond the preoccupation with autonomy. Such concerns can only have an effect if the preservation of autonomy is already linked with an awareness of a moral order that ultimately measures the use to which liberty is put. However unstated that awareness may be, it is nevertheless there and is ineradicable. To disconnect autonomy from a substantive moral order would be to eliminate its seriousness.[14] Not confined to the routine of instinct, human beings are engaged in the drama of self-disclosure and self-enactment by which they approach what is of transcendent goodness. The abbreviated character of liberal discourse, we now realize, is not truncated speech. Rather, it retains its implicit connectivity to the full range of moral truth that is drawn into its emphasis on autonomy and rights. The whole value of autonomy resonates with an openness to real moral growth. It is a connection that, however it may be obscured or forgotten, cannot be broken without evacuating the very purpose of self-responsibility.

For this reason, the priority of the right is less inimical to the order of the good than is often perceived. Far from being mutually opposed, they are inseparable partners. We recall that the dimension of self-responsibility is differentiated in the same context as the recognition of a teleological order of the good. In this sense liberal discourse belies the appearance it may suggest of a part adrift from the larger moral whole; the reality is that it still depends on the moral universe whence it has been derived. The major consequence of this recognition is that the unfolding of liberal injunctions entails the broader universe of moral discourse. Rights-talk cannot be severed from purpose-talk. We do not, therefore, have to fear disconnection between the two modes of expression, no more than we have to feel that the prominence of autonomy dooms all other moral intimations. The fragmentary character of rights language still remains, but it is not irretrievably incoherent. Through a patient willingness to explore the confusions, even a certain persistence in pursuing its debates, we will be led to discover the deeper coherence embedded within the framework the liberal mind cannot discard without forgoing its own resonance. The liberal language of rights can, in other words, be trusted to disclose and sustain the reality of moral truth.

Coherence Disclosed in Practice

The only condition for the articulation of such a luminous enlargement of rights is that we not lose faith in the liberal abbreviations as encapsulation of the moral truth of existence. A focus on rights can then become the means of resisting the distortions generated by a misapplication of rights claims. Perhaps the most instructive example of such reliance on the sufficiency of liberal rights in a moral conflict was Lincoln's approach to the institution of slavery. He understood what was widely sensed ever since the Philadelphia Convention of 1787—the incompatibility of slavery with the regime of equal rights and self-government. At the same time, he was confronted with a long-standing social reality that had acquired legal protection and intellectual rationalization. Liberal ideology was invoked to protect the rights of property and to insist on the rights of freedom of choice within the states. What is significant about Lincoln's strategy is that he did not despair of the incoherence of the available language when confronted with opposing rights claims. He was confident that their irreconcilability could be rendered transparent. Rather than reverting to some more comprehensive mode of discourse, such as the divine law of the Bible or some variant of natural law, he stuck with the superficially thinner but ultimately evocative terminology of the Declaration of Independence.[15]

The effect was to resuscitate the founding consensus in such a way as to activate its most powerful sentiments. Slavery was confronted with a forthrightness that had been largely avoided, so long as prevailing opinion had hoped it would simply fall away. The necessity had arisen as a result of its expansion, but the mode of confrontation was decisively shaped by Lincoln's leadership. He portrayed it no longer as an unfortunate historical remnant, but as a mortal threat to the very possibility of self-government. Denial of the rights of one human being was perceived as an assault on the rights of all. Whatever rags of justification might be invoked under property and choice, the liberty claim of slaveowners could not withstand the implication that they undermined the whole possibility of an order of rights. Preservation even of the right of popular liberty cannot be sustained when the choice extends to the derogation of the right of liberty. Slavery is incompatible with the notion of liberty since no one has the right to enslave themselves or others. Freedom is limited by the very presuppositions that make its exercise possible: the presence of self-responsible human beings. Lincoln saw to the depth of the liberal construction, that it is rooted in a moral order from which it cannot detach itself. Even when the abuse of human beings is relatively confined, the damage caused is universal since the abrogation of humanity in one instance eliminates the basis for opposing its extension to all others. Slavery constituted such a radical assault on the basis of liberty that the struggle against it, for all of its destructive consequences, called forth the deepest grounds of the liberal defense. Liberty is most powerfully invoked and illumined when it encounters its greatest threat.

The situation remains the same for us today. Not only has the language of human rights proved a durable and powerful source of the dissident movements that dealt the last blow to the totalitarian incubus, but it continues to be taken up as the sustaining political vocabulary in all contemporary confrontations with tyranny. Even within the established liberal democracies, the focus on rights recurrently demonstrates its interior moral conviction. One of the most divisive debates centers around the life issues, especially the legal endorsement of abortion as a right. Undeniably this distortion has a string of mischievous effects as it works its way through the institutions and affects the codification of rights more broadly. But what is the most effective rhetorical means of opposition? It does not lie in any broader moral appeal and especially not on the basis of religious premises. Such proposals play precisely into the strategy of those who would castigate the prioritization of life as a matter of private or religious disposition and therefore of no relevance in the arena of public argument. No, the most compelling basis for opposing abortion is that of human rights. What is at stake, we may claim, is far more important than any denominational perspective. It is nothing less than the integrity of our public conception of rights. To the extent that the most marginal members of our species are cast aside, the same specter of arbitrariness looms over the notion that any of us are entitled to inviolable dignity and respect. Not only is the language of rights the most publicly persuasive mode of argument; it also evinces the greater moral clarity of its focus on what is owed to human beings simply by virtue of their humanity.

In such demonstrations we begin to discern more clearly the secret of the liberal success as a moral and political form. Fragmentation of principles evokes a minimum consensus, but it also conceals a far deeper integrity of perspective, rooted in the most profound intimation of the transcendent inexhaustibility of the person. Even though that unspoken depth cannot be fully articulated, and certainly not through the compressed abbreviations of public exchanges, it can nevertheless be evoked through the intensity of the debates. Liberal formulations may suffer from excessive succinctness but they do not suffer from a lack of resonance. On the contrary, they work as effective symbols of the public order only because their rightness is beyond question. In practice no one requests a demonstration of the validity of the proposition that all men are created equal. Self-evidence of human rights can furnish our lingua franca only because it guards the full measure of the sense of ourselves and of the mystery in which we exist. Whatever else may be true, of this much at least we can be certain, that we ought to treat one another with unwavering dignity and respect. To doubt the validity of this conviction would be tantamount to undermining the possibility of reflection and discourse. Recognition of rights brings us to the boundary of what can be thought.

Growth of the Soul a Reality

Whence emerges that transcendent imperative within a seemingly flat assertion of rights? The answer, and the reason for the impressive resilience of liberal political regimes, is in the practical struggle for the right alignment of rights. The liberal practice, we have emphasized, repeatedly calls forth more than it seems to possess. The only way in which this is possible is through enacting what is never fully adumbrated in theory. Liberal politics is, as Twain quipped of Wagner's music, better than it sounds. What takes place in the invocation of rights, conscientiously pursued through robust public exchange, is an indefinable growth of the soul that escapes linguistic containment. It is not that further information is reached or that social reality is modified in any fundamental way. Growth of the soul is an enlargement of the human persons themselves rather than anything outside of them. All the great liberal thinkers are cognizant of this dimension, and Tocqueville most of all. He refers to the dynamic repeatedly and isolates "the dangerous exercise of liberty" as the pivotal means for the preservation of liberty. The change is inner, but the effect is far from private. It puts the individual participant in touch with the most real dimension of reality, providing an indubitable sense of contact with what is most enduring. The transformation is that which occurs when ordinarily self-absorbed individuals are galvanized into action in the service of what they perceive to be more important than their own private worlds. Suddenly the clarity of purpose and the difficulty of the struggle become quite secondary. It is not that the inconveniences disappear but that they are perceived differently. Now they are measured in the scale of what transcends them, because the human beings involved have made contact with a more real reality than what had hitherto dominated their consciousness. Externally nothing is new, but inwardly all is different.[16]

Even the crises that recurrently afflict liberal regimes, many of them self-generated, are thus not the worst outcome. Rightly viewed, the debates that fracture such polities can be the means of promoting a deeper grasp of the principles on which the whole construction depends. A far greater danger is that liberal societies might yield to the temptation of avoiding debate. Escapist illusions of a technical or neutral resolution of differences are always there, even when their appeal has considerably diminished. To eliminate such false hopes altogether it is necessary to see the contestation in a far more positive light. What needs to be recognized is that the abbreviations of a liberal order really generate coherent intimations only in the struggle with what threatens its core. The presence of robust moral challenges, though they can lead to increasing social cleavages, can also be the means by which they are surmounted in the attainment of a clearer and more firmly held unity. By compelling a liberal order to confront the ambiguities that may have remained unnoticed within it, sharp moral differences call forth the heightened awareness of the inviolable dignity of the person that lies at the liberal core. The growth of the soul is an event that the incompleteness of a liberal configuration invites, and virtually requires, as the means of surmounting the tendency toward disintegration. All that is required is the willingness to undertake the struggle and the confidence that below the surface are unsuspected moral resources for the revitalization of the present. The struggle with its own incoherence is both the necessity and the means by which liberal abbreviations are rendered coherent.

The task of enlarging the liberal soul through engagement with the challenges concretely presented to us does not imply any prediction, pessimistic or optimistic, concerning the outcome. What matters is that the strategy is the only viable one. Not only is the acceptance of the language of rights a pragmatic necessity of public discourse in the present, such acceptance is also morally compelling. Despite the abbreviated character of freedom and dignity, they are nevertheless the most appropriate means of confronting the threats of dehumanization that perennially haunt the modern world. Argument on the basis of membership in humanity as such most directly strikes at the attempts to redefine such membership, whether it comes in the form of disregarding the excessively young, infirm, or inconvenient. Once the challenge is taken up we discover the powerful resonances of all human rights affirmations. Will the appeal be successful? Probably never in any final and definitive way, given the capacity of human beings to find ever-new opportunities of dominating others, and always under the guise of a new badge of dehumanization. Resistance will always be in the name of defense of the rights of the concretely vulnerable. What is certain is that unless the challenge is faced, evil will flow unrestricted. Equally certain is that centers of resistance will be forthcoming, since the good too cannot be eliminated from history. The interesting political question is whether such centers of resistance will find an answering response in the wider social reality. Without making any claim to prophecy, I have tried to point toward the unsuspected possibilities of the liberal political tradition rooted in a reverence for the transcendent dignity of the person. At the very least this means that, if liberal polities cannot find their way toward a moral resolution of the conflicts that pervade them, they cannot find their way toward any resolutions at all. Conflict itself remains the most powerful evidence of the moral imperatives that liberal politics cannot discard without also rejecting its own most basic moral commitments.

When seen in the full amplitude of its dynamic, the liberal configuration exhibits a very different perspective than that suggested by its customary abbreviations. First, it becomes evident that the respect for individual dignity and autonomy is fully compatible with, although not necessarily cognizant of, the Christian or transcendent worldview. The genius of the liberal arrangement has been to detach itself from all theological reference, but its own performative coherence still strongly depends on the presence of such an intimation. The source of resonance with the inexhaustible depth of the person may remain inarticulate from a liberal perspective, but no one can doubt that this is the dynamic fount of its inspiration. The lack of explication may be viewed as a kind of weakness, but from another vantage point it is an incalculable strength since it removes the possibility of debilitating critique. Wittgenstein remarked in one of his wisest comments that we must remain silent on that about which we can say nothing. It is this very inarticulateness that guards the mystery of the person from which the liberal dynamic lives.

Second, despite the separation from its Christian background, the liberal construction, by virtue of its narrowness, accomplishes a heightening of the transcendent dignity of the person. There may not be the full amplitude of theological insight concerning man as the *imago Dei* or as the recipient of the redemptive divine outpouring in Christ, but there is a spotlight on the inviolability of the individual person. As a consequence, the issue of the appropriate treatment of human beings, by virtue of nothing more than their humanity, becomes a central focus. Without being Christian, it can nevertheless claim to have absorbed the Christian valuation of the human person. The imperative of respect for human dignity is what imparts to the liberal tradition the sense of constituting a moral advance. This can even extend to the claim of a superior standpoint to Christianity, a claim that depends on a forgetfulness of that which has been heightened. Yet even within the Christian tradition, the liberal elevation of the autonomy of the person can provide an invaluable clarification of the direction in which its own moral and political influence should unfold. This is an insight that has not been lost on the Christian churches, which now increasingly see the nexus of human rights as the primary focus of their public authority. The inexhaustible dignity and worth of each human being is the point at which the truth of God is most adequately reflected within this world.[17]

The third implication is, therefore, that the liberal order is the closest approximation of the Christian valuation of the human being. Liberal democracy cannot be regarded as a Christian political form, not only because no political expressions can adequately incarnate the spirit of Christ, but also because it is no longer explicitly connected with its Christian inspiration. A liberal order of rights is more appropriately viewed as a Christian refraction of politics. Like a light penetrating a medium that remains largely unaware of its source, Christianity nevertheless radiates its illuminative effect. Liberal democracy is a political form that no longer knows the inspiration from which it lives, but yet it has nevertheless absorbed that inspiration within its minimal principles. Like much else in our modern world, liberal politics is an expression of an anonymous faith. What matters is that the Christian resonances continue to be evoked through a language that bears intuitions no longer fully articulate within it.

From this recognition follows the fourth implication, that a liberal political order represents in a more profound sense the most adequate political expression of Christianity. Reverence for the dignity of the person is an oblique expression of reverence for that which is the source of human dignity. By naming the transcendent, human language and especially public language already renders it as something immanent.

Transcendence cannot be preserved once it is drawn into tangible public expression. Then it suffers the fate of everything finite; it becomes available for manipulation and devaluation. Reverence can be preserved only so long as the inexpressible mystery of God is not reduced to immanent expression. The failure of all political theologies is that they inevitably render the divine as a figure within the partisan conflicts of the day. God is hardly God when he becomes the deity of a particular people or party. He cannot be laid hold of through the clumsy hands of political representation. The best that can be done from a political perspective is to point silently toward that about which our mundane discourse can say nothing. In this way the liberal veneration of the inviolable dignity of the person preserves and conveys more powerfully the sense of awe before the mystery by which we are held. There is in this sense a distinct spiritual superiority to liberal reticence.

The only danger is that silence can lapse into ignorance. A fifth implication is that the preservation of the transcendent tension of a liberal order requires continuing openness to the appropriately transcendent symbolizations of the mystery. Agnosticism and a confused atheism are compatible with a liberal preservation of human dignity, but a dogmatic rejection of the transcendent is not. How can we sustain the notion that each human being is a center of infinite worth if we are certain that there is no such infinity? If the value of every single being can be exhausted, then there ceases to be any justification for treating humans as the exception. The rational calculation of costs and benefits must pervade everything, consuming even the calculator. An instinctual resistance wells up within us as we contemplate this prospect, but the liberal focus on rights strikes us as peculiarly ill-equipped to unfold the rationale for our opposition. For all of the vaunted merits of the essential consensus and the ray of light it casts on the indispensability of each one, it is still not a language in which the development of a meditative self-understanding can take place. Abbreviations may work well in practice but not when the question of justification arises. Then the liberal compression must look toward what is available in the great spiritual traditions of mankind, those streams in which the deepest and richest quest for self-understanding has taken place. Its own derivation from the resonances of transcendent openness makes liberal reflection a close relative of the world religions, especially Christianity from which it has originated. The viability of liberal convictions depends therefore on the preservation of this relation of friendship in which it recognizes its own inner filiation. The liberal language of rights may have been developed to avoid the necessity of taking determinate theological positions, but it cannot survive the utter rejection of all theological discourse. Beginning in the conviction that the value of the person matters more than all finite differences, liberal principles still find their deepest confirmation in the movement toward the transcendent God in whose love all humanity is united.

CHAPTER THREE

The Unattainability of What We Live Within

Liberal Democracy

Concern about the fragility of democracy, especially liberal democracy, has been an abiding feature since its inception. The simultaneous narrowing of principles toward an essential consensus and the heightening of their moral significance defined a liberal political order. It was an unstable enterprise from the start. Would the authoritative evocation be sufficient to sustain itself? Or would the incoherence of its abbreviations overwhelm its deeper resonances? Even to an exponent as confident as John Locke the answer was far from clear, despite the rhetorical cogency of the *Two Treatises of Government* (1689), for he still felt the need to explore the possibility of a more substantive philosophic and religious consensus. The need to resolve questions of moral and religious truth was, he explains in the "Epistle to the Reader," the genesis of his great philosophical inquiry, *An Essay Concerning Human Understanding* (1689). It was no doubt partly out of a sense of dissatisfaction with the fruits of that endeavor that he turned his attention to a "plain reading" of scripture as the basis for a latitudinarian Christianity. Unfortunately neither *On The Reasonableness of Christianity* (1695) nor the later *Paraphrase and Notes on the Epistles of Saint Paul* (1707) succeeded in establishing the theological universality his hermeneutic had promised.[1] All that remained was the political authority of the liberal democratic evocation without benefit of the philosophical and religious amplifications Locke had envisaged. Only the truth of its self-evidence could be evoked by Thomas Jefferson and others who would have to find their own way of dealing with the anxieties surrounding it. The quest for "foundations" had been set in motion as an arc that reaches all the way up to John Rawls and the present. Fragility has been the inescapable companion of democracy.

That awareness has hardly been absent from the great historic conflicts in which the democratic societies have been involved. One thinks of the rise of the totalitarian states in the twentieth century with their genesis in failed democracies. Or there was the shock engendered in the democracies that opposed them, uncertain at first if they possessed the resources to resist a foe armed with the ruthlessness of ideological invincibility. The flabbiness of liberal democratic societies has perennially provoked and prompted dreams of aggression against them. Viewed from the outside it was hard to imagine such regimes of private preoccupation as anything more than the final stages of declining decadence. Was there anything that could rouse their citizens to an effort of public sacrifice? Or, were they doomed to slumber into their inevitable demise? The less advanced cases of the democratic disease have since become capable of noticing their condition and fitfully rousing themselves against the "crisis of values" they sensed as engulfing them. A particularly striking example was the contrast between the United States and Europe in their different responses to the perceived deficit of civic virtue. In the former concern about such barometers as "bowling alone" called forth affirmations of religiosity that would appear distinctly unwelcome in the more secular indifference of the Old World. Neither case, however, provides much reassurance that the liberal democratic founding can be sustained in its own terms.[2] Whether support is sought outside the democratic frame of reference or whether the danger is simply ignored amounts largely to a difference of degree. The "crisis" of liberal democracy looms, and perhaps looms ever more ominously to the extent that its source within liberal principles is glimpsed so little. The irony of the situation cannot be overlooked. For it is precisely when liberal democracies have not only defeated their totalitarian foes but are engaged in a robust effort of self-rejuvenation that the core of their own success remains so elusive within them.

The problem of irony, however, is that it is rarely carried far enough. Often it is taken as an excuse for avoiding the opening irony has laid before us, as if by taking note we had ourselves escaped from the chasm between what is said and what is done. This was the insight that made Kierkegaard such an acute analyst of irony, a category that shaped his entire understanding of the modern world.[3] Ironic distance cannot enable us to bridge the abyss by which we are separated from our existence. Only the movement of existence itself can reconnect us to life, when "talk" of intervention has assumed the form of interminability. A similar paralysis can grip liberal democratic societies that contemplate their uncertainties while forgetting the struggles by which they became what they are. Irony always turns out to be a double-edged sword. The wielders of critical distance are invariably exposed as the ones who are furthest removed from the sources of their own critique. What, after all, could be more ironic than the discovery that the lessons in democratic virtue are to be taught most effectively by the very societies whose faltering steps are to be aided by the ostensible holders of the democratic mantle? Yet the pattern has been repeated more than once. Recall the witness to liberal democratic heroism exhibited by the dissident movements of the Cold War era. Andrei Sakharov lived it so deeply that he was virtually proclaimed a secular saint, while such leaders as Václav Havel could still speak with an authority far above the petty politics of Europe.[4] But nowhere is the astonishment as great as when we witness the seriousness with which the newly democratizing societies embrace the august responsibilities of voting. Turnout even in the 2005 election in Iraq, under the most adverse conditions, was far higher than it routinely is among our own more apathetic electorates. Disaffection runs highest where democracy is secured and is at its lowest when the democratic aspiration is most in jeopardy. Could it be that the ironic reversal of the roles of teacher and student is more than a coincidence? What is it about liberal democratic constitutions that makes their emergence easy and their preservation hard?

The pattern has certainly been noted before. Tocqueville made the appeal to return to the founding struggle for liberty the principal means by which he thought democracy might overcome its deleterious absorption with equality. Only the spirit of liberty could defeat the demand for equality that arose within it. He understood that the attainment of liberty was only the beginning and that its betrayal was the most fateful consequence of the modern democratic revolutions. Far more significant was the realization of what was entailed in the preservation of liberty, for it would require nothing less than the willingness to risk the very equality that had been its correlative. A society that places the primacy of emphasis on equality has already signaled its willingness to abandon liberty. But its equality can have no meaning unless it is rooted in the very liberty from which it has arisen. The tensions of the founding are never resolved or, to speak more precisely, they must be resolved in every moment. Success is no guarantee of success, for every generation must confront anew the issues that in one way or another spring from the very beginning of the constitution. Statesmanship is marked by the capacity to recognize that the struggles of the day are not simply what they appear to be but implicate us in the character of the regime in which we find ourselves. It was this capacity that distinguished Abraham Lincoln's response to the Civil War. He understood that the conflict was about neither regional tensions nor the abolition of slavery but about the meaning of the American founding. Was the United States to maintain itself as the union that had been constituted through the Declaration of Independence or would it simply disintegrate along increasingly factional lines? Democracy may have ignored the presence of slavery in its midst but could it countenance its expansion? The struggle that followed was all the more momentous because it was engaged as a refounding of what had not yet been adequately founded.

The question is whether democracy ever is adequately founded. Yet even when the question is raised, it is rarely confronted in its full force. We have not always been willing to think with the harrowing depth of Nietzsche, who saw that "disregard for and the decline and *death of the state*, the liberation of the private individual, is the consequence of the democratic conception of the state."[5] We prefer to comfort ourselves with the thought that the founding is secured in a past whose permanence we seek to make palpable in the monuments we erect to it. By remembering we try to forget what cannot be forgotten, that the past is no more. The future is not yet, for its arrival depends entirely on the response we make in the present. Our task is therefore not simply the transmission of some stable heritage we have received from the past but the invention of democracy anew in the present. The very meaning of history presupposes the openness of each generation to its possibilities, for we are not the products of predecessors who have fixed forever the range within which our nature will operate. (This is the nightmare possibility glimpsed in the contemporary cloning and genetic intervention debates.) We have a history just because we do not live in history as mutely assigned results. Instead we live in partnership, a partnership that presupposes freedom, with all who have come before us and all who will follow after us. None possess an exclusive superiority over the rest and none are compelled to live entirely on their own resources. Only beings who are free can possess a history, but it is only beings who are free that can live from history. We live within what we cannot fully understand, and we contribute to what cannot fully be stated. Without freedom there would neither be history nor the benefits to be derived from it. History may not be able to settle the questions that define our existence, but the movement toward settlement is drawn by the settlement that has already taken place within history.

Every generation is a founding generation, and every generation depends on the founders who came before it. We know this as a matter of general observation, but we have not necessarily grasped its significance. The inclination to see ourselves as mere caretakers of democracy has mitigated the realization that it is democracy that takes care of us. Democracy is not the issue, it is the "we" who are its putative guardians. Without democracy, would there even be a "we"? That is the question that all talk of preserving foundations overlooks in its easy assumption of a realm of fixed quantities. Forgotten is the realization that founding presupposes that there is no foundation, or at least not one that dispenses forever with the need to refound. Equally absent is the realization that no founding would be possible unless it had already occurred, as the point of recognition at which arrival is possible. In the movement of repetition there is not only the time of the founding but also the founding of time. What is present in eternity must be distended in time. Indeed, the possibility of time and existence is bound up with the nonpresence of what is present. It is because the founding of democracy is the work of democracy that it can have no foundations. To secure the foundations of democracy beyond peril is to lift it out of the movement by which it is constituted. It is to bring history to its conclusion. History itself has recurrently disabused us of our fantasies in such a direction in order to remind us bluntly that no generation escapes the burden of struggle that is tantamount to the work of founding. We are responsible because response-ability remains the dynamic of our existence. The work of preservation is the work of foundation from which no generation can excuse itself if it wishes to remain faithful to the undertow of its existence. Settlement in this sense presupposes the impossibility of settlement.

Paradox of the Person

The formulation is a paradox but only because it attempts to grasp the container within the contained. Taken as the tension that provides the possibility of existence, there is nothing inherently paradoxical about it. The rationale is eminently clear, as Kierkegaard understood in first announcing paradox as what structures our lives in every sphere.[6] That which we live within cannot be subsumed under the living of it. Everything we do presupposes the forgetfulness of self, otherwise the self interposes a distance that prevents the actual doing. Thought cannot think itself except by not thinking of its content, just as a gift cannot really be a gift if it calls attention to itself. Our goal is not defined by the activity, but the other way around. The more we attempt to close the circle and include one in the other, the more we botch the possibility of acting at all. So although science may aim at a comprehensive understanding of reality, its viability depends on avoiding its own consummation, for science would itself be over once the movement of inquiry no longer animates it. Thought thinking itself is the millennial theme of Western philosophy, but thinking depends on remaining within the suspension of its outcome. An equally enduring paradox has surrounded the theme of freedom, occupying ever more prominence as the symbol that has come to support an ever-greater weight in the modern world. The difficulty of distinguishing between freedom and arbitrariness has tarnished the valuation of freedom from which it springs. Debates over positive and negative liberty remain irresolvable so long as we fail to recognize their source within a paradox, that is, within irresolvability itself. Freedom can mean only our determination by chance so long as its meaning as nonfreedom is not recognized. To say we are obliged is to insist that we are not free.[7] Nothing prevents reneging on our obligation, but that is more properly characterized as a failure of freedom rather than its exercise. And freedom is not to be defined by its failure but by the possibility of transcending itself. Paradox is not in this sense the irrational, not even an antinomy, but the exceeding of existence that makes existence possible. It is the unattainability of what we live within, for to attain it would be to close off living it.

Ultimately it is the paradox of the person whose disclosure is never a disclosure. No matter how exhaustive the expression, the person who undertakes it remains outside of the expressed. We know that there is always more, inexhaustibly more. The person, in the words of St. Augustine, is "a mystery so deep as to be hid from him in whom it is."[8] Intuitively we know this, and we have given it conceptual shape in the language of human dignity. The impossibility of weighing one human being against another or even against all human beings has been enshrined within the liberal language of rights. Each human being is entitled to equal concern and respect simply by virtue of being human. Through such formulations we hold ourselves accountable before a high ideal, one so high that the greatest danger is that it trails off into realms of abstraction disconnected from the concrete complications of life. Indeed, talk of the mystery of the person or the sanctity of human life seems to suggest a remoteness from where we actually are. Ideals and aspirations insinuate alibis for failing them, even though this is quite contrary to the intentions that lie behind them. For we do not mean that it is desirable to treat every human being with equal dignity and respect, but that we must do so. Human rights are not "values" we have chosen to defend.[9] They are rather the imprescriptible boundaries of our very existence. We have no other choice but to live within the acknowledgment of their imperative. It is not we who have chosen them; it is they that have chosen us. Unfortunately, little of that moral compulsion is contained within the abstractions by which human infinity is expressed. Universality has betrayed us.

In seeking to connote the transcendence of the person, we all too readily assume the adequacy of the denotation. Confusing the signifier with the signified, we fall victim to the misplaced concreteness of our language. The failing only becomes egregious when the signified lies radically beyond all signification, when it is this transcendence, or "différance," that provides the possibility of signification.[10] The difficulties we encounter in giving linguistic finitude to the infinite depth of the person are related to the interpersonal possibility of all linguistic communication. We cannot speak of the inexhaustibility of the other because it is just this inexhaustibility that sustains all possibility of speaking. If we could reach that point in conversation where we meant what we said and said what we meant then conversation would cease. Fortunately this danger is of very little concern to us. We may get tired and break off because of the physical limits that impose a finitude on all communications between human beings. But we would not have begun to speak with one another if we were not drawn by the glimpse of the infinity of communication that underpins our mutuality. Faith in the resumption of our conversation after all inevitable interruptions is sustained by awareness that is prior to awareness. The romantic aspiration for perfect transparency between two human beings is just one such indication of the strength of the undertow. It is not by any means the most definitive testament to its force. Kierkegaard saw that the project of total communication could become so obsessive that it preferred the ideal to the reality. A far more authentic witness, he contended, was the acceptance of partial communication infinitely extended over a whole life. The very inexhaustibility of the relationship was given its truest expression by the choice of marriage over the romantic leap into perfection. What cannot be said cannot be "said" as art. It can only be lived, for in the living of it we invest our very selves as the most eloquent declaration of the impossibility of saying.[11] Living is indeed our saying.

Now, this is both an insight into the possibility of communication and into the meaning of marriage. But it yields an even greater insight into the meaning of time, the possibility of possibility, that underpins both of them. We need time, the flow of our existence, in order to unfold what cannot be unfolded: the unfathomable depth of the person. It is this unreachable horizon of the person that opens the time of our existence as the horizon of unreachability itself. We do of course live within physical time as measured by movement within space, for everything is chronologically datable, but this derives its meaning from interpersonal time as the only setting within which datability acquires significance. We do not live within the physical universe; we live within the interpersonal community. Exploration of the vastness of space is shot through by the possibility of contact with the other, as evidenced by the intense interest in extraterrestrial life as its pervasive accompaniment. Continuity with the personal is the primordial passion lodged even within our most impersonal modes of inquiry. The guiding intimation of meaning is the meaning of the person whose infinitude cannot be contained in any finite tangibilities but who, for that very reason, contains the possibility of just such an infinite in the finite. Only a person can open the infinite dimension of the finite. It is in this sense that the eschatology of the person, the impossible possibility of infinite self-giving, opens the mysterious interest of everything that draws us in existence. Impersonal mystery is sustained by the mystery of the person as gift.

The very language of gift is inseparable from the gift of self, for there is no gift, despite all appearances, unless there is such self-giving. This is why it is possible to give without giving, or to give only in appearance. Even our traditional understanding of existence as a gift or the other as a gift has often not fully developed its personal meaning. We talk about giving one's heart or giving one's whole self, but the conception is not easily articulated, since it is ultimately impossible to give oneself. Isn't the self what one possesses least, the unfathomable mystery of Augustine? And even if one wanted to give oneself, as in marriage, how can it be conveyed? All that one human being can give to another is particular and tangible. What lies behind cannot be conveyed, but, and this is the essential point, it must be conveyed. The only genuinely human communication is one in which there is a mutual giving of self. Communication therefore takes the form of noncommunication. Whatever gifts are given do not constitute true giving, for that entails the giving of all. Nevertheless, the finite containers must carry the infinite they cannot contain. The gift, we finally realize, is the gift of giving itself.[12] We possess it only as a gift, as what we do not possess, so that the giving consists in giving away what we cannot give away. There is thus nothing to receive, for the receiving consists in recognizing that it has already been received. We live in time only because we do not live in time but have already reached the end that is gifted to us as the unfolding of time. It is in this sense that the ideal of human dignity is misconceived when it is posed as a goal of our existence within time, for there would be no time of existence without the horizon of interpersonal infinity that is the invisible beyond of all horizons.

We do not sustain the moral imperatives of our lives; they sustain us. The philosophic revolution that began with Kant has largely been an effort to come to grips with this realization. Hegel's criticism of Kant was that he had left morality too much in the realm of aspiration and thereby missed its constitutive role within ethical life. Merely making that observation, however, was not enough, for it then transferred the aspirational character to ethical life or suggested the historical inevitability of its realization. What was needed was the more thoroughly existential development that has been the occupation of philosophy ever since and received its first definitive expression through Kierkegaard. The gap between "is" and "ought," between knowledge and deed, is then recognized as a gap that opens only from the perspective of contemplation, as if existence could be achieved merely by thinking it. Such an attitude, Kierkegaard diagnosed, was a postponement that ultimately could not postpone existence. The illusion of abstraction could only be overcome through the recognition that the imperatives were truly imperative. There was no escaping them, even by thinking, so long as we sought to exist. What that existence would be could only be determined by the responsive unfolding of the principles that offered us the possibility of existing. The "either/or" was not between good or evil but between existing or not existing, for there is no possibility of existing without accepting the responsibility it entails. The language of ideals always suggests that there is still an "I" after I turn my back on them and so suggests the capacity to hold them at a distance. But we can no more disregard the moral imperatives that draw us than we can leap outside of existence. The choice of good or evil is the choice of existence or nonexistence. We are constituted by the unfolding of moral responsibility toward the other, which, far from offering an option for the exercise of our freedom, is the very substance of our existence within time. Morality provides time, time does not provide morality.

The mastery we routinely exercise over the world of objects is inclined to lead us to overlook the momentous difference when the mastery is over ourselves. Our language is dominated by the subject–object model of relationship. In the realm of ethics the model has no relevance since there is no subject other than through the temporal exercise of responsibility. The fixities of philosophical language that have been developed to grapple, albeit inadequately, with this situation have yet to complete the transition to a language of paradox that incorporates the self-limitation of language as such. All that we have are the abbreviations or intuitions that glimpse what is already known as what remains to be known in the unfolding of time. The mystery of the person cannot be contained or exhausted. That is the bedrock from which our thinking begins because it is indeed the very possibility of thinking. Our problem is to secure it within a world of finitude and immanence. The challenge is both intellectual and political, and on both fronts progress has been made, but confusion remains, especially when we seek to explain ourselves to ourselves. Within a world of instrumental rationality, in which the efficient coordination of means and ends is the highest necessity, it is difficult to explain why human beings should alone escape cost-benefit analysis. How can there be ends-in-themselves when every end is subsumable as a means to a further end? What is it about the operators that releases them from the logic of the machine? Questions about the "iron cage," the catastrophes of the sorcerer's apprentice or of the Frankenstein monster, and all that menaces as the crisis of technology are familiar extrapolations of the condition in which we find ourselves. Their very ubiquity testifies to the degree to which we have overstepped the limits that threaten to engulf us. They are raised only because we cannot be held within the boundaries of a system and have erected a political order that, as far as possible, definitively places every single person beyond the calculation of utility. Besides the growth of impersonal rationality there has also emerged the awareness of the inviolability of the person.

The Impossibility of Giving Reasons

The person is at the core of the political paradox within which we live. Everything about the liberal democratic ordering we take as authoritative escapes the giving of reasons we might attempt. Perhaps this has something to do with the wreckage of liberal theorizing with which its history is strewn. Already in the famous "contract" theorists we discern the modulations away from the term toward "covenant," "compact," and anything that might avoid the implication of a contract rooted in self-interest. Eventually "contract" is rehabilitated as a moral or eternal contract before simply being dropped altogether.[13] It is not clear that liberal theorizing has ever adequately recovered from the demise of these first conceptualizations. Instead it has drifted through ever-more incoherent evocations of its own foundations to finally reach the point at which it has turned its back on the project as such. The only thing that is clear is that liberal democracy, for all its inadequacies, works far better in practice than it does in theory. More than a hint of suspicion is cast upon the enterprise of justification itself, as precisely what tends to call into question what is more safely secured by convictions that rest beyond question. Only one step remains to this line of reflection, namely, to recognize why the effort of rationalization must fail. The giving of reasons presupposes that the reasons adduced stand at a more fundamental level than what is being justified. But what can have a higher claim in priority than the respect that is owed to each person? Is there an ordering or summation of benefits that might finally conclude the measuring? Or is it not the case that the imprescriptibilty of persons has a claim on us that stands outside of both benefits and costs? That we are committed to it most of all when the costs outweigh the benefits? Granted that many positive consequences flow from a society of mutual respect, but they would hardly follow if the respect were conditional on the consequences.

We have no recourse but to admit that the most central conviction of our lives together cannot be explained further. Everything else can be referred to it, but the absolute priority of the person cannot lead beyond itself. Historically, the language of theology, of the *imago Dei*, has been available as a marker for what we cannot understand, and much has been made of its withdrawal from the public square. Often overlooked is that there were good reasons for that withdrawal, which is therefore not to be excessively lamented. It is not the demands of pluralism that foreclosed the possibility of theological translation but the realization that even theological justification detracted from the sheer primordiality of the person. Respect for the person is diminished if it is seen merely as a means toward an extraneous other, even when that third party is God. To put it most bluntly, persons command our unalloyed respect even if it were to entail the violation of a divine command. Nothing stands higher since unconditional valuation of the person is the condition of all valuation. A God who would command such disvaluation is not worthy of acknowledgment as God. That is not a plausible theology, but it does suggest an opening for the curious phenomenon of the revolt against God that arises in the name of God. An important strand of modern atheism reads itself in this light as the renunciation of God for the sake of God. These are simply dynamics of the shift in which theology too must become existential, taking its direction from the mystery within which it finds itself rather than from preexisting conceptual certainties. Liberal democratic forms are not so much antitheological as theological in their own right. Rather than depending on a theology outside of them, the understanding of man as *imago Dei*, they can more properly be seen as the route by which the meaning of the *imago Dei* is regained from within the encounter with the other. In prioritizing the other we glimpse God's prioritizing of all others.[14]

Nothing is thereby explained, rather we have entered more deeply into the mystery in which we live. Surely this is the real meaning of explanation and of the ever-unsuccessful search for foundations. Theological or philosophical glibness would only deflect the quest for what cannot be found but not answer it. Thinking, it has long been recognized, is not the attainment of a result. It is the movement or the activity toward it, as the very name of philosophy suggests. But this realization has often been mistaken for the ultimate result, the one by which the movement of the arrival could be eclipsed. The temptation is one with which philosophy has itself struggled from the Platonic Ideas to the Hegelian system, for it has never been easy to accept the implication of Socratic ignorance that is entailed in the activity of thought. Thinking can never really know itself, for it can never encompass that from which it derives. "The more we know, the less we know" has been a dearly bought concession that is one of the principal achievements of modern philosophy. Acceptance of it depends, as Kierkegaard above all saw, on the reversal from the negative to the positive connotations. The failure of thought to think itself does not finally emerge as a net loss but as an inestimable gain, one that ensures that the possibility of thinking is not foreclosed within some finite realm before us. We are saved from answers and liberated to questioning, for questioning is the only mode of answer available to us. It is the very meaning of existence that we exist from what we do not know and that our existence is guarded by the nonknowledge of its source. The unattainability of the centrality of the person within liberal democracy is not simply an instance of this existential ignorance. It is a heightening of it.

This has been the secret of the liberal democratic success. For it is not just a political form that "works" as confirmed by its widespread durability or appeal, but one that lives within the very principles it espouses. That has entailed the deepening of the mystery by which it is sustained, drawing ever closer to what it cannot comprehend, but in that failure realizing it more intensely. This is what explains the capacity of liberal democracy to deepen its inspiration without clarifying the source of that movement. The secret of its success, in other words, is that the secret cannot be penetrated or perhaps that there is no secret other than the living of it. At any rate, the living serves only to intensify the mystery by which it is constituted. Even the meaning of liberal democracy proves to be a moving target for definitional purposes, a source of dissatisfaction to categorizers who would prefer that it exhibit greater constancy of meaning. The pattern is well known—those who are revolutionary in one era become liberal in another, or liberal in one and conservative in another. Burke is, for example, a classic case of such shifting appellations, but one could hardly accuse him of inconsistency any more than the alterations in context are unrelated to a constancy of direction. The inviolable liberty of the person remains at the center, ready to be evoked anew in light of the challenges that confront it while never comprehended outside of the struggle to attain it. As a result, the definition of liberal democracy changes while its inspiration escapes encapsulation. Even the term "liberal" is a relatively late emergence and indicates a new awareness of the liberty of the person that must lie at the core of any genuine political liberty.[15]

The pattern is well illustrated in the major shift in the meaning of the term "liberal" itself. With its center of gravity located in the right of property as the primary means by which the property of one's person was protected, the implication of an absolute right to private property was quickly drawn. Locke's location of the right within the application of labor, by which objects in the state of nature are appropriated for individual use, seemed a plausible account. But it could not survive the full-scale development of an industrial-capitalist economy in the nineteenth century. Then the social consequences of private property and especially their effects on the concrete exercise of individual liberty became apparent. Political liberty, it was realized, could not endure unaccountable concentrations of economic power, and individual liberty would be set at naught without protection from the worst vulnerabilities to which it was exposed. The result was an extensive readjustment of modern liberal democracies that recognized the imperative of controlling private liberty in order to preserve it. Partial socialization, and the emergence of the regulatory and welfare state, were all part of the trial-and-error quest for a balance between the public and the private that aimed at the preservation of the liberty of each of them. No great theory exists to define or defend the outcome, and it is arguable that the search for a balance has not by any means been concluded. Adjustments and readjustments continue apace. But what is not at issue is that the state has a role in mitigating the worst excesses of a system of private liberty. That concession followed, as much as the political and economic shifts in which it was reflected, from the priority that had already been given to individual liberty. In order to preserve it we were prepared to limit it. Liberty could not extend to the annihilation of liberty that the commodification of human beings would entail. Freedom of contract required the acknowledgment of the limits of contractual freedom.

The question today is whether a similar resolve will emerge in response to the next great crisis that seems to endanger liberty. At the moment even the perception that we are in a crisis has not crystallized within public consciousness. Our politics is still looking in the rearview mirror at the battles of the past or, at best, scouring the horizon for their contemporary repetitions. Globalization and its attendant anxieties is a case in point, but it is not a case in principle. The issue that raises a crisis in principle for liberal democracy is the expanding possibility of biotechnological control over human beings. Again the issue is presumptively framed within the rights of private liberty, but the implications raise unsettling questions as to the very meaning of liberty. Does it extend to the exercise of control over the genetic endowments of other human beings? In the name of whose liberty are such interventions undertaken? Can there be a right to procure a clone of oneself? If not, on what basis is such a choice prohibited? And what about the permissibility of therapeutic cloning intended to promote the health of the fully present human being? Such are the questions that loom before us, and a resolution is crucially dependent on the recognition of their convergence on the inviolability of the person enshrined at the heart of our constitutional tradition. To the extent that the cases are viewed in isolation, the response will simply reflect popular or market forces, or the familiar vacillations of policy in response to pragmatic assessments of costs and benefits. In reality what is at stake is the viability of liberal democracy as such. Just as in the slavery crisis Lincoln understood that the ownership of one human being by another was radically incompatible with the very idea of democratic self-government. Is the design of one human being by another any more reconcilable? What then of the instrumentalization of the embryonic gestation of human beings?

Are there any limits to the manipulation of the biological processes on which human life depends? Does respect for persons entail respect for their nonpersonal constituents? Advancing scientific understanding is a necessary ingredient in reaching such decisions, but it is not sufficient to resolve questions that science itself has generated. Their only resolution must be political, that is, existential.[16] We are compelled to descend deeper into the convictions within which we live, conscious that the answers we retrieve implicate us to the very core. Information cannot settle the responsibility we alone can exercise.

Founding as Refounding

No generation is spared the burden of founding, least of all one that lives during a moment when the crisis of foundations looms. It is at such a time that the inescapability of founding becomes apparent. All founding is a refounding that is necessitated by the impossibility of founding. Just as there are no ready-made answers, so there is no already-made founding. The burden cannot be shifted to our predecessors for the life we are called to live. Surrogate living is not an option, especially when it is the very meaning of living that is at issue. It may be readily acknowledged that every individual is required to live his or her own life, but the implication, that every life exceeds the meaning of it, is less frequently adduced. There can be no guidance, however authoritative, that takes the place of the singular movement of self-realization. A blueprint to living would deprive living of its life, because living is precisely the capacity to follow more than a blueprint. This is the distinction between a mechanism and an organism. Teleology is merely a convenient way of conceiving the ordering process at work, but, from within, the movement is characterized by the supersession of all strictly teleological limits. Even the simplest organisms seem to delay rather than accelerate the movement toward their goal of expending themselves in the propagation of the species. Teleology then can mean the avoidance of a telos. Kierkegaard thought deeply about the way in which the individual, the religious, exceeds the universal, the ethical. In analyzing the story of Abraham's readiness to sacrifice Isaac he spoke of a "teleological suspension of the ethical."[17] The intuition that the individual is immediately related to the infinite arises from this insight. What has yet to emerge is the realization that it is this uncontainability of the individual that constitutes the very possibility of living. No matter how comprehensive the founding, the individual always stands outside of it, not as a defection from it, but as its supereminent realization.

The founding can therefore mean nothing apart from the persons whose founding it is. Nothing is founded as a product or result that exists outside of them. It is the founding that supports and sustains their being as what cannot be contained within it. Founding is always in the mode of nonfounding. Neither the burden of living nor the exercise of responsibility is lifted by the articulation of principles achieved. This is not just because principles must be implemented if they are to be taken seriously, but because over and above all realizations is the superabundance of the person who transcends and sustains them. Persons are contained, and they are not contained in the formulations they adduce, for the very meaning of their existence is the giving of what they cannot give, namely, themselves. We are all equal as persons, but this is not an abstract equality; it is the concreteness of our existence. Superiority or inferiority, founders or followers are categories that have no place when we meet as persons, or, at best, their place is strictly ancillary. Differences are quickly superseded as we recognize the mutuality of exchange that must take place. None can give only a part and none can be received only as a part. They are all wholes open to all other wholes and thus constituting a community of wholes. Not even the community as a whole outweighs such parts that, as Maritain expressed it, are themselves wholes.[18] Calling each one an infinite center of meaning and value in the universe is simply an attempt to evoke what cannot be said directly, but which can be approximated existentially. That is, to recognize that the founding is the work of every one of them, not because they are equally equipped to achieve it, but because it is equally present within them as the very essence of their being. The work of founding is the work of persons who can found because the possibility of self-donation is the foundation of a community of persons.

Theorists have expended a good deal of effort in trying to understand the process of community formation. Political leaders engaged in nation-building are naturally more than a little intrigued by the topic. Social science studies have identified an array of factors that enter into such an emergence, and much is to be learned from the fruit of such labors. Yet it is difficult not to feel that the essential has been missed. Having mastered all the incidentals that go into the growth of community, we have overlooked its core. The reason for this neglect, a notorious failing of social science, is not hard to discover. We are inclined to avoid what we cannot understand. Social science is in search of explanations, that is, the discovery that social processes are reducible to other more palpable processes. But the founding of community is not of that type. It cannot be understood in terms of anything other than itself. None of the explanations are ultimately sufficient, for it is a mystery that we live within. We cannot even reach, let alone reach beyond, the boundaries of our own existence. Founding can only be understood from within the struggle of founding, an act of such utter simplicity that it is available to every human being. We can understand the more elaborate and elaborately celebrated foundings of history only because that more elementary reality is readily available to us.[19] We know that the founding occurs whenever the miracle of generosity breaks through. The willingness to suffer for another, to put one's own existence at risk, is the unanticipated event that invites the formation of community between human beings. Nothing can predict it and nothing can explain it, for it is the basis of all predictability and explanation. A community of trust arises from the gift of vulnerability exceeding all expectation.

The founder is in this sense not the one who first signs the document but the one who lives it most deeply, a sentiment that is the secret of the Gettysburg Address. Lincoln had an uncanny affinity with this realization, but it is at the core of all authentic political rhetoric. Yet the appeal is not simply rhetorical. Reminders of the founding struggles are effective only if they are more than reminders; they must become invitations to outdo the founding in existential generosity. Without that inexplicable self-giving no amount of genius can effect a founding. The question inevitably is how such a spirit can be induced. Here it is very important not to diverge from the already intuited, for there is no way of communicating a spirit of generosity except through the spirit of generosity. Nothing extraneous can substitute. The mystery of the founding is thus inseparable from the mystery of the founding. It depends less on the attainments of the most visible participants than on the more numerous invisible participants whose unheralded generosity can neither be commanded nor anticipated. Conventionally we are inclined to applaud the notion that "everyone does their part" or that "every little bit counts." But here we are referring to much more. The little is indeed the all. Contributions are neither large nor small; they are all of irreplaceable value because they are nothing less than the persons who make them.

Measurement is not on the scale of the finite or the temporal but on the infinite and the eternal. We are not producing a product. The community we are founding is nothing less than a community of selves, constituted by the free gift of ourselves to one another. Such a community does not exist within its external trappings, nor is it to be identified with the most substantial professions of its presence, for the externalities are really the furthest from its essence. Community exists, we might say, most of all in the virtually inarticulate promptings of the heart by which it is concretely built up between human beings. Matryona, the woman who in Solzhenitsyn's story was universally overlooked in her insignificance, is the one who preserves the secret of community most faithfully with an inward purity of heart. She is the one just person without whom the city cannot stand.[20]

The power of the powerless turns out to be the only power that creates. This is not to suggest that the power of the "powerful" is a negligible factor in founding community; there is an ineliminable role for the power that removes the obstacles to the formation of community. Arresting the lawbreakers is indispensable to the reality of law, for it is not a wholly interior order but one that is reciprocally constituted through action. Only if law is reliable can it be relied upon. Without the hand of law everyone must take the law into their own hands. This is the state of mutual mistrust that Hobbes called the state of nature, a state that he understood could not be overcome simply by force. Whatever force was called upon to resist violence could not be the source of itself; the sovereign acquired power through consent and remained powerful only so long as trust in his power persisted. Even the Leviathan could not penetrate the mystery of his own genesis in an uncoerced act of freedom.[21] His power too arose from the power of the powerless, and he therefore must acknowledge its own dependent reality. The spectacle of dictators whose power melts away as soon as the first brittle periphery is breached confirms this. But it does not shed light on the positive formation of power, a process to which only those willing to risk their own vulnerability have any access. Democratic power has long been recognized as an awesome sight, for a community united in free self-sacrifice cannot easily be defeated. But how it emerges is a mystery even to those in whom it occurs. This is why we cannot readily export democracy. One human being cannot transfer the exercise of his freedom to another. All that we can do is suffer on behalf of another thereby becoming a suffering witness.

Shortcuts are anathema to the truth of the witness because they directly contradict it. A short-sighted pragmatism turns out to be the least pragmatic policy because it undermines the very possibility of what is aimed at. By placing the means ahead of the end, expediency demonstrates that the former is taken more seriously than the latter. Impatience with results and the pressure for accomplishments negate the very struggle they seek to consummate. Disappointment at the futility of our efforts to promote democracy arises because we have not fully counted the cost; it is a course we have embarked on without realizing that it may demand our all. Can we be in favor of democracy only if it does not demand too much of us? Or if it results in regimes we regard as acceptable? Or if it is a success? There is nothing unreasonable about such questions, for they are implicated in the value of democracy itself. After all, there is something horrible about a democratic revolution that devolves into brutality, oppression, and chaos. In politics the best is the enemy of the good, for the achievement of tangible human gains is far preferable to the obstinacy that must have all or nothing. The problem is that such reasonable judgments apply when we have placed a reasonable distance between ourselves and our existence. From within the perspective of existence no such detachment is possible because detachment is tantamount to the deferral of existence. Depth of conviction impinges directly on the unfolding of the reality in which we find ourselves. The emergence of democracy is utterly dependent on the unconditionality of our dedication to it. Anything less than a total commitment condemns its unseriousness from the start. Unconditional respect for the inviolable freedom of the other cannot be simultaneously conditional. Love is not love if it is within reason. Such complete self-giving is no guarantee of reciprocation, but yet it is the only possibility of evoking a response that is more than reciprocation.

Democracy as Eschatology

No one can determine the outcome, for it would be the height of madness to presume that our actions can determine the historical reality in which they take place. There will always be a role for the pragmatic humility that is willing to make adjustments along the way, but always without doing the slightest thing that might compromise the principles that lie at the core of democratic respect. A willingness to accept less perfect democracy in reality rather than an insistence on an unrealizable ideal is a fully consistent attitude. Indeed, it flows from the deepest commitment to the democratic idea. An acceptance of limits has historically been the route of the most democratic polities that, though never fully incarnating the principles that lie behind them, have never ceased to approach those limits in their concrete unfolding. What has sustained that movement, however, is neither an expectation of inevitable success nor a commitment to succeed at any cost. It is rather the realization that success is irrelevant, for it has already been achieved. What remains to be accomplished in time has already been accomplished in the eternity of its beginning. "Democracy to come" is eschatologically now.[22] External success, though not unimportant, is strictly secondary to the inner reality from which it derives. Democracy does not exist within institutions and places, but within the hearts and minds of the human beings who occupy them. Whether the number of adherents is many or few, so long as the democratic impulse lives within a single individual it has achieved its reality.[23] Plato struggled to articulate this insight in regard to the best constitution in the Republic and arrived at a roughly similar conclusion. Even for the man of preeminent goodness, the conviction of the best constitution is not simply an idea he carries within. He experiences it rather as the idea that carries him forward, one that would not have sustained him if it did not already exist before him. It is that insight into the priority of democracy over history that is the faith that underpins its historical emergence.

To the extent that we wish to be missionaries of the democratic idea we must be upheld by the faith that assures us of the attainment of the goal we seek. Not only is this the faith that alone can sustain the vicissitudes of the struggle, but it is the only faith that can preserve us from the temptation to sacrifice principle for the sake of short-term success. Expediency cannot deflect us from commitment to a goal that is already reached. How would it be possible to turn our backs on the reality we now know more thoroughly than any confirmation can provide? To betray it would indeed be the suicide of the spirit that only the spirit itself can commit. The mere nonemergence of a response, the historical failure of the democratic experiment in generosity, can work no such damage. When the end has already been reached in the first step, then the ill fortune of time, its trials and tribulations, can hardly reverse the direction. Democracy is already achieved once the readiness to suffer the consequences of freedom has been embraced. In recognizing the other as an inviolable center of the universe, the democratic ethos has dawned.[24] The mystery of that emergence, which cannot be penetrated further, is that, as an unconditional openness to the other, it is not conditioned on the response. A response would indeed be welcome, but it is not dependent upon it. Democracy will not emerge historically in its absence, but the invitation to it has already exceeded even the necessity of a response. This is the meaning of the only generosity that is appropriate toward the infinity of the person. Nothing can be predetermined in advance. Imposition of conditions would simply demonstrate that we did not believe what we said, that we were finally not unconditional in our conviction of the unconditional respect owed to each human being.

When we ask again how such faith can be sustained, how the foundation of democracy can be secured, we realize that the question has been misdirected. It is not we who sustain the faith, it is the faith that sustains us. We cannot comprehend it because it is what comprehends us. To say that we have through faith reached the goal toward which we strive is not quite correct, because it is more properly the case that the goal has reached us. Even the Kierkegaardian language of a leap, a term that is not quite so widely used by him as is often assumed, fails to capture the pre-leap toward us that is entailed. When we arrive at the democratic infinity of the other, it is not as the result of a ratiocinative movement on our part. Nor is it simply a leap in the sense of a raw decision, a will to believe. Instead it is the encounter with what has been present before we even began to search, what we have known from the start, and what we could not have known if we had not always known it. Modern philosophers since Kant have grappled with this conception that our decisions are not made in time but somehow in eternity, that it is the eternal rather than the temporal that constitutes the real boundary of our existence.[25] What might be meant by such a notion is perhaps best seen in the faith that sustains the democratic openness. We would not have been able to reach the opening if we had not already reached it, so that its actual discovery within the time of our existence carries the implication of arriving too late. The recognition entailed could not have taken place unless we knew without knowing it before. It is the realization that we are already within a state of community with all other human beings that provides the possibility of the formation of particular communities. While living in time we know that we do not live in time because we can become contemporaneous in the open understanding of every single person past, present, and future. Yet we cannot explain this possibility to ourselves. It remains the unsurpassable horizon of our existence. No one is in a better position to explain to anyone else what the formation of community is, otherwise we would not be equally positioned to bring it about within our own lives.

Everyone must begin anew to form the community in which he or she lives. All talk of schemes of perfection, or of historical crisis, merely defers the moment when that beginning must occur. Of all the political forms, liberal democracy is the one that most fully recognizes this existential imperative. It is not just a reflection of the liberal democratic reality that we must each day "improvise a government"[26] but that this is explicitly acknowledged as the principle within which we live. Crisis would then be the ordinary condition of liberal democracy. Jefferson's remark about every generation undertaking its own revolution may be taken as a rhetorical nod toward this unachievable ever-achievable revolution. The dignity of the individual within liberal democracy is directly related to this realization of the unique irreplaceable responsibility of each member. It is a political form that not only values the individual but one that is constituted by its valuation of the individual. To say that rights are indivisible is not to posit some mystical bond by which human beings are united. It is to recognize the very core of the democratic idea. Individuals found an order that acknowledges the dependence of its founding on individuals. This is why there is no founding before there is a founding, for it would be to place something before the inviolable reverence that is owed. Consent has long been recognized as its hallmark. But this is always more than a mere factual event. Within the requirement of consent is encapsulated a whole understanding of the irreducibility of the personal inwardness it entails. The movement of consent can be exercised in no other way than through the nontransferable authorization that the individual alone can make. To the extent that everything depends on the singular decision of each individual, it cannot be penetrated further than is available to every one who makes it.

From Democracy as Concept to Democracy as Existence

No one can ultimately tell us why we must respond to the call of the other. We simply know we must. To explain it further would be to step outside of the exercise of responsibility. Most men, Aristotle remarked, prefer to talk about ethics rather than to act, for the talking becomes a way of deferring what must be done. When we must move forward in action, the talking is left behind as a hindrance to where we have to go. All that is left is the inexorability of the imperative within which we find ourselves. Even the talking draws its luminosity from that imperative, but it runs the risk of deluding itself that it has escaped the imperative at the same time. Theorists have been grappling for some time now with the conundrum of why democracy works so much better in practice than it does in theory. It may well be that we are finally gaining an insight into the priority of life over reflection on it, especially through the recognition of the extent to which democracy is premised on that realization. A person is just what cannot be explained, not even to him- or herself. Infinitely eluding the movement of self-disclosure, a person is an unending movement of self-disclosure. Whatever identity is formulated or reached, there is always more, for, without the ever-going-beyond what he or she is, the person would scarcely exist. A person is in that sense what cannot actually exist as a fixed quantity. It is thus in the person that the very meaning of existence, of the movement by which it is constituted, is glimpsed. Existence is personal because the personal is existence. "Democracy" is both a term that names this process from the outside and the reality that is constituted by it from within. The ambivalence pervades our political language and the failure to grasp the distinction is the source of many of the confusions that afflict us.

Once we keep the distinction in mind, it is striking how many of the fractures that seem to define our democratic polities are resolved, or point the way toward a resolution that has yet to be reached. Most notably in the great crisis thrown up by the expansion of biotechnological control over human beings, it often appears as if our traditional language of individual rights has abandoned us. The right to have a baby of a particular kind seems to be merely an exercise of parental prerogatives over their own reproductive capacities. Yet the prospect of designer babies gives us pause, especially because it collides with the very notion of the absolute worth of each one. Do the rights of the parents trump the rights of the child? Can any rights be secure if they are variable across generations? The further we proceed, the more bewildering the outcome. It is no wonder that many have despaired of the coherence of the language of rights or of its capacity to respond to the novel challenges posed within it. Yet we are not simply in a position to invent a newly authoritative language. It begs credibility to suggest that we simply jettison the only viable moral language that constitutes the world in which we live. The impasse, however, can be resolved if we recognize that it has arisen because of a failure to distinguish between the conceptual and the existential meanings of our prevailing terminology. Rights are indeed prerogatives we can assert so long as we regard them as possessions whose objectivity must be acknowledged by all around us. Ownership of rights is an unfortunate implication of an "ownership society." The situation is quite different if we shift to the existential mode and recognize that rights own us. We are the possessed, not the possessors. Our rights cannot extend to the design of another human being because our very rights depend on the incapacity of anyone to determine the existence of another. We may be procreative but we are not creative. Our very humanity depends on the preservation of that limit. Once that line is crossed an abyss opens before us, for the other is then no longer a person, an inviolable source of self-disclosure in the universe. We would have destroyed the very principle from which we ourselves embark on the adventure of self-disclosure.

The possibility of that misstep is of course always present within the exercise of liberty protected by a regime of rights. An expansionist pressure on the boundaries of liberty is almost a given, for the boundaries receive their definition from that agonistic struggle. The pattern only becomes problematic when it contemplates the abolition of the boundaries as such, that is, when the balancing of rights permits one party to become the holder of the balance in relation to the other. No one can explain why this must not be permitted. We simply know that it cannot, for to be able to explain why would be to claim to have reached a viewpoint higher than the mutual inviolability of persons. Since there is nothing higher in the universe, such an explanation could only take the form of a descent below the level of the personal. The exercise of our liberty always implicates us in relation to the self-understanding of liberty. But when the application includes the very conditions from which liberty itself arises, then the prospect of dehumanization is intrinsic to the action and also intrinsic to its consequences. The bright line that demarcates the limits of genetic intervention in the life of an other must always be the imperative of the good of the other, uncontaminated by any further consideration. The liberty of parents and doctors must thus be wholly subordinated to the liberty of the child. To do anything less would be, not only to rob the child of the independence from subordination to which he or she has a right to expect, it would also be to rob the parents of the possibility of a relationship with their child that is unconditionally affirmed. Love can only love that which is utterly beyond our sphere of calculation and control, for it is only then that we can meet as equals in the equality of response to one another. To place any other factor ahead of the inviolability of the other is to lose the very possibility of love that loves the other beyond all reasons.

Resistance to the nightmare of instrumentalization that threatens to overwhelm our democratic liberties is the great struggle of the day. Resources may at times appear slender but that is only from the perspective of an external perspective. From within, the growth of the liberal democratic soul, as Tocqueville suggested, remains our highest possibility. To those who wish to bring it about, it is incumbent on them to trust in the principles they espouse to defend. A bemoaning of the problems must be exchanged for an inner immersion within them. Then the prospect of a founding opens up, as a new gleam of light. But it is not the light we shine on the issues that counts but the light that flashes back toward us. We find ourselves held fast by that which we dare not let go. The language of human rights turns out, as it did for the dissidents of the totalitarian regimes, to have more staying power than many had suspected. Not only is there the possibility of holding the line against some of the worst abuses of biotechnical manipulation, but the very struggle yields an unexpected benefit. There is now the possibility of reaching a clarification of the language of rights that had hitherto escaped the most astute theorists of the tradition. When the rights of one so totally threaten to envelop the rights of another, then we have no recourse but to bring forth the intimations that have led us to insist on the inviolability of the rights of all. It is a result that will have been reached, not by way of a philosophical meditation, but by virtue of the lived necessity within which we find ourselves. Principles will have been clarified by way of a new founding, one that now recognizes the origin of principles within the founding event. It is for this reason that the fragility that impels our efforts can be understood more profoundly, not as sheer fragility, but as the indispensable invitation to go beyond it. Fragility is strength when it prompts the founding in which we discover that we have found again what was never lost.

CHAPTER FOUR

The Person and the Common Good

Toward a Language of Paradox

The chapter title has been chosen to recall the masterpiece of concision that Jacques Maritain published under the same heading.[1] He too had concluded that the political language by which we juxtapose the "individual" and the "common good" had doomed the possibility of recomposing them. Confident that we know what we are talking about when we envisage individuals coming together for the sake of a common good, we fail to see that we have really confused two different orders of reality. The common good is something external to the individuals who constitute it, but the individuals themselves are not externalities at all. Not even the distinction between the public and the private can capture this incommensurability, or, rather, it captures it by way of obscuring the radical incommensurability involved. This was the contribution of Maritain's short book. He understood, almost as the culmination of his efforts to preserve and defend the modern heightening of respect for the individual, that the language by which that elevation was conventionally expressed had to be disrupted. This is why he invoked the tension between the person and the common good. As with much of the incomplete project of "personalism," Maritain saw that at least a beginning had to be made by insisting on the unbridgeability between every single human being and the political aggregation of the many. He understood that the politics he advocated, liberal democratic politics, revolved around the very recognition of that incommensurability.

The difficulty was that the liberal democratic language had never managed to achieve the transparence it sought to express. As it strained to relate the individual to the whole in such a way that the individual could never be subordinated to the whole, liberal democratic language had never found a way of capturing the uniqueness of the relationship. That is, as Maritain suggested, that the liberal democratic achievement is to have created "a whole composed of wholes."[2] No prescription of the common good, no matter how extensive the anticipated social rewards might be, can justify the abolition of the rights of a single individual along the way. The calculation of costs and benefits cannot be extended to human beings. Only the defense of particular rights can subtend the diminution of particular rights. Mere advancement of the collective welfare never provides a basis for a subordination that is tantamount to the devaluation of the single individual. This is the meaning of the liberal guarantee of the rights of equal dignity and respect. Only the rights of one can trump the rights of another. Nothing of merely collective significance, even happiness or welfare, occupies such a primary position. In weighing the rights of one against the rights of another we are engaged in weighing two infinities, so that the result is always the same. It is not that the result cannot be calculated but that the calculation cannot be resolved in anything less than equality. When considerations of the common or collective welfare enter in, we are immediately transferred to the realm of the finite, the calculable as such, and that is precisely what is forbidden. The individual and the common good measured in terms of anything other than their incommensurability is foreclosed. That is the innermost core of liberal democracy. Yet it must remain inaccessible to the publicly available language even in the practical acknowledgment of its imperative.

The Incomplete Development of Personalism

Maritain had a profound intuition of the paradox of liberal democracy, and he struggled, if not to resolve it, to render it more perspicuous at least. That was his achievement, especially in *The Person and the Common Good*, in which he introduced a more powerfully personalist language. The project can be seen as a first step beyond the philosophical language of substance. Maritain understood that the traditional understanding of man as *imago Dei*, even as that reached its culminating affirmation in the incarnation of Christ and his redemptive outpouring for all, could no longer function as the authoritative source for the public evocation of human dignity and respect. Not only was it a language tied to the orbit of Judaic and Christian faith, but, even for believers, there remained the problem of translating it into the concrete. The faithful witness of love in action still remained a powerful testament, but its source could not easily be articulated. Mother Teresa lived the imperative of the infinite dignity of every human being, but is it a principle that is founded on anything more than her unique personal commitment? This is the question confronting all Christian reflection on the political today, especially in light of the threat of instrumentalization confronting human dignity and the heightened awareness that Christians are the carriers of the unique divine affirmation of every human being. It is this challenge that shaped the profound nexus John Paul II sought to forge in his writings between the Christian truth about man and the contemporary affirmation of human rights. He was confident that Christianity contained a deeper justification for human rights than any purely secular perspective. Like Maritain he turned to the realm of the person, in his case the "acting person," to uncover the horizon within which our most powerful moral intuitions might become transparent for the source that lay beyond them. In other words, the turn toward the person as the region in which the mystery of the individual can be more perspicuously expressed has by now become an axiom of Catholic thought.

Yet the effect of this turn has been relatively slight. Readers of this personalist literature can discern that something new has begun, but they are unsure what to make of it. Personalism may simply be a concession to the dominant motif of autonomy or it may invite the descent into subjectivism that lurks behind the appeal to human rights. Is there a genuinely Christian retrieval of the respect for human dignity that has characterized the modern project? The inconclusiveness of the results, especially in light of the abandonment of a more rigorously natural law approach, may arise from the relative recency of the experiment. Even in the case of Maritain, the turn toward more personalist modes was a late development in his thought, while the earlier efforts of Scheler, Mounier, and others never seem to have delivered on their promise, at least not in the realm of moral and political language.³ Wojtyla's ambitious efforts were necessarily abbreviated through the genres of expression available to John Paul II, but taken as a whole his twenty-seven-year pontificate yielded a remarkable body of reflection.⁴ The challenge is to find the intellectual center from which they must be understood. The fact that admiration has so often substituted for understanding is an indication of the difficulty. A truly personalist mode of discourse requires a very different kind of thinking from the prevailing objectivist patterns. Correlatively, if we are to think about human beings in a different way, then we must develop the appropriate linguistic means, not simply make an alternative selection of terminology from the available possibilities. The inconclusiveness of the Catholic experiment with personalism, I suggest, has much to do with the failure to pay adequate attention to the philosophical and linguistic revolution it entailed. New wine cannot be put into old wineskins.

The tendency has been to assume that the shift to the perspective of the acting person would merely be a different way of doing philosophical anthropology. "Personal" and "individual" were simply interchangeable terms. What was overlooked is that the person is precisely what cannot be comprehended, what cannot be captured as an "anthropology" or "psychology" by which an explanation is reached. The perspective of the person is not one that can be reached by assuming an external vantage point, but rather it is one available to us only by virtue of our own reality as persons. It is a luminosity that is constitutive of what persons are, but it cannot extend beyond the perspective of our participation within its meaningful horizon. The more we talk about persons as if they were another species of objects, the further we recede from the only perspective on personal reality available to us. It is a common problem within the human sciences and goes a long way toward explaining why they are essentially sciences of the peripherally human. But in relation to the intended effort of fidelity to the personal reality of human beings, it is indispensable that it guards against the tendency to slide back into objectivist modes of analysis. The only effective means of resisting that undertow is to root the reflection firmly in the realization that we are ourselves the reality on which we seek to reflect. What this means is that our language does not refer to any preexisting entities but rather to the parameters of an existence that unfolds only through its own conscious self-enactment. Our best access to the acting person is through our own acting personhood, and this is also the limit of our access to what is emergent within the personal reality. We can give reasons for our actions, but we cannot penetrate beyond the reasons that provide the self-disclosure of a person.

A New Understanding of Language Required

Language is, in other words, not the means by which we define a reality that stands over against us. It is rather the means by which the interpersonal reality within which we find ourselves is constituted. Words themselves do not identify entities that are present before us, for they are part of the very process in which we aim at making present what can never really be present. Without that gap between the intention and its intended there could not be the space of the movement by which our existence is constituted. It is because the saying never overlaps with the said that our conversation can continue, endlessly, but not without the direction imparted by aspiration. Indeed, we might say that it is this impossibility of self-disclosure that above all marks the communication of persons. Over and above the nonpresence of the signified from which all our signifiers recede there is the special case of the nonpresence of the signified person. We might say that in the case of persons, the signified conspires to elude the capture of the present toward which our intentionality drives. Not only is each person a mystery, an abyss so deep as "to be hid from him in whom it is," in the words of St. Augustine, but even in the moment of self-disclosure what is most profoundly disclosed is that no disclosure has taken place. When a person expresses him- or herself, the uppermost meaning is that of the person who exceeds what has been expressed. The only thing we can know is that he or she is not present in the expressed. We might say that it is possible for human beings to express themselves because they never express themselves. Like God they remain hidden behind, yet present within, their creation. That incommunicability that ultimately characterizes the person can be known only through the capacity of persons to recognize what cannot be recognized in each of them. Only persons can know persons.

The problem with a language that talks "about" persons as if they were alternative essences or souls is that we recede further from the source of our discourse. Classical and Christian accounts of philosophical anthropology are not incorrect, they are simply opaque. What they neglect is their own awareness that the personal knowledge available to us arises because we ourselves are persons. Or, as is often the case, traditional anthropologies are prepared to concede the perspective of participation, but then they immediately ignore their own admission. Treating the individual as a specimen of a universal nature, they fail to acknowledge that the person in every instance exceeds the category of which it is an instance. This is the danger that arises when we forget that even the language we are using derives from the same participatory perspective as what we seek to articulate. Linguistic amnesia is not only a literary flaw, for it strikes at the very possibility of thinking through the issues that matter most to us. Assuming we have captured the mystery of the individual, the person, by naming it, we are confused by the incomprehensible notion that infinity can be contained in so little. Is it not strange that the rights of a single human being can outweigh the pressure of the entire world? We already know that it is impossible to kill a human being unless he or she has first been depersonalized. Are we not moving in that same direction when we take the "person" as a marker for the generically impersonal and forget that its very meaning arises out of the encounter by which the unique one surpasses all others in existence? There is no way to discourse generally about the personal without obscuring what the personal really is, and if we are to remain true to the presentiments that guide our discourse, then we must be prepared to guard against the tendency of our language to betray itself. Naming is in general fraught with difficulty, but the difficulty is insuperable when it seeks to name a person. Only by letting the name overwhelm can naming take place.[5]

Abortion as a Misunderstanding of the Person

A good example of the problems generated when the language of persons is transposed into the language of entities is seen in the abortion debate. The more linguistically aware formulations do not ask when life begins, since the aborting of life is precisely what is at issue. Rather, they pose it as the question of when the fetus becomes a person. This is also the point of engagement from the legally relevant perspective. So the endorsement of a personalist terminology seems to submit to the inspectors who would render judgment on when a person is actually present. The difficulty, as we have tried to suggest, is that the language of personhood is precisely the language of what is not present. If the person is what is signified, then it is just what escapes its signifier. How then can we know when the fetus becomes a person? The answer is that we cannot. No more than with the comatose can we tell whether a conscious other is there. This inaccessibility arises, not because we lack evidence in the particular cases, but because the relationship with persons is one that always goes beyond the evidence available. We do not love human beings because they have given us good reasons for doing so but because they are beyond all the reasons for doing so. Our relationship to others is unconditioned in the sense that it lies radically outside the satisfaction of conditions. Emmanuel Levinas has sought to articulate this priority of the other by saying that I am responsible for the other before I am even aware of myself.[6] I become a self in light of my responsibility for the other. Even our relationship to the corpse, from which we know the person is now definitively absent, is marked by reverence for what the body formerly invisibly contained. Of all the epiphanies of the person we might say that the vulnerability of the fetus is the one in which otherness is most deeply invoked. It is, after all, the beginning or as close as we can get to the beginning of the other.

The issue is not when personhood begins but the realization that personhood is what provides the possibility of beginning. This is not simply in the conventional sense that birth is the beginning of everything in human life, but in the more deeply metaphysical sense that each birth is somehow the beginning of being itself. The person is there even before he begins to be, for this is the very meaning of what it is to be a person. In thinking through the logic of what it means to be a person, to know one another as persons, we must be prepared to follow the implications that exceed our ordinary logic. This has been the great shortcoming of personalist reflection, which has not had the temerity to pursue its own intimations. Instead it has fallen back into more familiar patterns of thought by which thinking gives mastery over the objects of our thought. As a consequence, it is not surprising that the personalist turn is diverted into irresolvable debates about when a person begins, or even when human life begins, debates that always suggest that we have somehow stepped outside of all such parameters ourselves and can sit in judgment on what constitutes humanity. At this point it must be conceded that a large part of the philosophical tradition with its tendency toward definitional statement has encouraged such illusions. But what has always saved the tradition has been the inevitably unspoken awareness that such definitions were no more than derivative. Humanity can only be known from within, by becoming ourselves more human. This is why the status of the fetus can only be answered by the one who is in touch with it, one whose inwardness can respond to the inwardness that rises from the darkness itself. Only the mother can tell who the fetus is because it is in love that the otherness of the other is known. Outside of that the other can only be known as another, an indifferent clump of tissue. Only the latter can be aborted, for it is impossible (on all levels) to abort a person. But what might we say when the mother no longer loves the child within, when she asserts a right to abort the other?

Surely the same situation holds, that the fetus can only be recognized through the love of the mother, even if it is not always actual in the love of the "mother." We are each called to step into the place of the mother when mothers turn their backs on the others who make them who they are.[7] The only access available to us is the perspective of love, a love that is not conditioned by the attainments of the earliest zygote. We might even say that it is its incapacity to return the love that is lavished on him or her that is the greatest gift the embryo already offers toward the world. None of its potential achievements can surpass the pure gift of itself that it radiates from the very beginning. Children are loved and make it possible for us to love before they are even known. Only after they are born do they enter the world of visibility, the world of measuring and comparing in which even love can be tainted by the weight of tangibilities. Their life as human beings entering a finite social universe is then one long series of assessments. The fate would be insupportable if there was not at some point, at the very beginning, the one pure moment of unalloyed love for their own sake. Parental love, like all love, is only truly love if it is unconditioned. But when is it possible for us to affirm unconditioned love unconditionally? To answer truthfully we would have to say when there is no possibility of our knowledge of the other not introducing an element of judgment. Before we know who the other is, love must be called forth. This can only be when the other is present without being present. The unborn is in that sense the purest possibility of the person, of that which *is* without visible manifestation. The inwardness by which the child is known by the mother is the most elemental form of the inwardness by which every other is disclosed to us. Without the otherness of the fetus there would be no possibility of the purely other, the one who simply is apart from every characteristic that can finitize the relationship.

It is not therefore for us to determine the status of the fetus, for our own status as persons is determined by the fetus. Dehumanization has long been understood to be the main danger of the widespread practice of abortion. This is clearly the reason why it is not a mainstream procedure within medical schools or the profession. Even without back-alley abortions it is still a largely backdoor operation. By any stretch of the imagination this is surely a strange state of affairs for a procedure that has been widely hailed as a source of liberation. Not even its installation within the grandeur of constitutional rights has been able to rub out the taint of illegitimacy. Revulsion persists, not because of moral arguments, but because of the more elementary sense that our very humanity is implicated in the outcome. If we cannot love the unborn child, is it possible for us to love the born? Is love itself even a possibility? If the fetus is not a person, or is discounted as a person, is it possible for us to be persons, to be defined by the pure possibility of love? Seen in light of such reflections we begin to discern the real status of the fetus as the most inestimable gift bestowed upon us. New life is the unmerited gift of otherness that can arise in no other way, for the other cannot be other if he or she arises from our own deliberate action. Everything about us, including the possibility of intentional action, is conditioned by the priority of the other. We are not first of all responsible for the other, rather it is the other that provides us with the possibility of responsibility.

The Other Defines Me as a Person

To the extent that we turn our back on the other in his or her most elemental state, at the very beginning, we have not simply failed in our responsibility for the other. We have undermined the very possibility of responsibility. If responsibility toward the other precedes any knowledge we have of him or her, since it cannot depend on the verification of any particular conditions, then the pure precedence of the fetus is the ultimate case of our responsibility. The other at the moment of conception is the point from which responsibility must take its beginning. Prior to that there is no other. Through its status as pure otherness the fetus evokes responsibility in its most primordial form. We are responsible for responsibility. If we have in that moment foreclosed the possibility of responsibility, if we have placed preconditions on otherness, then we have abrogated the responsibility for the other who exceeds the limits we have imposed on him or her. A conditional responsibility is irresponsible. Its lack of seriousness is indicated by the conditioning of a response on our capacity or inclination to respond, rather than on the need with which the other stands before us. Responsibility cannot be conditional because we cannot determine in advance what may be asked of us. And who could ask more or need more than the fetus, who depends on others for everything? The asymmetry of the relationship cannot be captured through the weighing of rights. Indeed, the utter imbalance calls into question the notion of rights whose claims must be calibrated and adjusted. Vulnerability as sheer vulnerability upends the accommodation of equal claims, for it exposes the grounds of such entitlements within essential humanity.

What is owed to human beings by virtue of no other reason than their humanity is not in this sense a marginal or occasional issue. It is the bedrock of all human relationships and of all human discourse. Often we are inclined to think that our relationship to others is based on what we know of them, that there is a solidity of content that gives substance to the relationship. But this is to overlook that no relationship, even of the most superficial kind, is reducible to its tangible components. We might even say that it is the intangibility of relationships that furnishes the condition of their possibility. Anything can happen, as is the very nature of the encounter between infinities, for it is the openness to the unforeseeable that is the possibility of meeting. It is in that sense a meeting that never manages to enclose itself. Uncontained by the material, the finitely visible dimensions, a genuine meeting of persons can take place. That is, a meeting in which the meeting is never fully achieved. We never actually meet the other whose self-expression can never include the self presenting the expression. Yet we meet and greet one another. Glancing back at the event, however, we realize that we have met because we have never really met or rather that we have already met before the nonmeeting took place. In either case we recognize that what exceeds the meeting is the most decisive. Invocations of a "bond" or of "intersubjectivity" are frequently made in this context, but all such terminology merely conceals the extent to which language fails us, as it must, on such occasions. Instead we are left with the irreducibility of the other, the sheerly other, that is no different in the case of the fetus from any walking talking person we may care to name. The work of Levinas and Derrida on the impossibility of naming is a fascinating avenue on the eschatology of the person.[8] We can name the child only because we cannot name him or her in any adequate sense, for even proper names are not unique. Prior to the name is the other.

The Challenge: To Specify the Common Good as the Good of Persons Who Exceed It

The great difficulty with all such reference to the other is that it easily slips into the assumption that we know what we are talking about. Otherness has been specified, forgetting that we have been specified by the other. No more than the name gives us access to the innerness of the person, and the generic designation of the "other" does not provide us with any apprehension of what it means. The other is not a term we understand, for it is a term we stand under. As an irreducible, the other cannot be made a reference point of our thought. All our thinking takes place within the horizon opened to us by the other. This is the challenge of a personalist language of the person. It is nothing less than accepting the logic of its content and applying it to the form of its expression. If the other is primary, then he or she is prior even to our own consciousness, and what is prior to consciousness cannot be included within it. The container can never contain itself, for that is the possibility of containing anything else. How then can we talk about the other as what always exceeds our capacity to talk about it? The answer, as our reflection already suggests, is obliquely. Simply because the irreducibles of our thinking and speaking cannot be made the focus of our consciousness does not mean that they lie outside of all awareness. A sideways glance at what is not included within the horizon makes even the horizon itself visible. This is the very meaning of human thought and expression, that it somehow contains itself in the sense of containing the possibility of the enlargement that can include itself, but this is never the same as actually possessing itself. Only God contains the source of his own being. We are merely like God in the sense of possessing and yet not possessing ourselves. This is of course what makes it possible to be most God-like of all in giving ourselves to an other, but even this we know is never fully accomplished. Instead, we need a lifetime of giving of self, which is the only way we can express what we intend even while we recognize that it cannot be accomplished. The giving of self exceeds even time as that which makes time itself possible.

It is the same transcendence in regard to the person and the common good. Not only is the common good the means by which the person enacts the meaning of his or her existence, but that outpouring of service can never be completed within the finitude of the common good. The individual always exceeds the common good in the sense in which everything that is the source remains outside of that of which it is the source. No matter how the common good is defined, the person always remains more than the service he or she extends toward it. Of course, the individual may be used, may even be used up, by a political instrumentalization of his or her role within it. But that does not abolish the reality, the injustice of the part subsuming the burden of the whole. We talk of moral resistance to the deformation of humanity in such instances. It is always possible for the collective to emerge as a power over against the individual, to take the gift of self that is offered to the community and treat it as a mere expendability. What is of most interest in such instances is not that the injustice is condemned or resisted, but the source of such resistance. Whence does it spring? We can hardly think of the possibility of moral revolt except by virtue of the impossibility of the public force obliterating the transcendence of the personal it can never contain. What is most galling to every tyrant is that he cannot kill a person. He may put the human being to death but that is merely to put him or her out of sight. The dead haunt us, not because we see ghosts, as Macbeth did Banquo, but because the person as such can never be eliminated. Ghosts remain a possibility only because persons are encountered as more than themselves, more than the tangibilities of their lives. It is what makes them persons that cannot be killed, for it is ever what remains outside all that they are.

The common good of persons whose good always exceeds the common good consists therefore of the recognition that they constitute what Kant called a "kingdom of ends."[9] If each is an end in him- or herself, then no social or political necessity justifies the violation of their inviolability. Only the equal dignity and respect owed to an other could underpin such abrogation. No merely common enterprise, defined by the attainment of immanent historical goods, is sufficient.[10] We are familiar with such formulations in light of the invocation of rights in the tradition of liberal democracy. Yet the audacity of this recognition never ceases to astonish. Such a public order acknowledges, indeed is built on the acknowledgment, that its interests are outweighed by the priority of rights owed to its least significant member. Even projects that might hold untold benefits for millions do not allow us to set aside the fundamental rights of a single one. Human progress cannot be bought at the cost of the slightest inhumanity. By reflecting on this most basic principle of politics we begin to gain a sense of what the good of a community of persons must be. That is, the clear understanding that there is no commonality beyond the good of individual persons themselves. To the extent that persons are constitutive of the common good between them they cannot be reduced to their respective contributions. Over and above whatever they create there is the unsurpassable depth of persons who are its source. The situation is familiar to us as we reflect on any of the common enterprises in which we find ourselves engaged, whether it is building something, playing a game, or competing against one another. Even in war there is the ineliminable humanity of the other that calls forth our respect. All adumbrations of a just war are derived from this. The other who must be killed is yet an other. The common task has its imperatives built into it, but it can never include the abrogation of the persons who carry its imperative within them. The worker, as John Paul II formulated it, is always more than the work.[11]

Part of the problem in maintaining this distinction, the personalist distinction, is that our publicly available language has not yet managed to find its stable formulation, if indeed such a thing is possible. After all, we have to remain open to the possibility that our language best serves us through its instability at such junctures. However, we have made considerable progress. Over more than five centuries we have hammered out a language of individual rights and we have anchored our political constitutions within it. The inviolability of individual liberty, with its extension into the political liberty of self-government, is the very pivot of the modern political form of liberal democracy. Nor should we regard this as a wholly modern achievement, however regnant such a perception may be, for the language of rights is embedded in the idea of law and acquires its momentum once the transcendence of the individual is differentiated.[12] The challenge of explaining such convictions even to ourselves, however, should not be underestimated. This is the difficulty that remained at the heart of the entire liberal project with its focus on the definition and defense of rights occupying the center of attention. The question of why such rights or such a view of human nature is worthy of defense lay largely in the background. Now that the liberal assertion of rights has been so successful that few historical competitors remain, the problems generated by the obscurity of the source of rights can no longer be avoided. We simply have to explain, however linguistically vertiginous the effort, how it is that one can count for more than all.

That is where we stand today, on the threshold of a conversation to which Christians and Jews with their historic understanding of man as *imago Dei* have much to contribute. But the anchor of faith, an abiding intuition, is not yet the same as a teaching for the nations. Even Christians have to struggle to find the linguistic means to render their convictions more transparent. It must be possible to distinguish between the dual roles that human beings are called to perform within a world that is simultaneously engaged in the instrumentalization of everything and everyone, and yet committed to the recognition that every individual at his or her core escapes such calculation. Our political language struggles to maintain these distinctions as we find our way toward them in practice while never quite managing to articulate them conceptually. Few observers have the acuteness of Michael Oakeshott, who insisted that the "nation-state" is a contradiction in terms. The goal of the nation is the pursuit of its historical identity and destiny, for which it is prepared to call on individuals to subsume not only their interests but even themselves should it become necessary. By contrast, the state emerged as a realm of order between conflicting individuals and groups, drawing its raison d'être from the guarantee of equal liberty it provides for all. It is the difference between what Oakeshott calls an "enterprise association" and a "civil association."[13] The former is defined by its common purpose, that common good for which individuals have expressly subordinated their individual liberties. Within the organized world of work this is exactly how the common wealth is secured through that division of labor by which everyone does his part within the whole. But this is not how we wish to think of the political community. It is not an enterprise association serving a purpose beyond itself; its members are not a mere means to the attainment of its goals. Rather, the civil association has the freedom of its members as its purpose. In other words, the political community is what makes possible the attainment of the good of the individuals composing it, without bending them toward any end beyond their own self-direction. The rules of the civil association are like the rules of a language—they enable us to converse but they do not tell us what to say. Only such a conception of the common good as borne in every instance by the individuals who carry it within themselves is capable of defining a community of persons.

The organic analogy, invoked by the whole tradition from Aristotle on, only carries us a certain distance, for, like every metaphor, it also obscures what it portends to reveal. There is a sense in which the individuals depend on the whole and the whole on its members in the manner of a living organism. Yet even when the connection is severed between the citizen and the state there is still a sense in which it also remains. The "king's two bodies," his individual mortality and his political immortality, remind us of the limits of the organic metaphor. With difficulty we cast around for an alternative conception but find that none quite satisfies. It is simply not possible to understand the spiritual reality of the politically ordered community in terms of any other process but its own. How else are we to understand a social reality constituted by agreement that can be wholly present within individuals to such an extent that, even when it breaks down, they may be said to still carry it inwardly within them? The correlative side to this, as we have seen, is the recognition that the publicly constituted order has no other destiny than the preservation of its members whose rights exceed it. Where in nature do we find any suggestion that the whole must be subordinate to the part? The reason why we struggle so hard to find a way of comprehending this event is that the implication of individual priority over the common seems to overturn the possibility of a politically stable whole. Is individualism the consequence of liberal rights? How can such an order sustain itself? Is it not destined to disintegrate into a multiplicity of centers of desire, especially if there is no common good higher than the good of individuals?

We have a fairly clear conception of what the common good of a civil association is. Kant has formulated it as the "kingdom of ends" in which each individual is treated as an end in him- or herself, never as a means. What needs to be explained is how this common good is sustained within the individuals who constitute it. This is the conception of the whole that has proved so elusive in the history of reflection on it. Somehow the principle of unity must be carried within the individual human beings who realize it in their lives together. Recourse to the acting person or the dynamics of a practice have intimated what conceptually escapes us, and that may be the limit of what can be said on the subject. Yet even the acknowledgment of a limit suggests the possibility that it might yield more than a sheer limit. At the very minimum the situation calls our attention to the existential force for the common good in action. Like Tocqueville's observations on the exercise of freedom in cooperative action with others, we must be prepared to find in such climactic instances the wellspring of communal reality. He referred to it as the point at which the heart was enlarged beyond the boundaries of its own particular concerns, and he concluded that what made democracy work in the American case was that it recurrently called forth such possibilities.[14] In other words, the common good was evoked when individuals ceased to act merely as individuals but instead stepped out of their private sphere to take upon themselves responsibility for the common. Tocqueville's insight, which points all the way back to the Greek insistence that the political was the only meaningful realm of human action, was that the public good was sustained through the transformation its pursuit effected within individuals. From their perspective they no longer acted merely as individuals. Through the growth of the soul by which they acted on behalf of all, they now participated in an existence more real than the purely private. The capacity of human beings to be carried beyond themselves through self-transcendence is well known in many spheres. Tocqueville had simply recognized its crucial political significance. Yet despite the brilliance with which he elaborated his insight in terms of the role of intermediate and voluntary associations, by which the transition from the individual to the common good is accomplished, there is still a notable silence concerning the mysterious nexus that is thereby forged. It is almost as if the process by which we become more than we are through service toward the common good must remain a mystery to us.

Incomprehensibility of Self-Transcendence of Persons

The impenetrability is not all the fault of the abbreviated language of liberal politics. Instead, we are confronted with the limits of words themselves when they are the very words that make our lives together possible. For we are not here discoursing about objects or processes outside of ourselves, but about the very actions by which we enact our existence in common. Impenetrability is virtually a condition of such expressions, for if we were to penetrate their meaning from a viewpoint outside of them, we would no longer be engaged in their realization. The individual's service to the common good cannot be encompassed from the individual perspective without abolishing the very enlargement of the individual heart that is required. We have already glimpsed this insight in admitting the limitation of the organic analogy. The real application of the organic analogy would ask how it is possible for the blood vessels to understand the role that they play in the whole organism. To the extent that the sacrifice the individual makes on behalf of the common good is not an incidental or optional aspect of his existence, but the most indispensable means by which he becomes who he is, indeed becomes more than he is, then it can never be fully comprehended from his perspective. Even the most clear-sighted analysis cannot grasp the whole by which the analyst himself is sustained. The reciprocal relationship by which the individual supports the common good and the common good supports the individual can only be known from within its dynamics. To turn it into an object of examination would be to step outside of the process, an act that would not only be politically irresponsible but would fail to arrive at any higher insight than objectivization permits. Spiritual reality can only be known from within it. Spirit alone can know spirit.

This was an insight that was pursued far more philosophically by Hegel at almost the same time as Tocqueville was working on his *Democracy in America* (1835). Hegel's text is the *Philosophy of Right* (1821), which really was an expanded excerpt from his *Philosophy of Spirit*, the account of what the mind can know of itself from within its own self-unfolding within history. The *Philosophy of Right* is what Hegel called "Objective Mind" or mind/spirit expressed in the constitution of a publicly ordered liberty. His problem was the one we have been considering here, namely, how it is possible for individuals to find themselves within a legally constituted whole that is at the same time defined by its preservation of individual liberty. A merely formal relationship, a neutral framework that protected the satisfaction of private desires and interests,

Hegel understood would not work, as did Tocqueville. There must be a substantive bond between the individual and the whole, otherwise the relationship would easily fall apart. The difference was that Hegel sought to describe its dynamics from within. He understood that political reality is ultimately a spiritual relationship and, as such, no more accessible than it is to the persons who live within it. The difficulty of conveying Hegel's project is perhaps best demonstrated by the widespread underestimation of the *Philosophy of Right* as a book about the reciprocity of the individual and the political, just as Tocqueville is all too readily encapsulated by reference to the role of intermediate institutions. In each case it is not what we can so easily grasp about them that counts, but what we find ungraspable, what perhaps escaped Hegel and Tocqueville as they strained toward what pulled their thought forward. Thus it is not reciprocity or intermediate associations that are what we need to know, but how they work. What is their inner life? This is what is so difficult to get hold of, but Hegel made an impressive start on it in the third section, titled "The Ethical Life" (*Sittlichkeit*), of *Philosophy of Right*. This was his term for the concrete living whole of a way of life.

This is not the place to go into the details of its three dimensions of the family, civil society, and the state, but we can merely select the first of them by way of illustration. All three constitute a way of life integrating the individual and the common at successively more self-conscious levels. The analysis of the family is sufficient to gain a sense of the approach. Perhaps the most notable aspect is that the family is featured so prominently in an analysis of the state, and not as one of its preconditions but in many ways as its first stage. Certainly the family is not located within the private realm, but neither is it subsumed into the state. No, it is placed between the public and the private in a way that seems to point toward the intermediate status even of the state itself. The significance of the family for Hegel is that it is the state in miniature, or, more accurately, in its prereflective phase. What strikes him is that the family is based on freedom, the marriage between man and woman, but it also generates a bond in which the freedom of each has disappeared. Freely they submit their freedom and thereby preserve it. Neither partner calculates the return on contribution or considers the nurturing of offspring as accrual of debt. Private property, the very basis of individual claims, has been submerged. The reason is that the family is a real unity of persons. They no longer need to assert or defend their rights because they are fully protected, and more, within the whole in which each is valued as the whole. Conversely, the reciprocation of trust and love is never in doubt since the individual persons no longer look on themselves as such but as members of the whole, the family. It is the most complete integration of the individual and the common good because it is the most complete identification of the individual with the whole. No one knows where the interests, joys, and sorrows of one end and those of another begin, for they revolve in a continuous round of life. It is that integration in a living unity that points Hegel toward what sustains the common good in the more explicitly agonistic arenas of civil society and the state. He understood that these two spheres were not by any means comparable to the intense unity of the family, but he also saw that they shared an indispensable ingredient: love. If we want to understand even in part what makes it possible for individuals to subordinate themselves to the common good, then we must begin at the point where it is most inwardly present. We still may not have penetrated its source, but we at least know the mystery within which all union of persons must stand.

It must be a union that has no other good beyond that of the persons involved. By entering into the family, just as in civil society and the state, we have not "given hostages" to a future that no longer consults our interests as persons. Rather, it is by yielding our personal prerogatives that we have gained them more securely. This is, of course, the very pattern of the reciprocal grant of liberty that has been advanced by all the social contract conceptualizations of the common good. The difference is that Hegel has envisaged it as a living reality. Where his predecessors, Locke or Rousseau, envisaged an agreement that took place in time as founding civil society, Hegel has made the social agreement the very basis of the time of civil society. As with so much of his philosophy, he has put the concepts in motion. This is the source of his notorious difficulty for readers. Having become accustomed to thinking in fixed categories, we are ill-prepared to make the transition to the dynamic of living categories. Yet if we want to catch a glimpse of what sustains the world of meaning by which we are ourselves sustained, that is what we have to do. It is the nature of a common good that is borne within the persons who realize it in life that it can be known in no other way than through our participation within it. Any attempt to relegate its source to an event outside of the persons whose lives it make possible simply misses the reality. That has been the major failure of all contract "explanations" of political society. Such accounts are themselves as much in need of explanation since they do not make transparent how it is that human beings can experience the loss of liberty as their ultimate gain. Contracting parties must view themselves as fixed entities within a zero-sum game. It is quite different when the whole dynamic of their lives together is engaged. Then what might appear as a loss from one perspective is in the immediately following moment regained sevenfold in the enlargement of life together.

No beginning of the process can be found, for that would be to step outside of it. The parallel would be in thinking that the husband or wife could better understand the marriage by reducing it to the objective factors that went into it. This would strike us as a peculiar project, for it would withdraw such a person from the only source of meaning within the living relationship itself. Persons can only be understood from within the interiority by which their existence is borne. The same is true of their social and political unions. Hegel's remarkable innovation in the history of philosophy was, even if it has hitherto not been widely acknowledged, to make this necessity explicit. He understood that it inverted the meaning of most of the conventional terminology by which we discuss such matters. Where previously we had been inclined to assume that the concepts we used had originated within ourselves as a means of mastering the reality confronting us, now we are forced to acknowledge that such concepts constitute the reality within which we exist and can never hope to master in the slightest. The common good, a term that goes all the way back to the *res publica*, is one such instance. We do not possess the concept of the common good, it is rather the common good that possesses us. What does this mean? It means that the common good is what defines our existence. It is not up to us to define it. No one can claim to have superior knowledge of the common good but the person who bends him- or herself to realize it most completely. This is not a question of technique in which matters of greater or less might be judged. Ultimately, there is no special expertise that secures the common good other than the giving of self that is possible for every single one of us. No unique qualities are required beyond the uniqueness that is every person.

In many ways this community-forming role of virtue has been recognized in the tradition of political thought from the classical beginning. The problem is that it was no sooner recognized than it was promptly forgotten. Virtue began its meandering odyssey through all forms of instrumentality by which it became the basis for the assertion of one person's superiority over another. Little attention was devoted to how impossible such claims rendered a community of persons. Even Aristotle, who thought more profoundly about the nature of friendship than anyone and understood that it turned on the possibility of equality between human beings, promptly forgot about such implications when he turned his attention to political friendship. This is one of the reasons why being faithful to the Greek beginnings often requires us to be more faithful than the Greeks themselves.[15] The modern challenge to the hierarchical conception of classical political thought is driven in considerable measure by this logic. It recognizes that the core of virtue is always more than the specification of virtue. Nothing that we do can outweigh the person who does it, nor can it accomplish more than what the person seeks to achieve in the giving of self. Virtue is not a part of us, it is the whole. In that regard we are all equally situated. Our capacities may vary but not the self from which they spring. Even the lowliest, least effectual member of a society can give the incomparable gift of self by which the common good is founded. This is the element of unpredictability that exceeds all rational organization. The latter remains indispensable, for there must be an ordering of our lives together, but it can never preclude the eschatological flash of generosity by which every scale of value is transcended. What makes it possible for the authority of virtue to be recognized is this giving and receiving of self beyond all variations of attainment. The Greeks sought to designate this innermost core by the term *nous*, as distinct from the mere application of *logos*.

Christianity was, of course, the beginning of a wider awareness of the inexpressible depth of each human being. All were equal in their fallenness and their openness to grace. It was not simply that Christianity focuses on the transcendent destiny of each person but that it already lives within immeasurability. We are told not just to give our coats but to give ourselves to those in need. A fully personalist mode of discourse is already in evidence. Yet even Christianity did not follow out its implications for the world of politics, or even for the revised understanding of language that it contained. All communication between human beings exceeds what is said, for it involves the giving and receiving of selves, precisely what can never be given. The translation of this insight into political terms was the work of the modern liberal democratic development, which is, at its core, the most quixotic of all political forms. Liberal democracy takes its stand on a principle that departs utterly from any judgment of mundane success. Instead of focusing first on the pragmatic outcomes, it insists that, despite the consequences, human beings must be entrusted with their own responsibility. This does not mean that liberal democracy is utopian or unconcerned about adjusting to real conditions, or even with ensuring its own survival. It is simply that that is not its core and it is willing to endure considerable risks, the risk of political suicide, in embracing free elections. This is not because liberal democracy is sure of the likelihood of successful outcomes, that people will be better off if they themselves make the decisions affecting their lives. It is rather the conviction that such decisions are properly made by the individuals involved, not because they are likely to decide best, but simply because to be human is to live in such a way.[16] Liberal democracy is the political expression of the common good of persons, even if it still has a way to go to understand and develop a language of corresponding transparency. That is a language of paradox.

Not only is the liberal democratic form one in which the collective defers to the individual, "a whole of wholes" as Maritain suggested, but it is one in which the individual really is the whole. The paradox of a community of persons is that it surpasses all mathematical rationality. The individual is sustained by the common good; the common good is sustained by the individual. But it is not a relation of mutual dependence but rather of independent mutuality. Persons cannot exchange a part of themselves; they can only give themselves wholly to one another. This is why no economy can apply. In each instance the limits of reciprocation are exceeded. The consequence is that the common good of persons is always achieved and yet never achieved. To the extent that there is nothing over and above the mutual giving of selves that remains to be accomplished, then nothing more is needed. To the extent that the mutual giving of selves is never accomplished in the mere giving of tokens, the only means of conveyance, the community of persons is never achieved. The status is eschatological. This should not, however, be taken in the sense of what is not real or not yet. It is that existence occurs within the eschatological openness that can never be closed, a nonclosure that is the only surety of the openness of existence. The genius of liberal democracy has been to intuit this even if it has so far lacked the philosophic means of articulation. It is not that liberal polities constitute a neutral framework within which the plurality of private satisfactions can be pursued. That is only the most superficial appearance of liberal democracy. Its deepest truth is the realization that the only common good worthy of the name is the common good that involves the mutual giving and receiving of persons. It is not that one counts more than all but that only such a scale can adequately respect what is always owed in relation to persons. We become persons by giving ourselves. The political community simply announces and invites that possibility as its own deepest realization.

It is not, however, an invitation that is issued primarily through the medium of official pronouncements. We know that a written constitution does not exist in the document sealed under glass, but in the hearts and minds of the citizens. What then of the political community as such?

Does it have an existence beyond the inwardness by which it is carried? The logic of a community of persons, by which all are bound up in one, is fully reversible. The one is also somehow all. This is why the initiative and responsibility of every single member is so crucial, for each one bears the whole community within him or her. Each one literally is the whole. Obviously the articulated unity of all through effective representation is what makes it possible for the political community to act, to exist in the full sense. The United States is an actor on the world scene only because of that awesome unity of its members. Yet when we search for the beginning of that union we search in vain to find a point from which it took root, a beginning in time before which the union was not. In some sense it could not have occurred unless it was already there, a notorious source of difficulty for all historical and philosophical speculations on the origin of human societies. The process is mysterious because we can never find an absolute beginning but rather a slowly emergent recognition of what had been there before there was a there. No community between us would be possible unless we are already in community with one another before the possibility arises.[17] The question is not why community arises between human beings but rather why it gets restricted within such a narrow range. That is a question that lasts only until we realize that it undermines its own presupposition, for we are at least potentially also open to all others.

Persons bear community within them because they can communicate only through the giving of selves that constitutes community. In doing so, they have already realized the common good. It does not await us in the future since there is nothing more that can be given than ourselves, our all. In every action, to the extent that it is a fully human action, the whole of existence, eternity itself, is implicated. There is no founding in the past or fulfillment in the future that outweighs in seriousness the justice that must be respected in the present. "Everyone is responsible for all" is a saying of Dostoevsky's that can be received on many different levels. But surely its deepest is that all of goodness is gained or lost in the action of every individual. We each bear ultimate responsibility for all, not in the sense that we can effectively secure the welfare of all, but in that, as Kant would say, love toward all can be enacted in no other way. Organizations and states do not act, only individuals do. In our actions each one of us determines the good or evil of the whole universe, for in choosing we choose with whole selves that reach as far as the limits of all reality. This is the meaning of our God-given freedom, that we are free to turn away even from God himself. Good and evil are not decided at a particular point in time. Rather they are decided eternally at every point in time.

This is what it means to act as a person, to occupy the point of eternity from which all time is contained. Responsibility for the common good falls therefore to every individual, yet the power of realization lies within the capacity of every individual. Having given ourselves, there is nothing more to be given. It is accomplished. What the efficacy in time may be is not up to us to control, yet we must bend our efforts to the utmost. It is simply that nothing more can be added to the essential. In action from eternity the goal is already reached, while the unfolding over time remains to be determined. This is why the founding of states is not necessarily the work just of its founders. It can often happen that those who come later may found it more profoundly. This is the insight that is the secret of Lincoln's rhetoric in the Gettysburg Address. No honor can be bestowed on those whose own selflessness has surpassed all honors we might bestow.

CHAPTER FIVE

John Rawls's Personalist Faith

The discovery and publication of John Rawls's senior thesis can be compared to the influence of the early writings of Karl Marx. It was only with the appearance of the latter that readers could gain an appreciation of the humanist roots of Marxian thought, which, in its mature formulation, was more narrowly centered on economic theory. A similar pattern applies to the ever-more rigorous elaborations of Rawls's theory of justice, which, despite their prolixity, never quite capture the inspiration from which they spring. The publication of *A Brief Inquiry into the Meaning of Sin and Faith* enables us to glimpse the long-submerged origin in one of its most touchingly unguarded moments.[1] We are led into the inner hidden Rawls, and begin to see a whole new way of perceiving this emblematic figure of contemporary liberal political thought. Of course, this is not to suggest that the "discoverer," Eric Gregory, or the editor, Thomas Nagel, have let us in on a secret that ought not to have seen the light of day.[2] A senior thesis resting within the publicly accessible space of the Princeton library is hardly a private document, even if many Rawlsians might have preferred it remain within the darkness of the unread. It certainly complicates the notion of secular public reason to be reminded of its genesis within Christian theology, but that is equally a complication from the perspective of Christian theology. Yet it is not as if the affinity of Rawls's philosophy with a deeper spiritual strain was unknown. That was visible to any careful reader of the texts.[3] What is new in *A Brief Inquiry* is the revelation of just how many of the main parameters of his *philosophical* thought were worked out within a theological-personalist horizon.

This was something of which Rawls himself remained aware and in which he remained deeply interested. The accompanying document, "On My Religion," a private reflection on his own religious convictions from 1997 (at the latest), makes clear his continuing deep engagement with the Christian beginnings from which his odyssey had set forth. This too provides a fascinating perspective, comparable only to what we might have learned if the older Marx had penned a reflection titled "On My Judaism." Here Rawls shows that even what is left behind is never really left behind, for even when he concedes that he is no longer a Christian in any conventional sense, the question of his relationship to faith remains ineluctable. The invocation of Jean Bodin's *Heptaplomeres: A Colloquium of the Seven about the Secrets of the Sublime* (1588)—also unpublished (until the nineteenth century)—adds only a further layer of fascination to the unfolding mystery. Rawls singles out this conversation between representatives of different religions and none as most closely resembling his political liberalism. The first aspect he notes is that Bodin arrived at toleration, not on the basis of skepticism, but on the basis of faith: "Although he recognized the political importance of toleration, and held that the state should always uphold it, his belief in toleration was religious and not only political" ("On My Religion" included in *A Brief Inquiry*, 266). This observation leads Rawls to question the extent to which liberal politics still requires a foundation in faith. Not surprisingly, he concludes that even faith in the existence of God is no longer necessary for us to sustain the principles of mutual respect toward fellow creatures made in the divine image. "For my part," Rawls insists, "I don't see how it is possible that the content and validity of reason should be affected by whether God exists or not, thinking of God as a being with will" (268). Quite apart from the naïveté of this formulation ("whether God exists or not"), what is most striking is that Rawls is determined to hold onto the reasonableness of God even if he no longer holds onto God. It is this touching faith in God, when there is no "God," that attests to the remarkable spiritual journey Rawls navigated over a philosophic lifetime.

Beginning with a conventionally Christian upbringing, it was only in his last two years at Princeton that he "became deeply concerned about theology and its doctrines" ("On My Religion," 261). This was the time when he considered going into the seminary but decided to wait until World War II was over, characteristically, out of a sense of duty toward friends and classmates who had already signed up and because "I could not convince myself that my motives were sincere." It was only at the end of the war that his faith underwent a shattering change that marked not so much a loss as the realization that he was "no longer orthodox." Rawls recounts three incidents that precipitated this crisis. There was the Lutheran pastor who declared that God aimed American bullets at the Japanese but protected G.I.s from Japanese bullets. Then the incident in which another man, appropriately named Deacon, had been killed in his place merely because Rawls had had the good fortune to be selected as a blood donor. And there was the larger questioning of divine justice precipitated by the widespread realization of the scale of the Holocaust. Cumulatively they amounted to an assault on the very idea of divine justice: "To interpret history as expressing God's will, God's will must accord with the most basic ideas of justice as we know them. For what else can the most basic justice be? Thus, I soon came to reject the idea of the supremacy of the divine will as also hideous and evil" (263). It is not difficult to discern the unity of these incidents as defining the core preoccupation of Rawls's professional life: justice as fairness. There is more than a hint of revolt against the divine injustice that now must be surpassed by a more humane dispensation of justice. That might well have been the route of Karl Marx, but it was not to be that of John Rawls or, by extension, the liberal standard-bearers that take their lead from him.[4] Instead, both Rawls and liberal societies return to the question of their relationship to religion.

In this sense, only the opening statement of this remarkable testament fails to hit the mark. "My religion," Rawls begins, "is of interest only to me," but he left his thoughts about it in a way that was accessible to family and friends. Could it be that he suspected that his religion was of interest and of relevance to a far wider circle for whom he functioned as a preeminent theoretical voice? The very exercise of this autobiographical stock-taking seems to suggest a lacuna within the publicly elaborated accounts of justice. Perhaps there lay an injustice at the heart of a theory of justice? A debt that had not quite been repaid? Five years before his death, we encounter Rawls asking himself whether he has given God all that is his due. Such a meditation could only assume the form of a letter to oneself. Or perhaps it is a letter to God? At any rate it was not written for publication, even though it was available for publication. The delete button could have been pressed at any time. Perhaps it is testament to Rawls's own remarkable sense of justice that he never sought to suppress what could not be transacted within the parameters of the public discourse he had constructed. How could the thinker, who had explained so convincingly why no appeal to metaphysical or religious worldviews was permissible within the public square, deal with his own lingering entanglement with such "worldviews"? It is not that the theological resonances of *A Theory of Justice* were ever disguised. No Heideggerian erasure attempts to smooth the inconsistencies of liberal philosophical thought.[5] Complications are allowed to stand, and nowhere more poignantly than by the author who must write privately to himself about a "religion" for which he can no longer find a place within his public discourse. A consistent liberal would have no need to write about his religion, having firmly closed the door on all its confounding perplexities. But Rawls was no Rawlsian. He could not let go of what had after all been the wellspring from which his thought had flowed. This is the significance of the publication of the unnoticed thesis by a brilliant, deeply sensitive Princeton undergrad.

Without the simultaneous appearance of "On My Religion," the thesis could be given far less weight in an overall assessment. We might well have been inclined to regard it as a closed chapter to which he never looked back. But the later reflection demonstrates that the older Rawls did look back, prompted, not by nostalgia, but by a profound philosophical need to become clear about the character of his own thought. In undertaking our own review of that pathway we are perhaps best guided by one of the most striking cautions that Rawls issues to himself in the self-reflection. After noting that his religious views changed in 1945, he concedes his incapacity to comprehend the shift in any definitive way: "I don't profess to understand at all why my beliefs changed, or believe it is possible fully to comprehend such changes. We can record what happened, tell stories and make guesses, but they must be taken as such. There may be something in them, but probably not" (261). Rawls was sufficiently self-perceptive to recognize that there were limits to self-perception. Yet those limits were never absolute; their boundaries could be pushed back to catch a glimpse of what had not been glimpsed before. In this sense Rawls's exercise in self-interpretation is no different from the task of interpretation in general. We are continually on the track of the inspiration from which a text arose, a source that, because it lies beyond the text, can never be included within it, no matter how extended the latter becomes. Try as he or she might, the author can never include the point of view from which the work has emanated. Somehow its definitive formulation, its drive for self-expression, identical with the author him or herself, ever escapes capture. We may not reach the real Rawls in the undergraduate thesis, but we do catch something of the person who is far less visible in the writings of the professional philosopher. It brings us close to the motivating experience, even if such a core permanently eludes us, of the theory of justice.

Torturing Question of Public Reason

It is the representative significance of Rawls that makes this biographical self-disclosure of surpassing interest. As the voice of contemporary liberal political thought, Rawls is more than Rawls. What is hidden within him is, by extension, also hidden within contemporary liberalism, even one that embraces the full logic of a public reason shorn of theological adumbrations. His editors, Nagel and Cohen, both former students, intuit the deeper question *A Brief Inquiry* poses for the liberal secular self-understanding.[6] Is there any longer a secular public reason when its genealogy is tinged with neo-orthodox Christianity? Certainly we cannot accede to the conventional reading, facilitated by Rawls himself, that public reason eschews a theology.[7] Nor can we simply accept the opposing nostrum that liberal polities depend on transcendent foundations they can neither acknowledge nor sustain.[8] We seem to be close to Jürgen Habermas's concession that we live in a "post-secular" age, one in which the prevailing secularism is now incapable of identifying the source of its own self-understanding.[9] Rawls's affinity with Habermas is underscored by their mutual appreciation of one another's perspectives.[10] In different ways they struggle with the uncertainty of liberal reason that can no longer adduce what Rawls refers to as "comprehensive" religious or philosophical doctrines to support its convictions. In a final summative essay that "is the best statement I have written on the ideas of public reason and political liberalism,"[11] Rawls reveals something of what the long struggle for clarity had cost him: "Throughout I have been concerned with a torturing question in the contemporary world, namely: Can democracy and comprehensive doctrines, religious or nonreligious, be compatible? And if so, how?"[12] The end of Enlightenment hostility to religion, announced by both Rawls and Habermas, has made the path from *A Brief Inquiry* all the more relevant if we want to understand the faith that sustains political liberalism when faith in God can no longer be invoked. It may well be that *A Brief Inquiry* gives us the clearest insight into the faith of liberal democracy itself.

Previously, liberal dogmatism had seemed to echo the religious dogmatism it had opposed. The incontrovertibility of liberal faith merely substituted for the certitudes of theological faith. But why this must be so has not been well understood. Its explanation turns on the realization that a principle, no matter how authoritative, cannot furnish the grounds of its own authority. Ultimate principles are never more than penultimate. It is faith that holds them as ultimate, for that is what it means to be persons who bind themselves in relation to principles. This is an insight of Kant, who emphasized that it was the capacity to be bound by duty for its own sake that marked the highest dignity of human beings. They are the ones who respond to that transcendent call and thereby attest to their own transcendent dimension. Only persons can be obliged, for they are already obliged to obligation itself. There is no stepping outside of the grounds of obligation to interrogate its imperative, for any such maneuver presupposes a sense of obligation that makes it possible. Even argument is sustained by faith in its possibility. But where that faith is located or whence it is derived remains inaccessible. We can only say that faith is held by faith. As such it is the certainty that nothing is more certain than what lies on the far side of the possibility of doubt. Faith has already reached the goal of what it seeks through faith. It is thus not surprising that Rawls's own trajectory exemplifies the impossibility of jettisoning faith, even as it moves from a theological to a nontheological mode.

The case for returning to this earliest seedbed of his ideas is made all the more compelling by his continual rejection of any "comprehensive doctrine" that would account for their genesis. If there is a consistent thread to his intellectual development it is to find the basis for political philosophy outside of any metaphysical worldview. "Justice as Fairness: Political Not Metaphysical" is the title of one of his seminal essays. The most characteristic formulation of his intellectual position is that "the right is prior to the good." Liberal political society makes it possible for us to choose between rival conceptions of the good because it guarantees the right of self-determination. The question of what that assurance is based on, the question of its justification, is one with which Rawls and liberal political theory have continued to struggle. In *A Theory of Justice* he sought a universally acceptable account of the good in terms of principles of justice to which no one could object. Later he came to recognize that even that limited evocation entailed a comprehensive doctrine of the good. This set him on the path of a purely political agreement that avoided any moral presuppositions or only invoked them in the most narrowly tailored way. Rawls, we might say, engages in an act of such self-effacement that even the source of his conviction is withdrawn from view. The inexorability of his thought, and by extension the liberal arrangement he articulates, turns only on the faith in its own possibility. It cannot adduce any foundation beyond itself. It is a pure act of faith. This is why faith remains so pivotal for him even though he no longer called it such. The term he coined is "political constructivism," which he distinguished from the moral constructivism of Kant. In neither type of constructivism are political or moral principles simply "constructed" or made up, but they are, rather, discovered in the process of enacting them. Construction of a scheme of fair and mutual cooperation on the basis of guarantees of rights is the fruit of faith in action. It is objective in the sense of true but without laying claim to truth as such. For the political agreement, "the concept of the reasonable suffices."[13] When pressed to account for its genesis, political constructivism can only claim that it derives from faith in its own possibility. It is the horizon outside of which we cannot go because to depart from it would presuppose what we seek to do without. Reason, Kant understood, must ground itself. Rawls simply elevates political reason as the pivot on which justice, as fairness to all competing and diverging metaphysical doctrines, turns. Without any basis but itself the path of its emergence is the only access available to it. This is the significance of Rawls's initial attempt at evoking the faith that led him.

Sensing its importance, a number of other commentators have searched *A Brief Inquiry* for prefigurations of the conceptual apparatus elaborated by the mature Rawls. They have found, in the emphasis on community, equal respect for persons, the rejection of merit, and the notion of justice as fairness, striking anticipations of what is eloquently developed in the later writings. There have even been attempts to link the hallmark principle of the later Rawls, the priority of the right over the good, to the respect for persons as ends-in-themselves that we find in *A Brief Inquiry*. Robert Merrihew Adams has singled out the distinct personalism of the early Rawls, his explication of the difference between personal and natural relations, as "a point of originality" (38), in the early work. Indeed, *A Brief Inquiry* has consistently impressed readers with the theoretical penetration already evident in its youthful presentation. But what has not been attempted is any sustained examination of the inner continuity that extends to the mature philosophical work. In part this is because of Rawls's own disavowal, a disavowal that remained strangely incomplete, of his religious convictions. A greater part of the reason must, however, lie with the difficulty of tracing the continuity of an explicitly theological discourse into its strictly philosophical parallels. That is the challenge I assume here, fully aware that it can only be persuasive if it can be demonstrated in relation to the central line of Rawls's thought. What then is the status of the priority of the right over the good? Is it a thread that can be found in the very earliest attempt at a comprehensive formulation of his thought? And if it is, is it inexorably tied to its theological context there? Or does it constitute a bridge to the presumptively secular discourse Rawls embraces as public reason? What, in other words, is the faith that sustained the whole enterprise of reaching an account of justice free of any comprehensive doctrines that might be adduced to support it?

Priority of Right to the Good

The priority of the right over the good has been widely regarded as the overarching principle of Rawls's whole philosophical project.[14] It simultaneously defines his approach and articulates the self-understanding of contemporary liberal political thought. Even when he modulates away from insistence on a *theory* of justice, with its twin invocations of equal rights to liberty and the difference principle, or concedes that justice is grounded in no more than an overlapping political consensus, there is no retreat from the priority of right. This is because insistence on the priority of right is tantamount to what it means to constitute a liberal political order.[15] Government guarantees the right to pursue different and competing accounts of the good. It is the liberty to pursue irreducibly plural understandings of the good that is the distinguishing mark of liberal polities. In this sense, Rawls's principle is merely a variant of core invocations of the liberal political conception.[16] Yet its formulation strikes Anglophone ears as strange. They have heard of rights, but what of "the right"? The latter notion is one that emerges in the German and particularly the Kantian framework, where *das Recht* cannot readily be translated as either "the legal" or "the just" because it encompasses both. We often forget how thoroughly Rawls was steeped in that Continental mode of discourse. As a consequence, this pivotal notion of his thought has often been taken in a far more limited sense than it should be, when it functions as the linchpin of his entire theoretical framework. Usually it is treated merely as the assertion of liberal neutrality within a context of rival versions of the good. A liberal public order is one that maintains strict indifference over such divergent worldviews in order to maintain the peace within which individuals are free to pursue their respective choices. Frequently it is characterized as the tension between public indifference, which seems to suggest equal lack of merit within such private choices, and the maintenance of respect, which would seem to profess their worthiness of inexhaustible respect. Critics have cited the impossibility of maintaining a neutral view of the good without presupposing neutrality as a good.[17]

Rawls's own heroic effort to respond to this challenge in *A Theory of Justice*, by articulating an unobjectionable account of the just, and his subsequent concession that he had elaborated no more than a convergent consensus concerning the just in *Political Liberalism*, did not materially affect the core principle he thereby sought to defend. The priority of the right over the good endured despite the vicissitudes of its Rawlsian defense.[18] As a consequence we might suspect that there is more to it than either Rawls and his defenders or his critics had quite comprehended. Perhaps it is bigger even than the liberal self-conception it seems to define. Certainly it is more than a principle of neutrality, for despite the ease with which it is touted as the default conception of a liberal polity, it has always been evident that such regimes are far more than the houses of cards they are often reputed to be. Their history has demonstrated a remarkable capacity to rise in defense of the defenseless and often at considerable cost to their own tranquility. The patriotic generosity of the young Rawls in uniform was notable principally for its commonality, as was his resolve to hold liberal political society to a higher moral standard than it seemed to profess. But what was that standard if not the priority of the right above all other considerations of ideology, morality, or religion? Before the principle had been formulated, it had been discovered by him as the imperative of life. This is the inestimable value of the early thesis, for in its pages we see Rawls elaborating its central impulse outside of the interest in carving consensus from political pluralism, which later came to occupy him. To some extent his focus on the strictly moral, as opposed to the political, elevates his thought here to a spiritual purity not so easily discerned in the later work.

In *A Brief Inquiry* we see the priority of right over the good in a context far removed from disputes about liberal neutrality in which it is later ensnared. Here it is simply a fundamental principle of morality rather than a principle about morality. Perhaps it is because of the great difference in context that commentators have failed to note its emergence here, despite the fact that Rawls virtually declares it as the main point of his little work. In the preface he announces two aims, the first and most prominent of which is "to enter a strong protest against a certain scheme of thought which I have called naturalism." The second is to address specific problems of Christianity by avoiding the naturalistic terminology that has crept into it from Greek sources. Rawls acknowledges that what he advocates is "more or less of a 'revolution' by repudiating this traditional line of thought" (107). In place of the Greek appeal to nature and a natural good, Rawls proposes to make the categories of community and personality central. It is very much a strain of thought emanating from the neo-orthodoxy of Karl Barth, Anders Nygren, Emil Brunner, and others, who earlier in the century had set out to retrieve the radical difference of Christianity from the naturalistic compromise of liberal Protestantism and Catholic Thomism. Despite this theological lineage and the prevalence of its influence within the thesis, what is remarkable is that Rawls's interest flows in a far more philosophical direction. He is adamantly opposed to "natural ethics" and deeply committed to an account anchored in the centrality of personal relations and community: "Proper ethics is not the relating of a person to some objective 'good' for which he should strive, but is the relating of person to person and finally to God" (114). The theological terminology is only incidental to what is essentially a personalist philosophy worked out without benefit of any personalist philosophies. Yet, as in the personalism announced by Max Scheler, Rawls was very much aware of the deep departure it entailed with the entire philosophic tradition that appealed to an order of nature.[19]

It required no great leap to assert the priority of the right over the good when one had already discarded the whole notion of an orientation toward the highest good. This had nothing to do with the Hobbesian abandonment of a *summum bonum*, but arose from a far deeper realization that any account of the good has failed to take account of the person through whom it is apprehended as good. Apart from the person, whose free acknowledgment is the turning point, the highest good is a mere externality indifferent to the persons without whom it is scarcely of value. Rejecting the whole language of the good as anything outside of persons, Rawls boldly declares his position: "(a) We do not believe that the so-called 'good life' (detestable phrase) consists in seeking any object, but that it is rather something totally different, a matter of personal relations; and (b) we deny that men seek the 'good' so named" (161). There is no doubt that Rawls's neo-orthodox influences turned him away from classical and Scholastic thought to such an extent that he seems to have never entertained a serious reexamination. As a consequence he could not perceive the extent to which his own prioritization of the person only became possible through the Greek discovery of *nous*, and through the Christian discovery of interiority.[20] Modern personalism rests on an account of the person made possible by the encounter with the personal God. At best Rawls evinces only a dim awareness of this in the thesis, and it scarcely surfaces in his later lectures. He is, we might say, so gripped by the novelty of his discovery of the person, especially of personal relations as the very meaning of community, that he brusquely declares that "all natural systems lose communality, personality, and the true nature of God, and are therefore not really Christian but individualistic" (178).

Thus long before Rawls became a liberal he had ceased to be a Lockean. No account of individuals in a state of nature, arranging their mutual relations by way of a contract (126), could be adequate to one who understood that true community only exists within the inwardness of the person. *A Theory of Justice* and its later incarnation, *Justice as Fairness*, look very different when seen, not as an effort to negotiate differences, but to bring about an interior state within the persons who bear liberal communities within them. Even the famous "veil of ignorance" can be seen as a meditative exercise in bringing about an awareness of another person's social point of view.[21] The community at which Rawls aims throughout his work is one in which the mutuality of persons in relation to one another exists nowhere but within each of them as persons. A community of persons is one in which the right of the other has assumed the same primacy as my own. It is above all a community of right. Some commentators have pointed out how the essentially communitarian character of Rawls's vision only becomes clear in *A Brief Inquiry*. Standard objections to the unencumbered, punctuated, or isolated self of the Rawlsian calculations will no longer be possible. Now it is clear that even the thin community of the overlapping consensus is a genuine community in which each has taken on board the perspective of the other. Despite the externality of an order of right, the adjustment of mutual freedoms it entails, its most crucial feature is the inwardness by which every person is held by every other. Persons who are not mutually present are nevertheless present to one another within the order of right. That narrower, political, conception still lay further down the road, but it was continuous with the early discovery that "a person is not a person apart from community and also that true community does not absorb the individual but rather makes his personality possible" (127). A liberal community is one in which persons always take precedence over their convictions and commitments.

Priority of Person to the Good

The priority of right is really the priority of persons over the good. What appears as indifference is really affirmation of a far deeper bond that unites human beings beyond everything that divides them. The reason for the notorious difficulty in finding a language that can explicate commonality is that any language already takes its stand within a realm of objectivity. An appeal to nature or to nature's God raises the questions of meaning around which divisions turn. Yet the question of foundations cannot simply be ignored without suggesting the vacuity of an order of right. The mature Rawls certainly understood this, and he sought, in the various revisions through which his thought moved, to infuse the notion of right with a moral primacy that could withstand the solvent of doubt lapping against it. The priority of the right was for him a moral priority. This was what imbued it with an authority that could not be doubted, for no account of the good that failed to meet the test of the inviolability of persons could be regarded as legitimate. It is that heightened certainty of the principle of individual dignity and worth that has long functioned as the central axis of the liberal political tradition. But there is a big difference between a principle whose implementation demonstrates its validity and the elaboration of a theoretical account adequate to it. The latter was Rawls's project, and his enunciation of the priority of the right over the good is as successful a thematization as we have reached. Its durability, however, does not imply that the author had plumbed the depth of his own formulation. The reason for this, as it is for the broader liberal self-understanding, is that the principle represents the limit of the horizon within which we must contemplate it. We are persons and we must think within the awareness of what it means to be a person in relationship to other persons. The horizon of faith remains ineluctable.

It is only if we see this inescapably meditative character of his unfolding that we can follow the trajectory of Rawls's thought. Persons mark the boundary of that meditation because we know persons even before we raise questions about the true or the good. The person precedes the thinker. For Rawls there are none of the solipsistic questions about how we know other minds, the kind of intellectual isolationism from which there is no exit, since no proof can definitively put the uncertainties to rest. From the beginning he is a moral philosopher for whom obligation is the given within which he thinks. But it is only in *A Brief Inquiry*, so far as I know, that he explains why knowledge of other persons does not depend on me. The young Rawls brilliantly perceives that persons cannot be known at all except through their self-disclosure and that that, when it occurs, is irrefutable: "Natural objects immediately reveal their nature as being colored in such a way, as such and such a shape, and so forth. But personal relations are different; what the person feels cannot be seen as a sense-datum, but that person must reveal his feelings to us by means of sense-data, using those which have been determined by convention as representing the feeling and state of mind in question" (153).²² This may not have the full force of the Levinasian insistence on the primacy of the face of the other, but it is impressively convergent with it.²³ "We have bodies, then, as signs which make community possible," says Rawls (153). Individualism is never seriously entertained by Rawls because his thought moves entirely within the priority of community.

The problem with this realization is that there can never be an account of the obligation that has been imposed on us before we have even begun to contemplate it. On the contrary, it is our notion of obligation that must withstand the severe judgment under which it is unfolded. Right, in the schema of Rawls, is an inexorability before which our account of the good must answer. Far from being an evasion of responsibility, it is a heightening of it to such an extent that we stand naked before its imperative. In his early work, Rawls had no hesitation in acknowledging that this is tantamount to the inescapability of divine judgment. This is why he emphasized that there is no separation between religion and ethics. But this is not a God located far from the center of action. Rather, he is thoroughly disclosed within the personalist horizon within which he unfolds. It is because God is personal and therefore intimately related to all other persons that he is implicated in our mutual relations with one another. What we do to one person affects all others to whom that person is united: "Ultimately all personal relations are so connected for the reason that we all exist before God, and by being related to Him we are all related to each other although we may never have met one another. That personal relations form such a nexus leads to the conclusion that religion and ethics cannot be separated" (116; see also 204–5). It might not be too much of a stretch to conclude that even after Rawls could no longer regard his religion as orthodox, he nevertheless understood ethics as replete with attenuations into a religious sphere. The God of *A Brief Inquiry* was so thoroughly manifest within a personal universe that it would be virtually impossible to eradicate him from it. Without God the voice of God is still heard within, as the one who insists on the right treatment of persons above all other natural or social goods.²⁴ Even the break with religious language, in the announcement of public reason as the only authoritative discourse, is one that can be viewed as the final logic of the transcendent imperative.²⁵ The God who respects persons in their irrefragable autonomy cannot impose himself upon them. He is the seal of their inviolability.

Reason Making Room for Faith

It is possible that this is too smooth a construction to place on Rawls's more fitfully transacted odyssey, an odyssey that for all his formidable philosophical power was not in touch with the full reach of the Greek and Christian tradition or with the full range of philosophic developments in the contemporary period. Yet it was not entirely parochial, for unlike many of his admirers, Rawls was deeply immersed in the history of modern moral philosophy. It is particularly in the lectures on Kant, which take up almost half of the published version of his lectures, that we see him working out the wider parameters of his own thought. In this he attests to the impossibility of doing philosophy except in relation to the greatest philosophic minds of the past. Even if, as Rawls concedes, "I never felt satisfied with the understanding I achieved of Kant's doctrine as a whole,"[26] he nevertheless managed to work out how the famous postulates of God, immortality, and freedom could be understood in a way that was unobjectionable to his own evolving public reason. The focus on Kant is not surprising, for he was a thinker whose core convictions center on the person. Kant is not only the one who elevates the dignity of the person to its modern philosophic prominence, but he is virtually the origin of a personalist turn that recognizes consciousness, in its theoretical and practical enactments, as the horizon from which philosophic reflection unfolds.[27] But what particularly absorbs the interest of Rawls is the thorny issue of how the postulates of practical reason are to be understood. It is here that Kant, who "limited reason in order to make room for faith," discloses the kind of faith that endures beyond dogma and metaphysics. For the author of *A Brief Inquiry* this was the path that drew him irresistibly.

Rawls refers to it as "reasonable faith," which he wishes to distinguish from *Vernunftglaube*, a terminological distinction he introduces to Kant rather than finds within him. This is done because Rawls wants to differentiate between Kant's faith in a highest good (labeled by Rawls *Vernunftglaube*) and in the postulates proper. The result is a subtle and useful delineation of what are probably tensions within Kant's treatment, but we do not need to examine the merits of that suggestion here. We need only note its convergence with Rawls's overarching conceptualization in which the good, and accounts of the highest good, are continually de-emphasized in favor of recognition of the priority of right. He finds the grounds of this understanding in the Kantian "paradox of method," which is formulated in the *Critique of Practical Reason*'s insistence that good and evil do not define the moral law but are rather defined by it. "Kant believed," Rawls explains, "that once we start from the good as a prior and independently given object, the moral conception must be heteronomous."[28] Whatever is presented to practical reason as good, even God, must first be assessed in light of the imperative of goodness within us that is the autonomous enactment of the moral law. "Even the Holy One of the Gospel," Kant explains in the *Groundwork*, "must be compared with our idea of moral perfection before he can be recognized as such."[29] It is because of Rawls's more consistent commitment to the primacy of autonomy that he is sensitive to Kant's own occasional slippages into the older formulations of nature and the highest good. Rawls is, in other words, still on the determinedly personalist path he had first embraced in *A Brief Inquiry*, and he finds in Kant the indispensable means for its sustained elaboration. But that does not mean that Rawls opts for a purely secular rationalist account of Kant, for he takes *Religion within the Limits of Reason Alone* very seriously and mounts a considerable effort to include the famous postulates of God, immortality, and freedom as a whole. Even though he is willing to discard the *Vernunftglaube* that looks toward a highest good, Rawls seeks to sketch a reasonable faith in the postulates that does not overstep the secular boundaries.

Certainly he is scrupulous to avoid giving the impression that he is smuggling in religion or metaphysics by the back door of practical reason once the front door of theoretical reason has been closed against them. Even when Rawls finds himself in the minority position of rejecting the metaphysical construction of Kant's assertion that the origin of action must be located outside of time, he simply concedes that he does not regard such an implication as necessary to render Kant consistent with himself: "I believe that he is describing beliefs and attitudes that we are to adopt and cultivate so as to act from the practical point of view."[30] Rawls is, in other words, unusual among Kant interpreters in taking the postulates and their metaphysical adumbrations seriously yet not in a metaphysical way. We might also add that, like most Kant specialists, he does not look to Hegel or Kant's other successors for a solution to these problems. He continues to take "metaphysics" in a conventionally Kantian sense that suggests it is a supersensible realm no longer accessible through sense intuitions. The question-begging response as to what we might do with such a parallel universe does not seem to occur. Yet despite this lack of sophistication, there is something quite impressive about Rawls's determination to live with the manifest tensions of Kant that sustain a reasonable faith in the face of its rational demolition. It is as a result of that perseverance that Rawls arrives at a kind of metaphysical or religious openness that can find no justification within the strict secular limits of his thought. A metaphysics of practice has replaced a metaphysics of theory. It cannot be rendered intellectually coherent without taking stock of why such a logic is unavoidable, namely, because the horizon within which we live cannot be comprehended from within it. But that does not render the context within which we exist unreal. It is, on the contrary, the most real reality there is.

In many respects the early Rawls seemed to be surer of the status of that reality within which human beings live. He had named it as the "personal" that he distinguished sharply from the "natural," a division that gave him a rather firm grasp of the priority that must be maintained between them. The problem was that the later Rawls focused more narrowly on the autonomy of the person, without much reference to the contrast with the nonautonomous surrounding reality, and certainly without any extended effort to unravel the relationship between them. He eschews a broader account of autonomy to emphasize the narrower political conception of persons who "can be full participants in a fair system of social cooperation."[31] As a consequence, the best he can do is concede the inconclusiveness of his own intellectual position. This is the conception of a reasonable faith that he carves out by way of his reading of Kant. Far more is involved, Rawls explains, than the Tocquevillian notion that religion is an indispensable support of morality, for otherwise we would be inclined toward cynicism or despair. Rawls is willing to accept "that it would be better to maintain our religious faith, for then we would preserve our allegiance to justice and virtue."[32] But then he goes on to explain that such "religious beliefs would not be postulates in Kant's sense, since for him, postulates specify conditions necessary for us to conceive how the a priori object of the moral law is possible; religious beliefs are not needed for this when that object is the realm of ends."[33] This is because a "realm of ends" is not a good or a goal at which our actions aim but the very source from which they spring. In regarding every other as ends-in-themselves, we act as if we are bringing about a realm of ends-in-themselves.[34] This is not an event that lies in the future, for which we must hope and therefore require some grounds for hoping for it, but the reality within which we exist. The realm of ends is already accomplished within our action. This is why Rawls concludes by insisting that "Kant's reasonable faith is more than simply belief necessary for us to uphold our moral integrity." Reasonable faith thus turns out to be eschatological faith, a faith that is "the assurance of things hoped for, the conviction of things not seen (Heb. 11:1)." It is a faith that cannot be dislodged because it is impervious to refutation. In the instant of action it has been fully realized and does not await any consequence beyond itself.

Priority of Right as Eschatological

Now, it is not clear that Rawls realized the eschatological character of this faith, that as the wellspring of the moral law it evinces its definitive consummation. Certainly he seems to have thought that he was hoeing more narrowly to the expectations of a secular discourse.[35] Yet it is hard to resist the sense that he follows that line in part from a desire to preserve the conviction of right from the uncertainties to which any transcendent appeal would expose it.[36] The right that is prior to the good is the surest safeguard against the divisions that confront any specification of the good. Right as the a priori is unassailable. Beyond that it is probably not possible to go in Rawls's deliberately minimalist reading of the postulates of God, immortality, and freedom. In the end it is only freedom and its role in enacting a realm of ends that he seeks to defend along Kantian lines, a defense that he readily admits many will find less than adequate. Given the inability to mount a theoretical defense of freedom without invoking the categories of causation, the most that can be done is to indemnify moral action against the collapse that the denial of freedom would bring about. This is the role of reasonable faith that accepts our inability to bring theoretical and practical reason into a unified point of view: "While we cannot give a theoretical proof of the possibility of freedom, it suffices to assure ourselves that there is no such proof of its impossibility; and the fact of reason then allows us to assume it."[37] In the language of the young Rawls, there is no naturalistic demonstration of the freedom upon which alone personal existence depends. What it means to be a person, a self-enacting source of our own existence, can only be held by faith. Given the degree of his self-identification with Kant, we are inclined to conclude that this declaration of reasonable faith also represents the limits of Rawls's own thought. The concession that "many will find this view unsatisfactory" in its inability to resolve the tensions must be taken as an acknowledgment of his own limits. Yet even such disarming frankness need not be taken as the last word.

For one thing, there is the question of how Kant and Rawls could reach a position they discerned to be unsatisfactory and thereby hold the irreconcilables simultaneously apart and together. How could he know about the antinomy without in some sense going beyond it? One does not have to be a Hegelian to recognize that an antinomy one beholds has in some sense been transcended. The question is, what is that sense? Fundamentally this is the limit to which Rawls admits, a limit that refuses to reflect on itself. It simply takes note of the momentous historical significance of this bifurcation of theoretical and practical reason that Kant accomplishes. Acknowledgment of our inability to bring them together into "one unified theoretical account of the world" is the point at which "Kant breaks with the long tradition of Western metaphysics and theology."[38] The equivalent formulation in Rawls is surely his principle of the priority of the right over the good, for the entire tradition is premised on the capacity of theoretical reason to give authoritative direction to the moral life. Now, the good cannot be demonstrated but must rather be discovered, or "constructed" in Rawls's terminology, within the implementation of the right. The primacy of practical reason that subsumes theoretical reason under its guidance is indeed the revolution in thought signaled by Kant. It marks a break with the prevailing tradition as it has been conventionally understood, but a deeper examination would discover that it is more in line with what was implicit in the Greek beginning.[39] Rawls is certainly a partner within this development, yet a partner with distinct limitations in his own self-awareness. It is not clear, for example, that he saw his own central principle in terms of the shift from theoretical to practical reason. But what secures his position within the historical unfolding is that he may well be the first thinker since Kant to concede the core implication of the prioritization of practical reason. That is, without its theoretical underpinning, practical reason can only sustain its rationality by means of a faith that is more than it can justify. This is the significance of the trajectory we have sketched from the Christian personalism of his undergraduate thesis to the reasonable faith of his lectures on Kant. Even as Rawls narrows the application of that faith, over the course of his elaboration he seeks to secure it more impregnably against the objections of reason. Like Kant, he too has placed limits on the reach of reason in order to more thoroughly confirm faith. And as with Kant, one wonders whether the narrowly tailored faith he has embraced is up to the formidable responsibility he has placed upon it. Is a "reasonable faith" faith at all? Or does faith not necessarily entail a move beyond reason?

Perspective of the Person

The questions accumulate, but this is not the place to address them. Here we may only insert a coda that may be of relevance to those further considerations. It is an afterthought that is suggested by the continuity from Rawls's early thesis on faith to his late thesis on reasonable faith. Continuity always raises the question of discontinuity. What is the promise that has not been delivered upon? Over and above the departure from orthodox Christianity, the major discontinuity is in Rawls's abandonment of the language of personalism. That may be of a piece with his theological rupture, but it is not necessarily implied in it. What makes it of relevance here is that the question of the viability of Rawls's reasonable faith is surely connected with the question of whether faith can be viewed apart from faith in a person. Given that only persons have faith, is it not also inevitable that faith is centered on persons? What does it mean to have faith if faith does not open us to the community of persons? This is close to the position of the Rawls of *A Brief Inquiry into the Meaning of Sin and Faith*, for whom faith is an openness to the self-revelation of others that can be grasped only as faith. As such, persons are untroubled by an inability to bring their theoretical apprehensions of the sense data of others into coincidence with the practical faith by which they hold the others in inwardness. For them there is no question of the viability of their faith since it forms the axis on which their existence turns. Persons live by faith. But where does that faith come from, especially if the believer cannot fully account for its origin? If it is a gift, who is the gift-giver? The young Rawls seemed to have no difficulty acknowledging that it is only in community with others that the person acquires that openness to others that defines what it is to be a person. It is through others that we discern what inwardness is, as the horizon that holds us in relation to one another. The later Rawls struggled with freedom as a more solitary event in a world largely indifferent to its splendor. Without an affirmation of the mutual transparency of persons as the horizon of reality, the freedom they exemplify can scarcely convince us of its reality. Who we are recedes into impenetrable mystery.

In this sense, the younger Rawls possessed a far stronger intuition that the later Rawls could not philosophically retain. The tools of Kant proved, as Kant himself seemed to admit, inadequate to the task set for them. Freedom as a postulate, the faith that dare not speak its name as faith, is all that remained. It could not account for whence it had come or, more importantly, why it had generated an imperative to respect it that must not be breached. Nature still weighed too heavily in framing the sense of reality for it to be displaced by the persons who disclose it from within. Yet it is the presence of persons and their mutual openness that finally demonstrates the nonfinality of nature that can never contain them. Persons contain nature. This was the insight that the young Rawls glimpsed and the mature Rawls still struggled to articulate. To say that persons are different from nature is only the beginning of that reflection. Its elaboration would require a more thorough admission of the priority of practical reason that Rawls recognizes in Kant without grasping the shape of its consequences. Reason, in its practical mode, is moral reason that is seized by obligation before its reflection begins. Otherness is a faith that takes hold of us in advance of our taking hold of ourselves. It is the Thou we hear before we overhear the I. But without that substantial prioritization of ethics to ontology, as Levinas conceives it, we are left with the aspirations that characterize Rawls's reasonable faith. Then the inability to defend responsibility before the scrutiny of theoretical reason, even before public reason, weighs more heavily upon us. The thread of faith is strained when the call of the other remains beyond confirmation by the sensible. It arises from a faith that rests on nothing but a faith that, for all its nobility, is tenuous nevertheless. One wonders whether the burden of excessive narrowness that Rawls imposes on a liberal polity is one it is capable of sustaining. Yet the concern is one that virtually answers itself, for to become the kind of person who requires no more justification than public reason supplies, who has accepted the impossibility of rendering its practical convictions theoretically coherent, is to have demonstrated the transcendence that marks the fullest meaning of what it is to be a person. When one lives by the conviction of the priority of the right over the good, one has actualized a faith that affirms the person as more than he or she can say. The poignancy of Rawls is that his humanity exceeded the capacity of his thought. He could affirm that the imprescriptibility of the right surpasses all capacity to justify it, but he could not explicate the source of his insight. This is not necessarily to claim that philosophy has elsewhere accomplished as much. It is simply to take note of the possibility of a greater recognition of its possibility.

CHAPTER SIX

Dignity as an Eschatological Concept

An eschatological concept is one that cannot be fully known because we live within it. One day its meaning will be disclosed, but for now we see through a glass darkly. Human dignity is such a concept because it says what we cannot fully say—that each human being is sacrosanct. There is a zone of inviolability we must not cross because it would be to deny the very meaning of what it is to be a person. We must not take away that inviolability, which they hold in their own hands, by treating them as objects of control. "Autonomy" is too thin a word for what autonomy identifies. It is the whole metaphysical significance of the person that is at issue when we confront the question of human dignity. Our difficulty is that we live in a world without metaphysics and therefore have to say what cannot be said.[1] In this chapter, I take up the challenge by pointing to eschatology as the horizon of saying because it is the horizon of our existence. We begin by reflecting on what it means to live within an understanding we do not fully penetrate and thereby enlarge the possibility of truth. Then we examine the regime of rights that is our authoritative moral language, yet one that acknowledges its own incompleteness. When pressed to explain what rights are imputed to defend our rights talk can only point to the dignity of the person. This is why the topic of human dignity has in the last few decades surfaced with new prominence. The problem, third, is that dignity proves more elusive than its invocation might suggest because it protects what is most invisible of all, namely, the true self that even the person him- or herself never fully apprehends. In avoiding metaphysics we have evoked it even more deeply. We cannot finally deny, fourth, that dignity derives from the transcendence of the person by which each of us approaches the transcendence of God. Human dignity names our capacity to go beyond the claim to dignity through total self-emptying. It is thus what constitutes the transcendence of the person and can therefore never really be lost. That is why, most of all, human dignity must be preserved as the framework of rights.

Primacy of the Practical

We begin by noting that the notion of dignity has migrated from a social setting where the assertion of status was all important to one in which it is precisely the capacity to transcend any status claim. Rather than a world-immanent concept, dignity has become an eschatological proclamation. Each one of us exceeds the whole world, because we are called to exceed all limits in self-giving. There is no worldly limit to our capacity to love. It is that eschatological flash that we glimpse when we glimpse the reality of the person, or rather the nonreality of the person who transcends every boundary assigned in advance. The inexhaustibility of the person, the inwardness within which everything is contained, is familiarly intuited in the persons we know. We might say that we hardly know them until we encounter them as individual abysses of unknowability. This is why we cannot know persons except personally. Then we at least gain a sense of each person's unique unfathomability. The problem is that we have no philosophical language that can access that mutuality of persons that is more than words can say. Even worse, philosophy has often despaired of the task. It concedes the death of metaphysics, the opaqueness of the language of substance and the language of God, and betrays a singular lack of interest even in attempting to say what cannot be said about itself. Wittgenstein is one of the few exceptions, at least in calling attention to the problem.[2] But this is where politics enters the scene. In the political realm, philosophical limits cannot define the human limits. We cannot await the theoretical breakthroughs that would prove sufficiently compelling, but we must forge a meaning from the remnants that still retain the evocative moral authority that wins our consent. In politics we do not agree on foundations and then erect the principles by which a publicly representative order is affirmed. The theoretical comprehension arises, like the owl of Minerva, only late in the day, and even then it does not entirely detach itself from the principles whose emergence has been the condition of their own possibility. Before we reflect on who we are and whither we are going, we are already bound by certain moral and political convictions with which we cannot dispense. Truthfulness cannot be grounded unless we are prepared to do so truthfully. Loyalty cannot be discussed unless we are already pledged to its requirement. This is why politics is always in advance of its philosophy and the prayer life of the Church is prior to its theology. What theoretical reflection provides is not the first principles of what it examines but a meditation on what it finds as already obliging its own exercise. Philosophy can never contain that wherein it too is contained. It is bound by the primacy of the practical that receives its public authorization only within politics.

A case in point is the unsurpassability of human rights. The mutual recognition of rights is not only entailed within the logic of discourse in general, as Habermas suggests, but it is even more deeply entailed within the moral imperative of the human community.[3] It is difficult, if not impossible, for us to conceive of a human community that would not value each and every member as unique, irreplaceable, and immeasurable. Of course, we know of societies that devalue and dehumanize their members, but we cannot regard them as anything but perverse. What is decisive, however, is that we cannot conceive of any higher notion of community than the one that puts the neediest member first, the one whose rights are in any instant most in need of defending. This does not mean that every member is preoccupied with the protection and the assertion of their individual rights. On the contrary, the reciprocity that a regime of rights requires consists in the mutual self-restraint by which the rights of all are recognized. Rights are permissive; they are not unlimited claims. We are free to exercise them or not, but we are not free to abrogate them in others. It may indeed be that in defending my rights I defend the rights of all, and that when the rights of one are threatened the rights of all are placed in jeopardy, but this is not a prescription for collective self-interest. Our interests are served only within a regime founded on fairness because it is only then that the right to what each is owed is sufficiently guaranteed. Interest is served only when justice takes precedence. A system of rights is the way in which this relationship gains recognition. Its discovery, however, has largely been the fruit of historical practice for which the theoretical justification has continued to lag.[4] The pattern is detailed in Brian Tierney's *The Idea of Natural Right*, where he traces the rise of natural rights largely outside of medieval political theory to show that rights can be invoked within any expansive theoretical framework.[5] The canonists distinguished between the ownership of property and its use, and thereby established the notion of a right from which others could be excluded. It was only a small step for William of Ockham to establish the idea of a right that could not be alienated in his dispute with Pope John XXII over Franciscan poverty. The most that the vow of poverty could entail is a renunciation of the legal right to property, since the natural right to the use of property for the sake of life could never be renounced. From there the idea migrated to the conciliarist disputes in which the right of the Church, and of any community, to govern itself could not be renounced. This in turn created difficulty for the Spanish monarchy in the sixteenth century when Francisco de Vitoria and the Spanish Scholastics insisted that conquest of the Americas had not abrogated the natural rights of the Indians to property and self-government. In other words, long before political theory had begun its quest for the foundations of rights, the discourse had emerged in practical disputes in which inalienability had become starkly visible.

Dignity as the Invisible Source of Rights

To call these "subjective rights," as even Tierney does, is to suggest that they have no other basis than the mere assertion of claims. But they are not subjective in this relativist sense. Rather, they are simply the result of adopting the perspective of the person affected, the individual subject whose humanity is under threat. In effect they are objective rights, the ineradicable rights that attach to a human being simply in virtue of his or her humanity without subtraction or addition. When all else is lost or renounced they are the rights that remain to denote the inexhaustible reality of the person. The problem is that the source of that inexhaustibility remains strangely invisible. We are hard-pressed to locate what cannot be located or to measure what cannot be measured. It is only in the heightened intensity of the disputes, in which the notion of natural rights arises, that their imprescriptible reality is clearly glimpsed. Once the high drama of defense has passed, rights recede into the inaccessible. It is no wonder that they generate a rich trail of theoretical adumbrations even if none have succeeded in establishing their formulations definitively.

More recently, that awareness of intellectual fragility has begun to surface within the practical realm in which the priority of rights must be implemented. It is no accident that the UN Universal Declaration of Human Rights simultaneously avoids any indication of the source of justification of rights while also invoking the substantive notion of human dignity as their background. The same pattern is repeated in other contemporary constitutions, notably the German and Israeli ones, in which the protection of rights is deemed to be insufficient protection for what must be protected. Over the past twenty-five years the theme of dignity has become pervasive in charters and courts as they concede the insufficiency of a rights jurisprudence. Dignity is required to name what must be preserved over and above the preservation of rights. Only if dignity is named can the source of rights be adequately guarded.

The difficulties that this movement beyond the specificity of rights generates are readily accepted as the price that must be paid for what is priceless.[6] It is an impressive testament to deeper resonances within liberal discourse. Where philosophy has failed and religion has been unable to generalize its insights, the law must invoke what cannot readily be invoked. Dignity is surely the most elusive concept of all. Its presence within legal briefs and judicial opinions signals a felt need that is otherwise unmet within the public square. Somehow the harm that the deprivation of rights inflicts must be resisted not just in the name of what is right but in relation to what the right seeks to shield. That evolution was amply displayed in the thought of Immanuel Kant, who was the one who introduced the notion of universal human dignity, in contrast to prior conceptions of dignity as specific to a particular office or station in life. Where previously dignity was precisely what attached to the role a person played in society, now it would arise from the person who stood apart from the multiplicity of roles in which he or she might appear. Rather than turn to the dignity of what is visible, Kant would direct us toward the dignity that exceeds all visibility. Kant may not be thinking juristically, but the same inexorability is at work in both cases. When we think about the respect that is owed to each human being, we realize that it cannot be limited to the finite contribution each has made. When someone is no longer marked by his or her role, we are required even more to respect the person who plays it. Entitlement to dignity is by virtue of his or her humanity. The sharp distinction we had made between social status and human status begins to melt away as we realize that the latter is the ground of the former. There are no pure role-players.[7] All are persons who first possess the dignity of persons.

It is their integrity as persons, their inwardness, that the notion of dignity seeks to guard. Rights are merely the external barriers against the infringement of what is, strictly speaking, internal. This is what makes the protection of dignity so notoriously difficult, because what may be an infringement to one may not be so to another. Dignity is not contained in any of the codifiable attributes that make a legal code possible. What may be an insupportable burden to one may be a matter of indifference to another. A prohibition against turbans falls more heavily on Sikh men than on other men, just as a ban on head scarves affects Muslim women differently than other women. In each case it is not the specific character of the burden that is at issue, but the way in which it infringes upon the inner freedom to be oneself. Without intending it, requirements that on their face may be trivial or neutral can have the effect of abrogating the most sacrosanct imperative of self-determination. Of course each individual remains capable of an interior refusal to obey, but one cannot manifest that within the external world. People are deprived of the possibility of presenting themselves in public, which is more than the loss of what they would present. It is a denial of the self as the source of all self-presentation. To denigrate or diminish that innermost self, the self from which all self-expression arises while it itself remains beyond expression, is to strike at the core of the person. It is to deny the dignity of that which enacts its own being. This is the awesome stature of the person for whom no one is entitled to speak but the person him- or herself. The person denied does not disappear but is prevented from appearing. It is the objectification of what cannot and should not be objectified. But what of the possibility that the person might choose that path of diminished personhood?

Dignity as Invisible

This was the great difficulty that Kant intuited and struggled against. Indeed, his whole discourse about human dignity can be read as a protracted effort to heighten the awareness of dignity as a bulwark against its deliberate devaluation.[8] Even when we must allow ourselves to be used as objects, as in his strangely objectivist conception of marriage, we must take steps to ensure that the person is not reduced to that status as object. Marriage is the only way that the sexual relationship of men and women can affirm that they are more than what they do.[9] In marriage the partners are received as wholes and never as parts. The person who presents him- or herself to the other is acknowledged as what can never be fully presented. That is what is absent from the contract of prostitution. Even the term "prostitution" carries disavowal within it, for in that case the partners have only presented themselves in the form of economic exchange. Any service that entails the whole person cannot be reduced to the coin of barter. Persons can engage in economic exchanges precisely because they cannot exchange themselves. An economy requires persons who stand outside of it as enactors of the freedom that makes it all possible. The person who remains beyond every action can neither be subsumed into the transaction nor excluded from it. Dignity is the path by which what cannot be said, what can neither be preserved nor abolished, is irrefutably displayed. Autonomy, Kant discovered, cannot be exercised in disregard of its own meaning. What remains to be discovered is how self-determination is bounded by what makes it possible.

In the absence of any comprehensive philosophical defense of the dignity of the person, we must be particularly alert to the insights that are generated in the field of practice. Real-life controversies, especially as they are encountered in courts of law, are an invaluable guide, for they arise not only from the law but also from the most elementary human responses. What cannot be concealed or denied is very often what makes its way into raw judicial decisions. One thinks of the famous body-tossing case in which no amount of protest of liberty interests could override the sense that here a human had been utterly reduced to an object.[10] Could the assimilation to a piece of inert matter have gone any further? Perhaps only mutilation or the sale of body parts could suggest a further disdain, which, characteristically, has also prompted a similar revulsion. At such points all that is interior to a person seems to have been drained away. These are practices we would have difficulty contemplating even in relation to a corpse, so that it is inconceivable that they should be perpetrated on one who is alive. It is the loss of the person to whom one can relate that is the most devastating. Like torture or degradation, we can only engage in such practices when we have been able to cast aside any suggestion that this other is an other, another human being.[11] Even killing in war can often retain more of a sense of the nobility of the other as a worthy opponent who must not be gratuitously or inhumanly mistreated. "Crimes against humanity" that "shock the conscience" are terms arising from such historical moments of revulsion, and, like many things said in the heat of emotion, they do not necessarily reveal their own genealogy. The formulations suffer from an excessive abstraction, as if humanity could be assaulted or conscience shocked in general. The truth is that it is only individual human beings that can be killed, and we can be revolted only by the destruction of each unspeakably precious life. This is why the aggregate number of exterminations and casualties numb the imagination. We can be stirred to indignation only when we behold the misery of a single one. What is true of one is true of all, that each one carries a whole interiority within and that it is its denial that is the ultimate indignity. Their suffering has ceased to count. Thus it is not that they suffered but that they are no longer regarded as persons. The ultimate indignity points us toward what dignity is intended to guard.

Such a route is needed because dignity names what is invisible. The person is the source of all that is visible, but the person therefore remains beyond visibility. We often resort to the notion of a "transcendent core" of the person to suggest what it is that dignity seeks to protect, but that language has understandably lost its evocative power. This is not necessarily to be regretted, because the term is a contradiction. A "core" indicates an irreducible bedrock, while "transcendent" suggests that it lies beyond all fixity. Besides, we have become accustomed to conceiving of the philosophical alternatives as either deontological or consequential, both alternatives that eschew any appeal to ontology. What we have not considered is that the dignity of the person may not need any grounding in terms of ontological status. Just as the person lies beyond any social status, and thus can be regarded in relation to his human dignity quite apart from the dignity of his particular office or role, so the person can be seen as standing outside of all ontological status, as incapable of containment within any horizon to which he or she may be assigned. Indeed, persons can consider their ontological status precisely because they are not simply confined to it. Dignity can be gained or lost because we are beyond dignity as such. We have already seen that the person is what eludes all the enactments and expressions to which he or she gives rise. There would be no "giving rise" if there was not first what is not given rise to. Now we must be prepared to take the next step to which we have been led. We must dispense with the metaphysical crutch that there is nevertheless some innermost core, some primordial stuff, from which the person emerges and on which he or she is grounded. The extraordinary thing about persons is that they hold their existence in their own hands. They can give themselves or they can withhold themselves, so that no one else can bear responsibility for them. Even God is not responsible for them, for he has left them free. Nothing is prior to the person who thus shares in the primordiality of God. In other words, the status of the person is of that which is beyond all status. Whatever is adduced as the ground of the value of the person, even the love of God, remains available to the person to be accepted or rejected. The demise of ontology (itself a hybrid invention) is therefore not to be lamented for it always stood in the way of glimpsing that which it sought to articulate. Metaphysics (another surrogate) must finally yield to eschatology as we admit that the person arises from what is not, as befits the proper meaning of what is transcendent.

Persons Transcend All Saying and Doing

Perhaps it is time too to shed the connection that the term "human dignity" has with any notion of status. Granted that it has already eliminated the vestiges of special status in favor of a universal human status from which no one is excluded. But this still may suggest something too worldly. It leaves something tangible, even if it is universally human, on which the person may stake his or her dignity. In doing so, however, we betray the dignity of the person that does not turn on any particular features or qualities the person may possess. Even the dignity of a rational being, so important to Kant, seems to suggest that it must be accorded only so long as we retain the capacity to reason. This is, of course, the error into which the inclination to define what it means to be a person, and therefore an agent of dignity, inevitably leads. It is not what we intend in invoking the term "human dignity," for we mean precisely the opposite of any scale of measurement. Even those who fall short of displaying their full personhood are somehow persons, and we affirm this in according them the dignity of persons. We do not ask them to produce proof of personhood. Instead we are inclined to accept that they most of all are persons, for they allow us to relate directly to them in all their invisibility. By saying nothing, they have said everything. They show that, above all, persons just are, most of all when they are not expressed in anything present. Even without consciousness, they give themselves through their breathing until they yield up their last breath. Theirs is the dignity of having yielded all, and we realize that there is nothing in which they can be contained. This is why we reverence their remains as what still speak to us even after the person is gone. Not even death can defeat the person who, somehow, is deathless. This is why the distinctive mark of all human societies is remembrance of the dead. We are inclined to think that thinking about the afterlife is the result of religion, but it is really the converse. Religion arises because we already know about the afterlife through our experience as persons who are never fully here and therefore are never fully departed.

To be a person is to be transcendent. We therefore know about the transcendent, God, only because we participate in that mode of being. Whatever we have said or done, we have gone beyond it as that which can never be identical with the said or done. Persons thus exist nowhere. It is futile to ask for a metaphysics of the person, as if anything more substantive could explain the transcendence of the person. We can understand metaphysics, the possibility of transcendence, because we are persons capable of containing the whole world inwardly only because we are not present within it. This is the *imago Dei*, but the formula already suffers from the defect of suggesting that there is a likeness for what has no likeness. But the term also works because it shows that we have been able to glimpse the transcendent by virtue of our own transcendence. God can be known only by persons who are God-like. That is their dignity. They are beyond any claim to dignity in this world. It is the dignity of those whose dignity does not turn on any display of dignity. They hold their dignity within their own hands and can freely take it up or surrender it. For this reason it does not arise from our acknowledgment. Persons cannot lose dignity, but we may fail to stand within its imperative. The dignity of persons is that they are deathless, that they stand outside of all that they are. They cannot lose what never is. This is why, no matter what indignity they may suffer, they can never lose their dignity. Of course, a human being may lose control, may be overwhelmed by suffering and devastation, but that is only a possibility for one who is not defined by that extremity of misery. Only persons can suffer because they are not identical with pain. Animals are engulfed in their pain. This is why we put them out of their pain. We cannot do that for a human being, who always remains beyond the pain he or she undergoes. It is why persons have faith, a faith by which their suffering is transcendence.[12]

This is exemplified by Christ, who not only lays aside the dignity of God to become man but even sets aside the prerogatives of a human being through his death on the cross. It is a death utterly without dignity because it is public. Crucifixion is certainly among the most excruciating ways to die, but it is intensified when it is undergone before a hostile public gaze.[13] The innermost agony of the person is exposed. That moment when the person is most vulnerable, when the precious loss of life that must be shielded from the stare of indifferent onlookers, has been ripped open. What should be observed only by those who can share in the suffering of the dying is exhibited for all to see. Not only is death inflicted but the person is annihilated as a person. The interior life is denied when it is objectified. Like one of Francis Bacon's carcass paintings, everything says this was not a human being. That is precisely Bacon's point—we cannot look upon a human being in that way. Yet it is the way willingly undergone by Jesus. He not only suffered and died but did so in such a way that he abandoned all human dignity. Yet he simultaneously regained all that had been lost. In giving himself up, shedding not only the last drop of blood but also the last vestige of human dignity, Christ showed the real character of human dignity. It is the dignity of yielding up one's dignity completely. It is the dignity of God that carries nothing of self-concern within it, but freely gives itself on behalf of all. No greater triumph over evil is possible than the divine action in which God sacrifices himself completely. Nor is there any greater meaning to human dignity than the capacity to share in that total outpouring that is the life of God. This is why human dignity is an eschatological concept. It cannot be described in the terminology of this world, for it has exceeded every finite measurement. It is the dignity of the immeasurable, the dignity of that which has renounced all claims to dignity. That is its dignity. It is the dignity of what is beyond dignity.

This does not mean that it is only in the renunciation of dignity that dignity is realized. An even worse implication would be to suggest that dignity must not be safeguarded because it cannot ultimately be lost. The highest aspiration of our humanity would be taken as an invitation for its worst desecration. What could be worse than the blatant disregard of the best? Generosity is not an invitation to robbery. It may indeed be, as Plato saw, that the evildoers are even more severely injured than those whom they injure, but we cannot countenance their actions without complicity in them. Dignity, the dignity that cannot be lost, must be saved most of all. The challenge is to find a means of saving it when it appears to have no worldly presence at all. Dignity may be eschatological, but it is not for that reason any the less real or any the less present. We encounter it in every person whose inviolability we are charged with protecting. Their self-presentation must remain sacrosanct. No one can subsume the innermost self from whom all of their existence flows. To do so would be to abrogate their existence as persons, that is, as beings who have no existence but what they put themselves into. Their interiority must be guarded as the highest, uncontainable in anything but itself. But this means that we must be hesitant in imposing our judgment of what dignity requires in place of the person's own. We can easily see that there are many situations that might be deemed undignified or even degrading to outsiders, but not to the responsible individuals themselves. Human dignity cannot be so serious that it prohibits all undignified behavior—a bar that would eliminate many of the activities in which we engage. Nor can human dignity lack the highest seriousness of the capacity to surrender all claims to dignity, to exercise dignity in its most transcendent form. The turning point in each of these cases is to judge the validity of the claim to be exercising the highest form of self-responsibility.

The eschatological moment in which the whole of a person's existence is contained is neither private nor solitary. It is the meeting place of all human beings past, present, and future under the gaze of irrevocable judgment. All have become judges who must place themselves in the position of the other. We cannot avoid rendering a judgment on the judgment that the person him- or herself must render. Have I put myself wholly into this action? If I have then there is nothing that can diminish the dignity invested. Even letting oneself be demeaned to the level of an inanimate object can be accepted so long as it is a full expression of the self. But that does not mean that we must support every degradation to which a person may volunteer. It is only those losses to which a person has wholly submitted that can be regarded as retaining the dignity of a human being. The whole person must be given in the action. That is not possible if the indignity is merely an economic transaction, for no one can give him- or herself for the sake of an object. One can only give oneself for the sake of a person, including one's own person. Then one is giving what cannot be given and yet must be given in a human relationship. In an economic exchange, at most we can give our time, ourselves in part. Material transactions are somehow beneath the dignity of persons, who reside forever outside of them. It is only if the meaning of an action rises above the economic level that it is an appropriate communication of the person as such. This is why it is possible to sacrifice oneself for another, but it is impossible to sell oneself to another. Paradoxical as it may be, one can give away what cannot be sold. That which is priceless cannot be bought. Anything into which the person places the whole self, which is precisely what cannot be contained in anything finite, must not be reduced to the terms of conveyance. The person always communicates by going beyond all that is said. By contrast, an exchange is what can be reduced to the terms of a contract. Marriage is virtually an overturning of its contract because it is unconditional. Organ donation is bedeviled by the same impossibility of reducing it to an economy. It may indeed be the case that everyone else in an operation gets paid but the donor, but has not the donor demonstrated that he or she has given more than can be repaid in giving life? The dignity of the immeasurable cannot be measured.

Rights as Guarding the Invisible

The person who exceeds all that is given must nevertheless be preserved in his or her excessiveness. Has the giving been in the name of what cannot be given or only in the guise of what can be given and which is thus not given at all? It is in that eschatological arc that the dignity of the person lies. Is the uncontainable self contained in the action? That is the only relevant question, for we cannot prejudge in advance what form the gift of self may assume. This is why it is difficult to judge an affront to dignity, but it is not by any means impossible. We know what the gift is when we receive it. All we have to do is oppose its being counterfeited. This may still not forestall the possibility that counterfeit can be employed as the only available medium of truth. Humiliation may be redeemed by the giving that transfigures it or by the laughter that detonates it. We cannot fix the criteria of authenticity in advance of the event, but we can insist on its applicability. In doing so we have established a boundary of dignity that, though it may be breached, has nevertheless marked what must be defended. Dignity, in the end, recedes into the indefinable, but that is why it must nevertheless be defined. We cannot protect the dignity that includes the possibility of its own abandonment as its highest possibility, but it is just for that reason that we must make the attempt. Law must define the indefinable in the only way that it can. It must acknowledge that law itself is overtaken by the dignity of the self that exceeds its own dignity. The legislation of dignity cannot in the final analysis escape the eschatological character of its subject. Law too must exceed its own limits.

Law must acknowledge that human dignity cannot be alienated even when it is legally alienated. This is the core of the famous dispute of the Franciscans with John XXII when it was precisely their determination to renounce all that brought inalienability into focus. They could only alienate a legal right to property but never the inalienable right to the means necessary for life. Law encounters the limits of law in the notion of natural rights, which are not subject to the conveyance of law. Dignity as the unfathomable depth of the person, the container of the interior presentation of self, is the flash of transcendence that is glimpsed in the prohibitions against the violation of human rights. What is not present anywhere may nevertheless be intuited in the barriers it provokes. The discovery of natural and human rights is just such a moment. It is the point at which the law acknowledges its insufficiency as law, when it is itself measured by an order of right beyond it. Law cannot be used to alienate the inalienable. On the contrary, it is pledged to preserve what it cannot but preserve. Dignity has been invoked as what exceeds a mere catalog of rights, but it is in their recognition that dignity looms as the inexhaustible source. What cannot be alienated cannot be fully named. Rights are not the same as dignity, for dignity requires us to go beyond the mere acknowledgment of rights, but rights are the epiphany of the dignity of the person. Rights are inviolable. They cannot be balanced against some larger social good, nor is there a point at which the individual ceases to count as much as others or even as much as all others combined. Infinity cannot be calculated. It is that affirmation of the incalculability of each one that is the primary legal affirmation of human dignity. When it has said more than can be said, what more can the law say? It has wholly subordinated itself to the dignity of the person, who is alone capable of giving him- or herself on behalf of the whole. Rights are our refusal to trade in the untradeable. It is in the defense of rights that dignity is resplendent.

PART 2

The Philosophical Discovery

CHAPTER SEVEN

Voegelin's Path from Philosophy of Consciousness to Philosophy of the Person

Political theorists, like literary and social theorists, occupy a kind of twilight zone in relation to philosophy. Their disciplines are at once empirical and philosophical, an indeterminate status compared to the strictly autonomous unfolding of philosophy. Yet it is by virtue of this difference of perspective that they may have something to contribute to philosophy. The problem, however, is that the contribution remains largely invisible to the philosophical core. As practitioners of these twilight disciplines, we may be acutely aware of their potential application to philosophy itself, but it is difficult for philosophers to grasp the implications for their discipline in the work of Tocqueville, Weber, or Derrida. The same is surely the case with Eric Voegelin. His work may indeed be philosophical, but it is not philosophy and, therefore, does not necessitate a philosophical taking notice. For philosophers this is a reassuring state of affairs. Not having to take account of every thinker who has philosophical thoughts allows them to concentrate their efforts on the canon of bona fide members. Professional narrowness is a welcome time-saver, but that excuse is not our principal concern here. Our focus is less on the consequences for philosophy of neglecting its neighboring disciplines than it is on the reverse. The consequences seem larger if social, literary, or political theory fail to take philosophy as fully into account as is possible. That is the justification for the present reflection on Voegelin's relationship to modern philosophy.

Professional Context

It is a relationship that goes far deeper than mere professional association, but that is a context worthy of note. The fact that Voegelin's work was not exposed to regular philosophical critique is a factor that must not be overlooked. It meant that he did not have to pass muster before the most intellectually rigorous scrutiny. The chances of professional historians, the proprietary practitioners of the empirical side, paying attention were even less. Instead, Voegelin's work was left to fend for itself among the ignoranti of political science. It was among the latter that he appeared as a figure of philosophical weight, an estimate that reaches no higher than its source. Even practitioners of political theory, Voegelin's own subfield within the discipline, are not well equipped to furnish philosophical critique. Having only recently stepped outside the boundaries of constitutional theory, political theory has sought to live off an acquaintance with only one strand of the larger philosophical tradition. A focus on the strictly political texts has been deemed to be sufficient. Voegelin at any rate cannot be accused of that kind of parochialism. His omnivorous interests ranged far and wide and certainly included the centrally philosophical texts, not just their political applications. The problem was that he rarely encountered professional situations in which his broader philosophical interpretations were subjected to challenge. As a consequence, his approach to the history of philosophy became peculiarly settled. Having once mapped out a line of interpretation, there was little provocation to reconsider it, especially as it was readily taken as dispositive by readers who had even less philosophical training. This is no doubt a hazard of the disciplinary setting within which Voegelin worked. It is a situation that was no different for such mentors as Max Weber. Both were clearly men with a good grasp of the history of philosophy, but that was never enough to enable them to make philosophical progress on the problems to which they addressed themselves.

In the case of Voegelin, the situation is even more remarkable. Despite the fact that he locates himself outside of the discipline of philosophy, he nevertheless persists in working his way toward the resolution of philosophical problems. He still interacts with philosophical texts, but it is not an interaction that is connected with any contemporary conversation. Instead it is an isolated inner conversation in which Voegelin occasionally makes contact with fragments from the great thinkers. His final work, *In Search of Order*, gives the very strong impression of a man working almost completely alone. A tendency toward isolation may well be a trait of great thinkers who find no adequate partners for their work. Yet there is something more than the vicissitudes of greatness at work here. Looking back over Voegelin's career, we see that there has been a deliberate turning away from the modern philosophical conversation, even while remaining sensitive to its echoes in his own work. A rejection of the modern philosophic project remains so strong a note in his thought that most readers have inferred his avowed opposition to modernity as such. The characterization of modernity as "Gnostic" was only the most notorious indication. Much of this impression has to derive from the totalitarian crisis that became the lens through which Voegelin viewed the modern civilizational development. To the extent that totalitarianism was the defining feature of the era in which he lived, it was hard to shake the sense that everything else was implicated either positively or negatively in its unfolding. It remained difficult to integrate those other counterbalancing assessments of modernity that he was always careful to insert. Focusing on the extreme instances that illuminated the essence, he tended to let the intermediate developments slip from view. As a result, we are left not only with an overwhelmingly negative assessment of modernity but with a suspicion that the disorder extends to the very core. For Voegelin, what is positive in the philosophical achievements of modernity still carries the taint within it. Little can be expected therefore by way of a genuine restoration of order from the philosophic enterprise it has simultaneously sustained.

Negative Assessment of Modernity

We need only recall how few were the unalloyed heroes in the struggle for order in the modern world. Voegelin singled out Bodin, Vico, Schelling, and Bergson, a line of equally solitary figures whose connection with their own times had also been among the most tenuous. What he admired most about them was their achievement of a degree of detachment that made it possible to invoke a sense of universal humanity. Epitomized by the mysticism of Bodin, they had all found a way beyond the chaotic disintegration of symbols to an unassailable reality forever on the other side of them. This was an insight that informed all of Voegelin's work because it undergirded the possibility of communication across historical differences. It is no accident that the major turning points in Voegelin's own intellectual odyssey came through his reading of these thinkers. The engagement with Schelling, for example, caused him to jettison the project of *The History of Political Ideas*, although he held on to the manuscript. Philosophy had lost its "Last Orientation" and now moved within the realm of solitary seers who might preserve its truth for an unforeseeable future. Absent was any sense that its movement might be carried forward through a broader collaborative process. The reason for this assessment, I suspect, was Voegelin's reluctance to accept the notion that the modern world might be engaged in the struggle for order while at the same time germinating the totalitarian eruption of disorder. Even for a mind of Voegelin's evident flexibility, that seemed too unlikely a prospect. Yet we could document exactly such a pattern in his own observations. Witness the very different assessments of Hegel that emerge in *The Ecumenic Age* and in *In Search of Order*. It is worthwhile to contemplate how different Voegelin's treatment of the modern world might have been if he had discovered that Schelling marked, not a departure from German idealism, but its culmination. That would have necessitated a revision in his assessment of Hegel and might possibly have raised the status of Kant within the whole account.

He might then have seen that modernity is not just a darkness punctuated by a few bright spots, but a luminosity that, even though it may come into focus in a few instances, is far more widely dispersed than we had suspected. It would not then have been for Voegelin to single-handedly rebuild the edifice of order but to realize that it is already being built from within the world that had previously only exhibited a drive to destroy itself. The two dimensions cannot be separated, as Voegelin ultimately recognizes. The difficulty is that he often seems to give the impression that they can. This is when the historian of ideas comes up against the meditative philosopher within him, a conflict he struggled to reconcile over a long career without ever permitting definitive victory to the latter. If he had managed to reconcile the objectifying tendency of scholarship with the existential requirements of philosophy, then he would have been able to perceive the tragic-comic character of modernity more fully. As it was, that sympathetic reading was continually present without ever managing to recognize its full implication. Modernity, he often seems to suggest, is neither a problem nor a solution—it is the condition of our very existence. To frame it either way is to preempt existence within it. Rather, it is for us to gain a sense of the impenetrable mystery, simultaneously tragic and comic, by which our existence is guarded. It is then no more puzzling that the figures who perpetrate the most destructive consequences are also the ones in whom the overcoming of those consequences lies closest. Or that it is at the point where the struggle against evil reaches its apex that the danger of evil is at its greatest. An abundance of his own comments demonstrate Voegelin's awareness of this tragic-comic character of the messianic figures of modernity. It is just that it is not clear that Voegelin himself has taken on board the full significance of that concession.

More often than not, he judged that the opening toward order had failed to overcome the tendencies toward closure of which he remained acutely aware. The return of philosophy toward its existential source, a challenge virtually defined by the end of Scholasticism, had never been more than partially accomplished. Almost as soon as the imperative of life had been grasped, a new conceptual mummification had overtaken it. So although the aspiration of Hegel might be admired, his accomplishment fell far short of its promise. The temptation, as Voegelin saw it, to render the openness Hegel had gained a permanent achievement proved too much. Fantasies of the stop-history variety vitiated the truthfulness from which they began. Even Heidegger, who abjures the very notion of a system, does not escape its seductive hold, for he projects what Voegelin called a philosophy of "parousiastic expectation."[1] It is not necessary to profess an ideological faith to fall under its spell. The fatality can take many forms, including an infatuation with National Socialism. But the mistake, in Voegelin's mind, consists less in making political misjudgments than in the prior readiness to entertain totalizing solutions. It was therefore a philosophic error that paved the way for the political one. Clearly, this was a view of the flawed genius of German philosophy that was widely shared. Confirmation by the facts themselves seemed to decide the issue. Yet there is something vaguely unsettling about such a tidy disposition. Hegel, Nietzsche, and Heidegger were not peddlers of an ideological cure-all. They were genuinely philosophical figures in whom the original *eros* still lived. How then was it possible for them to be so profoundly deluded? To delude themselves along the path of sorcery? The frequency with which Voegelin returns to ponder this question suggests its obstinate persistence within his interpretation. Yet it is not quite inconvenient enough to cause him to reconsider his dismissal of their failures. Other than the exemplification of what to avoid, they provide in his view only limited positive guidance.

What Voegelin does not do is think through the logic of the critique he has made. If Hegel is, for example, a flawed genius, then the error does not necessarily affect the fundamental thrust of his thought. It merely constitutes a failure to follow it out. To the extent that he has grasped the direction in which philosophy must unfold, his achievement remains indispensable. The fact that he may have strayed from his own intuition does not mean that the intuition is itself flawed. Voegelin no doubt senses this complexity, but not enough to take seriously its implication. He concedes his admiration for dimensions of Hegel's thought, although there is little that is taken up into his own work. A curious detachment from the work of his predecessors often permeates Voegelin's work, but it is most in evidence in the case of the great modern figures, whom he holds at arm's length. Reporting on a conversation rather than participating in it, he finds himself carrying on the philosophical project with few vital partners. It is a tension between the Voegelin of the history of ideas, who can comfortably stand outside of the process he is mapping, and the Voegelin who recognizes that he stands within the differentiations that constitute the boundaries of his own thought. The tension can be sustained more readily when he is dealing with a problem case, such as the Greek *polis*, that is already defined by a certain historical distance. In the case of the modern context that is Voegelin's own, there is far less possibility of detachment. Embedded within the historical and philosophical context in which we find ourselves, we simply depend on the luminosity that has already emerged within it. A mere cursory acknowledgment of the legitimacy of the modern age is not enough to satisfy this requirement. Blumenberg sensed this withholding of legitimacy within the critiques of modernity wider than, but parallel with, Voegelin's, and it is difficult to deny the overall validity of his objection. How can illegitimacy infect a whole age? Does the very notion of illegitimacy not presuppose a legitimate modernity within it?

Philosophic Project of Modernity

Derailment is only possible if one is already on the rails. A root and branch dismissal of the aberrations eliminates the very reality that became aberrated in the first place. The result is not only the isolation of the remedial or reformative efforts we have already noted, but the even more serious disconnection between those efforts and the reality they are intended to address. That sense of removal from the age whose crisis Voegelin addresses has long struck readers, even if they have not always been able to articulate it to themselves. Over time we learn not to look for prescriptions, to accept the long-term character of Voegelin's contributions, and simply to accept the limitation any thinker has of not being able to do everything. But not to be able to do anything is a different matter. The inability increases as a thinker can find no point of contact with the problematic he addresses. That notable absence in Voegelin's work is of course evident in the case of his engagement with the tradition of liberal democracy. His readers know by now that they will find no more than a few passing remarks of relevance to the principal political form that now dominates our world.[2] One expects, therefore, that his contribution will intersect with the larger philosophical project of modernity, and there is no doubt that Voegelin understood himself as engaged in this enterprise. Knowledge of the empirical materials of history would continue to advance, but his theoretical approach to them was likely to endure. More than anything, Voegelin had opened up a way of understanding history and therefore a fundamental philosophy of existence. He discovered that there really was no such "thing" as history, but that history provided the very possibility of knowing the past and orienting ourselves toward the future. To the extent that historical research was possible, it was because of the contemporaneity of understanding that made the encounter with other persons possible. His own investigation could be both philosophic and empirical, drawing on the meditative immediacy of his own experience while reaching toward the enlargement achieved by the great spiritual adventurers.

It was a conception of order that recognized the impossibility of congealment within any fixed incarnation. History remained the horizon of an order that could never definitively be achieved. The elevation of history as the constitutive framework for every emergence of meaning was in line with the prominence it was accorded within post-Kantian philosophy. Voegelin recognized his affinity with Hegel in this regard. But he was hesitant to contemplate the relationship further. Beyond an appreciation for historical context, he failed to see how far the idealists had traveled in explicating its philosophical implications. To the extent that history had become the horizon of human existence it ceased to become an object external to the subject who contemplates it. This was the great philosophical project underway within that still unassimilated movement we know as German idealism. The Cartesian subject, the self whose domination of reality had marked the modernity of the scientific revolution, was undergoing a profound displacement. Its revolutionary significance was not by any means fully grasped at the time, and the subsequent history of philosophy is still in the midst of grappling with it. Voegelin only seems to have been dimly aware of the pivotal dimension of this turn that philosophy takes from Kant onward, even though his own efforts virtually parallel it. The failure is important not because it constitutes a shortcoming in his interpretive practice, but because it suggests the possibility of advancing that project beyond where Voegelin was able to bring it. To overlook the modern philosophic revolution was to lose out on the enlargement his own project might have received. Voegelin was sufficiently attuned to the direction philosophy had to travel in the modern world, but neither he nor anyone else is adequate to the task of unfolding all of the possibilities of that enterprise. Rather than merely seeing modern philosophy as implicated in the totalitarian convulsion it failed to avert, it might be possible to discern the direction its unfolding would resume once the crisis had passed. Astonishing as it may seem to most readers of Voegelin, the path philosophy has trod in the twentieth century converges almost exactly with the trajectory of his inquiry.

We are familiar with his late ruminations on the "It-reality," or his accounts of a "subjectless" and "objectless" event in being as constituting the experience of order, and of the impossibility of linguistic reference to anything outside of the participation it makes possible. The eerie similarity of such reflections to the poetic metaphysics of Heidegger or the tortuous semiotics of Jacques Derrida has been noted more than once. The possibility that Voegelin might himself occupy some space within the mansion of postmodern philosophy flutters across our minds. But we have not been able to pierce the bewilderment other than to note the affinity between their respective critiques of modernity. Missing has been any clear insight into the challenge that has occupied philosophy since Kant. Having been misled by the Cartesian phase that seemed to install the dominance of the subject at the center of reality, we have failed to see to what extent more recent efforts have amounted to an almost complete reversal of the subject–object model. Rather than talking about the anthropocentric character of modernity, preoccupied with the self and its sources, we should begin to recognize the extent to which the priority of the self has been almost completely displaced. Our failure to understand this development and, by implication, the course of modern philosophy arises from our preoccupation with the early modern primacy of the subject. As a consequence, the later efforts to displace it simply look like a series of ever-widening circles of incoherence.

Absent is an appreciation of the task that philosophy has accomplished. That has been nothing less than the reversal of the assumption that epistemology precedes metaphysics, the very rock on which pre-Kantian philosophy sought to rescue certainty from the uncertainties to which probabilistic science had so thoroughly exposed it. The hopeless naïveté of the notion that knowledge might be secured in advance of its assault on the great questions of existence has been demolished. How can the justification of knowledge prescind from the reliability of knowledge on which its justification depends? Knowing is an irreducibly existential reality behind which knowing itself cannot go. Descartes had inverted the priority in his famous *Cogito ergo sum*, for there could not be a thinking subject unless he already was. The subject is not primary and therefore does not have the problem of establishing its relationship to reality. Rather, the subject is already within being and must take its orientation from within the pregiven relationship of existence. No contemplation of being is possible from a perspective outside of it. Existence is the priority behind which it is not possible to go. Heidegger's famous "Kehre" consisted in sloughing off the last shred of subjectivity that still attached to that recognition. To exist is not to hold one's existence within one's control but to recognize that all possibility of control is contained within the relationship to being. There literally is no existence apart from the openness toward being. The unencompassability of being, the impossibility of containing it within an idea, is the boundary of all language that cannot itself be referenced within the medium of language. Philosophy now must avoid the implication that it is contained within subjective mind but must strain its utmost to show that the mind of philosophy is contained within being. That is the horizon of the person.

What this displacement of the subject really means was already clear in Kant, even if he did not fully recognize the logic of what he had accomplished. It meant the priority of practical reason over theoretical reason. Indeed, Kant's "Copernican revolution" in the *Critique of Pure Reason* ultimately consisted of recognizing theoretical reason as itself a genre of practical reason. Before it could be a means of accessing reality, reason had to assume the form of a practice. It was hardly surprising therefore that the metaphysics Kant sought to save found its emergence most fully embraced within his other two critiques of practical reason, the *Critique of Practical Reason* and the *Critique of Judgment*. In the former it was the famous "postulates" of God, immortality, and freedom that were salvaged; in the latter he found his way toward beauty and order as regulative ideas through which our reflection operates. The caution with which

Kant proposed such "metaphysical" conceptions demonstrated the hold that the earlier identification of thought with subjectivity still had over him. His successors evinced far less hesitation in entering on the path he had opened up. The metaphysics that had been definitively foreclosed by Kant's recognition of the impossibility of overstepping the bounds of empirical knowledge was now regained as the ineluctable boundary of existence that included the possibility of empirical knowledge itself. Besides the knowledge of intentionality, as Voegelin came to formulate it, there was also the more embracing knowledge of luminosity. But what Voegelin did not do was to follow out the logic of this realization within the existential metaphysics, the metaphysics of the person, that characterizes philosophy after Kant. Voegelin's place in modern philosophy is peculiarly tied to the Kantian moment in which metaphysics had still not clearly separated from the presumptively foundational questions of epistemology. As a result, the issues are framed in terms of "experience," an avenue still predisposed toward the subjectivity of the experience itself. Largely overlooked by Voegelin, though he continually charts an independent course toward it, is the more radical attempt of philosophy to think the question of truth apart from all reference to the subject. Nowhere was this more evident than in the case of Nietzsche.

Failure to Recognize Postsubjective Metaphysics

In other words, by neglecting the main line of philosophy after Kant, Voegelin passed up the assistance he might have derived from its intensive unfolding. Only occasional concessions of admiration give any evidence that Voegelin was even dimly aware of the large parallel enterprise to overcome "propositional metaphysics." He seems to have no clear idea of how far modern philosophy had succeeded in the task. Even his early study of Husserl betrays little recognition of the achievement of the latter's phenomenology regarding the centrality of ontology.[3] There is only a brief acknowledgment of Husserl's achievement, followed by astonishment at the possibility of its chiliastic misdirection, from which Voegelin draws the conclusion of the necessity of embarking on a new beginning. Nowhere is there the suggestion by Voegelin that Husserl might have provided an indispensable clarification from which a new beginning might be taken. As a consequence, Voegelin's own application of the phenomenological method reverts to its experiential applications rather than to its ontological primordiality. He is more like his friend Schütz than the philosopher of primordiality, Heidegger. It was only later as Voegelin approached the end of his project that he began to realize the necessity of inventing a new philosophic language by which the postsubjective understanding of order might be expressed. "Eternal Being in Time," the penultimate essay of *Anamnesis*, may be taken as the marker for this phase. It is no accident that its formulation is redolent with Heideggerian overtones. One senses Voegelin realized that what he had sought to do in the empirical investigation of order as a living reality within *Order and History* could never really be clarified until it had found philosophic formulation. What is remarkable about "Eternal Being in Time" is the extent to which it echoes all of the language of postsubjective metaphysics with little overt reference to its extensive literature. Again, Voegelin is alone in his meditation with only the classic philosophers to guide him. This is all the while acknowledging, in a characteristically contemporary vein, that neither Plato nor Aristotle saw the way through to the development of an adequately nonobjective metaphysics.

Yet Voegelin is hardly to be blamed for missing the turn toward a metaphysics of existence in contemporary philosophy. The extent to which a stable consensus has still to emerge may be measured by Derrida's remark toward the end of his life that he was less well understood then than he had been twenty years before.[4] It is simply that closer attention to this mainline of Continental thought would have assisted Voegelin enormously in breaking free from the subjectivity of experience, a burden that still affects the reception of his thought. His insistence on the triad of "reality-experience-symbol" does not quite capture the dynamic character of existence by which reality as such is never present. We are always too late to encounter it, and it is precisely this lateness that opens the possibility of existence, for we exist within the unending movement toward what can never finally be reached. Something of this insight is certainly present within Voegelin's conception of the transcendent ground as constituting the boundary of existence, but it is still too much attached to the spatiality of substantial presence. He seems not to have thought through what the meaning of transcendent being must entail. As transcendent it is just what cannot become present, what cannot be revealed. His approach to the question of Being remains too closely tied to the historic reception in texts formed around the aspiration of naming it. Too much emphasis is still attached to the project of naming when the very meaning of naming has not yet been subjected to radical examination. By uncritically accepting the language of substantial identities the problem of the possibility of naming is overlooked, for naming can only take place when not everything can be named. Beyond the name there is always what exceeds the name.[5] If this is the situation with persons who always retain a mysterious depth that belies the identity of a name, then it is preeminently true of the divine name that opens an infinite abyss of mystery. Voegelin was certainly aware of such issues, but that is not quite the same as following out their full linguistic consequences. He had not seen that the language of substance and identity must be replaced by the language of persons and relations.[6]

Truth as Prior to Experience

One of the most significant possibilities of development is indicated by the question of how the nontransparency of language permits the possibility of any transparence? How is it possible that we nevertheless can apprehend what cannot be apprehended because it is transcendent? Is there a revelation of what is not revealed? The question is one that lies at the heart of German idealism, that flowering that has increasingly come to be recognized as the seedbed of the contemporary philosophic revolution. It was the genius of the idealists to recognize that the question of how meaning is apprehended could not be resolved in subjective or psychological terms. Ultimately the provenance lay within the realm of metaphysics. When we ask how it is possible for us to grasp what lies beyond appearance, what cannot be revealed, we are directed toward that within us which is derived from what is there before the beginning. Schelling in particular made this realization the focus of his meditation. We know that we do not live within the world of appearances, that beyond the symbols we can grasp what cannot be symbolized, because there is in us what is derived from that primordiality. Unravelling the meaning of that observation occupied the postidealist history of philosophy. The task took the form of despatializing such metaphors as "within us" or "outside of us" until the point is reached when all subject–object reference has virtually been eliminated. This is the achievement of a truly postsubjective metaphysics, which though its formulations may initially bewilder nevertheless manages to penetrate to the truth that has been the aim of all previous metaphysics. That is, that truth is not a condition internal to our consciousness but the very reality within which consciousness exists.

A good contemporary example is provided by the work of Emmanuel Levinas. His formulation that "ethics precedes ontology" captures the thoroughly existential thrust. There is no neutral "ontology," a condition of existence that permits the subject to dispute with itself before it resolves on the direction on which it will bestow its favor, for we have already arrived at obligation too late. We have no choice but to assume responsibility for what makes us responsible even before we have arrived. It is not as if we have to prove the existence of persons before we determine the limits of our responsibility toward them. There is no conditioning of responses when we are called by the unconditional. To say that we are obliged is to recognize that we are not free to disregard what is required of us, that the imperative within which we find ourselves is far more real than the subjective freedom of the possibility of turning away from the other. None of this is any longer the language of impulses and motivations that still envisage a subject capable of walling himself up within his subjectivity. Rather, we live within a moral-metaphysical universe whose truth is not contained within us but contains us as the very condition of our existence. Some adjustment is no doubt required to think in such a thoroughly desubjectified manner, but it is probably far less of a shift once the power of its moral truth has penetrated. The dislocation of philosophical reflection over the past two centuries then strikes us as less disorienting, for it has become the means of reaching a more profound orientation within existence. Thinkers, who had previously been perceived only vaguely, suddenly come sharply into focus as harbingers of this most profound transition. Kierkegaard stands out as perhaps the most prominent such instance. His reception has been peculiarly delayed as it has been assimilated to contexts that were not yet ripe for the full realization of his achievement. In many ways he represents the epitome of the shift, not to a metaphysics of existence, but to existence within metaphysics. It is no accident that our contemporary postsubjectivists have rediscovered him as already there at the end of their own meditations.

Kierkegaard provides the clearest and most persuasive illustration of the distance Voegelin still had to travel. The affinity between them has long been noted and includes Voegelin's own engagement with the language of the great existentialist. It was, however, an engagement that did not pursue the deeper intimations of Kierkegaard. Like many other readers, Voegelin appears to have assumed he knew all that there was in him. This is perhaps why his engagement breaks off before Voegelin faces Kierkegaard's challenge to the centrality of religious experience. One might have thought that a thinker who places the relationship of the individual to God at the center of his reflection would privilege those moments in which the encounter becomes manifest. Similarly, we might have expected that much would turn on those modes of life that seem wholly dedicated to divine worship, as in the practice of monasticism. Yet Kierkegaard firmly renounces such avenues to faith, insisting that faith itself takes priority over them. He does not want the experience of God to supplant the God of experience. It is an admirable grounding of thought within truth that completely understands the impossibility of thought grounding truth. When we begin with the subject, Kierkegaard recognized, we rarely get outside of it. Instead, endless debates about the truth of truth endlessly postpone existence within truth. Preoccupation with experience had been the fatal flaw of Romanticism, a fatality abundantly evidenced in its turning away from existence for the sake of its distillation. In the name of existence, existence was deferred. The bankruptcy of subjectivity was virtually complete. Because he was living in the Romantic age, the necessity of confronting the ubiquitousness of experience had thoroughly cured Kierkegaard of any misconceptions concerning its primacy. By recognizing that existence within truth could not be postponed, he became the first and, in many ways, the greatest postsubjective thinker. It is for that reason that we must identify Kierkegaard as the one who establishes the priority of the person. His focus on existence does not so much foreground the passing moment as illuminate the person who holds all of the moments in responsibility. He thereby brings the person as such into view.

History No Longer Outside but What We Live Within

Voegelin by contrast still remained entangled by the linguistic vagueness of "experience." Symptomatic of the problems is the common objection that all experience is private, a difficulty that is not quite overcome by the response that it is universally available or recognizable by all human beings. Of far greater weight is the objection that the experience cannot authenticate its own truth, that there is no way of establishing the transition from what is within to a reality that lies beyond the subject. How do I know that a correspondence holds? Philosophy of consciousness reflections may alleviate, but they cannot resolve, the difficulty that beginning with consciousness has already established an unbridgeability. Voegelin's intention is obviously to avoid any such suggestion. The difficulty is that he has not found the philosophical means; he has not quite thought his way through to the priority of truth over consciousness. Breaking with the conventions of subjectivity has proved to be more difficult than expected, for it requires a radical departure from prevailing patterns of thought. Some measure of what is entailed may be gained by considering what the experience of transcendent being must involve. To speak of it as an "experience" is already to move into the realm of metaphor, for we can hardly experience what cannot be contained within us, that which itself contains us and provides the possibility of all experience. How then do we know or recognize it as transcendent being, as God? Surely not in virtue of something immanent to our consciousness. When we use the term "revelation" we are more appropriately on track, especially insofar as we acknowledge that the initiative lies wholly on the side of the divine. But how then is it possible for us to receive such a revelation of the transcendent? The difficulty seems to have merely been moved further ahead as the question we cannot finally avoid. Revelation seems then to be an event that occurs to persons who already exist within the luminosity of revelation. They have simply not yet awoken to it. There is then no event of revelation within time, there is only revelation that has already happened before and perhaps even as the condition of time itself.

Such reflections hardly surprise any close reader of the later Voegelin, but, I would suggest, they clarify one of the great unresolved tensions that remain within him to the very end. It goes back to the tension between the historian of ideas and the meditative philosopher. Voegelin may have surmounted it at one level, but there were yet other layers to maneuver. Nor is this a tension that is peculiar to Voegelin, for we encounter it every day within philosophical discussions. Heidegger expressed it best when he pointed out that it is impossible to recount the history of philosophy from the outside, no matter how erudite the scholarship. It is a history that can only adequately be narrated from within its movement, that is, philosophically, for it has no reference but to the very movement by which it is constituted. In this regard Voegelin consistently found himself on the side of Heidegger, but that was never quite enough to completely shake the alternative model of Ernst Cassirer.[7] Perhaps it is Hegel who provides the most telling example of the effort to hold together the empirical and the philosophical in some final resolution. So although Voegelin might abandon his *History of Political Ideas* project, he would only revise, not abandon, its successor, *Order and History*. The form that the project took in the final volume, *In Search of Order*, had of course rendered the conception of a material philosophy of history all but unrecognizable. Voegelin might still insist on its empirical content, but its meditative movement had virtually absorbed it all. Only a slight step remained to the recognition of its virtual impossibility. History, Voegelin came increasingly to concede, is not something outside of us but what we live within. It is that contiguity that provides the possibility of understanding history, of placing ourselves within it. Scholarship on its externalities may yield enormous troves of information, but it cannot provide access to its inner life. Voegelin's own insistence on the perspective of participation as the only avenue of interpretation recognized this, but he did not carry that recognition to the conclusion of the diminished value of all external mappings. His own evolution may have indicated as much, yet it never rose to the level of principle. One wonders if the crucial factor was his failure to grasp the pivotal insight of post-Kantian philosophy that thought is already an openness to being even before it begins to raise the question of being.

Philosophy of consciousness must ultimately find its basis in a philosophy of the person. There is no getting behind the person who is prior to and the condition of all experience. Voegelin acknowledged as much in his insistence that philosophy of consciousness must derive from the concrete consciousness of the philosopher. But the latter is not merely a consciousness, for he or she is a person who in everything has already transcended consciousness. Voegelin's own anamnetic experiments attest to this insight as he returned to his own earliest memories as a child. A similar prioritizing of the person occurred in his revulsion at the progressivist scheme of history endorsed by Husserl. It was enough to prompt a decisive break, for Voegelin sensed that all such constructions regard human beings as a means to some historical end that is transacted over their heads. He repeatedly references Kant's admission that this prospect had "disconcerted" (*befremdend*) him, for it called into question the value of a progress that no longer serves the fulfillment of individual persons.[8] Husserl, Voegelin judged, whether fairly or not, had failed to demonstrate the requisite sensitivity that should have recoiled at the instrumentalization of human beings. It was a turning point in Voegelin's odyssey when, even if it meant embracing a more solitary path, he resolved to pursue a horizon of openness to all human beings rather than restrict them to a predetermined meaning and significance. In every respect Voegelin had embraced the priority of the person, even if he had not yet risen to the explication of it as a principle. His own moral alertness had demonstrated the structures of transcendence his philosophy of consciousness sought to articulate. It would have taken only a minor adjustment to realize that his project consisted in the prioritization of persons over their consciousness.

CHAPTER EIGHT

The Turn toward Existence as Existence in the Turn

The crisis of meaning that has confronted modernity is inseparable from the technological drive. Not only can nature no longer provide a guide when we subject it to universal dominion, but even the coherence of nature as a concept begins to fall apart. Nature may be the means by which we dominate nature, but the boundary between the natural and the artificial can then scarcely be maintained. All becomes raw material for homogenization and manipulation. Nothing is simply given as a fixed or permanent nature; everything is drawn into the process of transformation. The dream of universal mastery finds no limit except one. Mastery cannot master itself. In the end the vast expansion of power is itself unmastered because it is left without purpose or guide. Technology has no goal. But in this realization our philosophical reflection has at the same time illuminated the self-limitation of all instrumentality. Nothing can really be an instrument unless it somehow serves a goal that is not instrumental. Just as in each case the object pursued is regarded as a relative end, so the scheme of instrumentality as such can only function if it is embedded in an order of things that limit its expansion. The process cannot continue indefinitely. It is only because of the overwhelming power of technological development that we gain a sense of its omnivorousness. The reality is that the whole structure quickly crumbles unless it is sustained by an order of limits which define and guide it. Formal rationality may seem to exercise unchallenged dominance, but without a substance of ends it falls apart. The pursuit of means is always structured by ends.

Correlative with the great philosophic critique of instrumentalization is the growth of the alternative by which it is judged. The still incompletely acknowledged revolution in modern philosophy consists in the progressive articulation of substantive reason. Modern science may have succeeded by virtue of its confinement to the world of phenomena, but modern philosophy has correspondingly found itself within a substantive reality that it knows from within. Technology too is ultimately known from the inner perspective of participation, and this in turn is what enables our philosophical reflection to escape the realm of technique. Unlike the superficial expectation that a technical solution may be found to all the problems of technology, our philosophical meditation unfolds at the heart of the technological project. Refusing to be limited to the realm of appearance, the philosophical penetration of the underlying reality is an opening toward being as such. It is a disclosure of reality from within, in contrast to the illusion of domination from without. In place of the subject standing over against a world of objects, we expand the meditative knowledge of our participation within existence. Illusory superiority is replaced by submission to truth. This is the shift of perspective that has been underway in modern philosophy as it struggled against the subject–object model, whose dominance has been so great that the countermovement has scarcely been noticed.

To really comprehend the far reaching implications of this philosophic revolution, a revolution that does indeed return us to the very beginning of philosophy, we must be prepared to follow out the many threads by which it is unfolded. All that can be attempted here is a sketch, but it cannot be only a sketch. In keeping with the existential shift in philosophy itself, we cannot avoid an actual beginning. Philosophy can no longer be talked about, it can only be discussed from within. A non-philosophic account of the movement of modern philosophy would be like discoursing about an event of which we had no experience. No doubt much useful information could be assembled by such a strictly historical approach, but it would miss the core that justifies attention lavished on the periphery. Philosophy can only be understood by participating in it. This is a principle that increasingly informs and identifies the philosophic revolution of the modern period as the accent shifts from discourse to its existential roots. Once we become self-conscious in our discourse, attention turns toward the conditions of philosophical reflection. Among the conditions that cannot be overleaped is the existence of the philosopher himself. It is in this way that philosophy returns to its classical conception of a way of life. But merely recognizing the indispensability of the existential perspective does not mean that a thinker will fully recognize the implications of the shift. Indeed, one of the patterns we will discern is that the modern philosophic revolution is often characterized by the struggle, not always successful, to remain true to itself. If we are to uncover the full dimensions of this movement, we cannot remain at the level of the intellectual formulations left by the respective thinkers. We must reach beyond what they said to the dynamic of questioning that in many cases yielded developments that had never been acknowledged and sometimes even distorted by the thinkers themselves. Given the inconclusive state of much contemporary philosophical discussion, the notion that a unifying pattern exists at all is a claim requiring some justification. For now all we can do is prepare the way by taking note of the fundamental condition for perceiving its plausibility. We must be prepared to exist within the mode of philosophy. To understand those who worked toward this new way of conceiving philosophy we must place ourselves within the same dynamic. We must be prepared to philosophize about philosophy.

The recognition of this necessity is slow to emerge in the history of modern philosophy, but it clearly antedates the "existentialists" of the twentieth century. A persuasive case can be made that Kant marks the beginning of the return of philosophy, more explicitly than the classical thinkers, to the primacy of existence. The shift is proclaimed in Kant's assertion of the superiority of practical reason for the disclosure of being. God, the immortality of the soul, and the reality of human freedom are postulates of the moral life, and Kant is very careful to emphasize that they provide no theoretical knowledge of their truth. Since all of our knowledge comes through our sensible intuitions, that of which we can have no experience can never become an object of knowledge. This is the famous end of metaphysics in the sense of a claim to know entities that exist in some abstract realm apart from all possibility of experience. Kant inaugurates the liberation from unreal entities that Nietzsche continues to celebrate. Relief from the burden of unreality is seen as a break from a long imposition dating to Plato. Yet as every reader of Kant can recognize, he does not thereby abandon his concern with faith or metaphysics, for he brings them to a deeper level. This is not merely a haunting of the past. Both in tone and in substance Kant displays the new seriousness about getting at the real truth of things, even to the extent of proclaiming his own search for the pure a priori of reason to be the only adequate metaphysics. What makes him sanguine about the possibility of thereby bringing about a fundamental advance in philosophy is his conviction that the critique of pure reason, both theoretical and practical, puts us in touch with the thing in itself. It is reality known from within, knowledge of the *noumenon* rather than the *phenomenon*. In reflecting on the a priori of pure reason, whether in its theoretical or practical mode, we are no longer apprehending the appearance of what is intended, but we know it as it is. This means that what is discovered in this noumenal reflection of the self on itself carries with it a force of reality that breaks through the barrier of the phenomenal. We still have no phenomenal basis for our assertions concerning God, immortality, or freedom, but we are profoundly convinced of their reality. As "postulates" of practical reason, they are the indispensable continuities from the reality that is most powerfully evident in our own existence. To the extent that Kant struggles to heighten the human dignity that realizes itself exclusively through the exercise of self-responsibility, he at the same time intensifies the awareness of the dimensions of reality into which human being extends.

This is the excitement that took hold of philosophy in the movement known as idealism. A whole generation of thinkers looked on the completion of Kant's philosophical revolution as their project. They understood that Kant had placed the subject, the transcendental ego, at the center of reality and had thereby resolved the gulf that seemed irresolvable within all correspondence theories of knowledge. By making knowledge of the world derive from the subject, he had redefined the nature of the problem. Knowledge now meant the categories we impose on sensible intuitions, which removes entirely the mystery of how they connect us with the world outside ourselves. Rather than conceive knowledge as something that comes from a source outside, he showed that it is essentially the order we impose on the world of our experience. That left the great problem of truth. If knowledge consists of the imposition of categories on data, how do we know if our imposition is true in some sense? What does truth mean in this context? These are the questions with which Kant himself struggled in his last great critique, *The Critique of Judgment*, which was the point of departure for the idealists. Comprehension of reality by means of our categories is true only if our reason is itself continuous with the structure of reality itself. Recourse to a postulate of teleology is again the way in which Kant formulated this derivation, but the idealists made the existential leap to grasp that this is no longer a claim about knowledge but about human being. Our categories can comprehend reality, not because we can bridge the separation of subject and object, but because our being is already the unity of the two. Human existence is never simply a fact within a world of other discrete facts, but is already that which can see facts as facts. The way to understand reality, the idealists concluded from Kant, was not to contemplate it as a whole outside of the subject, but to recognize that the subject was already the whole or the point through which its self-disclosure took place most completely. They saw that it is practical reason that holds the key to theoretical reason and turned their attention to the process of history in which the self-realization of man unfolds into the self-disclosure of reality.

When human self-consciousness occupied such a pivotal role, the temptation to claim possession of absolute knowledge proved irresistible. But this distortion should not devalue the philosophic shift toward existence that lies behind it. Before Hegel's claim to absolute knowledge could be rendered plausible, there had to be the prior recognition of man's openness toward the absolute. It is not our knowledge that makes this relationship possible, but our participation in the absolute mode of being that makes the knowledge of it possible. Hegel gave voice to the turn toward existence as the mode of knowing by his insistence that knowledge could no longer be apprehended as a result. Propositions had to be replaced by the movement that catches truth as it discloses itself in the unfolding movement of reality. We know ourselves, not by contemplating the self objectively, but by the process of self-realization. Truth is in the movement, never in the dead result. It is unfortunate that this profound insight, which sought to restore philosophy to its original understanding of the love of wisdom, was overshadowed by the counterpull within Hegel to bring the movement to its completion within his system. He thus is the first of the ironic exemplars whose intention of countering the objectifying tendency of thought is subverted by his own inclination to commit the same mistake. Nevertheless, Hegel does stamp the history of philosophy with the discovery of its dynamic quality. Reality is not a fixed condition but one that discloses itself through its movement. This is the turning point in which philosophy becomes historical. The entire empirical course of events becomes material for philosophic reflection because it is in this existential course that the truth of being emerges. Correcting for the Hegelian distortions, even though it has taken much of the succeeding two centuries, does not entail a rejection of his fundamental project.

It was his colleague Schelling who first separated what is living from what is dead in Hegel. Although he never brought his own project to a satisfactory conclusion, Schelling directed single-minded attention to the point from which he departed from Hegel. It is an issue of fundamental importance that utterly eliminates the possibility of philosophy collapsing back into the deadness of a system, and the real point of departure for the history of contemporary philosophy. Schelling has quite rightly been hailed as the source both for the existential turn and for the postmodern emphasis on the dynamic. He is the one who insists that reality always escapes speculation. No matter how comprehensive the speculative grasp may be, it cannot include the reality from which it itself is derived. As soon as it makes an attempt to include that wherein it itself stands, it has merely rendered its own ground as no longer its ground, only the marker of where the ground had been. Speculation that attempts to include the living process in which it exists is left only with the dead remains. Living life always escapes the attempt to capture it; to the extent it is captured it is no longer living. Schelling understood that this had been the tragic flaw of Hegel's temptation to yield to the definitiveness of system. Existence always lies outside of that which it has created. Philosophy must therefore bow to this necessity and concede that it can be no more than the love of wisdom. Schelling did not embrace the full existential implications of this recognition, and thereby proved both an inspiration and disappointment to Kierkegaard, but he did demonstrate the inability of speculation to overleap the boundary that includes itself. The best that philosophy could do was to turn to life, to catch the disclosure of being in act, and to respect the narrative of myth, which is the mode of discourse concerning what is beyond all discourse.

The priority of existential knowledge is inescapable. Contrary to the conventional notion that we recognize ourselves in a mirror by seeing our reflection, it is doubtful that we would know who it is we see there unless we had a prereflective knowledge of the self. We cannot claim to have seen ourselves before, since it is precisely that claim to self-recognition that is in question. At best the image we contemplate in the mirror is only an image. It is never the self that does the contemplating, which remains radically beyond the boundary. This is what the infinite means. It can never be fully unfolded into its creations. Schelling saw this truth with a blinding clarity while Hegel periodically lost sight of it. Where Hegel allowed the possibility of self-consciousness reaching its culmination, Schelling insisted that the goal could never be attained. This is why Schelling could insist that history can never be reduced to the inner dynamics of consciousness. There is always the irreducible beyond of the process. The ironic consequence is that this preserves history, while the attempt to draw everything into history abolishes it. Now existence is not merely a phase in the production of the end, but an irreplaceable expression of what can never be fully expressed. History as the trace of the infinite renders all existence as a luminous sign. The possibility that human consciousness could capture that by which it is held is an utter impossibility. Only the movement of existential disclosure, responding to the invitation of being, reveals what is contained from the beginning. Schelling's insistence on the unsurpassability of the order in which human consciousness is embedded is the point at which the primacy of existential disclosure is established within modern philosophy.

Not all of the subsequent turn toward existence took its lead from Schelling. Much of the movement flowed directly from the reaction to the self-enclosure of the Hegelian system. Marx is the most famous among a very talented group of Young Hegelians who saw rather clearly that their master had comprehended everything except life itself. The scandal was that the great culmination of philosophy had not effected the slightest change in how men live. Philosophy had been seduced by the perfection of the system. Now the task was to make philosophy real again by engaging in the struggle to transform the conditions in which human beings found themselves. Rather than permit the theoretical reconciliation to conceal the extent of real social and economic conflict, theory must now be directed toward the unremitting dialectic of history itself. No more would philosophy allow itself to be used as a tool of oppression. Unfortunately, Marxist philosophy ended by legitimizing a far more extensive regime of oppression. The unmasking of ideology recurrently gives way to a more extreme ideology. When philosophy has embarked on an activist course, the relapse into systematization can prove deadly. So long as theory sought only a contemplative transfiguration of all things, the result was relatively harmless. Once the same drive was manifested among individuals bent on the real transfiguration of reality, we end with the totalitarian nightmare. The theoretical impulse to master being ends in the activist drive to remake the world. But this perversion does not minimize the initial realization that theory had failed to transform reality. The totalitarian debacle simply reveals that there is also no reason to expect revolutionary action to accomplish the same goal.

We are thrown back on the only route of transformation that remains. The individual can work on him- or herself and from there begin to effect some wider social change. This is the path of Marx's great unnoticed contemporary, Kierkegaard, who understood the problem so profoundly that he hoped his books would not become popular. If they did, then they would be swept up in a social movement and no longer address their real target, the solitary individual. In many respects Kierkegaard had understood the modern condition of philosophy most completely. It had to remain a philosophy of existence, neither forgetting itself in the realm of concepts nor imagining its superiority through systems. Yet despite his unique position and, perhaps, because of it, Kierkegaard is the least understood of modern philosophers. He is familiar through a few slogans about the absurd and the leap of faith, which, when one actually reads him, one fails to recognize. Even the ubiquitous three stages turn out not to function as such within his thought. What Kierkegaard feared in his cultivated obscurity has indeed happened to him. By becoming popular he has become misunderstood. The first wave of that popularity was his identification with the twentieth-century existentialists. Once such a movement has taken shape it is inevitable that its members, including its putative antecedents such as Kierkegaard, are all reworked to fit the mold. What they actually said becomes far less important. This has certainly been the fate of the pseudonymous Dane whose strategy of publishing under other names was intended to warn of the difficulty of understanding existential philosophy. Only now with the passage of time has he begun to be read more carefully and in his own right. The result has been a renewed appreciation of his status as a thinker that has placed him at the very center of the postmodern debate.

The failure to recognize the full measure of Kierkegaard's achievement curiously begins with Kierkegaard himself. His own focus on the existential, on the struggle of the individual to live the life of fidelity, tended to forget the implications of this new approach for philosophy. Socrates and Jesus both figure prominently in his writings, but the notion that he was setting both philosophy and Christianity on the course of renewing their foundations emerged only occasionally. Kierkegaard would no doubt have seen such a perspective as a temptation away from his existential task. To this extent, however, one might say that he did not fully understand his role. For it was not simply to become a better person, which could have been accomplished without all the voluminous writings. It was surely to chart a path of meaning within the modern world where the historical symbols of philosophy and Christianity had become opaque, and where modern men seemed capable of only constructing ever-more horrific schemes of instrumentalization. Kierkegaard can rightly be regarded as the first postmodern thinker because he is the first to take up the challenge of meaning in a context where all meaning has collapsed. He knows that all talk of finding a beginning is not only interminable but is merely a way of deferring a beginning. There is no beginning for discourse or action because we have already begun. We are in existence. Our task is to remain faithful to the truth that discloses itself within the process and resist the pull of untruth. Among the latter is the temptation to control the process in which we find ourselves, to make it instrumental to our own purposes rather than to submit to its exigencies. Communication about this condition is itself one of the variants of the temptation. By talking we avoid doing. How can we talk about living without sidestepping what we want to communicate? How do we communicate that which cannot be communicated, which can only be shown, but really only discovered? A profound understanding of language lies behind Kierkegaard's extensive ruminations on how one talks about Christianity within a society of Christians.

The attempt to seize existence on the run is also what animated the other great nineteenth-century loner, Friedrich Nietzsche. It is well known that Nietzsche exalts life over its conceptualization. He abandoned art in the Wagnerian sense because, although it brought us closer to heroic life, it too served only as another form of escape. If he was going to arrive at truth it would have to be by living it. For this reason, Zarathustra can never be any more than a bridge toward the goal that lies beyond all writing. The best that literature can capture is the radiance from life, and for this Nietzsche developed the aphoristic style. We might view him therefore, not as the theorist of nihilism by which he is conventionally identified, but as he claimed himself to have become, the first European to have gone beyond nihilism. The tortured quality of his thought arises as much from Nietzsche's own inability to understand the novelty of his project as from the failure to break through the boundary of the self. Nietzsche is left railing against truth in the objectivist sense while unable to recognize his own achievement of truth in the existential sense. It is because he cannot bring the tension between them to any resolution that he suffers the conflict so intensely and becomes, as a consequence, the paradigmatic figure of modern and postmodern philosophy. In retrospect we can see, as Heidegger observes, that Nietzsche had thought through a metaphysics beyond metaphysics. The "death of God" had never really meant the death of God. It only meant that a spatially imagined divinity was no longer credible, not that Nietzsche himself was no longer held by a mysterious fullness of life. Indeed, it is the contrast between the denunciation of truth and the living commitment to truth that attests the utterly existential character of his faith, a faith that would not even permit itself the luxury of acknowledging itself.

The same fear of betraying the existential quest marks the unremitting struggle of Heidegger to unfold the Nietzschean project. It is also unclear to what extent the obstacles are self-created, to what extent the very intensity of the battle each of them wages for fidelity to the luminosity of existence masks an unwillingness to follow the full logic of openness to which they have committed themselves. This inscrutability has made both of them notoriously difficult to interpret. But in another sense, such contested interpretations remain beside the point. If we have learned anything from either of them, it is that the value of a thinker is not defined by where he ends up. It is where his thought leads. This is for us the primary concern, but it can be expected that extending the direction in which they move will provide a unique vantage point for an overall assessment of what they accomplished. It may indeed turn out that it was the tenacity of their blind spots that accounts for the depth of the struggle in which they articulated the existential exigence of truth. A thinker with fewer hangups, who reached the goal of existential disclosure more easily, might have been less useful to us. In philosophy the results are best when they do not come readily. Those who present themselves to us with all of their glaring flaws not only compel themselves to wrestle with the blockages but, more importantly, impose on us the obligation of extending their thought into regions they were themselves not always prepared to go.

This must surely be our attitude toward the great flawed genius of twentieth-century philosophy. Like it or not, Heidegger's towering presence arises from his extended meditation on what philosophy must be when it has definitively adopted the original perspective of existence. Even in his earlier "existentialist" phase, Heidegger shied away from the label, knowing that it still preserved too much of the isolated subject for whom the whole of being could become an object. Heidegger continuously worked to eliminate any such suggestion of subjectivity from his thought. It was at the core of his famous turn from the existential phenomenology of *Being and Time* to the meditative opening toward Being as what made all reflection possible. It was the truth of Being rather than the intentionality of the subject that made human knowledge and existence possible. *Being and Time* could still suggest a self-contained subject who must anxiously project or decide the meaning of its existence without resort to any disclosure beyond the self. Later, Heidegger came to see that even the self-contemplating subject was never locked within itself. From the very beginning it stood within the opening of Being, which made all contemplation possible. In order for us to become conscious of anything, we must first be able to think about it as such, that is, as standing in the light of Being. Not only does everything that exists participate in being, without being Being, but it is that relationship that enables us to know what exists, as what is in being. Human being enjoys the special privilege not only of participating in being but of seeing that it does so. From this all of the special features of human existence follow. Animals may live in the world, exist in time, and end in death, but it is only for man that the world, time, and death exist. He alone confronts them as such because he alone beholds them in the light of Being.

But this does not mean that man contains or comprehends the light of Being. Heidegger mightily opposes the tendency to objectify Being, which he regards as the fatal misstep within the history of philosophy, a derailment that begins almost as soon as the difference between Being and beings is first encountered. The modern revolution is to return again to that first moment with a new self-consciousness of the imperative of resisting the assimilation of Being to beings. This "ontological difference" becomes the core of Heidegger's project. In this way he sought to make the modern shift from intentionality to luminosity definitive. Not only would philosophy not revert to an objectivist metaphysics, but the modern crisis of meaning would have reached a decisive turning point. The enthronement of instrumental rationality, as confirmed by the technological success of the contemporary world, would no longer prevail unchecked. Man's capacity to dominate reality would be seen as itself dependent on the prior openness toward Being that enables him to contemplate things as they are. The great problem, of furnishing the regime of instrumentalization with an end that would not itself be instrumentalized, had been solved. Being, in Heidegger's articulation, could never be absorbed into the stream of beings available for manipulation and control because it was itself what made such processes possible. Technological rationality is itself a mode of being, and it is the history of man's engagement with Being that is being realized within this modern manifestation. History is in this sense, not the history of man, but the history of Being in which man is the point at which the process becomes self-conscious. Hegel had made the mistake of claiming that Being itself had become self-conscious, but Heidegger understood that it is only the participation of beings in Being that reaches luminosity.

Being itself cannot become self-conscious because it cannot be in the mode of a being. This is what turns Heidegger against all forms of ontotheology that assimilate Being to God. But this, of course, does not mean that Heidegger was an atheist. He could more accurately be described, as he occasionally admitted, as a negative theologian. Out of faithfulness to God, we might say, he refuses to name him. If Being is that in the light of which everything else is seen, then Being itself cannot be illuminated. Being is what brings beings into unconcealment but remains itself in concealment, otherwise it would become a being. Heidegger resolutely struggles against the conventional understanding of revelation because he sought to understand how the transcendent could be known as transcendent once it had been mediated by the immanent. How can Being be revealed through a being? Being is what can never be revealed no matter how many beings come forward to disclose it. So how then do we know about Being at all? Our knowledge derives from the trace of Being that remains in beings, for they point beyond themselves. Only in man, however, does this directionality become knowledge. He alone not only points but is aware of it. It is for this reason that man plays a special role in relation to Being. He is the "shepherd" or "guardian" of Being because it is only in him that Being is disclosed and nowhere else in existence. All other beings provide a mute testament to Being, that by which they are disclosed, but only man can give voice to that awareness through language. This special relationship, however, is not made possible because man has the capacity for articulation, rather he has the capacity for speaking because of his relationship with Being. This is a point that Heidegger struggled mightily to make clear as he sought to complete the shift from a self-contained subject to a subject already constituted by its openness toward Being.

The question of Being cannot be separated from the question of man. In his exploration of the dynamics of revelation, Heidegger shows, the "revelation" of Being is possible only because man is already constituted by the revelation of Being from the beginning. Problems arise for Heidegger, we might say, because of the very relentlessness of his pursuit of revelation in the original sense. He cannot abide any of the stopping points along the way in what Judaism or Christianity call revelation. None of these satisfy the requirement that revelation must bend its efforts toward what cannot be revealed. The result is an intoxicating and disorienting pursuit of what cannot be reached. In the name of sustaining a tension that is unsustainable, Heidegger loses all points of reference within existence. His notorious political misjudgments are not the cause of this; they are its symptom. Nor do the blunders represent only an occasional lapse. They seem to form a pattern that his best critics have discerned as the betrayal of his own fundamental impulse. It seems as if the refusal of all intermediaries makes the tension toward a revelation of Being that cannot be revealed so unsupportable that it collapses into some intramundane manifestations as an all too welcome substitute. The danger of apocalyptic thinking is that it tends toward various forms of an immanent apocalypse. It is for this reason, Heidegger's critics have suggested, that all of his strictures against the metaphysics of presence have not been enough to prevent him from falling victim to the same tendency. The Being that lies perpetually beyond disclosure is increasingly burdened with the expectation of its disclosure. Once that pressure has mounted, the danger of opting for a substitute becomes almost irresistible.

The scandal of Heidegger's dalliance with Nazism has been the most notorious case. Apocalyptic thinking veers precipitously close to the pseudo-apocalypse. The fact that a Heidegger was repeatedly prepared to run the risk says something about the hold of such thinking on the modern imagination. In many ways the style of immanent apocalypse can be seen as the culmination of the modern drive for mastery. What, after all, could be more gratifying than to be the individual or the generation that extends its control over reality totally? Behind the urge for technical control lurks the dream of comprehensive domination. The impulse can be so overwhelming that it blocks out all other considerations, including the realization that the achievement of total control abolishes any further technological progress. A willingness to obliterate the very process from which science itself has derived is mirrored in the willingness to obliterate the planet in the name of the final transfiguration of all things. What is fascinating about Heidegger's case is not the banality of evil into which he was drawn, but the fact that he was susceptible to the lure of the false apocalypse despite the contrary implications of his own thought. Public attention has naturally been drawn to the spectacle of his astonishing political collaboration with the worst totalitarian regime of the century, as if one more tale of human wickedness would somehow insulate us from the enormity of the events. The challenge by contrast is to understand how a man like Heidegger could yield, indeed cheer, the advent of evil despite his own ability to unmask it. It is surely not our place to sit in judgment on Heidegger since we are not privy to his soul. We do, however, have access to his thought where the task is more straightforward. It is to understand how even a philosophic mind that strains against the closure of existence can nevertheless succumb to precisely the same temptation. How was it possible for Heidegger to perceive the *parousia* of Being in the beings of the Third Reich?

The journalistic side of philosophy has been preoccupied periodically with Heidegger's failure as a man. But philosophy itself has always needed to pursue the more indispensable question of the failure of his philosophy, for there it is *our* humanity that is at stake. If Heidegger represents the limit of philosophy, we have to ask whether it is sufficient for the task it has set itself. Is the case of Heidegger merely the failure of the man or is philosophy itself implicated? This is the question with which philosophy has wrestled increasingly as it has come to recognize the stature of his achievement. It would hardly be an exaggeration to say that he has carried the modern philosophic revolution the furthest. The shift from subjectivity dominating a world of objects to the luminosity of existence that never succeeds in grounding itself has been brought to its fullest realization in his thought. Many others have made the leap intuitively, but Heidegger, perhaps by dint of the obstinacy of his struggle with objectification, has made the transition to the perspective of participation inescapably articulate. This is why he is the defining philosophic mind of the century. Without displaying an extensive range of philosophic interests, Heidegger has nevertheless compelled us to recognize the necessity of moving from the contemplation of reality to the reality of contemplation. Prior to all knowledge there is the existence that therefore can never be fully known but can become luminous. How then was it possible for Heidegger to fall back into the claim of the primacy of knowledge? If we take seriously the direction on which he had set philosophy, then we must take equally seriously the necessity of preserving philosophy from the pitfalls into which philosophers too may fall.

Instead of simply dismissing Heidegger as a "historicist" or a "decisionist," the most acute readers have acknowledged the necessity of going beyond him by going through him. The issue becomes that of carrying Heidegger's project beyond himself by mounting a critique from within. In this way the transformation of philosophy that had been underway is carried forward by arguing that Heidegger had not been Heideggerian enough. This is why the leading postmodern thinkers are both under the shadow of Heidegger and his most vigorous critics. They take him to task for capitulating, despite his protestations, to an immanent apocalypse. His talk of the concealment of Being that makes all unconcealment or truth possible still suggests the *parousia* of Being. In part this is an inevitable consequence of the language he employs, which is still very much tied to a metaphysics of presence, as if an object were present before the subject. For all of his efforts to resist subjectivity, Heidegger still thinks of philosophy in a contemplative mode, which privileges the perspective of the contemplator, who is thus outside of Being. The consequence was not only the tilt toward the intramundane apocalypse of National Socialism, but the more profound closure toward existence once the tension toward Being had been abolished. When the eschaton is drawn into time, there is no more possibility. Existence is closed by its completion. This totalizing tendency of even Heidegger is perceptively discerned by Levinas and Derrida, both of whom in their respective ways insist on a nonattainable eschaton as the only adequate horizon for humanity. What an "apocalypse without apocalypse" means in its specifics may not always be clear from their formulations, but it does mark a definitive turn away from any possibility of revelation.

The apophatic quality of this orientation has often been viewed as merely inscrutable rhetoric. Such an accusation, however, misses the crucial advance that a thinker like Levinas introduces into the theoretical complex delineated by Heidegger. Levinas represents a shift toward a more decisively existential perspective. Where Heidegger had used the existential emphasis as a starting point for a philosophic meditation that ultimately remained contemplative, Levinas insists that the extraction of a contemplative fruit constitutes a betrayal of the existential impulse. His famous formulation that he is prioritizing ethics over ontology captures the essence of the move. Levinas leaves the philosopher no room for relaxation. There is never a moment of escape in which he would be free to calculate or contemplate because there is never a point at which the debt of moral obligation has been satisfied. Wherever we construct a compound of privacy, the face of the other is already there before us. Responsibility toward the other is the condition of our existence that can be neither abandoned nor abolished. Philosophy becomes therefore not a disclosure of existence but existence is itself the disclosure of philosophy. There is no independent mode of philosophy apart from the imperative of living out the imperatives of our moral life. Levinas thus brings the turn toward existence to its completion by showing that a merely theoretic philosophy has become impossible. It is no accident that the contemplative mode has derailed into the totalizing because it has turned its back on the primordial structure that is there before all possibility of structure. We never in this sense find what we are looking for in philosophy, according to Levinas, but are always on the way toward it. Even the way cannot be hypostasized because then it would cease to be the way and have become a rest stop.

To accuse Heidegger of such reification may be a bit disingenuous since he is the one who most emphasizes the dynamic character of philosophy, but the critique does call attention to the difficulty of maintaining the purity of the event. If even Heidegger could end by tilting toward an external perspective on it, then the danger of dominating the other is very real. Levinas finds a crucial safeguard against this tendency by going behind domination itself. The possibility of domination arises from its impossibility. We can dominate the other only because we are already in a relation of responsibility toward him; we can turn our backs on the person who calls us by turning away from the face. What we cannot do is eliminate the relation that makes domination possible. Without the priority of the face of the other, placing us under obligation before all freedom, there would not be the possibility of rejection. Levinas has thought through the primordial character of transcendence in a way that is more originary than Heidegger's explorations.

Where Heidegger had sought the openness toward Being by going through beings, Levinas focused on the being of the other as the movement beyond Being. Now it may be that the difference between them is not large, and it may turn out that Levinas's "otherwise than Being" overlaps with Heidegger's "Being beyond beings," but the dynamic of responsibility toward the other more adequately marks the existential character of the disclosure. Levinas eliminates the possibility that we might withdraw to a viewpoint outside of Being by identifying the relationship as one of responsibility. We are already called to act on behalf of the other before we can even think of who we are. There is no self that is prior to the relation to the other.

It is the unsurpassability of this relationship that makes it impossible for domination to succeed. We can never get back to the point at which the self exists in splendid isolation, as if there could be a moment at which the demand of the other ceased to be. Is it ever possible to maintain we have given enough? Surely "enough" is measured by the need of the other rather than our inclination or capacity for sacrifice. Before and beyond any state from which domination could be imposed there is the face of the other. We are never free to dominate. That realization, however, is not reached from within some independent perspective, itself suggesting a superior starting point. Our involvement is rather disclosed within the movement in which we are already engaged. Existence, in which we are already related through the face of the other, will not leave us alone. The vantage point of theory on which Western metaphysics has been based for more than two millennia is permanently displaced. No higher viewpoint is available than the truth of ethics, which, as Aristotle emphasized, takes priority over all general propositions. This is also the culmination of Heidegger's resistance to all forms of the metaphysics of presence. Being as Levinas conceives it is nothing at all like a presence but is rather what draws us into presence. We do not behold a reality before us but are ourselves brought into a fuller reality than we are. Luminosity does not precede our existence but is its unfolding direction.

The effort to reverse a pattern of thought that assimilates Being to beings or that remains tied to a world of objects is in large measure a struggle against language. Metaphor is the trap that language sets for us. Perhaps no one has devoted more attention to the constrictions of language than Jacques Derrida. In many respects his preoccupation with the limits of semiology can be viewed as a continuation of the critique of a metaphysics of presence on which the conventional conception of language is based. Naming is the preeminent model from which this misdirection originates, for nothing seems more obvious than that denomination is a way of making present that which is not. It easily misleads us into thinking that the mere practice of naming conjures the reality to which it refers, rather than merely represents what can no longer present itself. The critique of language, especially of the privilege that the spoken word always seems to exercise over the written one, is a continuation of the assault on the objectification of Being. Derrida takes over the indications of Heidegger and Levinas, while giving their existential shift an essentially linguistic application. This is no mere sidetrack but an essential completion of the project of removing the centrality of the all-seeing subject. Without the linguistic instruments of its domination of reality the subject is left forlorn, longing for a presence that it can no longer make real because the very means of its control have betrayed it. Derrida shows that language, far from delivering on its promise of making present what is absent, is itself a response to the problem of absence. Nouns cannot provide the security we seek, for we are adrift in a sea of verbs and adverbs that move us along. The final chapter for the dislocated subject is surely provided by Derrida's analysis of the incapacity of language to refer to what we thought it refers.

In place of reference he emphasizes *différance*, a neologism that combines the senses of difference and deferral. That to which language refers is both different from it and deferred by it at the same time. This failure of intentionality to achieve its object is not, however, a sheer negative, for it also opens up the space for elaboration. Without the gap between signifier and signified there would, according to Derrida, hardly be room for an unfolding of the language relationship within reality. If the project of definition had succeeded, then discussion would cease. Absolute knowledge in the Hegelian sense has the perverse consequence of terminating the search for knowledge, and without the search for knowledge we no longer actually know. Derrida thus emphasizes the penultimate character of language as the indispensable openness that makes the search for knowledge possible. Of course, many readers have concluded that he renders all knowledge ultimately inconclusive. His own style of reflection often suggests an interminable digressiveness that has come to typify "postmodern" thought, but this is surely a misimpression. It would be more accurate to say that Derrida's main concern has been with preserving the space for signification even at the cost of suggesting its provisional character. The difficulty, as many commentators have noted, is that he must use language in order to discuss the limits of language. How can he refer to an absence in the language of presence? His project would have been better served if he distinguished more clearly between the ordinary context of language that refers to the world of objects and the existential context in which that ordinary use occurs. The difficulty is at this point a long-standing one in the history of modern philosophy and is at the heart of the reorientation on which it has been engaged. Derrida's work is one more aspect of the multifaceted shift from intentionality to luminosity.

The central issue may be identified as the absence that makes all movement toward presence possible but which is itself neither an absence nor a presence. In his later work Derrida has utilized the language of religion as the most suitable mode of discourse. He had always alluded to the theological parallels with deconstruction, declaring that it was a form of negative theology, but now he has adopted the full-blown language of revelation. Messianic, apocalyptic, and eschatological vocabularies figure prominently in his thought to such an extent that he might be regarded as a religious thinker. This is a strange turn for a thinker who acknowledges that he is not quite a believer, but certainly not a disbeliever. His is a religion without God, an apocalypse without apocalypse, that is, more than a substitutional piety. It is an attitude that arises when God is no longer believable as a projection of spatio-temporal imagination, yet remains indispensable as the assurance of possibility by virtue of its impossibility. Without the unreachable horizon of transcendence, the movement of *différance* could not even begin, but if the divine were reached, the movement could no longer continue. Derrida himself remains puzzled by the status of his faith, and we see in this bewilderment the incompletely understood character of the existential turn in philosophy. Even a thinker of his theoretical acuity cannot adequately locate his project so long as he remains tied to the understanding of presence as objective. His railing against objective signification does not save him from captivation by the same model.

Derrida has difficulty conceiving of a pleromatic mode of presence, that is, of a presence that is so complete that it draws all else into presence and cannot therefore be one of the things that become present. We cannot know about it as an object out there. Rather, we are already constituted by its pull before we even begin to search for it. We are the ones who are differed and deferred until we have begun to attune our existence toward its luminosity. It is not absent, we are. This is the meditative unfolding articulated by the first existentialist, St. Augustine. His development of the language of interiority was in response to the discovery that he had found himself only when he found himself in God. The process did not consist of the subject turning his light inward, though it did provide the language of introspection, but of realizing that the interiority in which he was contained was not his own: I would not have found myself if you had not found me first. The absence to which Derrida and Heidegger refer is not an absence as such but our inability to ever catch up with that which is so fully present we can never outrun it. This better explains how that which is absent can exert such a powerful pull toward presence, for if it were a sheer absence, it could never exercise an endless fascination. Only that which is somehow more present than the things that are present can do this, as Heidegger's lifelong occupation with the mystery of Being attests. So although the transcendent cannot be present in the mode of a thing, or else reality would shrink into a black hole without movement or light, it cannot be so transcendent that it fails to draw all things toward itself. The only way to conceive of God is, not as lying outside of us, but as that outside of which we lie. God is not the problem, we are.

The theoretical dead end into which deconstruction seems to lead modern philosophy arises from the search for a theoretical resolution. Once we realize that practice resolves what in theory remains impenetrable, the impasse is removed. This does not mean that practice has become an instrument for a theoretical goal, but rather the reverse, that in abandoning the insistence on achieving a theoretical solution, we have opened the way for the luminosity of life itself. A profound revision of the prevailing primacy of theory is contained in such a move. We seem to be turning our backs on the contemplative life as it was exalted by the classics, in which *theoria* is alone pursued for its own sake, but the shift can also be regarded as a more profound appropriation of philosophy. In contrast to the conventional conception of philosophy, as a result, we begin to see that there is no philosophy apart from the appropriation of it. This is the direction of the modern existential revolution, to catch philosophy in living life, only now with the realization that this brings us back to the beginning. It is not, as Derrida suggests, that we expect to arrive at a beginning before philosophy, only that we recognize that philosophy has no beginning before itself. The theoretical enterprise that extends its reach to include the birth of philosophy itself is already a misstep. Philosophy is in act, not in theory. Plato and Aristotle both struggle in different ways to maintain the truth of action rather than the discursive movement away from doing. The life of virtue lies in activity rather than in discussion, which thus makes philosophy a mode of discussion that must constantly move beyond itself. Paradox is the structure of philosophy, not a modern discovery about it. The derailment into the supplementarity of theorizing is not an accidental development within the history of philosophy, but the central danger against which the discourse must perpetually struggle if it is not to lose the existential direction it seeks to articulate.

The modern revolution in philosophy does not so much introduce something new as bring us back, in the manner of revolutions, to the point from which it began. Return is in this sense never simply a return to the beginning. It is a new beginning, a re-appropriation, made all the more necessary by the deficiencies of the first beginning. A re-initiation of philosophy is a genuinely philosophical act. Derrida's famous remark, "nothing outside the text," leaves itself open to a number of possible interpretations. Among the most compelling is the existential one that insists there is no point of reference that would relieve us of responsibility or permit us to dominate the meaning it provides. We cannot abandon our existence to a totality that would enclose it, not without ceasing to exist entirely. It is not that we are, in the cruder formulation of Sartre, "condemned to be free," but that we are condemned to exist in openness because that is the mode of human existence. Not only is there nothing outside the text, we are not even outside of it. The text is our existence. We can only get outside of it by existing, that is, by extending the text of our lives. A resting point, a security nook, could only be a falling away from the task. Sleep interrupts our consciousness, but we can hardly regard it as anything more than a necessary and inevitable break in the endeavor of freely and humanly becoming who we are. There is no point before the beginning that would make the beginning happen and relieve us of the burden of beginning ourselves, just as there is no end point that will allow us to rest in the easy release from all effort by having become all that is possible. Human existence is a mystery or, rather, since it is not a thing, human existence is caught within a mystery that can neither be fathomed nor exhausted. For this reason there is nothing outside the text, since the text encompasses the unreachable whole. If it did not, then we would be constantly tempted, as indeed we are, to settle down in the satisfaction of achieving our goal. All that saves us from spiritual suicide is the impossibility of finding a definitive point of reference outside the text.

We are the text, as Kierkegaard insisted, and the effort to stand outside of it is the refusal of existence. He may not have explicated the full extent of the revolution in philosophy that this recognition implied, but he is probably the one who carried it out most completely in his own life. It may be that it was Kierkegaard's willingness to think through the issues within Christian categories that saved him from the tentativeness that characterizes most of his successors, just as it is the same openly "religious" character of his thought that remains the principal obstacle to the appreciation of his philosophic achievement. But if Derrida, Levinas, and Heidegger are correct in seeing philosophy as implicated in the drama of revelation, then Kierkegaard may be one of the most underappreciated contributors to the discussion. For Kierkegaard it was no scandal that revelation had occurred. This was what enabled him to surmount the obstacle that loomed so large for many others. A historical revelation seemed so absurd because it could not be assimilated within any conceptual scheme. Kierkegaard even embraced the category of the absurd to talk about revelation, but he thereby also left himself open to the long-standing misimpression that he regarded revelation as irrational. What he really meant was that revelation escaped the categories of human reason. It definitively demoted reason from its central theoretical role and made reason itself dependent on the opening toward what is beyond it. By acknowledging revelation, reason was saved from itself. In place of the illusion of a control that could be imaginatively projected over the whole of reality, reason now had regained the rationality of its ever-incomplete capacity to comprehend reality. The key is the existential submission of reason itself. Only by abandoning the impulse to dominate could reason avoid its own distortions and obtain the only access to reality available to it.

By accepting the participatory requirement of knowledge, Kierkegaard overcame the obstacles that still stood in the way so long as thinkers held onto the model of theoretic intentionality. In the process he introduced a far-reaching revision in the language of philosophy that has still not been absorbed. It has proved more convenient to classify him as an "irrationalist," a "decisionist," or an "existentialist" rather than grapple with the profound changes he introduced. We have still not understood his insistence that we do not really live in time but that, for the most important relationships, our context is already eternity. Whereas we conventionally imagine eternity as something other than time, Kierkegaard is already showing us that time is itself a derivative of eternity. A human being is not really a creature of time and its effects. In every important respect we are transacting an eternal reality, of which the temporal passage is just a series of attenuations. This is why Kierkegaard can assert that there is no beginning before the beginning of decision itself, which often makes him sound like an advocate of arbitrary leaps. In reality what he is saying is that the leap has already taken place. The commitment to marriage, which seems so improbable from the perspective of creatures who are the contingent playthings of temporality, makes perfect sense when we see that the decision was never actually made in time. How can you make a commitment at a particular point in time to remain steadfast to what also dissolves with time? The task seems nonsensical and futile, as we daily acknowledge in facilitating "no-fault" divorce. Yet we also insist on retaining the fig leaf of marriage as a lifelong commitment. The reason, Kierkegaard explains, is that we know that nothing that is done in time can be serious. It is only if we invest the resolution with eternity that it can encompass all that we are. We know that we live, in every dimension that matters, in eternity rather than in time. It is eternity that makes every present possible.

Contingency is not itself contingent. Once we realize that what characterizes the flow of things does not necessarily, and cannot necessarily, be extended to the whole itself, we are no longer so lost in the cosmos. Kierkegaard, who was a great student of irony, would surely have delighted in the irony of the limits of irony. There has always been an element of this recognition in the objection that skepticism depends on not extending to itself, but there is more to it than mere cleverness. A philosophical revolution of the kind that has been two millennia in the making does not result from a brilliant turn of logic. A far deeper meditation is involved in which we lay hold of the utterly noncontingent reality of our lives. When we acknowledge that the value of a human being outweighs all the progress of history, we are not simply voicing an aspiration. We are giving expression to a reality that makes possible the whole of history in the inexhaustibility of each human being. Human beings have history because they are not historical. They are never captured by the finitude of history because they exist in relation to the eternal. However much they may forget their participation in the eternal, falling into the inauthentic amnesia of time, they cannot sever the remembrance of the pull that makes this awareness possible. Kierkegaard was the one who definitively eliminated the imaginary space and time that attached to the discussion of souls and their afterlife. He made it clear that the language of Christian spirituality had its source in the existential now. We could conceive of an afterlife only because we already live in relation to eternity. Human life, every human life, is crucial because it is the arena in which good and evil are irrevocably chosen. Reading Kierkegaard, we experience a shudder of the numinous, which, though it may have been reinforced by his personal sensitivities, finds a resonance in us because it is an inescapable dimension of every human existence. We know that what we do matters more than life.

What was an antinomy for Kant had become transparent for Kierkegaard. Kant struggled mightily with the impenetrability of the opposition between human freedom and spatio-temporal causality. If human action was subject to the causal exigencies of everything within this world, then it could not be free, but the essence of human action is autonomous self-determination, which can never be subject to extraneous factors. He resolved it by maintaining that human freedom does not occur in space and time, but has its locus in eternity. The decision to act in a certain way could not be subject to causal necessities because it had already occurred before or outside of that realm. Kant's problem, as most of his readers recognized, was that he had made the spatio-temporal realm so real that anything beyond it seemed peculiarly attenuated. Kierkegaard had reversed this emphasis by contemplating the relativity of the space–time continuum. By beginning from the perspective of eternity, he had been able to see the conditionality of time. Without the overarching-never-moving context of eternity there would not even be time. Heidegger would later make a great deal of temporality, as what can be grasped as such only from the perspective of nontemporality, but Kierkegaard had exemplified this understanding through his existence. In this sense Kierkegaard had leapt over the temptation, still present in Heidegger, to turn this conditionality of time into a new mode of presence. Without really explaining that this would be to make eternity another mode of time, Kierkegaard ignored the suggestion by virtue of his existential struggle to live out the meaning of eternity. Once we take seriously the revolutionary insight that there is no way of stepping outside of ourselves to view the whole in which we are, then we recognize that the only perspective available is through our participation in existence. Kierkegaard resolutely insists that that participation requires our all.

There can be no holding back, as if we might yet be able to secure a corner of detachment from which our contemplative domination could expand. We must not yield to the final temptation of doing the right thing for the wrong reason. Ever since Hegel, the philosophic revolution has wavered around the possibility of turning the existential movement into a mode of absolute knowledge. It is no accident that Kierkegaard took Hegel as the great other of his struggle, and consequently managed to extricate himself from the fascination more successfully than most who have tried. He acknowledged his debt to Hegel by not becoming a Hegelian. Absolute knowledge must remain absolute, even while it provides the possibility of all other knowledge. What makes possible the whole movement of existence cannot become an object of attention without ceasing to be the source of all. This is the key challenge within the modern philosophic shift away from the mode of intentionality. Fidelity to the basic insight that the process cannot be apprehended from within it, except through the movement itself, requires a resolute avoidance of the attempt to surreptitiously permit its objectification. Hegel had seen that what provides the possibility must be beyond the possible, but he persisted in dreaming that he nevertheless could comprehend it. It was because Kierkegaard's resolve was more wholehearted, informed less by the contemplative quest than by the need for existence, that he could prove the more exemplary figure of the modern philosophic revolution. By being less of a philosopher he became more of one. The existential shift means that philosophy itself must become something of an aftereffect. Kierkegaard shows that it is only by becoming a man that one can become a philosopher.

Yet it is possible that he also shows that the demand is too great. It may well be that the modern shift of primacy toward existence will therefore mean that the revolution will always remain incomplete. That would not be a surprising outcome, especially given that philosophy itself is peculiarly implicated in the eternal. We should perhaps be more cautious about attributing so temporal a metaphor to its movements and, as a consequence, entertain some second thoughts concerning such a study. The burden of demonstrating that there has been a revolution accomplished by modern philosophy is not the essential point. It is rather that philosophy in the modern era has set itself the task of revolutionizing itself. By shifting the burden to philosophy, the task of scholarship is lightened. But this is in no way to ensure the project against failure. Scholarship about philosophy cannot ultimately shrink from the challenge of philosophy, and philosophy, as Kierkegaard and his collaborators have taught us, cannot absolve us of the obligation of being human. The revolution in philosophy is truly revolutionary, touching all aspects of the discipline. Even the account of the change cannot ignore the logic of what it contains. Once we have eliminated the possibility of contemplation furnishing the meaning in which we live, we undertake the task of living first in the meaning from which contemplation can follow. By acknowledging the primacy of existence we have accepted the impossibility of reflection apprehending it in advance. Philosophy can now only be a matter of catching reality on the wing. Participation means there is nothing living beforehand and nothing living afterward. We may be released from the millennial illusion that we could contemplate the whole from the perspective of God. But we now must move toward God as the only mode in which the whole is at all apprehensible. The security of meaning is traded for a meaning that seeks security. We may be animated by the bonds of faith and trust that support us but we cannot reach any surety without giving ourselves to them. To the extent that the nature of philosophy has now coincided with the nature of human existence we may be sure only of one thing: the goal of each cannot be reached in time. This is what makes them both impossible and possible.

CHAPTER NINE

The Indispensability of Modern Philosophy

Philosophy remains an indispensable perspective because it provides access to what cannot be accessed in any other way. Every discipline and practice possesses its specific subject matter. We are familiar with the distribution of fields encompassed by the contemporary university. Our knowledge-driven economy demands ever-more refined modes of specialization that underpin its astonishing advances. What we lack is the viewpoint from which the proliferation of viewpoints can be apprehended. We seem to know more and more about everything in the universe except what it means to be capable of such knowledge. Despite becoming ever-more confident masters of our fate, we cannot quite shake the sense that something has eluded us. No matter how far and how fast we travel, we seem to be going nowhere. We are, in Walker Percy's phrase, "lost in the cosmos." The world around us is thoroughly dissected, yet we remain an insuperable mystery. Technique, we discover, provides no guidance to the technicians. Our mastery serves only to reveal the extent to which we ourselves are unmastered. Without purpose the power we have acquired has rendered us powerless. That is the crisis that has formed modern philosophy and at the same time called forth its most impressive achievement.

That may strike us as an unfamiliar assertion. We are accustomed to noting the shortcomings of philosophical positions and often view the history of philosophy as a succession of mutual repudiations. Yet that cannot be the whole story. Critique implies engagement on a common project, employment of a common language, and convergence on a common goal. Philosophy is more than philosophers. It is the great collaborative enterprise on which they expend themselves. That is why even the most devastating analysis remains at its core a contribution to the field. The failure of philosophers is not a failure of philosophy, which advances over the wreckage they leave behind. It is for this reason that we must be prepared to read each contribution in the light of what it could potentially be. The defects are incidental. It is the horizon toward which they strain, even without attaining it, that is their real significance. Otherwise the history of philosophy is a mere spectator sport where collisions and pileups serve only to confirm the superiority of those who do not participate. For the contestants, the mistakes of one's fellows are an indispensable source of instruction. Such was undoubtedly the attitude of Aristotle, Aquinas, or Hegel, for whom thinkers' shortcomings were merely an invitation to remediate them, and each undertook the enterprise with the awareness that he too would surely fall short. What could not be abandoned is the philosophical adventure itself. If we want to rationally apprehend the horizon within which we exist, no alternative is available. This is why even in an age when empirical science has acquired preeminence, philosophy still manages to assert itself. It knows that the reign of quantity is not itself a quantitative proposition, for it too has its feet planted in the ground of philosophical reflection. Philosophy cannot be superseded without invoking it.

In the words of Heidegger: when the danger looms, the saving power draws even closer. It is perhaps not so inaccurate to characterize him as just such a saving figure within philosophical discourse. Admittedly, Heidegger was a flawed messiah, yet one whose sustained meditation on being justifies his ranking among the greats of the history of thought. It is no accident that he occupies that position within our world, or that science, theology, art, and politics look to him for an account of themselves. Philosophy in the hands of its most penetrating practitioners is the perspective that tells us what perspectives are possible. When it is carried on as an indefatigable inquiry into what is, the state of affairs in which we find ourselves, then it reveals what can arise in no other mode. All other investigations uncover what is within being, only philosophy prevails as a reflection on being as such. Heidegger was the one, among contemporary thinkers, who saw this most clearly. This was why he became a thinker with only one theme, albeit a theme that remains indispensable to all others. Philosophy, Heidegger showed, deals with what no other discipline can address: the possibility of addressing as such. It is a meditation on what can scarcely be apprehended because all modes of apprehension remain within it. This is the line of continuity from the Greeks up to the present. Despite the admixture with various contents, whether natural or divine, philosophy has nevertheless been able to preserve the axis on which its distinctive turn occurs. In essence, philosophy is a glimpse of what cannot be glimpsed because we are always within it. That is the horizon of being. This is why it remains indispensable to clarifying our orientation. Without philosophy the sciences and intellectual disciplines are blind. They can know their respective objects but they cannot know themselves. They cannot know how they stand as such, that is, how they stand within being.

Even the question of being itself, as within being, cannot plumb the condition of its own possibility. Yet it is the only question that preserves the openness to its mystery. All other paths take the mystery of their own possibility for granted. They step over themselves. This is why philosophy remains the irreplaceable guide to who we are and to the age within which we find ourselves. When we inquire about the character of modernity as a means of locating the framework of our life together, we do not turn to the dramatically visible manifestations. The astonishing reach of instrumental rationality, the global expansion of markets, or the relentless march of technological prowess cannot exhaust the essence of who we are. For that we must reach deeper to what the creative and destructive powers portend. What is the meaning of our universal domination of the world? Only a philosophical term can capture what it is about, and such was pronounced by the philosopher who was present at the dawn of the crisis. Friedrich Nietzsche did not invent the term "nihilism," but he did seize upon its emblematic significance. Ours, he declared, is the first thoroughly nihilistic age in which all possible access to meaning has been blocked. Nothing is true and everything is permitted, as Ivan Karamazov brusquely declared. Once it is thus announced, we sense the misgiving that has accompanied modernity from its inception, now suddenly confirmed. The great quest for foundations launched in the Renaissance and the Reformation with such heady expectations now lies before us in ruins. We had set out without a strong enough faith in our destiny. It had all had been mere bravado to disguise the nagging anxiety that the foundations were no longer available. But then the gloomiest of all prospects begins to strike. Perhaps it is that the lost foundations had never been what we thought they were. Even the Greek and Christian edifices had been infected by the doubt that gnaws away at the possibility of any of the claims to truth they so valiantly asserted. Could it have been a gigantic sham? This was the thought that assailed the most intrepid explorer. Nietzsche did not shrink from the implication that nihilism had not only become the truth of our world but had always been so. The crisis that long rippled through the modern centuries now bursts into the open because it has been seized upon in its philosophical essence. We do not stand in relation to being, because there is neither being nor standing as such.

That realization is not the exclusive province of philosophy. In many respects it is a pervasive mood of a civilization that must ceaselessly work, and never so ceaselessly as when it is at leisure, to avoid confronting its inability to confront anything. All our vaunted freedom contains only one injunction. We are not free to be idle. For it is only in that condition that awareness of our condition is likely to assail us. Philosophy may bring into focus what is inchoate in contemporary society, but it is by no means the only mode of resistance to the cage of instrumental rationality. Art in all of its proliferations also arises as a counterthrust to the drive for efficiency. By its essence art aims at the nonutility of what is pursued for its own sake. That means that art evokes the broader rationality beyond the merely calculable. It releases us into a realm of freedom because it emerges from the free interplay between mind and material. The beautiful is beyond what need requires, which is why it is needed all the more. In a similar way faith, or religion (as it is less aptly termed), also draws us into the supererogatory, that which goes beyond all we are required to do. Neither recompense nor return can be invoked when it is a matter of exceeding all that merit might claim. Giving without counting the cost is the path that overturns calculation by rendering it incalculable. The gift that is outside of any economy is the definitive overturning of the limits that contract our existence. Through the encounter with transcendence we are thus launched on the trajectory of transcendence.

It cannot be said that art and faith are in any way lacking in the struggle against the reductionist mentality that would shrink human life within the boundaries of the causal and the measureable. In many respects they possess formidable powers of penetrating all the barriers posed against them. Art is the universal language of the spirit and faith locates itself within the innermost life of the soul. Neither can be suppressed, for their suppression deepens their endurance. Yet they lack that final degree of self-awareness that is so all-important to their constancy. Art and faith cannot finally say what they are. That alone is the task of philosophy, which must perceive them as equivalents of itself. They too stand within being and must know that orientation as the source of their truth.

Truth is the common ground, but only philosophy can effectively mount its defense, because it stands explicitly within the horizon of truth. It remains to philosophy to determine if we live within an age of nihilism, to decide if nihilism is to be our fate. It is no accident, for example, that Benedict XVI in his encyclicals turned repeatedly to his Frankfurt colleagues, Horkheimer and Adorno, to take the measure of contemporary atheism. They were the ones who not only had lost faith but proclaimed its impossibility. The meaning of faith must be found by going through and beyond that renunciation of its possibility, but the task remains within the charge of philosophy. Theology may be grounded in faith, but it cannot say what faith is. If theology contemplates the nature of faith within scripture, it does so by way of a philosophic reflection on the scriptural text. Benedict performs such a philosophical exegesis on the most famous passage of Hebrews 11:1: "Faith is the substance of things hoped for, and the conviction of things unseen." Even the scriptural text itself cannot avoid the philosophical term *ousia* (substance) to name what it intends. The larger issue, however, is whether theology now must carry on the philosophical enlargement without the assistance of its philosophical partner. There is more than a hint of this in the culminating encyclical of John Paul II, *Fides et ratio*. Reason, the philosophical path, has led to a dead end attributable to its closure against transcendence. Yet *Fides et ratio* also emphasizes that theology cannot mount its own rescue operation without drawing upon the resources of philosophy too. For better or worse, even revelation depends on philosophy for its self-understanding in the most comprehensive sense.

We remain with Nietzsche and his question of the age of nihilism. Any advance beyond him requires an advance with him, for, as he recognized, by becoming the first nihilist of Europe he had also become the first to go beyond nihilism. The question of nihilism cannot, as Heidegger said, remain nihilistic. To raise it is already to step outside of it. Diagnosis is inseparable from therapy. Nietzsche understood this in his admission that he too worshipped at the same altar of truth as Plato had. Metaphysics that had so publicly been dismissed now seemed to return almost unnoticed. It may be that Nietzsche was alone in realizing that the elimination of metaphysics could not occur without invoking metaphysics. Our own forgetfulness consists in the wholesale elevation of empirical science that cannot itself be empirically established. It remains a matter of faith for us, that is, of that which is beyond knowledge. The problem for Nietzsche is that he could not quite perceive the status of his own misgiving. He simply knew that nihilism is "the uncanniest of guests," because it brought about its own overturning. The identification of nihilism could not rest on nihilism but must somehow resume the standing in relation to being. What had not yet come into focus, and may even today have escaped realization, is that truth remains the limit of thinking. We cannot question the validity of truth unless we do so truthfully. Similarly we cannot interrogate the value of goodness unless we have already made goodness our criterion. The transcendentals cannot become a topic of reflection for they are its horizon. But how then do we know them? This is the great question that has agitated Western philosophy ever since Plato suggested that they might be Forms enduring beyond all particularities. In the process he injected the fruitless visualization of a reality beyond reality that has most often been identified with the vexed term "metaphysics." It is from this misstep that Kant and his successors, including Nietzsche, have sought to rescue us. Their achievement is nothing less than a correction of the misconception that the classical world had unwittingly sowed within it.

The continuity with the Greek and Christian understanding is in other words far greater than the discontinuity so noisily touted. Not only does this represent the formal necessity that difference presupposes an underlying identity, but it arises from the substantive contribution that modern philosophy makes to the classical articulation of the unseen measure within which we are held. The intangible horizon of transcendence continually wavered between its skeptical dissolution and its overly concrete identification. Too little or too much present, classical metaphysics always ran the risk of irrelevance. Its final test emerged in the modern period when the death of metaphysics is pronounced. Then at last we arrive at a trial of the claim of metaphysics to denote a reality more real than all reality. What is not prevails more assuredly than all that is. But how can this be? Metaphysics surpasses its own demise only by virtue of its deathlessness. What is not cannot die. This has been the paradoxical outcome of the modern philosophical revolution that, for all of its readiness to abandon the horizon of transcendence, demonstrates even more emphatically the impossibility of its renunciation. We have already remarked on the naïveté of those who would dismiss philosophy without recognizing their own commitment to it. For the breakthrough to be completed they have only to recognize that their disavowal serves to reinforce the contrary. What cannot be disavowed is avowed. Metaphysics cannot die because it has never assimilated to the mode of what merely exists. As the condition of the possibility of existence, of the true, the good, the beautiful, it is beyond their vicissitudes. Even when Heidegger complains bitterly about the reign of technology in which the coordination of means and ends has supplanted philosophy, his own words challenge and overturn the assertion they make. We cannot be trapped in an iron cage once we have begun to perceive it. Unlike actual cages, the putative imprisonment that Weber identified is primarily in the realm of thought. Thinking remains our way beyond it. Now there only remains the step of apprehending the realm of freedom at which we have arrived.

In the end it is the opening of the horizon of the spirit that is the principal achievement of the modern philosophical unfolding. Not only has ideology been expelled but the fundamental incompatibility between thought and its constraint has become abundantly clear. This is always more than the abstract triumph of liberty. It is the attachment of liberty to the transcendent pull of existence itself. When the meditation unfolds from the zero point of the meaningless and the absurd, as Albert Camus suggested, it nevertheless unfolds under an imperative buried within it. It cannot end in suicide or murder because the abundance of being from which it arises draws it into the enlargement of the soul in which it begins to glimpse the mystery by which it is held. This is not to comprehend, far less to master, the horizon in which we exist. It is simply to recognize the peculiar privilege that belongs to beings who do not simply exist but are capable of perceiving their own existence. Transparence is the possibility of transcendence, and it is the only perspective in which transcendence is not simply a figment. God is not an idea or an image in our minds, and eternity is neither a place nor time. Before they are visualizations, they are first of all intimations we know because we are within them. Nor can they easily be dislodged as empty musings without any surety, for they are realizations of the imperative that is more intimate to us than we are to ourselves. It is in this sense that Kant's famous postulates of God, freedom, and immortality must be taken. Whenever he returns to them, it becomes clear that they are far from stipulations. They have become the insuperable parameters within which we enact our lives, and their function is to bring home to us the deep seriousness of the task. In the case of Kant, the postulates serve to remind us of the unreality of the space–time universe our moral actions inhabit. Such action, he explains, is underpinned by the voice of God, who calls us in the full rigor of eternity to fulfill our inescapable responsibility. The metaphysical horizon within us surpasses the physical horizon around us.

Far from abandoning metaphysics, Kant has enhanced its hold upon us. In this sense his thought is, his own demurrals to the contrary notwithstanding, fully congruent with the historical tradition of philosophy. He has made it clear that it is the invisible that rules the visible and that it is our participation in what transcends the finite that defines our true significance. It is thus no accident that he is the one who most thoroughly invokes the idea of human dignity as the constitutive self-understanding of our world. The difference between this conception and its premodern equivalents, whether as the *imago Dei* or the rational animal, is that the Kantian formulation emerges without any prior metaphysical commitments, which arise only in the course of reflection on the exercise of self-responsibility. God is not the beginning, nor is eternity the end. They are rather disclosures that accompany the enactment of universal legislation. In deciding for myself, I simultaneously decide for all similarly situated human beings and thus assume the kind of awe-ful responsibility that is the divine governance. Only the perspective of God can adequately account for the full ramifications of human action. Inevitably they trail off into a level of mystery not fully accessible to us. But their beginning remains within the clear awareness that we are charged with primordial responsibility for good and evil. Even God cannot interfere. Otherwise we would not be full participants in the original freedom that is the life of God. All of this explains why Kant repeatedly returns, no matter how puzzling to his secular readers, to the theological framework that exceeds purely moral considerations. It is also why Kant could so unerringly pinpoint the centrality of human dignity.

In this way, Kant and his successors have managed to illumine the source of the insights that had also been reached by their predecessors. Participation in the divine *nous* may have been the result of the classical inquiry, but the path into it had largely been obscured by the focus on its conceptualization. Without that prior experiential opening, the symbolic elaborations become opaque. This is the great failing that prompted Eric Voegelin to remark that the history of philosophy had largely been the history of its derailment. A focus on propositions and arguments had eclipsed the movement of inquiry by which they had been reached. It was in this way that "metaphysics" could emerge as a teaching, rather than the horizon that makes all teaching possible. Without turning metaphysics into a set of contents, the idealists could cast a glance at the condition of possibility within which they thought and lived. What could not be said could nevertheless be indicated. This explains the dynamic quality that Hegel imparts to philosophical language where meaning lies in the movement rather than in the conclusion. A similar preference for movement is displayed in the development of an aphoristic style by Nietzsche and the elevation of paradox in Kierkegaard. Eventually it would reach the high point of Heidegger's meditation on truth as *al-atheia*, an opening that precedes its opening. To relate these bewildering linguistic gyrations to the earlier tradition, we need only recognize the echoes of Platonic dialectic within them. Indirect communication has always been a philosophical vehicle, but it is only in the late modern period that its necessity has become thematic. Even the vaunted clarity of Aristotle's teleological analysis turns out, on closer examination, not to be so sharply defined. The telos of living beings may guide them, but it cannot be attained without annihilating their existence. It is for this reason that *eudaimonia* is a horizon, but not one that can be reached in this life. Even to say that the Good is experienced is not quite accurate, for it is what structures experience and thus lies strictly speaking beyond it. In the encounter we glimpse what cannot be known in any satisfactory sense.

This is what Kant meant by insisting that we could have no theoretical knowledge of what lies beyond the reach of the categories of our understanding as they order our sensible intuitions. There can be no metaphysical knowledge. Yet we continue to have metaphysical intimations of what is beyond the boundaries of our thought. Even the assertion of such boundaries does not lie, strictly speaking, within them. Kant distinguished *Vernunft* from *Verstand* and understood the former as the principal source of the synthetic a priori propositions he denoted as metaphysics. It was in this way that he expanded the boundaries he had initially set for thought. Beyond what is known is the practice of thought that thereby glimpses the condition of its own possibility. The shift that Kant thus inaugurates is a momentous reversal in the history of philosophy that had privileged the contemplative life over the active and saw the former as the grounds for the latter. Now, whether that self-understanding of philosophy had ever adequately captured its situation is, as we have suggested, open to question. Philosophy has always understood itself as primarily a way of life before it becomes a body of thought. Its animating center had always been the movement toward transcendence rather than the application of transcendence as a first principle. Teleology had always functioned as a boundary rather than a goal possessed. What classical philosophy had never done, however, is bring its own existential dynamic into line with its explicit account of the order of things. Somehow it always conveyed the impression that thinking is outside of what it thinks about, the subject confronting the object, as it has evolved in our latter-day formulation. It is this notorious separation from being, as Heidegger explained, that has become the principal source of our disorientation in the modern world. Kant and the philosophical movement that follows him represent an impressive correction to the misperception that philosophy at its start had allowed to slip in. Modern philosophy affirms, in contrast, that practical reason is prior to its theoretical implementation because theoretical reason is itself a mode of practice. What we know of being we know through our participation within it, not by stepping outside of it.

The center of gravity has shifted from metaphysics to ethics. This was the reversal announced in "The Earliest System Program of German Idealism," a text so widely representative that even today we cannot be sure of its authorship.[1] Later Levinas would proclaim it as the realization that "ethics is prior to ontology." But it was Kant who inaugurated the revolution that, as the term suggests, returns philosophy to its starting point. The elevation of contemplation over action always sat uneasily within the classical account, once it was conceded that contemplation was itself a form of action. Participation (*metalepsis*) could hardly be known without entering upon the movement in which being is disclosed ever-more fully as its ground of possibility. It is only with Kant, however, that it becomes clear why this must be so. Theory cannot furnish a beginning for action because no matter what point of origin is selected we must still be prepared to ask whether it too is good. Even if God is taken as the starting point we must already have judged that God is good ("why call me good?").[2] There is no getting behind the imperative to act in accordance with goodness. It is prior to the order of being and suggests that we are capable of standing outside of being. Or at the very least, it is from that vantage point that being comes into sight. This is why for Kant the moral life is the heart of his thought. No speculation penetrates further. It is when we are compelled to bend our will to the uttermost requirement of duty that we begin to glimpse the order in which we are held. The antinomy of freedom exercised within a causally determined world is resolved as we perceive that the source of our action lies outside of space and time. This is why the call of duty comes to us as the voice of God and we realize the immortal character of the consequences. When all else has fallen away, the import of good or bad action remains as an eternal reality. Without divine mercy, reconciliation to our failures would be impossible. There could be no new beginning through which we set out again to correct and overcome the mistakes of the past. The full panoply of the Christian drama of creation and redemption is somehow imparted as an inescapable attenuation of the moral life.[3]

The transcendent horizon cannot be shaken because it is the one we live within. Even when the divine is explicitly excluded, as it is within the ostensibly secular mentality of our world, it returns in the only way in which the transcendent can. Absence is its mode of presence. Again we are at the heart of a long-standing struggle within the spiritual tradition. Ever since God revealed himself to the Israelites, the problem of his representation and his presence with a particular people has vexed our best symbolizing efforts. The medieval Church thought it had resolved the challenge by clearly demarcating a spiritual realm in relation to the finite material world. But demarcation itself entailed a worldly application. The cathedrals are still physical. What could not be conveyed is the God who can be worshipped only in spirit and truth. Interiority offered itself as an alternate locale but could hardly resist the descent into subjectivity. What could not be accessed is the mode of presence of that which cannot be present. This is the great achievement of modern philosophy. Much of it, including the culminating effort of Heidegger, addresses the impossibility of God. Its real effect, however, is to underline what God must be since he cannot be "God." In many respects the self-understanding of the secular world is ideally suited to conveyance of the transcendent as transcendent. Without the possibility of mixture with anything immanent, God can be known as God. This explains too why religion has returned with such vehemence to a world that is marked by its absence. An awareness of what is missing pervades, as Jürgen Habermas has noted, our "postsecular age." But apprehension of the duality remains a philosophical problem. Only philosophy can give an account of what is beyond all giving of account, since it glimpses the condition of its own possibility. In the full rigor of the Socratic maxim, philosophy too is ignorant of what is beyond it, but it possesses the incomparable advantage of knowing its ignorance. Once again, the transcendent is grasped as transcendent. It is present nowhere but within the movement of its disclosure as what cannot be disclosed.

The further step remains for philosophy, to explain how it itself is possible. How is it that we do not exist in sheer ignorance? That we can hear the call that comes to us from beyond all possibility of hearing or calling? That is a step that remains to be taken as philosophy discovers that it is only the language of the person that can grasp the paradoxical perspective it seeks to express. The ontological difference, so intensely ruminated by Heidegger, underlines the difference between being and beings and regards its forgetting as the great misstep in Western philosophy. By recalling it he hoped to reverse the disorientation that marks the modern world in which mastery of objects is accompanied by evacuation of purpose. Yet despite his formidable determination to regain the perspective of being, occluded by attention to beings, Heidegger nowhere manages to explain how the task is possible for us who are after all still beings ourselves. *Dasein* may raise the question of being, but Heidegger did not seem to seize upon the condition of its possibility. That is, that a person is not simply a being but is always already outside of it. Only a person can grasp the ontological difference because persons exist within it. Like being, they are not what they are. Whatever is disclosed by the *prosōpon*, the mask/*persona*, is not what the person is. We know this as the very meaning of what it is to be a person. We meet one another, not through what is said or transacted, but by virtue of what cannot be said or transacted. The person him- or herself is utterly beyond all that is done. To meet another is to encounter an utterly beyond that is neither a core nor a totality but the person him- or herself. Whatever attributes a person may possess, he or she is capable of considering them as if they were not of them. Identity is a notorious philosophical problem because the person transcends identity. He or she can only be known in themselves, as the whole that includes being itself. Each is a whole world, inexhaustible and infinite in themselves. Like God they can contemplate being because they are ever beyond it. There is, in other words, no analogue for the person, but the person whose exemplification of the ontological difference makes possible its apprehension.

The only place where philosophy has incontestably reached this insight into its own personalist horizon is within politics. Consistent with the prioritizing of the moral life we might expect practice to be ahead of theory, and that expectation is not disappointed. Our political life does not depend on a prior theoretical underpinning, for like the prayer life of the Church that is always in advance of its theology, politics already evinces principles whose full justification has yet to be reached. As persons we know one another as persons, and therefore we know how persons must be treated in the third-party arena that is public life. Our inviolability must be guarded by the guarantee of imprescriptible dignity and rights. Within a world in which everything is subsumed in the relentless coordination of means and ends, persons alone stand outside of the demand for rational efficiency. They cannot be commodified. Nor can they be sacrificed for the sake of the greater social good, for each is a whole that outweighs the whole. There is no point at which their utility, even to themselves, has been exhausted. Each is a unique irreplaceable member of the human family that must mourn the loss of every one as if he or she alone mattered in the world. That is what the discourse of equal rights and liberty enunciates. It is a language that has accumulated, through reflection on the recurrent irritations of political life, a priceless pearl. Such has been the achievement of a world that has brought forth an authoritative understanding of the person that both philosophy and theology are compelled to acknowledge as their own. It may indeed be that liberal political principles do not attain the transparence sought by philosophy and theology. Yet they contain the public affirmation of the person whose standing outside of all being is the condition of the possibility of their reflection on the whole. Philosophy may, as Hegel observed, always come on the scene too late to change it, but that does not mean that it cannot find itself reflected within it and thereby perform the inestimable service of confirming what has hitherto only been intuited.

CHAPTER TEN

The Turn to the Subject as the Turn to the Person

The turn to the subject is a defining feature of the modern world. More than the pervasive secularization of human life, there is the subject who is the driver of that development. When the symbols of transcendence have become opaque they lose their hold, but the experience behind them does not disappear. It is simply that the traditional forms of expression are no longer adequate. Attention turns increasingly to the inner life of the subject now embarked on the search for new evocations. The crisis of meaning so characteristic of modernity exposes the subject as the site of its eruption. Even science, the one indisputable point of clarity, is surrounded by confusion about itself. Having disavowed ultimate questions, it can neither tell us whence we have come nor where we are going. Science cannot even understand itself. The subject alone must begin the reflection on the whole in which we find ourselves. That point of departure was emblematically captured in Descartes's *Meditations* (1641), in which philosophy was to begin anew from the certainty of the *cogito*. A similar reliance on the self is also the basis on which the social contract theorists sought a mutual accommodation of rights. When an authoritative foundation of order is lacking, there is always resort to each individual's interest in self-preservation. Along the way we discover that this elevation of the individual opens a perspective on a rich and fascinating interior life, as it has been chronicled in the distinctively modern literary form of the novel. The subject, it would seem, now encompasses the whole universe.

Yet it would be a mistake to regard this as a novelty. The subject has been present from the beginning, ever since human beings emerged with minds. Indeed, the modern turn to the subject is itself preceded by the more profound discovery of mind in the spiritual outbursts of the first millennium before Christ. A special case of this development is the Greek differentiation of reason, of *nous*, in which individual mind replaces all cosmological mediation of order. That astonishing emergence of a language of self-consciousness is the real source on which the modern shift to interiority is based. In the discovery of mind human beings can for the first time control the activity of thinking. Philosophy may have been Greek in its inception but its application is universal. Anywhere thinking about thinking occurs it unfolds within the categories of Greek thought. Knowing or acting are no longer simply activities of mind but can now be grasped within the principles of their respective sciences. Perhaps the most impressive instance of this advance in self-control is to be found in Aristotelian logic, which was so definitive that it endured without historical improvement virtually to the present.[1] At the same time, however, that example also suggests the limits of the classical opening of mind.

Thinking is more than logic, just as acting is more than habit. Each arises from depths only vaguely under our control and only dimly sensed in their effect. The opening of mind goes beyond intellectual wonder. It encompasses the full gift of self, an act that, as Christianity showed, requires more than the self-determination of which the self is capable. Where philosophy could initiate the discovery of transcendence, whereby inwardness is apprehended, it had not been able to seize the full implication of the encounter. Its epochal experience of the beyond, of *nous* participating in *nous*, was too readily confined within the *logos* of speculation. Christianity and the revelatory events had found the path of faith by which the interior response becomes crucial, but they too tended to assimilate the opening to an orthodoxy of content. Only with difficulty and prodding could theology be compelled to yield up its own mystical foundation. In many respects this is the burden of the countless reformers who would not permit the ecclesiastical community to limit itself to the structures it had erected. Finally, the bonds of spiritual unity were burst asunder in the reform that became the Reformation. At that point we have reached the modern demand for inner conviction as the one indispensable touchstone of faith.

The modern turn to the subject is of a piece with the millennial opening of the spirit that preceded our world yet failed to arrive at its full realization. Whether our own fitful and chaotic search, for a new foundation within the self, will succeed remains to be seen. So far the results are hardly dispositive. A widespread view is that the modern emphasis on inwardness and autonomy has failed to reach anything higher than the abyss of selfishness that had always lurked in the background. In this assessment the modern turn to the subject, its anthropocentric pivot, has failed to reach any foundation within the order of being.[2] On the contrary, it has made it impossible for nature or spirit or God to function as an authority over against the individual, who is continually reminded of his or her own ultimacy of judgment. Can being in any sense disclose its order when the individual stands imperiously above it? Is not the turn to the subject confirmation of the unassailable superiority of the self? Politically we are confronted by the parallel conundrum that the language of individual rights has prompted an increasing sense of entitlement. When individual human beings have been assured of their primacy within the existing order, is there any way by which they can be dislodged to assume responsibility for its maintenance? The outbreak of nihilism that Nietzsche detected as the corrosive solvent of modernity seems to have become our truth. In a world of particular selves and interests, the possibility of community seems to have disappeared. Mutuality has become impossible. It would seem that, far from completing the Greek and Christian discovery of self, the modern turn to the subject has botched it in irretrievable subjectivism. The self, no longer anchored in anything beyond, can scarcely even value itself.

The Subject as the Path of Philosophical Return

That is the challenge taken up by a disparate group of thinkers who share the conviction that the modern turn to the subject is not wholly mistaken and that the earlier neglect of the subject is not wholly correct. They sought a way of mediating the opposition, by showing that the subject was just as much present in the classical sources while the disclosure of order was just as accessible from the standpoint of the subject. Even while siding with the ancients, Voegelin, Strauss, Lonergan, Finnis, and others demonstrated that the quarrel with the moderns had been resolved. This is not simply in the superficial sense of their own modern embrace of classical and Scholastic thought, but in the far deeper sense that they had bridged the central divide between the perspective of the self and of the whole that contains it. How is it possible for a part to extend its penetration to the whole? This was the great issue left unresolved in the classical sources. They may have enacted such an attunement with eternal wisdom, but they could not explain how that had been possible. It had simply been a glimpse or vision by which the limits of mortality had been breached, but that had not altered the condition of mortality in which they found themselves. Plato had coined the *daimonios anēr*, or "spiritual man," as the new type of human being who is neither mortal nor immortal, but between them. What is the status of that *metaxu*? Socrates could only accept the Delphic estimate of his wisdom as the realization that he had no wisdom. He could exemplify but not explain what this meant. It was left to his latter-day followers to probe what had been left unsaid because, although for Socrates it had marked the limits of what could be said, the demarcation of a limit is already a step beyond it. The contemporary revival of classical thought is no mere return to its Greek formulations. It is an enlargement to the full self-consciousness of what it entailed. That is, that the source of philosophical illumination must now be firmly located within the subjective realm. The Forms are no longer the focus in this contemporary elaboration that now pursues the question of our access to them.[3]

The return to the philosophic and revelatory sources is no merely antiquarian exercise. It is a full-scale integration that now takes account of the experiential movements from which they arose. Ancient wisdom is recovered with a far more articulate grasp of its own emergence and can now more readily address the loss of being within the modern world. Philosophy has returned to its existential beginning as a way of life, rather than a speculation apart from its vital responsibilities. The setting in life has become explicit. What for the Greeks could be assumed and therefore omitted, as is still the case in the professionalized discipline of philosophy, now has regained its centrality as the knowledge by which we live.[4] It is no wonder that the members of our modern orthodox cohort are either centrally concerned with political disorder or have made the requisite conversion thematic. The perspective of the subject who must decide is not remote for them. They already locate themselves as bearers of existential responsibility. Their achievement is to show that ancient wisdom arose out of just such an impending crisis. Philosophy, before it is a speculation on the order of being, is first a response to the world whose collapse necessitates such knowledge. Resistance to disorder and the imperative of inquiry are the great constants that reach across the millennia. Now it has become clear that the modern turn to the subject arises from the same imperative. It also explains why this particular recovery of orthodoxy deliberately eschews discursive elaboration. Rather than penning systematic treatises, our contemporary exponents focus on the underpinning sources. It is enough if the central principles are sketched, a method suggested, or vital beginnings illuminated. The details can be unfolded as befits a wisdom that arises as a way of life, rather than its congealed results. Life has taken priority over its conceptualization. The difference is that now it has become clear that it was always so.

The gain to the modern world is evident, for it can now access the fount of wisdom on which it had always drawn even without full acknowledgment. But the gain to the sapiential tradition is also large, for it recovers the vitality of its beginning with an explicitness that cannot be gainsaid. Once the interiority of classical philosophy has been regained, it will no longer be possible to overlook the extent to which it can be found only within interiority. It is this realization that transforms ancient learning into a resource for the present. Greek thought does not remain in the world from which it arose. It can migrate into every age in which human beings resume its discourse in response to the challenges with which they are confronted. Philosophy lives in interiority, not in space and time. This is what Leo Strauss sought to suggest with his observation that the ideas unfolded by the great thinkers of history are not confined to their historical setting. They endure in splendid independence, to be perceived by readers with the requisite acuity to engage them. Historicism, the notion that ideas are contingently related to the circumstances of their genesis, is diametrically at odds with the nature of ideas, which is precisely to endure beyond the particularities of their emergence. In this way Strauss gave voice to the consensus underlying the common retrieval of a wisdom the passage of time had rendered opaque. Our neo-orthodox cohort demonstrates the transhistorical nature of ideas. But in fact they did much more. They affirmed that it was not only the ideas that were constantly available but the process of their discovery itself. To recover them meant, not plucking them from an eternal realm, but reembarking on the original encounter of their conception. Curiously, however, it is at this point that the consensus among our reenactors begins to break down. They are in agreement on the practice, but they cannot quite agree on the description of it. Strauss, for example, accuses Voegelin of historicism by paying attention to the process of historical differentiation, even though Strauss himself repeats the same pattern in his recovery of the permanent principles of philosophy.[5]

The disagreement, even if it turns out to be more apparent than real, nevertheless reveals a deeper confusion concerning the character of the enterprise our exemplars of orthodoxy are engaged on. Intent on finding a subjective path into authoritative truth, they often neglected reflection on the status of their own inquiry. It may indeed be that they have grasped the compelling force of truth in texts long relegated to merely historical interest, but have they done anything more than set aside their own misgivings at the possibility that these contents too might be superseded by others? What is it that renders their own discovery of authoritative truth more than authoritative for themselves? Have they finally been able to set aside the interminable subjectivism of their starting point? When the turn to the subject has become the inescapable path for the recovery of truth that has been lost, there is no guarantee that the truth that is gained is anything more than subjective. Perhaps it may be that the ancient neglect of the subject, whereby the full force of truth is allowed to penetrate us, is preferable to the labored musings of those who must wrestle with the suspicion of entrapment within the subject. These are surely the misgivings, whether voiced or not, that often impel our mentors to more vociferous expressions of their orthodoxy than they have been able to warrant. "Natural right" and "absolute moral principles" and "the truth of existence" remain assertions even when their indispensability has been fully conceded. Could it be that a desideratum has substituted for a foundation? The impression can easily be taken from a careful reading of Strauss's *Natural Right and History* or Voegelin's *The New Science of Politics*. Neither establishes what it claims as irrefutable.

No doubt that impression would be unfair, and not least because the authors were fully aware of the deficiency. Philosophy cannot establish what it presupposes. This is the great difficulty that they navigated as they sought to illumine the horizon within which philosophic thinking occurs. It is at this point that their reflection moves away from its identification with the subject, since it is really the case that the subject is now invited to think within the framework of what is beyond it. Rather than term this subjective, they are more inclined to favor the classical designation of *methexis* or *metalepsis*, "participation." Yet it is accessed through the experiential movement that remains inward. Thinking in the end is within being rather than outside of it. Even Voegelin, however, does not embrace the full implication of that realization, but he comes tantalizingly close on a number of occasions. In general, he is content to acknowledge the circularity of philosophical experience and reasoning. The ground, he explains in "Reason: The Classic Experience," is already present within the question that seeks it.[6] There would be no search for the ground of existence if the ground was not already known, indeed even active, as the revelatory force that stirs up the questioning. Meditative questioning moves, not from ignorance, but from knowledge of what it seeks, until it touches what is beyond it as the disclosure that has drawn it from the beginning. The ground is already present as the moving force in the revelatory encounter. Voegelin places great weight on the meditative structure of the experience precisely because it allows him to answer the question of its truth. There is no outside vantage point from which its truth can be assessed. It is only by participation in it that the affirmation can be reached. Even the questioning of truth is itself a moment within the unfolding. To raise the question of the truth of the experience is to raise the question of the ground oneself. The criterion of the ground is internal to the question. Lonergan initiates a similar move in his disavowal of any questioning of the structure of consciousness that does not move through the same structure: "All special methods consist in making specific the transcendental precepts, Be attentive, Be intelligent, Be reasonable, Be responsible."[7] Questions of meaning and judgment are imprescriptible. It is the impossibility of a higher viewpoint than the question of truth that renders the experience of more than individual significance. Transcendent truth carries representative significance because it is the point at which being becomes transparent. The judgment of truth may be an interior movement, but its possibility arises from the openness of reality to itself.

Beyond the Subject

Yet there remains a hesitation to dwell too intently on that pivotal realization. Perhaps nothing supports, albeit unfairly, the charge of reverting to private experience than Voegelin's readiness to move on to its categorization as an event within history, one that sets up a range of other relations. History seems to hold more interest than the events that, as Voegelin is the first to insist, constitute history. In this regard he is far from alone. Most scholars are far more comfortable in dealing with the peripheral than with the most intimate. How can we even talk about what is closer to us than our own selves? "Debate and Existence" is one essay in which Voegelin seems to be at last confronting the most crucial matter. How is it possible for us to engage in rational debate when we have such divergent accounts of the reality in which we find ourselves? In particular, how is it possible to talk of God when science has deliberately excluded any reference to final causes? Voegelin acknowledges the weight of the objection and concedes that the symbols of transcendence have become opaque. Much of the essay is devoted to the impossibility of debate when there is no longer any possibility of invoking a summum bonum. There are even extensive suggestions that reason itself has broken down when it has been reduced to its purely formal exposition. Yet that is not what Voegelin dwells upon. Instead, we are treated to an exegesis of a passage from Aristotle's *Metaphysics* in which the necessity of a limit is explained to be inherent to the nature of reason: "Those who maintain an infinite series do not realize that they are destroying the nature of the Good, although no one would try to do anything if he were not likely to reach some limit [*peras*], nor would there be reason [*nous*] in the world, for the reasonable man always acts for the sake of an end—which is a limit [*peras*] (*Metaphysics* 994b10–15)." After noting that here we have reached the core of the Aristotelian analysis of existence, Voegelin returns to the depiction of the stalemate he had earlier elaborated in the essay. It is almost as if retrieval of the Aristotelian "truth of existence" has no application in the present. This is all the more remarkable in light of Voegelin's own personal response that is sensitive enough to discern how Aristotle's style of discourse had changed in the passage. He avers how "all of a sudden it becomes warm and incisive as if now we had reached the heart of the problem; and it becomes discursive enough to make it clear that here indeed we touch human existence at its center."[8] One would have expected that recovery of such a centerpiece would merit a fuller unfolding. Perhaps there was nothing more to say. Or it may be that the interest in locating the event within a wider narrative overshadowed the discovery itself. Whatever the reason, the reader is inclined to feel that an opportunity for deeper probing has been lost. Some may even be forgiven for concluding that Voegelin too has his own allegiances to maintain.

It may be that nothing is further from the truth than this impression. Yet it is a persistent one across the exemplars of modern orthodoxy. They may have arrived at their convictions through the most unbiased personal inquiry, but it is often difficult to convey that transparency to readers who may not have the same readiness to follow them. In the end, our salvagers cannot even be approached without giving them the benefit of the doubt that they are worth approaching. Trust is a prerequisite to judging trustworthiness. In the end there is a gap between their personal odyssey and the responsiveness of readers, even when, or especially when, the indispensability of the personal dimension has been made explicit. The careful reader might suspect that our exemplars have gone as far as they dare in raising the inescapably personal dimension, including their own pathway to truth, but that once it had been announced the centrality of the personal had been promptly forgotten. The pattern is strikingly repeated by the group of thinkers who are identified as personalists. In the end they talk about the person but not out of the person. The source of their own thinking has been closed over in much the same way as the first opening within the Greek discovery of mind had congealed. To talk about mind is not always to be mindful of what a mind is. It is easier to talk about mind as if it is a thing. The turn to the subject has thereby failed to deliver on its promise, for it becomes a mere talking about the subject that remains vulnerable to the charge of subjectivism. Indeed, to embrace the subjective point of view is to deprive it of all value.

    Our modern orthodox retrievers do not go that far, for they are determined to resist the charge of subjectivism. Yet as we have seen, they leave themselves open to it because they cannot provide an account of the source of their own apprehension. Strauss merely asserts natural right, while Voegelin acknowledges the circularity of meditative participation; Finnis and Lonergan accept the imperative of practical reasonableness without considering it needs any further elaboration. What they cannot say is whence their convictions have arisen. They know that they possess an indubitable apprehension of the order of things, but they cannot account for that possibility. This is why they unfailingly convey the sense of having merely decided to adopt a point of view. They cannot explain the mode of access to it, and so it must inevitably appear as private and capricious. No amount of protest that they have nevertheless reached science or wisdom can alleviate this impression. They know that the indispensable moment is the internalization of truth, but how can truth be anything more than internal? On what basis does it have a status as reality? Why does it not remain what it at one level is, a privately appropriated conviction with no basis other than what seemed compelling to each individual? How does it rise to something of universal significance? How does truth become authoritative? These are certainly troubling questions that were both familiar and disturbing to our orthodox proponents. Acknowledgments of their validity surface on more than a few occasions in the texts. Yet they refrain from exploring them any further. A limit has been reached that they conclude cannot be overcome. Instead they accept the necessity of thinking within its parameters. Already they have gone pretty far in conceding the inescapably subjective character of thought, further than the originators of the convictions to which they hold firm, but they cannot see their way to the realization that thought is also and of necessity a movement beyond the subjective. In thinking, we are already anchored in that which is beyond thinking. It is the point at which being begins to lay hold of itself, not subjectively, but in the inwardness that is the being of thought.

Admittedly, this intuition is tantalizingly close to our orthodox cohort. Voegelin in particular has formulations that acknowledge the irrelevance of the subject–object dichotomy.[9] The notion of *nous* as the point, not simply of our thinking about being, but the point at which being becomes transparent to itself reverberates through the whole history of Western thought. Not only are there allusions to the incomplete project of German idealism, but the echoes reach all the way back to Aristotle's famous formulation of thought thinking itself (*Metaphysics* 1072b–20ff.). At the same time we are also reminded that this intuition never succeeded in finding appropriate conceptualization throughout its long unfolding. Somehow a stable formulation eluded the tradition, including its most authentic exemplars in the present. Talk of participation in being could never articulate its own possibility. When the pattern of incapacity is so extensive, we are inclined to suspect that it does not simply arise from the inability of particular thinkers to penetrate its mystery. The cause must lie within the terms that have conventionally been employed to do justice to what is sought. Heidegger virtually made a career of the complaint that we had forgotten being, pointing by way of example to the inability of science to understand itself. To the extent that science comprehends reality it cannot be comprehended in the same way. What is outside the frame of reference, as science by definition is, cannot be included in it.[10] It is no wonder that we are dazed by such lesser challenges as pondering the relationship between brain activity and consciousness. The imponderability is so pervasive that one is inclined to attribute it, as Wittgenstein did, to an underlying conceptual confusion. We conceive of science and mind as if they are things with the same solidity of presence as balls and bicycles. In truth, we know that that which grasps cannot itself be grasped. It has always ever evaded the possibility. Indeed, neither mind nor science is anywhere, which is why they can be everywhere at every time.

The problem is that we have long lacked a term that would identify what escapes every corner of reality and yet can reach into every corner. Merely calling it "mind" does not solve the problem, for we have simply given a name to what it does. But what is the entity itself that is mind? How can we even conceive of mind? What kind of reality is it that can stand outside of all reality? The term "being" or "substance," *ousia*, was early seized upon because mind, *nous* or *logos*, must possess the same kind of self-subsistence as the things it studied. The intuition was a good one, for certainly mind possesses a kind of permanence and identity that seems most durable. It would be much later that the notorious problems of self-identity would arise, especially when the credibility of soul or psyche as container of mind had begun to wane. Such objections would unravel the notion that mind was such a stable entity, but they would do nothing to disavow the underlying assumption that, whatever mind is, it must be some form of substance. The problem was, not that we could not discover the substance of mind, but that we increasingly came to discard the notion of substance as such. Even the *subiectum*, the source of our modern terminology of the subject, had begun to dissolve.[11] Descartes's turn to the subject seemed increasingly unpromising. The cogito could not be sure of its agent. The dissolution of the subject, under the withering scrutiny of its claim to identity, casts suspicion on the entire project of taking the subject as a point of departure. Calls for an ontological foundation, a source of the self beyond the empirical self, have been frequent. Yet none of our orthodox cadre seemed particularly enamored of the suggestion. One suspects they regarded it as a fool's errand, a need they had already surpassed by leaping directly into the existential horizon of practical reason and participation in being. What they did not do is make their misgivings explicit. They did not explain that the effort to understand mind in terms of substance is a fundamental reversal of the order. Substance is not the basis for an understanding of mind because it is from mind that we derive the notion of substance. That which appears and yet remains the same as it undergoes changes of appearance is preeminently the case for mind, which is never contained in all that it says and does. Other notions of substance, including the idea of self-subsistence, are diminished versions of this supreme self-possession of mind. Yet we have assimilated mind to the model of other persisting entities. What we lack is a way of assimilating them to mind as the highest disclosure of being. We must be prepared to abandon the primacy of substance to put in its place the other term that at the beginning it had displaced. That is, the notion of the person.

Person as Prior to Being

It is in the person that the problems of the subject/substance are resolved. The futile quest for the substratum beyond which there is no other disappears. The person is contained in nothing beyond him- or herself. There is no other beyond the other. Each is a whole containing him- or herself as a whole. The question of who he or she really is, the question of the true or innermost self, cannot be answered in a final way because it is out of that question that the person lives. Who he or she is remains a question to each. Every person can raise it because he or she already stands outside of their being. They contain their own existence. This is the condition of their enactments and disclosures that cumulatively answer the primary question yet never exhaust it.[12] In every aspect, thus, the person is in being and yet already outside of it. This is why he or she is not reducible to the presence of an entity that merely is. The self that would assert such solidity is not the self that makes the assertion. The turn to the subject that inaugurates modern philosophy, as a way of completing the earlier discovery of mind, had been led by the intuition of that innermost source from which all thinking and saying arises. But it could not be found.[13] Every candidate proved to be provisional and incapable of supporting the ultimacy required. Only the series of discarded possibilities as a whole stands as mute testament to the self that has undertaken the most rigorous self-inquiry. Like the contemporary analytic debates about the ground of self-identity, nothing endures except the self that has undertaken the debate from start to finish.[14] The self stands irrevocably outside of all that is said.

That is what it means to be a person. There is nothing higher, for nothing can contain the self but the self itself. There is no analogue in being for what can contemplate being as a whole. In that act the person is definitively beyond being. But how then do we know about what cannot be in being and nowhere present? We know only because we too are persons and, as such, continually in touch with all other persons. They are known, not as appearances or quantities, not in anything that they manifest, but in themselves, in what definitively transcends even themselves. We cannot claim to know another until we know him or her personally. Voegelin at one time referred to this mutual openness as part of the pregivenness of consciousness, a structure of transcendence in which the subject is already engaged before any reflection on it takes place.[15] It is for this reason that the knowledge of other selves presented such a philosophically insuperable problem. No accumulation of evidence seemed sufficient to warrant the conclusion that the other is a self, just like me. The same applies even to my self, since the underlying continuity falls short of a justification of identity. But instead of foreclosing further reflection through the erection of the boundary of the pregiven, it would have been preferable to regard this as an invaluable invitation to peer beyond such limits. How do we know about them except by exceeding them? Is there not something of that excessiveness in every meeting in which persons glimpse one another as persons, as what must be exceeded to be known? Instead of becoming a problem within philosophical analysis, the person might be embraced as the inexhaustible source of reflection itself. Persons cannot be explained because they are the possibility of explanation. Nothing in reality can account for them because they escape every limit enlisted to account for them.[16] Even this insight itself cannot be accounted for. It is a glimpse of the self-containment of persons available only to persons.

Is this then subjective? Is it merely an inner feeling we wish were true? What basis does it have other than my longing for it? Obviously there is no absolutely compelling fact to which we could point. Yet there is the undeniable reality of the question itself. Whence does it arise if not from the infinite capacity of the questioner to put him- or herself aside in order to reach the truth? It is that unrestricted openness that distinguishes a person and, at the same time, provides the link to all other persons who of necessity must be similarly situated. Transcendence may not be the most obvious feature of persons, but it is what pervades all of their features. Standing within truth is thus not something purely subjective, an option that persons may or may not exercise as they wish. It is what marks their relationship to truth even when they seek to avoid it. Only persons can lie, for only one who knows the truth can present it as false. Truth remains deeper than the lie. This is why it is persons alone who exist within truth.[17] Even to ask whether their convictions are merely subjective is already to discard the subjective perspective. How then can we describe that mode of being if it is not the mode of truth? Categories such as "subjective" and "objective" have become irrelevant. This is why it is possible to have endless philosophical debates about the problem of knowledge—because we studiously avoid asking how the inquiry is possible. Kant was the first to fully explicate the impossibility of providing a defense of knowledge without presupposing it. The question that has endured is what the status of his insight is. Clearly it is not simply a form of knowledge because, as Plato too recognized, it is a glimpse beyond knowledge. Heidegger insisted that such a glimpse is no longer internal to the subject; it is not in our minds because it locates our minds within being. It is the point at which being is transparent to itself. Unfortunately, Heidegger could not see his way through to the realization that transparence is what marks the person. Being is a person. He could not take that step because he thought that to be a person is to be a being within being. This was also why God too had to be displaced by the horizon of being. Instead Heidegger went on to discourse about the unconcealment of Being, the truth of being, or be-ing, as if it was contained entirely within itself. He could not recognize that it is only because he too is a person that it was possible for a part to attain a glimpse of the whole. To concede that he would only have to leave behind his prejudice that persons are beings. His own example demonstrates, however, that the ontological difference between being and beings is accessible only to that which is not a being.[18] How can there even be a hint of the partial and subjective in persons who take their stand in that which is beyond all beings? They may fail to live within the light of truth, but that is only a possibility because they can depart from who they are.

It is thus never a matter of showing that persons can arrive at the true or the good. Arrival is possible only because they have never left. Not only is the possibility of reaching the true and the good implicit in every exhortation to reach them, but the true and the good are already there as what calls forth even that exhortation itself. The appeal to foundations has all along presupposed the foundations themselves. It is not our minds that arrive at truth and goodness but truth and goodness that enable the arrival. Rather than thinking of the journey that must be undertaken to attain its goal, we should think of the goal as what is prior to the journey it sustains. We arrive at what we know. This is the circularity of thought so well identified by Voegelin and the others. It is a meditative movement toward what already stirs before the beginning. The classical notion of *anamnesis* is one of the ways to describe what is sought, and can be attained, because it has never fully been lost. Voegelin turns the Platonic *metaxu* into a quasi-technical term to name the same movement. Yet it remains difficult to shake the notion that this remains a movement within thought. Of course, there are assertions that "the between" represents the structure of existence, but what has not been confronted is how we can have knowledge of this knowledge. Surely that too cannot be a form of knowledge. Echoes of the Platonic struggle to find the right formulation of that which is beyond being in dignity and power are still present. To resolve them, and to penetrate our grasp of the between that is not simply a vantage point within it, requires a more radical realization that we too are not within being. As persons we are not what we are. It is because we are beyond being that we can apprehend it in its transcendentals.

We bear responsibility for truth and goodness and beauty, not because we contain them, but because we are contained by them. It is truth and goodness and beauty that call us into being, for they are prior, in just the same way as every person is prior to me. Responsibility is not up to me for it is precisely my discretion that responsibility has taken away. I am responsible before I have *become* responsible. It is the former that is the ground of the latter. There is nothing subjective about it, for responsibility has been thrust upon me even before I have had time to consider it. Otherwise I would not be responsible. It would be up to someone else to assume responsibility. What makes me responsible is that I have been chosen and there is no way of evading it. I cannot avoid accepting truth, acting well, and responding to beauty. Even when I fail I have not been able to remove my responsibility, which remains implacable. Before there is an I, there is responsibility. It is responsibility that makes me who I am. Or, more accurately, it is what makes me more than I am. The transcendentals are the possibility of my self-transcendence, but this is never a pure possibility. There would be no transcendence of the self unless it had already happened. Possibility is provided by actuality. Even the Aristotelian categories lose some of their fixity within this existential dynamic. How can we talk about that which is coming into existence? The problem was one that Aristotle intuited even though he did not fully confront it. Nevertheless, he broached it in wondering how it is possible for one who does not possess nobility of character to be drawn toward it.[19] Somehow nobility must yet be present within one who is not yet noble. He is not a sheer potency because act has already slipped in. It is on that basis that he is able to move toward what he is not. Unlike all other transitions from potency to act, for the person the transition is in germ before any movement takes place. As the source of its own action, the person is both potency and act simultaneously. The categories of immanent reality hardly apply to one who creates him- or herself.

The Person as Transcendence

The person is God-like without being God, who is all act without any potency remaining. For us the self-enactment may derail, and for that reason it is extended over time. Yet the reality remains the same. Eternity is within our hands. Nothing can explain the deviation by which we let it slip away. The moment of decision is not a moment within time but the moment that constitutes time. It is a decision that is valid for all time and thus not an arbitrary event, but rather the turning point in which everything is held together. Kant possessed an intimation of this in suggesting that moral action is one in which we simultaneously enact a universal law. It is not that we conform to a universal; it is that we bring it forth. But from where? Kant struggled to suggest that the origin of moral action must be conceived as outside of time if freedom is to be maintained. He too was entangled in the idea of the subject whose interior life must be the source of the outward movement. What had yet to be recognized is that there could be no externalization unless the subject was already embedded in it. Inwardness had yet to find its anchor in the transcendent, as Kierkegaard was the first to clearly understand. Human consciousness is not properly speaking something internal but a stepping into the perspective of the transcendent that is beyond all vantage points. It is the vantage point of God, in himself. Thus we do not occasionally decide to consider things *sub specie aeternitatis*, for all considering is from that indispensable standpoint. We may, of course, drift into subjectivity and merely dream or float, but even that is an option because of the priority of the really real that is eternity. The priority of the eternal is what allows us to recede from it into a merely subjective state. Even that, however, is still known from a vantage point outside of it. In essence, there is no pure subjectivity that does not know itself as such, that is, from beyond it. The topic we have been asked to consider, the turn to the subject, already takes its stand from outside of the subject. We can consider the subject because we are not imprisoned within it.

The transcendent is the perspective from which we think about everything. We know it, not by stepping outside to take a look, as Lonergan would put it, but by glimpsing what it is that makes all thinking and doing possible. It cannot be known, as Plato conceded (*Republic* 509a-b), but it can be perceived in a sideways glance as we stand upon its indubitability. Metaphysics is thus not another realm toward which we are striving but the condition of possibility of everything we do. It is not another thing but the boundary within which all things are. We possess the peculiar capacity to apprehend that in which we are apprehended. This is the transparence that is synonymous with consciousness. The turn to the subject was not mistaken in the intuition that here we would find the point of access to the transcendent. It was only mistaken in holding it to be an event *within* the subject. Here, by contrast, we find that the subject transcends itself and knows it as its own truth. Inwardness is not a holding within but a going beyond in which the self sets itself aside for the sake of what it holds within. It is the self in the other and the other in the self. The meeting place is neither in one nor the other. Rather, it is in the self-outpouring that exists nowhere but within itself. Transcendence is what makes transcendence possible. No laborious explanation is capable of explaining what requires no explanation because it precedes any that could be given.[20] What could sufficiently account for the moment in which self-interest is set aside to grasp what *is* apart from our grasping it? Can an act of unbidden kindness have any source but itself? Is there anything more generous or more open from which it could arise? What is that supreme gift of self that enables all consciousness of others if not transcendence as such? Whence derives that gift of giving we cannot say, but we do know that we have been given it. In that our transcendence is transparent. It includes the possibility of turning away from openness to hold itself within the subject. But then the subject has failed to be itself, for there is no subject apart from the opening to all in love.[21]

Even our champions of orthodoxy are inclined to preserve a subjective path toward it, not wishing to take the most daring leap of acknowledging that it is orthodoxy that subtends the subject. Unconditionality cannot be conditioned. They know that truth and goodness and beauty are there before the subject arrives at them. Arrival, they sense, is premised on having arrived. Yet there is no way that the eschaton can be present within the subject before the process has unfolded. How can a subject be what it is not yet? That is the question around which I have continually circled and it is now time to concede that it cannot be answered within the terms of the debate. The subject cannot be more than it is. A fixed quantity may set out on its journey equipped only with the vague intimations of the goal toward which it is drawn. Yet is that not to depart from the conception of a finite self? Surely it already lives in relation to what it is not, thereby demonstrating that the subject is not what it is. But what then is it? The need for a reconceptualization is now more pressing than ever. Having reached the limits of the paradigm of the subject as a thing, it is perhaps time to explode the limits in the direction of the unlimited. The subject-substance model that has dogged our inquiry, and the long historical tradition, must be confronted with one that begins not with its self-preservation but with self-transcendence. All along, however, the difficulty has been that nothing presents itself as having already surpassed its being. Everything is a being that seeks to maintain itself in being. What kind of being can be characterized as a movement beyond being? Intimations of such a reality, or nonreality, have already been dispersed in the characterization of the subject as not yet what it will be, as defined by the movement of the in-between. Yet even those suggestions still carry within them the notion of a finality to be achieved. What kind of subject will it be when it is no longer marked by the ceaseless movement that has hitherto marked it? One would be inclined to suspect that it would be a subject that ceased to be what it is. So what then must it be?

It must be a person. The word is almost interchangeable with subject and self, but not quite. It carries an alternative genealogy. Where substance-subject denoted the hidden reality behind appearances, person depicted the movement of revelation itself. The person is the *prosōpon*, or "mask," the persona, that must be carried by the actor who is thus concealed behind it. It is thus the perfect term for the interplay between closure and disclosure. The actor reveals by not revealing, for he is at once incapable of self-revelation and capable of it. He is neither in the mask nor what is behind the mask, but is the one who mediates between them, the one who can be known in no other way except by that mediation in which he himself is. The person, we know, is always more than he or she has said. There is neither a point where everything has been disclosed nor a point where nothing has been disclosed. What matters is neither what is said nor what is left unsaid, but everything that is outside of it all. That is the person in him- or herself who must be known as each is in themselves. Nothing can contain them and nothing can fail to contain them, once they have put themselves wholly into it. And we too are capable of beholding them even when we see nothing at all. Transcendence, we may say, is not a goal toward which persons strive. It is the ground of their possibility as persons. It is that flash of revelation in which externally nothing has transpired and yet everything has been communicated. Without information the person is given and received. Vastly surpassing all that is said and done is the saying and doing that intimates an infinity beyond it. Unlike the subject who must contemplate his or her openness to all others, the person is already open to them as requiring no intermediate connection. As one who nowhere exists, the person is already beyond existence. A metaphysics of the person is not a prerequisite, since the person is the prerequisite of metaphysics.

The problem that so dogged our archaeologists of orthodoxy can now be resolved. Having reached the truth of existence, they need no longer struggle against the objection that they have only arrived at a subjective perception of it. They have rather arrived at the condition of their own possibility of arrival. It is prior to their thinking about it, in the same way as eternity is what makes it possible for us to think about time. This is not a logical priority but an ontological one. Only that which is not in time can grasp time. Kant struggled with such thoughts but only reached a moment of clarity in the realization that justice does not depend on an afterlife but rather the reverse.[22] It is from the conception of justice that an idea of eternity is generated. In thinking of justice we already stand outside of time. For the subject it may be impossible, but to the person it is eminently the mode of its being. The transcendence that can contain the whole is already there within the part. We may already continue to think of ourselves merely as parts within the whole, but that is already a view from the perspective that is beyond parts and wholes. The person includes all, not as a subjective moment, but as the transcendence that makes even subjectivity possible. Skepticism, we know, includes itself. But this is not just to perform a cheap intellectual trick to defeat an opponent. It is to advert to the condition of the possibility of such self-examination. We are not confined to the self. When we ask then wherein we are, we are left with a vague puzzlement. Yes, we are within ourselves, but wherein is that? To be a person is to live within that inexhaustible mystery. To trace it back to God is not to ultimately resolve it, for God too lives out of what he is not. Even his Godhead is not something to which he wishes to cling, for it is in giving himself away that he is himself most fully. It may be that every reality strives toward that transparence and can be understood in such terms, but how we are to understand transparence itself is certainly not in terms of anything further.[23] The limits of the mystery can only be reached by a person who cannot simply be limited by them.

In the end this is the witness demonstrated by the retrievers of orthodoxy. The discovery of mind that had forgotten the minds in whom it occurred had now regained its source. No longer would the doctrines that issued from the event take precedence over the event itself. Teleology, whatever its status as a metaphysical principle, originated in the immediacy of human action that cannot unfold without a summum bonum. There was no ground of reason apart from the exercise of attention, understanding, judgment, and decision. The appeal is not to some disputed concept of nature but to the imperative of practical reason embedded within it. And it is the permanent character of the ethical and political challenges that bring home their ineradicably existential character. A good deal of the intellectual excitement of this group of experientially vibrant thinkers is that they managed to complete the turn to the subject overlooked in ancient and only incompletely realized in modern thought. They demonstrated that it is possible to make texts from times and places far away from us as current as the morning newspaper, once one had pierced the interior movement from which they had emerged. Nothing that is human is foreign to me.[24] The past had ceased to be past when it has entered the problematic of the present. What they had not done was consider the condition of possibility of that mutuality that abolishes all distance in time and space. They had not considered the astonishing character of their own work, in setting themselves aside to enter so fully into the world of others who had also done the same for them. It was a singular shedding of their own singularity. How was that possible? It can only be because they are not Eric, Leo, Bernard, and John, but already beyond any identity assigned to them. The whole is available to each person because each person is already more than the whole.[25] Yes, they called attention to the existential opening, but they could do that only because they could even stand outside of that. Thus it is not experience that is primary but the person who can discourse about it. It is the person that is irreducible.

CHAPTER ELEVEN

Why Kierkegaard Is the Culminating Figure of the Modern Philosophical Revolution

When I wrote a book on what I termed "the modern philosophical revolution," it came as something of a surprise to discover that Kierkegaard was its culmination.[1] I had not planned on assigning him the final chapter since every other thinker was treated in chronological order. To the extent that there is a coherent unfolding of modern philosophy, one would expect it to be a succession of ever-more penetrating accounts. The arc of thinkers from Kant to Derrida can be seen as converging on an ever-more adequate conception of their common project. However we define it, there can be little doubt that they are in a conversation driven by mutual critique. The successors correct and enlarge on their predecessors. None can overleap the process by which its inspiration unfolds. Yet that is what occurs in the case of Søren Kierkegaard. He is the exception who arrives largely unnoticed at the end point before the dialectic of philosophy has reached it. Not only is his voice diminished because of its publication in Danish, but, when it does join the European mainstream through Jaspers and Heidegger, it serves the purpose of the later underwriters. It is no longer the astonishing apprehension of the path that includes them. The successors cannot be eclipsed by the predecessor on whom they build. For that to occur we must be prepared to revise our narrative or at least remain open to its possibility. That is the task of this chapter, as we attempt to rescue Kierkegaard from the labels of irrational decisionist and also unreconstructed religionist. Perhaps more than 200 years after his birth we are finally in a position to consider how one who pondered the modern problematic most deeply could thereby stand most fully within it.

To suggest that Kierkegaard reached the limit of the modern philosophical revolution requires first that we sketch what that singular development has entailed.[2] This may require some indulgence since it is hardly a universal consensus that modern philosophy follows an overarching narrative. Certainly there are many threads to the unfolding of modernity, but part of the challenge has always been to identify the turning points in which their convergence comes into view. Once that is done, the structure of the modern philosophical revolution can be grasped. If Kierkegaard is one of those pivots, then he also brings the process as a whole more readily into view. Our second step will be to suggest how he completes the movement of thought that comes after him. In its simplest formulation we may identify his achievement as the breakthrough to the paradox of faith, that "the single individual is higher than the universal."[3] The singular individual now becomes the horizon within which reflection occurs. Yet it would not resolve the aporias of identity and meaning so well documented in the ensuing philosophical development if it did not go beyond the isolated individual. Somehow the individual must disclose the inwardness of the person in whom the relationship to others is already contained. Our third step will follow Kierkegaard's discovery of the God relationship as the one in which the individual is most fully revealed. The individual becomes the person who inwardly contains the whole of being as he or she is held within the inwardness of being that is God. Kierkegaard is thus the one who points the way beyond a metaphysics of presence to the mutuality of persons that had always been its source.

Elements of the Modern Philosophical Revolution

The conventional narrative of modern philosophy and, by extension, modernity itself begins with Descartes, who famously declares *cogito ergo sum*. By turning to the self or subject he seeks to ground certainty on what cannot be doubted. When everything else has become questionable, there is still the indubitability of the questioner. From there the validation of our knowledge of reality and our place within it must be erected on the one indefeasible foundation of the self. The autonomous subject becomes the center from which order extends into social and political reality. Eventually the crisis of the isolated subject becomes apparent when it discovers it can neither find its way toward a sustaining metaphysical horizon nor manage to live without one. The mastery of nature by modern science does nothing to mitigate the unmastery of reason now deprived of any guiding purpose. The forlornness of reason over against the world it dominates is well recognized. Less clearly perceived is the partial character of this observation itself. Omitted is any account of the resistance to groundlessness that has remained a feature of the same philosophical unfolding. The dramatic rupture with theology and metaphysics has obscured the extent to which they endure, and not simply as a remnant increasingly discarded by an ever-more virulent rationalism.[4] Awareness of the unsustainability of a truncated reason is present from the very beginning. Not only does Descartes turn toward God as the foundation in the Third Meditation, but the impossibility of reason furnishing its own justification only deepens. Kant is surely the high point of its explicit recognition. He is the one who demonstrates that reason would have to presuppose its validity in order to establish it. From that crucial concession philosophy moves toward an ever-deeper realization of reason as itself a part of the reality it investigates. Having previously forgotten its own being, reason now opens toward the horizon of being as such.

That is a formulation reminiscent of the thought of Martin Heidegger, whose own trajectory virtually repeats the transition. Beginning with the subjectivity of *Dasein* he came to see that existence could never provide the category of its own thinking about itself. The condition of the possibility of existence is that which does not exist because it simply is. *Sein* is the horizon of *Dasein*. But how *Dasein* might know *Sein* when it is constituted by it is one of the most puzzling questions in Heidegger's reflection. It is the central question around which his thought revolves, as it is for the whole transcendental movement launched by Kant.[5] Just as Wittgenstein grapples with the question of what language can say about itself, the results may be elusive, even inconclusive, but they cannot be regarded as incoherent. Heidegger may be on a track that is difficult to map, for it is being uncovered in the process of walking it, but that does not in any sense render it a figment. It is real because it is the reality of subjectivity. When thought thinks of itself, it no longer revolves within its own thought world but reaches toward the horizon of being. It was Parmenides, in Heidegger's judgment, who uttered the inceptional proposition of philosophy. To think and to be are the same (Fragment B 3). But what is the being that is the possibility of thought? How can it be thought? Heidegger well knew that the thinking of being is within the horizon of being, not within the horizon of thought alone. It is the stretching of thought beyond itself that is possible because thought moves beyond itself and being opens itself to the glimpse. It is the event in which meeting takes place. What cannot be met is encountered. This is where all of the paradoxical language of *Vom Ereignis*, the long withheld *Contributions to Philosophy*, is first fully employed.[6] The traces of that shift from talking about being to talking out of being would be enigmatically evident in the many exoteric writings of the succeeding years. But it was only with the eventual publication of *Vom Ereignis* that they could be properly deciphered. Then we would see that philosophy is precisely the accomplishment of the impossible. It says what cannot be said, the word of being that makes its saying possible.

All that is overlooked in the oracular pronouncement of being is the figure who undertakes it. Heidegger himself is missing from the Heideggerian philosophy. This explains the tone of apocalyptic detected by his most acute successors, who take note of the inflated self-importance present within it. Vanity even when not unjustified, perhaps most all then, remains vanity. It is the fatal misstep that leads a great thinker to presume his superiority to actual historical reality. Not only does this lead to the appalling misjudgments of the practical sphere that taint the name of Heidegger, but it can even contaminate the core of his philosophical project. If the latter is to be rescued, then it requires acknowledgment of what Heidegger fails to acknowledge. That is, that despite the world historic significance of his apprehension of being, as what cannot appear even as it opens the possibility of appearance, he remains a man within the world. Without a superior claim on reality he remains the servant of being. It is indeed the modesty of his own status that most profoundly guards the transcendence he reveals. In this respect he is no differently situated than any other human being. The shepherd of being remains a shepherd. It is precisely when he puts himself first, when he allows his own finitude to intrude on his message, that he most decisively betrays it. If the call of being means anything, it surely means that the one who responds has irrevocably put himself aside. Neither he nor his local cohort can emit any hint of self-aggrandizement. Being that transcends even appearance can be reached only by the readiness to transcend all appearance. Eternity definitively surpasses time. Nothing in time can represent it.

These are not necessarily new problems. Apocalypse has been on the boundary of revelation ever since the rupture of the transcendent intersection with time. What is new is the clarity, an almost unmistakable clarity, Heidegger has brought to bear on it, despite a readiness to deflect his own insight. Yet an inclination to betray an illumination does not in any way detract from its imperative. Rather, it sends us in search of what is missing in Heidegger's thought that would preserve it from the fate of self-distortion. Heidegger's failure to live up to the call of his illumination is emblematic of the failure of the great spiritual aspiration that defines modernity at its best. Impatience at the failure of justice has too often collapsed into an embrace of injustice as the means of securing justice. Mundane success became the measure of a call that is utterly beyond the mundane. In each case the crucial mistake had been to absolve the particular carrier of transformation from the necessity of submission to its imperative. Goodness could be short-circuited without the necessity of becoming good. The individual had ceased to live under the judgment he proclaimed. The absence of an ethics from Heidegger's thought has long been remarked, and the response he offered strangely unpersuasive, amounting to a kind of abdication of responsibility for holding one.[7] If one's allegiance is to the ground of ethics within the opening of being, then one would seem to bear an even greater responsibility. Responseability to being remains responsibility.

The latter was the path pursued by Heidegger's most penetrating successors, Levinas and Derrida. They were his deepest critics because they followed him by going beyond him. Levinas broke new ground by insisting that opening toward being requires a response to the call of the other that comes from beyond being. Heidegger's still contemplative priority is overtaken by the primacy of action that precedes it. Before there is even an I to open toward being, the face of the other is disclosed to me. The other is closer to me than I am to myself. The leisure of beholding has been taken from me by the urgency of the call that compels my response. Heidegger's prioritization of being to the self that opens has been transformed into the priority of the other whose need breaks in upon me. Being that is more me than my self is identical with the other who is more intimate to me than I am. In each case the I that contemplates has been shattered by the breakthrough from beyond. But where Heidegger's rupture of the primordial still permits a relaxation into the self, Levinas permits no such retreat. The ethics that had eluded Heidegger because it could not establish its priority within being has now gained that indefeasible status. Even the disclosure of being cannot eclipse the other who comes from before it. Being is the face of the other.[8] Ethics is prior to ontology, to use a favored formulation. The tradition that had always based practical reason on its theoretical foundations could now be secured, if still by no means universally, by the priority of the call of a practical imperative. There is no stepping outside of obligation. What has yet to be explained is how it is possible for me to recognize this. How can I know myself as the holder of an unlimited debt? It must surely have something to do with who I uniquely am, for no one can substitute for me in its discharge.

This is the aporia that Derrida zeroes in on in the Levinasian enlargement of being to the other. At first it is merely to point out that Levinas cannot even maintain the priority of the other without a corresponding extension of the understanding of language. The asymmetry of the other to me can hardly even be expressed unless we concede that all of our language is somehow incapable of performing its role. If the other is before I can even pronounce a name, then he also overturns the competence of naming. *Sauf le nom* is one of the reflections in which Derrida accomplishes this endless destabilization of the mastery the name seems to provide.[9] The title, playing on "save the name" and "except for the name," suggests that the name can be saved only by excepting it from being named. The other exceeds all language that might denote. This is more than a semiotic subversion of the claim of proper names to name what is proper to the person named. Derrida goes on to unfold the existential horizon within which the consequences must be lived out. He develops, for example, an elaborate account of hospitality as the relationship in which the host becomes hostage to the guest. What is owed to the other can never be sufficiently repaid since the only basis on which the relationship can exist is the admission that there is no point at which the claim of the other has been met. Something similar applies to the practice of giving that can never give sufficiently, no matter how much is given. Excessiveness is embedded in the relationship to the other before it has even begun. This is why Derrida turns increasingly toward the divine horizon in his later years, including Kierkegaard's meditation on Abraham's sacrifice of Isaac, as the only possible means of containing the impossible dynamic in which his thought unfolded.[10] He sensed, without fully conceding, that Kierkegaard was the one who had taken the fullest measure of the reorientation that the modern prioritization of being and the other thrusts upon us. Not only could the foundation of order no longer begin with the I, but even the possibility of claiming authorship of the works we pen was subverted.

Unlike Levinas, who hesitated to embrace the thought of Kierkegaard, possibly out of dislike for the decisionist reputation attached to it, Derrida displayed a far more uncomplicated admiration. He understood the convergence both in the style of literary self-distancing and in the existential purpose it served. Every text opens up the space of *différance* as the possibility from which it arises and is thus incapable of containing. Existence is irrevocably outside the text. Kierkegaard insisted that he was not the author of the works he had written because he was just as much the learner in the process. Writing is itself an opening of existence that occurs in no other way. Derrida's concept of *différance* carries this Kierkegaardian notion of the impossible possibility of writing, as he continually points to the aporias that infect every text. Deconstruction is precisely their reading in this light. Yet despite the increasing seriousness with which Derrida embraces the existential implications of this grammatological beginning, a deepening well attested by the religious turn in his last two decades, the full realization of the consequences eludes him. At best Derrida is serious about remaining unserious. Ironic self-distancing has not, in Kierkegaard's formulation, gone far enough to include itself. Then he would realize that there is no leisure to consider the aporias when one is in aporia. He is the text that must be written, for the deficiency of all written texts has been established. No writing can contain the author whose narrative must arise in living it out. Not even the estimable personal qualities of a Derrida, with his lifelong penchant for inserting himself into various social and political challenges, can reach the limit of complete self-giving. It may be that this has something to do with his inability to arrive at God, who alone could receive him completely. Without the God relationship, the self that can give and receive is hardly real. This is the culmination reached only by Kierkegaard.

Individual Exceeds Universal

The problem for deconstruction is that the semiotic shortfall that infects all communication seems to rebound on the subject, who must also fail to become present. Aporetic expression applies equally to the self that utters it. Neither the meaning nor the speaker acquires presence. What is overlooked is that this very analysis derives from a meaning and a self that are knowable despite their defectiveness. The condition of the possibility of deconstruction, as Derrida admitted, is that not everything can be deconstructed. Justice is such an unassailable measure.[11] Everything else can be seen as deviating from it but only because *it* cannot deviate. Skepticism concerning personal identity arises from our inability to denote an indubitable carrier of identity that is not itself simply imputed. Deep down there is nothing deep down, as our house nihilist, Richard Rorty, ruefully intoned. No matter how uneasy we may be about accepting the consequences of the view that we are nothing more than the contingent assembly of our parts, we have real difficulty in constructing an alternative. A metaphysical soul seems too remote a concept to be of any value. Certainly Kierkegaard has no use for it. His reflections head straight for the reality that is emergent in the whole process, for he knew that the soul or self was not a beginning but an end. It is not so much that we are in danger of losing our souls as we are in danger of not having them at all. The ethical life and the soul are correlative. It is by means of right living that we gain our souls, not in the sense of saving them, but of making them real. The ethical life is the attainment of the immortal.

But contrary to the conventional view, this has nothing to do with the future. It is a present reality. In fact, immortality is the condition of the possibility of acting well, as Kierkegaard made plain in *Either/Or*. The Seducer of Kierkegaard's "The Seducer's Diary" can scarcely even be named, for the web of deceptions occludes even his own identity. He etherealizes in concealment, deceiving even himself. Like Don Giovanni who dissolves in a welter of music, he continually modulates away from who he is. The condition of gaining a substantial presence in himself and in the world is, as Judge William demonstrates, the willingness to make a lifelong commitment. By contrast, the Seducer is incapable of the constancy that friendship requires. The point of Kierkegaard's meditation on the juxtaposition of character types is, however, not to denote them as the result of opposing choices. Either/Or are not the alternatives with which we are confronted but the possibility of choosing at all. In this sense the choice is not the arbitrary leap Kierkegaard is so notoriously thought to propose but the realization that nothing in time can overcome the inconstancy of time. Only eternity can save time from itself. This is what Judge William (both in *Either/Or* and *Stages on Life's Way*) explains in his discourse on marriage, a commitment that on its face carries no surety of its accomplishment. Indeed, everything seems to indicate its unreliability. What makes it possible for one moment to contain all the moments of a life is that we already stand outside the whole of existence. Kant was right in suggesting that free action begins in eternity, but he lacked the linguistic means of expressing it.[12] Kierkegaard found it in the exchange of wedding vows that would otherwise be a reckless leap into uncertainty, if it were not "signed in heaven, and then it is countersigned in temporality."[13] The translation of the man and woman into eternity is not an event ahead of them but the condition of binding their lives in mutuality. It is because they are capable of holding the whole of their lives in that moment that they can present it to one another. Marriage transcends the existence it makes possible.

In this way it brings to light the inner reality of every ethical action in which the character or ethos of a person comes into view. But this is not simply a reality to be observed from the outside, as the returning symposiasts of "In Vino Veritas" (in *Stages on Life's Way*) do in taking note of the domesticity of Judge William's house, for they cannot know what is going on within the inwardness of husband and wife. All they can know is that before a marriage has become a public phenomenon it must first have been conceived by its participants, who, strictly speaking, are not simply within the lives they are leading. Capable of comprehending the whole of their existence, they do not fully exist anywhere within it. Rather than dissolving into the multiplicity of their unfolding, they have emerged at the turning point that embraces it all. By taking responsibility, they have become the persons who transcend the temporality in which it is undertaken. If they had not instituted such a moment of encompassing commitment, they would not cease to be persons, but their hold on personhood would have become correspondingly attenuated. It is only by losing one's life that one saves it. Paradoxical language has traditionally been employed to convey what cannot so readily be conveyed, even though it is intuited universally. Kierkegaard understood this well, for he knew that it was paradox that held the whole movement together and permitted us to talk about it. The self that is gained in self-giving is clearly not the momentary self of our awareness.

It is a far more substantial reality. This is what Judge William knows most clearly, but it is only dimly grasped by Johannes the Seducer (from "The Seducer's Diary," in *Either/Or*). It is the latter who seeks to retain existence from a standpoint within it, to make the moment into a frozen instant of eternity. But the moment cannot be made to last, and the attempt to hold onto it results in losing even the fleeting enjoyment that marks the esthetic life. At least Don Giovanni did not make that mistake as he cast himself headlong into the exhilarating rush so perfectly depicted by Mozart's music. The Seducer is incapable of pleasure, consumed as he is by the need to prevent its passing. Judge William, by contrast, relishes the esthetic life because he has demonstrated his readiness to go beyond it. Without craving its pleasures he can affirm their reality. Instead of believing that the erotic finds its consummation, and thereby its collapse, in marriage, he is able to assert that it is marriage that provides the possibility of an erotic continuity. It is the institution outside of time that has made the unfolding of time possible. For this reason it cannot be entered into with a partial self. Nothing can be held in reserve as if providing an escape hatch. It is only if one has become the kind of person who can hold the whole of existence in one's hands that one's whole life can be bound. Then, and then alone, have you become the self that, although it exists nowhere within time, makes a lifetime possible. No doubt this is a highly paradoxical conception. It amounts to the claim that we are already at the end before we have set out on the journey. We have no mundane analogue for a transcendence that is prior to itself. But this is, Kierkegaard insists, where a steadfast conviction of the ethical leads us. It is in light of the eternal that our temporal existence is possible. Who we are is disclosed most profoundly in the ideality of our becoming it.

That is all we know, for Kierkegaard refuses to enlist the language of metaphysics that, since Kant, has become an extinct tongue.[14] Yet the problem of a metaphysics that foreswears metaphysics is that it is perpetually in danger of lapsing into solipsism. When nothing can be said, we are inclined to concede that nothing can be known. The great challenge is to hold onto permanence when it can no longer be assigned to permanent things. How can there be the identity of self or soul when we have conceded their unattainability? It is in rising to meet this challenge that the real greatness of Kierkegaard lies, for he not only recognized the nonviability of metaphysics but arrived at the horizon that had all along been its source. Existence cannot be comprehended along the lines of an alternative universe outside of the one we inhabit, but it must be understood as the unsurpassable boundary of the existence we continually unfold. In answering the question of where the anchor of that which cannot be anchored lies, the center of a centerless reality, he returns us to the only whole in which the whole can be contained: the person. This is the absence that has been present from the very beginning. All of the discussion of being and beings, of God and the soul and the whole furniture of ontology, has been carried on by persons who remain outside of what they say. Yet they are in no way ethereal or uncertain. Nothing could be more substantive than the person who endures beyond all the changes they undergo. Capable of containing it all, they are themselves uncontained. Indeed, they surpass the universal since they are capable of contemplating it. Persons are the ultimate particularities since each is unique and irreplaceable. Contrary to the prevailing notion that ideas of being, substance, or identity are necessary to comprehend the reality of persons, we realize that it is the reverse. Our metaphysical conceptions are derived from our self-knowledge as persons who somehow contain their own being and remain the same throughout all of the vicissitudes of their existence. We still do not have knowledge of that which makes our knowledge possible, but we do know it as what must be the case. To speak of this as the core of the person is always to suggest an identity that might be extracted, which is just what is impossible. The self that expresses itself is not the self that is expressed.

Kierkegaard may not have elaborated that focus on the inexpressibility of the person, but he did bring to light the inner dynamic that underlies it. Nothing can contain the person who contains all. This is the insight that makes him the true originator of the philosophic movement known as "personalism," but yet he is often not fully recognized within its genealogy. It is true that he does not use the term "person," preferring usually to talk about the "individual." This is among the most decisive concerns for the personalists, who understand the individual as what is interchangeable, the instance that can be duplicated elsewhere, while "person" signifies the unique and irreplaceable one that each of us is.[15] It is a crucial, if still not a widely embraced, distinction, in part because its philosophic significance has not been fully grasped. Even the relevance of the person to the discourse of being that dispenses with metaphysics has yet to be taken on board. But when those acknowledgments are duly made, the singular role of Kierkegaard becomes evident. He is the one who most thoroughly elaborates the interior movement by which in grasping the universality of the ethical life, the person not only gains a foothold in the eternal, but becomes indeed the substantial reality that is its indispensable concomitant. In making a lifetime commitment, one becomes more than one is. The self is the self who not only expresses itself but binds itself. Kant had earlier suggested the same in explaining moral action as the enactment of a universal maxim, for it has simultaneously enacted the self that is beyond the self. By thinking through the issue in individual cases, Kierkegaard made the eternity of the self an unmistakable theme.

Yet even that is not the summit of his achievement. There still remains the moment in which the eternity of the self is gained precisely as mine, not to be replaced by any other. The eternal must be contained nowhere but within the "I" that is invisible to the external world, for I have become the carrier of the whole. This is the disclosure of the horizon of the person within which Kierkegaard's thought unfolds. The obligation that is assumed in light of the eternal demand of duty must be made my own. Otherwise the ethical capacity to stand outside of all conceptions of the good to interrogate their goodness could become an evasion of responsibility. The arrow of obligation strikes home only when it has become my inescapable obligation from which I cannot turn aside. Without possibility of avoidance, I have become the uniquely responsible one. The meaning of the ethical life is that it can terminate only in the call that I alone can hear. Beyond the question of whether what is proposed is good, is the question as to whether it is intended for me. Have I been called before the judgment seat? In asking about the good I am simultaneously asked by it. The voice of conscience is ultimately not my voice. It reaches me from the Other who is more within me than I am myself. What makes Kierkegaard the great navigator of inwardness is that he brings out the full weight of this realization. Thought can never dispense with the self within which it arises. But what imparts to that momentary self the realization that it is far more consequential than its present emergence is that it has been called forth by that which is beyond all emergence. The command of God is what secures the eternity of the self. I know who I am within the unsurpassability of the call. It is in this way that the self exists beyond itself as that which shares in the eternity of God. The God relationship is the horizon of the person.

God Relationship as the Horizon of the Person

The person is affirmed as a person. There is no greater metaphysical reality or more deeply disclosed core. It is the God relationship that constitutes the horizon of the person. This is the realization that made Kierkegaard a religious thinker. He could not speak on behalf of religion, for that would be to claim its authority, an authority of which he himself was just as much in need. The *Upbuilding Discourses*, his most religious works and published under his own name, were written in the knowledge that he too stood just as much in need of upbuilding. His original plan of writing pseudonymously as a way of disguising the religious perspective of his authorship suffered an ironic reversal when he discovered that he could not so easily jettison the arrangement. When Kierkegaard came to write in his own voice, he discovered that it was premature to claim what such authorship implied. It would be tantamount to speaking for God. At best, he could aspire toward the divine perspective on things. How indeed can we speak of God when it is the God relationship that is the horizon of our existence? This was the staggering implication of his displacement of metaphysics with religion, a displacement that the unfolding of metaphysics had made inexorable. Terminologically, "religion" and "metaphysics" effect their own overturning since they render external what can only be grasped from within. But the deeper issue is that no one can claim mastery of what is of God. When the substance of our existence turns, not on the achievement of moral heroism, but on the impossibility of measuring up to a relationship that utterly exceeds it, then there is no possibility of reaching a vantage point from which it can be comprehended. The best we can say is that "in relation to God we are always in the wrong."[16] When the God relationship constitutes the core of our existence it cannot be pronounced. This is an insight, not only into religious language, but into the inaccessibility of that by which we are constituted. The innermost can never be said.

It can, however, be shown. The poetic presentation that Kierkegaard thought would be a stage eventually left behind turned out to say more deeply what could not be said. Nowhere was this more the case than in the meditation that even at the time he knew would make his name immortal, *Fear and Trembling*. Abraham's sacrifice of Isaac was the story that brought the God relationship into focus because it departed so radically from the ethical universal. What was Abraham to hold onto when he could no longer hold onto the imperative of duty, the duty above all of preserving his son? The episode not only unhinges our connection with duty but makes it clear that it never was so firmly established. It had always been up to us to maintain it. The duty of following duty remained our responsibility.[17] Nothing could determine that inexplicable free initiative that arises from we know-not-where. Often, accomplishment of duty is as much of a surprise to us as it is to the rest of the world. We do not know what we are capable of, good or bad, before we have undertaken it. Freedom is unfathomable. This is the abyss that all moral philosophy had sought to avoid, preferring to take refuge in talk about nature, sentiment, or inclination. Almost anything might occupy the ontic black hole so long as it saved us from contemplating it. Whatever ground is attributed to goodness, we can always ask whether it too is good. Indeed, ever since Plato first turned our thought to the good as the highest, this has been the ominous threat at the heart of our philosophical reflection. Is the good itself good? Now it can no longer be avoided. This was the crisis that hung over the modern understanding of morality as it became apparent that the questioner stands outside of the good. But unlike Nietzsche, Kierkegaard did not despair of arriving at an answer. Despite his reputation as an existentialist, for whom nothing is higher than the decision of the moment, he had found his way through to what is beyond existence. It was the relationship to God that secures the individual who "exceeds the universal."

Beyond universal law are the individuals who enact it. They continually exceed it, not only in the generosity that goes beyond what the law requires, but in the impossibility of anything determining their freedom in advance of its exercise. Kant shows more than a glimpse of this in his marveling at the impossibility of anything determining the will to action but the will itself. Nothing stands higher in his estimation than a good will. What he did not contemplate is how such a good will might contemplate itself. What could preserve it from the abyss of arbitrariness that its supremacy seemed to open before it? It would have to find a way of putting itself aside so that no hint of superiority could taint its devotion to the good, no whiff of self-approval mar its impeccability. To accomplish this, something more than self-restraint is required, for there must be nothing of self left in its actions. That can occur only if the place of the self is entirely occupied by the other. It is relationship to the other that holds it decisively away from itself. Now action springs from the other, from the priority of the other, rather than from the self. That priority becomes all-encompassing only when the other encompasses the whole of the self. This is preeminently the case of the God relationship, the One who calls on us to respond with nothing less than the whole self. Even in the call of others, it is God who calls on us to respond with complete self-giving. It may indeed seem paradoxical to suggest that the solitary individual on whom the entire burden of responsibility rested is now profoundly displaced. Yet that is what has occurred, and it is Kierkegaard's genius to have grasped what the modern elevation of freedom requires. Freedom must be prepared to go beyond itself. Only then is it free, when not even a regard for freedom itself stands in the way. By ceasing to be a self it becomes a self most completely. Rather than hold onto its identity, the self must be prepared to transcend it. When we ask where then does it exist, we can only say that it exists solely within itself. Inwardness is the mode in which the self has already gone beyond itself.

To erect freedom on this singular foundation of relationship to the other is of course to anticipate the course of philosophy up to the present. We have scarcely even reached the point at which he seemed to arrive. This is because we lack the conceptual means of explaining to ourselves how the one who has given away the most *is* most all. It seems contrary to the law of being, certainly to the economy of loss and gain. Only in the economy of relationship does it make any sense. But then it remains invisible to the external world since relating is only possible in inwardness. External expression may be a way of marking it, but that remains an external marking. Nothing of the reality that transpires can be accessed from outside. Only those who are prepared to enter into the relationship can know what it is and what it contains. This has always been known within the history of revelation, even if it could not withstand the inclination to think that we could nevertheless find an external measure. To Kierkegaard this was the problem of Christendom, the enduring misconception by which the Church armed for its defense without realizing it had thereby lost what was worth defending. In the logic of relationship, loss is gain and gain is loss. Those who love cannot be deceived, nor can they lose. The self has so completely been displaced that there is not even a self to calculate the cost. Each has exceeded itself and installed the other in its place. They are in one another. Containing one another inwardly, they hardly exist in the realm of the external, for only traces of what they have left behind remain. But the whole possibility of self-transcendence is that there is an other to whom the self can give itself. This is why the God relationship is so foundational. It is the relationship that includes all other relationships. God is the guarantee of mutuality when the mutuality of others has not even been disclosed. Openness is already there because it is the openness of God. He is the one who is present in the relationship to every other, not as a universal principle, but as the one who enfolds them more fully than they do one another. Mutuality is of God.

The inwardness by which we hold all others is a participation in the inwardness of God. It is because we share in the divine inwardness that we can relate to one another inwardly. Within marriage this occurs without the partners realizing they have thereby become selves that can only hold one another in inwardness. It is only when they transcend even their relationship that they realize that they are marked by the God relation. Each holds the whole of being within him- or herself because there is nothing that may not be asked of them. By going beyond the finite each has become the infinite to whom God can give himself. This is the identity of the self that no longer seeks to preserve its identity. It is in the God relation that it has most truly become an "I." In asking the question of every instance of the good whether it is good, the self has only dimly begun to realize what it is. That is, that the self is in every instance the one whose responsibility for the good surpasses every instance of the good. No instantiation of the good will be sufficient to extinguish the demand for even more goodness. The partners in the marriage who enact an unconditional commitment had not quite realized what this entailed. Not only are they capable of containing the whole of their existence in that moment, but they are also incapable of containing the whole of their existence in that instant. Nothing can contain them.

The condition of the possibility of the ethical life is that the partners in relationship bear an unconditional responsibility toward it. They can be bound by the ethical because they stand outside of its bounds. It is their capacity to relate to the infinite, the God relation, that discloses who they are. Nothing they do sufficiently measures up to what has been required of them. Even marriage is not a finite commitment, one they might eventually discharge as one might amortize a debt. Rather they have entered upon a debt that mounts continually. Even when the partners hold one another through their finite actions, they are themselves held in an infinite relation that remains their true reality. Nowhere visible in the external world, they have begun to disclose their infinity. It is only in their relation to the infinite, the God relation, that they can perceive who they really are. The unconditionality of their commitment arises from the unconditioned in which they exist. It is the God relation, the relation to the One who may require more than they are prepared to give, that defines who they are. That is, as persons who must always be prepared to be more than they are.[18] Excessiveness is not only a possibility but the very ground of their possibility. The self that may claim its substance is always eclipsed by the self that is called to surrender it. Responsibility means the impossibility of limiting responsibility in advance. That is the unattainable self, the self of the God relation, that Kierkegaard so unfailingly targets. It is not only that the individual exceeds the universal but the universal continually points to its own overcoming.

This is why it is silence that marks the knight of faith. Nothing can be said for nothing can convey what must be held inwardly. The case of Abraham fascinated Kierkegaard because he so perfectly exemplified the pure inwardness of the God relation. Not even the law could become a means of externalizing it. God had commanded him even to go against the law, or at least to demonstrate he was prepared for that extreme. The greatness of Kierkegaard's account is that he respects the impenetrability of inwardness. We do not perceive Abraham's experience. For us the externality of the poetic is the only means of glimpsing what occurs. Even less can we penetrate it from the side of God. We do not know why God issued such a command, a "teleological suspension of the ethical" that sails dangerously close to overturning it. All we know is that Abraham did not take offense. His heart did not rebel against the divine command or presume to measure it in his own finite judgment. He simply yielded and thereby became the knight of faith. When all was lost he resolved to hold fast to the call that he alone could hear. He could not even cling to the law that had all along been synonymous with the voice of God. Yet it was not the voice of God, who may call on us to act differently. But what did that mean, "a teleological suspension of the ethical"? The paradoxical formulation—since the ethical is the teleological—is a way of acknowledging the penultimacy of the ethical. Beyond it is the One who is its source. Nothing is higher than the personal relationship to God. Teleology points beyond itself.

Whether God will require the abrogation of the teleological is not for us to know. He could command the impossible and we have no assurance against it, except for the assurance of faith. This is what above all, on Kierkegaard's reading, characterizes Abraham. He is the knight of faith. He trusts that God will not require what God has required of him, to kill his own son in whom the promise of his descendants is contained. Yet nothing provides a ground for that faith, nothing, that is, but God himself. The God whom Abraham knows would not require it of him. He might require that sacrifice of himself, but not of Abraham. Indeed he *would* require it of himself before he would require it of Abraham. Toward Abraham it would only be one more gesture of the love that wishes to draw him near but can scarcely risk its disclosure, lest it overwhelm him. The love that cannot be expressed can only be inwardly embraced. That is the life of faith. Faith is the inwardness that holds fast to the inwardness of God.[19] It is not a holding of beliefs, of propositions, but of the other who is beyond them. This is why no one can substitute for another, for each must enter personally into the relationship. God cannot be known in any other way. Everything else can be known through the mastery that knowledge provides, but the person can only be known through the unmastery by which each cedes place to the other. Personal knowledge is the knowledge of personal uniqueness. The whole can only be known as a whole, as it is in itself.

It is through faith that Abraham opens the whole of his existence to God and receives the whole of God in return. Neither side holds anything back. When we ask what it is that God reveals to Abraham, we can only say that he reveals his heart. That is, he reveals nothing or at least nothing that we could say. The revelation of God has no content, for any content would merely be something more about God. It would not be God himself. That which expresses is inexpressible. Even the divine call, the divine instruction, contains the specific. But how we know it is from God cannot be explained except by knowing God. Only one who knows God can hear the command and follow it out. Faith is that heart knowledge. It is through faith that Abraham reached it. From the beginning it was faith that led him to trust in God who already revealed himself in the first prompting of faith. By following the path of faith Abraham would arrive at the disclosure of God as the God who can only be known by faith. That is, as the God who can only be known in himself. To say that this is mystical is to use a term that Kierkegaard disliked, for it suggests that it is secret or hidden, but it is indeed open and available. Abraham may not have been able to say what he knew of God, but he did know God. That was enough, for nothing could authenticate the message more truthfully than God himself. God is the message. Faith is its reception. The invitation to open toward it is the path of faith that Abraham followed in order to arrive at the God who had issued the invitation. He became the knight of faith because he showed that faith is the opening through which every individual can gain all by surrendering all. By responding to the call he became the individual who stood outside the whole. He had definitively surpassed the substance of his ethical identity.

To arrive at a theoretical penetration it would be necessary to go beyond Kierkegaard's focus on the individual (*den enkelte*), a term that already arises from the discourse of beings. If the individual bearing of responsibility is to become a paradigm of being beyond beings, then it would have to reach for the language of the person. The person is already what is not in being because it is the mask (*prosōpon*) or persona through which it appears. This is how it can grasp what is beyond being. Beyond all that is said or done is the person who is never reducible to what is said and done. It is for this reason that the person bears responsibility. The "beyond being" is thus not a vague aspiration toward what cannot be said, but the quite concrete reality in which the person is. We know it through the experience of living within it, but there is no "it" apart from the reality of the person. When we think about such categories as substance, that which endures beyond the changes it undergoes, the suppositum of accidents, it is the durability of the person that is the controlling paradigm. This is not the soul or psyche or "I" in any empirical or specific sense, for they too can be interrogated as to who the person is. The possibility of asking who a person is derives not only from the inexhaustibility of the person, but much more fundamentally from the unique totality that the person is. We know the person beyond all that the person presents as appearance, for the person cannot simply be in the appearance. The very meaning of the mask is that it is held by that which is not mask. This is not an abstraction, but the concrete truth that each one of us is. My call to responsibility is the voice of God who, beyond the law, calls me to be uniquely responsible. No one else can take my place, for it exists nowhere but within the call. Responsibility is not located in being but rather being within responsibility.

That is what Kierkegaard saw, even if he did not fully elaborate it within the language of the person. He not only called our attention to the personal dimension of all thought but realized that it is the personal that is the horizon of thought. All thinking begins within the movement by which I assume responsibility for it. To say that all that we do or say is a mode of existence suggests that it might be assimilated to some general pattern of reality. But that is to overlook the extent to which the "I" that attends has stepped outside of what occupies its attention. I can attend precisely because I am not within it. The individual exceeds the universal and yet is not dispersed as if it were universal. By embracing all, I affirm that I am even more the unique one. Nothing and no one can take my place. This is the point at which the language of being has been eclipsed, just as it is the place where the incomprehensibility of the unique has erupted. Yet that defeat of generality has not rendered it inaccessible, for it has been transcended by the leap of the personal beyond it. What cannot be said can be grasped. Persons know one another as persons outside the boundaries of the universal to which they are assimilated. We know one another as unique others, without any science to explain it. That is the horizon of all communication between us even though it cannot be included within any horizon. The indispensable cannot be contained. It is the "I" that can assume responsibility for the whole because it is somehow the whole of reality. That is how God addresses us, as it is also the way that we turn to God. Without intermediaries we encounter one another as utterly unique. There can be no danger of forgetting or losing ourselves in that encounter, since it revolves around the impossibility of avoiding the whole that each of us is. Even without fully embracing the language of the person, Kierkegaard had hit upon its most central feature. Each person is the whole of being. By assuming sole responsibility each one stands outside the whole of being. Those who know this already think within the horizon of the person.

PART 3

The Historical Discovery

CHAPTER TWELVE

Epic as the Saving Truth of History
Solzhenitsyn's *Red Wheel*

If we think of revolution as the force that has shaped and continues to shape our world, then the response of an artist of Solzhenitsyn's caliber to its cataclysmic effect is surely of the first importance. That is why *The Red Wheel* is a project of more than Russian significance. Not only did the effects of the Russian Revolution wash over peoples far removed from it in space and time, but it remained the emblematic instance of apocalyptic transformation that has haunted politics in the modern era. If our politics perpetually begins in upheaval, then the Russian Revolution is its epitome. The French Revolution may have been the decisive destruction of the old aristocratic order, but the Russian Revolution is the point at which the messianic transformation of society and history is inaugurated. The titanic drive of modernity is sent forth in all its limitless ambition. How art can sit in judgment over such a shattering overwhelming event is one of the most interesting question raised by Solzhenitsyn's project. It can do so only by dint of the fairness of its comprehensive judgment.

Solzhenitsyn would have to show that he has pondered the sources, influences, and emphases more deeply and sympathetically than all of the alternative accounts. Within that immersion in the pathos of revolution, he would have to draw up the principles by which actions and events would be judged. Such principles must come from the participants themselves in all of their far-flung but inescapably shared responsibility. The artist cannot evoke an authority outside of his or her subject matter. This is what makes such a formidable opponent, as Solzhenitsyn demonstrated in his own life. The calf carries no other weapon but the crunching impact of his own skull in butting the oak.[1] But what a power that turns out to be, for art contains the possibility of surpassing the reality on which it operates. Real revolution, it seems to say, is a largely inward event, for the artist has effected just such a transformation in our understanding of the convulsion that had seemed to overwhelm us. We see it all in a new light. And in that light we glimpse the only possibility of a new life, if there is to be a new life. It is widely recognized that Solzhenitsyn was one of the great prophetic voices of our time, but how he managed to exercise that role through his literary work is far less well understood. In particular, we must ask how his greatest project, *The Red Wheel*, functions as the evocative epic of our age.

We begin by confronting the greatest challenge that any account of history must overcome: Can there be any stable account of what happened that is not itself overtaken by the continuing shifts of historical perspective? Is every account of history historically relative? Is truth accessible from within history? Here the contrast with Tolstoy, first, brings out the greater philosophical awareness of Solzhenitsyn's project. Once that most fundamental question of historical truth is addressed, we can then explore, second, the literary heightening of truth that goes beyond a mere historiographic narrative. Solzhenitsyn's conception of historical "knots" is of particular importance in this regard, but it will be considered within the wider development of his juxtapositional form throughout *The Red Wheel*. It is that form that makes possible, third, the realization that the epic is the point at which history itself is transcended. Historical action attains its significance when it has emerged as of more than historical significance. It is in the light of eternity that history is illumined. Art is particularly well equipped to reveal that perspective because it aims at its own eternal truth. But historiography too partakes of the same framework of relevance as it reaches toward the form of the historical epic. The account of history cannot be separated from responsibility for it. If the epic is written from the standpoint of our continuity with the past, then it imposes on us a responsibility for the future.

Is a Truth of History Possible?

The construction of a historical narrative is in its very nature fraught with the question of its truth. By suggesting a perspective on events that was not available to the participants, we already cast uncertainty on our own application of a perspective. What is it that makes our perspective so superior that it will not be overtaken by later events and subsequent historians? Is an account of history anything more than a subjective viewpoint destined to be succeeded by other equally partial accounts? Surely none of us escapes the limitations of our setting within history that prevent us from comprehending its order as a whole. We cannot perceive the part we play within a grander plan. This was the problem that so preoccupied Tolstoy in *War and Peace* that he felt compelled to append an epilogue on the philosophical conundrum of freedom and necessity. If there is a great historical purpose at work unknown to its participants, then this surely means that their conviction of acting freely is an illusion. Even framing a historical narrative serves to reinforce the conception of a pattern of causality within which individual freedom counts very little. Explanation is sought, Tolstoy insisted, in terms of forces larger than particular persons. History itself "moves" from west to east and back again with an inexorability that individuals, even leaders, were incapable of resisting. How else could the narrative be framed? Conceived as a series of wholly free choices, the account could scarcely hang together as anything more than a random concurrence. Particular actions are intelligible only when seen as part of a wider pattern that reduces individual variance to irrelevance. The problem is that once we depart from that individual perspective, we have no means of comprehending the actions and events at all. Even the historian who imposes a putatively higher viewpoint on the events, who perceives a pattern where none was perceived before, has no certainty that the preferred configuration is itself ultimate. The provisionality of every historical perspective seems inescapable.

This was the great insight of Tolstoy, who declared it impossible to reach any definitive grasp of historical significance: "Only by renouncing the claim to knowledge of an ultimate aim immediately intelligible to us, and admitting the ultimate purpose to be beyond our comprehension, may we discern the logical consistency and expediency of the lives of historical personages."² Inscrutable divine providence is the limit beyond which we cannot penetrate, even though we may be able to reach evermore comprehensive surmises as to the pattern of the whole. The ultimate whole remains beyond our reach. In this respect modern historians have not surpassed their ancient predecessors, who attributed to the gods the directive role in the affairs of men. But in another sense, the moderns are inferior in thinking they have understood history as the outcome of leaders' intentions and abstract forces: "Modern history has rejected the beliefs of the ancients without providing a new conception to replace them; and then the logic of the situation has obliged the historians . . . to come by another path to the same conclusion: the recognition (1) that nations are guided by individual men, and (2) that a goal exists toward which humanity and those nations are moving."³ In essence, the historians are no better off than the participants, who are drawn by an inexorability they can neither discern nor resist. To underline the inevitability at work is hardly to comprehend it. It is indeed to submit to it, as the inevitable condition of developing a historiographic account.

The only difficulty with this familiar Tolstoyan elevation of fate is that it cannot be sustained, for its formulation undermines it. Once fate is acknowledged to be irresistible, a beachhead of resistance has already been established. One cannot simultaneously declaim against our imprisonment within the unbreakable chain of causality, as Tolstoy does in his epilogue, and at the same time think that this thought itself is the one instance of pure liberation. The answer to the undergraduate essay topic of free will versus determinism is to recognize that the question has already resolved itself. Freedom is the only perspective of thought. It cannot therefore be put in question. When he enters upon his great literary exploration of war and peace, this is precisely what Tolstoy demonstrates. Whatever "history" is, there is no point at which the freedom of human beings has been completely eradicated. Even when circumstances have severely circumscribed the options remaining, human beings still retain the inextinguishable freedom of how they are to regard them. It is this enduring capacity for a response that in many respects constitutes the enduring interest of history. We may be powerless to redirect the course of events, but we never lose the power to accept or oppose them. As our interest is drawn toward that most decisive of all levels, the interior of the human soul, the source from which freedom springs, we begin to suspect that history is not about external events at all, or at least not ultimately. This is the conclusion reached by Tolstoy when he is guided by his art rather than by half-baked fragments of philosophy. When pressed to pierce the meaning of the events that overwhelm them, his heroes move inexorably toward the perspective that transcends history. Prince Andrei in the operating tent glances over at a man whose leg has just been amputated and recognizes Anatol Kuragin. The encounter brings back a flood of memories through which Andrei sees clearly what is really real: "Compassion, love for our brothers, for those who love us, and for those who hate us, love for our enemies—yes, that is the love which God preached on earth, and which Princess Marya tried to teach me and I did not understand; that is what remained for me had I lived. But now it is too late. I know it."[4]

The truth of history, despite the determinism Tolstoy cannot quite shake off, bursts through as a truth beyond history. In that moment the whole of history is illumined by a perspective that rises definitively above it. What happens in history, and therefore the varying perspectives it presents depending on our vantage point within it, fades in significance compared to the one point toward which all of history strains. It turns out that the meaning of events and patterns is no more than provisional, for they may lead to consequences that remain unforeseen. Good can come from evil and evil from good. But what cannot change is the truth of good and evil as such. The judgment under which history exists does not await an apocalypse that brings it to an end. It is the revelation under which history is enacted in every moment. When we narrate the course of history, we do so in the form of a series of intersections of the timeless with time. Despite the impression that we are describing a flow of events, we are really stepping outside of them to glance over the whole. Historiography is in this sense not historical. It is itself one of the timeless moments from which the course of things can be apprehended. The project appears self-defeating only if we immerse the narration of history within the sequence itself. Then it seems destined to be overtaken by later developments. But what even makes it possible to describe what has happened is that we can have recourse to a perspective that transcends history. At their core the actions of human beings are moral events; they are not simply the unconscious motions of automatons. We may not be able to embrace the furthest ramification of the Czar's abdication, but we are able to recognize it as the moral failure that it was. Historiography is possible because neither we nor the participants exist wholly within history. It is rather the case that we make history and remember it by virtue of the inexorable judgment under which all equally stand. Historical recollection breaks down only when we assume that it must lead toward a viewpoint definitively unavailable to those who made history.

Once the search for the meaning of history has been abandoned, then the meaning of the events within history can be explored. The question of the truth of the historical narrative does not then depend on our reaching a comprehensive account of all that has happened. It turns on our recognition that there is no higher viewpoint than the perspective of eternity from which history is judged. What happens in history matters much less than what outweighs every historical outcome. It is the relationship to what is beyond history that marks the line of meaning within history. Of course, the events that are memorable are the ones that produce enormous consequences within history, but their meaning is not exhausted by that long train of effects they set in motion. Nor can we disdain the largely minor incidents simply because the fruit they bear appears to be more modest on the world scene. History is composed of the great and the small events such that they mutually illumine one another. Selection of historical events is indeed the task of the historiographer, and this entails a judgment of significance in light of what is known about the subsequent course of events. The Napoleonic Wars and the Russian Revolution each constitute such meaningful units within history. But even the most comprehensive treatment can scarcely account for the profound moral impulses, for good and bad, that have shaped the historical pattern itself. Historical explanation stops at the level of causal factors but shies away from what renders them decisive in that particular instance. This was the difficulty Tolstoy sensed in the glib assignment of causes by modern historians. Yet he was unable to explicate the deeper intuition (which nevertheless guided his artistic construction) that no causal analysis could ever account for what lies beyond the control of causality. At issue in history is always how we are to stand in relation to causes or objective factors. Is history the effect of social forces, economic motives, the vainglory of leadership, or anything else without our ceding responsibility to them? How indeed could the historian account for moral growth or decline when he or she is equally liable before the same imperatives? There is finally no historical perspective apart from the perspective from which history is made. The epic is the appropriate form of historical recollection because it eschews the distance of the professional historian to acknowledge what even the latter is compelled to concede. That is, that the author and the community for which he or she writes belong to the same moral universe.

The artist is for this reason freed from the burden of explanation and can therefore turn to the illumination of the spiritual horizon within which human beings enact their historical existence. The writing of history too does not escape the imperative of moral responsibility. The only difference is that the artist must include the warrant of truth within the work itself. Professional historians are validated by the confirmation echoed by their professional peers, and only secondarily by the consensual judgment of the society for which they write. Art never places itself above the material it explores but rather finds its voice within the work itself. When it succeeds, art can therefore function as the representative account of the community itself. It is the voice neither of God nor of impersonal forces of reality, but remains the voice of a human being who has miraculously discovered a resonance with others, perhaps all others. Art is in this sense an ideal medium for moral exploration because it neither preaches nor teaches. Instead, it radiates and it sings of what is memorable as such. It thereby furnishes the truth by which its own achievement is to be judged. There is no need of higher authority or external validation, for they too would stand in need of authentication. Art in this way exemplifies the deepest meaning of history as the eternal presence, the timeless moment, in which we are all contemporaries, none with a superior insight. The later in time do have the benefit of a more extended contemplation of the course of historical consequences, but this scarcely affords any advantage in respect to the moral fidelity or failure that is most deeply at issue. Virtue remains the measure of all human beings, just as Homer understood in elevating it to the central place in the epics. How men live counts for more than what they accomplish. In the end it is that acknowledgment, shared by the poet, that elevates the truth of the poem above a flatly historical account, which may aim at something similar but is less surely guided by the moral principles that measure the historical reality it contemplates.

Literary Heightening of Truth

If the role of art is to show the truth it cannot say, because it too is governed by the same truth, then the literary form must reflect this inescapable continuity. The author is no longer the undisputed master of the material presenting the definitive viewpoint from which it is all comprehended. Tolstoy understood that this was the fatal defect of the professional historian for whom history unfolded toward his own idiosyncratic vantage point. Yet despite the polemic Tolstoy conducted against this specialist genre, he never succeeded in finding the literary form that would disrupt it. Despite his best efforts, his own authorial voice drifted toward that imperious perspective. His fascination with the great men of history, Napoleon and Tsar Aleksandr, belied his denunciation of great men explanations. It was only when he allowed himself to enter the interior life of his characters that their transcendence of all historical forces comes into view. Each is irreducibly a center of history in his or her enactment of responsibility for the course of events in which they are engaged. It is only indirectly therefore that we glimpse an account of history that Tolstoy is never fully able to admit to himself: that history is the realm in which, for all of the powerful collective influences at work, individuals remain free to define their response to the challenges that confront them. No explanation for their decisions that seeks to aggregate them under some objective logic can surpass the inescapable moral responsibility by which they must explain them to themselves. How can anything within history interpret the exercise of responsibility that is greater than all of history? A very different literary form would be required to contemplate the historical sweep in which every human being is an irreplaceable center of history. This realization is what distinguishes Solzhenitsyn's *Red Wheel*.

The historical novel already contains within it the seeds of its own evolution into the historical epic in which author and characters occupy the same realm of truth. When characters become the means of probing historical truth, of plumbing the moral depth from which historical events arise, then it is only a matter of time before such multiple individualities surpass the narrative movement. What can narrative add to the acceptance or betrayal of obligation? This diminished role of narrative is surely what accounts for the juxtapositional form that Solzhenitsyn favors in *The Red Wheel*. Narrative has not entirely disappeared, but now it is confined within the respective episodes. It is no longer the voice that seems in control of the account as a whole, capable of guiding us because it has comprehended the unfolding from beginning to end. Now the narrative is itself embedded in the incidents by which the wheel rolls. We do not even have access to the movement in any continuous sense but are instead drawn into the knots in which its most intense self-revelations take place. What is the Russian Revolution as Solzhenitsyn conceives it? If we are to take seriously his original project of a work with up to twenty knots, we realize that the revolution is a series of events whose boundaries are not easily demarcated. Even the very scale of the work suggests something of the challenge it presented to the author. He was willing to risk the weariness of readers for the sake of remaining true to the upheaval that overflows all possibility of a narrative unity. But this is not to suggest that the sheer abundance of materials overwhelmed the author. Solzhenitsyn is far too deliberate in his approach to the defining enterprise of his life for this to be the case. The careful elaboration of incidents, along with the manifold variety of literary techniques, are too well considered for them to be the result of anything but a deep estimation of their significance. Besides, we have the main structural device of knots to confirm that the principle is the self-interpretation of history. They are the culminating moments when all of the elements at work have come into view.

In essence, the knots are the narrative. Assimilating them to the homogeneity of a narrative would rob them of their irruptive effect. Solzhenitsyn evidently did not want them reduced to the uniform level of significance that is the inevitable smoothing effect of a narrative. All that occurs, such monotone expositions seem to say, has found its place within the omniscience of the narrator. In *The Red Wheel*, both author and reader occupy the same level, as shaken witnesses of shattering events. No doubt the episodic heightening of the drama lends considerable interest to the account. But there is something more than a mere literary device at work. The knots are a fundamental structural form for the conception of history, or at least for the history of "R-17." History, they seem to say, is punctuated by irruptions in which the meaning of what is taking place bursts on the scene. Time continues at its ordinary pace, but for the participants it intermittently seems to slow down in order to process the vast new developments it is bringing forth. Or it may seem suddenly accelerated in the multiplicity of events taking place that seem to far exceed the transactions of a more routine timeframe. At any rate, the knots are those compressed periods in which the momentous transpires. What is happening in history becomes manifest.[5] The connections between widely scattered fragments are unexpectedly revealed and the direction of the historical epoch aligns its focus. The truth of events is grasped. History has interpreted itself. This is why there is no need for a narrator, for there is no curtain to be thrown back when history has performed its own denouement. The author recedes to the status of an observer, little different from the reader before whom the whole is unfolded. Yet the withdrawal of the author must not be mistaken for absence. He is the one who has assembled the dizzying succession of scenes. His judgment and skill have brought their components together, an achievement that is all the more impressive for the degree to which his creation can function without him. In letting history speak for itself, he identifies with Kierkegaard's remark in the *Upbuilding Discourses*, that he has been as much the learner as the author.[6]

Authorial recession is a familiar means of establishing the truth of what is said. It is what underpins the polyphonic novel so favored by Dostoevsky, by which the center of action is carried forward not by one particular hero but instead by a succession of characters each presenting their own unique perspective. The result is a polyphony of voices in which the absence of a dominant presence precludes the possibility of identifying any one of them with that of the author. He is strangely absent from his own creation. Instead, the author risks the defeat of his own cherished convictions by insisting that truth emerges from a clash of perspectives without any predetermined outcome. Dostoevsky notoriously worried about this juxtaposition in which his own convictions might lose out. Yet it was a risk he thought worth taking for the sake of the authoritative establishment of truth. What emerged from the winnowing of positions would stand without need of authorial support. This notion of the truth of "living life" is one that Solzhenitsyn readily embraced in his novels.[7] He knew and appreciated the polyphonic approach. One suspects that Solzhenitsyn understood that all writing is polyphonic, for the author's voice cannot be carried by any of the characters he creates. They are needed precisely because none of them can say what he aims at saying. Only the text as a whole comes close to what has been intended. Even then there remains the endless possibility of extending it, a prospect Solzhenitsyn seems to have contemplated in the even more voluminous projections of *The Red Wheel* he had considered. The finitude of the human life span, and, possibly, a merciful regard for the overburdened reader, imposed a limit on the work. Yet the central idea of polyphony remains in the principle of the knots. History revolves around multiple epiphanies, which it is the duty of the author to treat as comprehensively as possible. History is studded with apocalyptic breakthroughs.

The whole is contained in the part or, rather, in the moment that reflects the whole. But this is because the whole is nowhere present. No account, no matter how comprehensive, can do justice to history as a whole. We are left then with the moments when its innermost truth flashes forth and they are each indispensable, for none of them contains the whole. Our only access to the meaning of the whole is in those precious glimpses when it comes into view. Narrative that seems to parallel the stream of historical time somehow fails to capture what is decisive, for it reduces everything to the one homogeneous level. But that is not the time in which we live. It is not that of the calendar or the clock. Instead the time of existence and of its memory bursts ecstatically with what it contains, often with such intensity that the outburst cannot be confined within any of the forms toward which it radiates. Within the knots all of the forces at work have reached their highest intensity, but in such a way that they can no longer be held together. They must fly apart. The knots are the moments when history has leapt outside of itself. Participants and observers have become contemporaries in that ecstatic leap by which they have left the steady beat of the narrative far behind. Now all that matters is inescapably laid bare. The way that things are has become inescapably clear because it stands revealed in the light of an eternal judgment. That is what fixes the knots as the moments of arrested time. They are the points at which we see plainly that history does not occur in time, our everyday impression to the contrary notwithstanding, but within the irrefutable light of moral truth. Above all, the knots are the moral epiphanies of history, but not epiphanies the author has constructed. They are the flashes by which the author brings together the disparate threads that hold everything fast.

Everything works toward that leap of insight by which connections are grasped that scarcely exist at the level of chronology. This is why fictional characters must be invented to supplement what history has supplied. Such a man is Colonel Vorotyntsev, the energetic and brilliant staff officer who plays such a prominent but ineffectual role in the first knot, *August 1914*, and remains a recurrent presence throughout the cycle. We recall that the same Vorotyntsev was a character in the 1953 play *The Prisoners*, set in 1945 when the Soviet army captured Russians who had fought for liberation with the Germans. Vorotyntsev confirms that he had fought during the Russian Civil War on the "White" side. If we conceive this play, as Klimoff and Ericson do, as an epilogue to *The Red Wheel*, we see that the whole work is conceived in light of what might have been.[8] It is history as seen from the perspective of a man who had no effect upon it but who represents its tantalizing other possibility. What if the Russian officer corps had been composed of men such as Vorotyntsev rather than time-servers, sycophants, and incompetents? Even in 1953, Solzhenitsyn's imagination had already crystallized around the character who would be among the most penetrating figures of *The Red Wheel*. Gradually such fictional characters are reduced in significance as the knots proceed, but Vorotyntsev does not disappear completely. He is still present at the end of the fourth knot to provide some musings on the future direction of Russia and of his own potential role within it. It has been noted that the later knots are more heavily and consistently historical, as if the author no longer needs the extrahistorical perspectives to illuminate what has happened. The outcome has been decided and fewer options remain for altering it. History had provided its own Vorotyntsevs, but now their range of action is far more severely limited. Often it consists simply of holding their station in the face of the cataclysm that engulfs them. This was all that was possible for Colonel Balkashin and the soldiers of the Wheeled Battalion who were beaten to death by a mob.[9] Yet that elemental steadfastness, perhaps most of all when it is powerless, is enough to establish the truth. Juxtaposition is the principle out of which the knots are constructed.

What has happened can never be contained in its factual report. Somehow it must be heightened to elicit its defining character. That is what juxtaposition accomplishes. It enables Solzhenitsyn to present what happened in relation to what might have been, but not as a purely imaginary alternative. To work, juxtaposition must invoke what really might have altered the situation. It must be a real possibility in the moment, not simply an impossible wish fulfillment. Vorotyntsev is not therefore a purely fictional character but the truth of a possibility that remained. Men of his caliber with the requisite skill and energy might well have been able to form themselves into a cohesive force sufficient to overcome the debility of the sclerotic regime. The failure of their emergence is, however, not simply accidental or personal. It is bound up with the forces of inertia posed against it, a general mood of passivity that eventually even reaches those most capable individuals. Solzhenitsyn allows his hero to slide into the distraction of a private passion, his affair, that is symptomatic of the wider lassitude that invades Russian society from the top down. Even a Vorotyntsev succumbs to its enervating spirit. Where does Russia exist, Solzhenitsyn seems to ask, when its most devoted members have been overtaken by a paralyzing drift into the world of private dissipation? Yet the question could not even be asked unless there existed that cadre of individuals for whom the possibility of heroic vitality had not vanished entirely. They may have been powerless to reverse the mounting forces arrayed against them, but they were not powerless to choose their response to them. They could still attest to the truth by which history, and they too, are judged. Judgment is juxtaposition, for art can invoke no criterion beyond the truth emergent within it. Verisimilitude, the touchstone of the writer's code, requires nothing less than refusal of the manufactured point of view. We are confident in the judgment rendered because we can behold the balancing of perspectives from which it has been drawn.

Juxtaposition, one is inclined to suggest, is Solzhenitsyn's principal literary technique. A comprehensive weighing of experiences and views is surely what renders the *Gulag Archipelago* such a powerful testament.[10]

It becomes apparent too in the smaller-scale writings to which Solzhenitsyn returned after *The Red Wheel*, especially the miniatures and short stories. We begin to see that the author of one of the most extended literary works of the century is at heart a miniaturist, capable of seeing the whole in the smallest instances. This was after all the secret of *The Red Wheel*, not that it is composed as one long tale, but as an assemblage of many, many much shorter ones. Each of them is essentially "binary," depending for their meaning on a relationship to a whole that is not fully adumbrated. The technique is amply displayed in the later collection of short stories Solzhenitsyn referred to as "binary tales," *Apricot Jam and Other Stories*.[11] Many of the stories seem to deal with events and material that may have been left over from or were part of the larger projected version of *The Red Wheel*. In them the juxtapositional technique is developed as a structural device whereby the same event is viewed from two very different perspectives. The opening story, "Apricot Jam," begins with a desperate emaciated peasant who writes a letter appealing to a famous writer for help, while the second half recounts a conversation between the famous writer and his neighbors in which the letter features as a splendid example of raw Russian language that the writer intends to use. When asked if he will answer the man's plea for help, the writer simply dismisses the suggestion as he cannot regard himself as having anything in common with a dispossessed kulak. They live in such completely different worlds, the story seems to say, that their lives scarcely touch one another. Yet they inhabit the same world, the world that the story has laid before us. The truth that neither side can grasp about the other is contained in their juxtaposition. Indeed, it is their juxtaposition that brings out a depth in the kulak and the writer, whether it is of openness or closure, that would not have been apparent in their isolation. History, in this case a very minor episode within it, has effected an epiphany not so much of character but of the human condition. Behind the multiplicity of perspectives that divide human beings there lies the common humanity that binds or fails us. Juxtaposition is in the service of that common humanity. That is the source of its truth.

History Is Transcended in Truth

Juxtaposition is elaborated, not only in the system of knots and such dialectical forms as the binary stories, but in the whole array of techniques, from historical documents, to cinematic montages, to epigrammatic folk sayings that Solzhenitsyn uses in his vast work. Everything is designed to elicit that moment of epiphany in which what has happened in history is rendered luminous. What is worth remembering, he seems to say, is not so much the bare events and outcomes as the meaning through which they are grasped. Even to see it all as constituting one great convulsion, a rolling of the red wheel, is already to step back from the details to comprehend them. In that moment, history is arrested, for it is only then that the wheel is glimpsed apart from the blur of its movement. The wheel that moves so inexorably, crushing all that lies in its path, is held fast in the moment of its beholding. History itself is thereby transformed so that it is not simply the whirring buzzing confusion experienced by the participants as they are trampled to death by mobs or forced to flee from palaces their families had occupied forever. It is not the immediacy of events that is recorded but their meaning within a wider drama of which they are a part. Even the participants themselves seek out that larger significance as they attempt to probe the meaning of what has happened. They too bear witness to the realization that they are not simply in history but are also somehow always outside of it. It is in becoming clear, if only in part, on why and how all that has transpired in their lives has occurred that they gain a release from it. They reach, if not the perspective of eternity on the events of their lives, at least the distance afforded by that perspective. It is not simply the author, Solzhenitsyn, who has transmuted their suffering into something beautiful, for they have already begun the process themselves. Even in losing the thread of meaning, in failing to break through to any ultimate significance, they have nevertheless preserved the imperative of that transcendent quest. History is in this sense a ceaseless quest for the moment in which history is transcended.

It is reached when what has happened is grasped in its universal significance. That is when it stands under the moral judgment that attempts to plumb the depths of good and evil that lie within it. How does it appear sub specie aeternitatis? This does not mean that the question is ever fully answered, for, in an important sense, no definitive judgment can be rendered while history continues to unfold. Yet the question must be posed and it must be posed of that sphere of responsibility within which each person acts. The treatment of General Samsonov, the figure responsible for the Second Army in *August 1914*, exemplifies this relentless self-examination. For Solzhenitsyn it was not enough to catalogue the unhappy general's military blunders. It was necessary to probe their source. Did they lie in ineptitude, a failure of diligence, or some deeper character flaw? To what extent was the catastrophe that resulted in the loss of the Second Army assignable to a more extensive collapse of responsibility within the

Russian high command? Solzhenitsyn leaves us in no doubt that the contagion of feckless incompetence was widely shared, almost as if everything conspired to ensure a defeat and demoralization of Russia that was in no sense inevitable. How differently it would have turned out, he seems to say, if only the tsar had displayed more resolute judgment in his military appointments, if only the senior military ranks had been populated with fewer blockheads who cared less about saving their own precious hides, and if only the wider political circles had glimpsed something of their own precarious position in the ensuing collapse the disaster would visit upon them. To single out one individual for most of the blame, however pivotal his role, would seem to misread the constellation of forces at work. Yet Solzhenitsyn comes close to doing just that. He refuses the Tolstoyan invocation of historical necessity in insisting that Samsonov could have done otherwise. Indeed, he preserves his responsibility by demonstrating the extent to which Samsonov sought to honestly fulfill his duty. He was not one of the cowardly incompetent flatterers that proliferated in the tsar's headquarters. He was a soldier who knew that his first duty was to remain with his men, and he sought to do so. Nevertheless, he was drawn toward the disastrous decision by which he moved to the front himself and thereby lost communication with army group headquarters. When one of the colonels pointed out how such an action was contrary to all military rationality, that he was "neglecting the army commander's duty to control the *whole* army," he would not be dissuaded. Yet even in that final imbecility Solzhenitsyn does not condemn the doomed general outright. Instead he probes deeper into the mood that could so possess Samsonov that he departed from the most elementary rule of command.

What had been a colossal blunder could still be viewed in the higher light that had already been vouchsafed to Samsonov in prayer. He had sought to "lay the whole of his life and the present suffering, before God"[12] in a way that made his prayer one offered on behalf of all of Russia. It was no longer for himself alone that he prayed, for he had united himself with Russia as a whole, taking upon himself the burden of suffering it would have to endure as it descended into the maelstrom in which nothing could be known of its future. Everything was dark except for the certainty that somehow Russia would be redeemed. He had no basis for this but the assurance he had received that his own suffering would be united with the divine saving action by which sacrifice is the path toward resurrection. In surrendering everything, Samsonov had gained his release from all that held him earthbound. The whole burden of the moment, in which the fate of Russia was dependent on this one man seemed, in Solzhenitsyn's account, to become bearable. Even his body became "less cumbersome, his soul less dark: all the weight and darkness soundlessly and invisibly fell away from him, evaporated, was drawn heavenwards. God who could assume all burdens was taking this burden to Himself."[13] This is surely the meaning of the voice that Samsonov hears in a dream on the night before the crucial battle, which intones, "Thou shalt be assumed," until he finally bolts upright with the realization of what it means. To be "taken up," on the Feast of the Assumption, meant that he would die. It was under the influence of that shattering revelation that Samsonov undertook his last disastrous step of moving up to the front, thereby breaking off communication with army group headquarters. The contrast between what happens in history and the transcendence of history could not be greater.

What at the level of historical action appears as culpable ineptitude assumes a very different appearance when seen in the light of eternity. What matters in that transcendent perspective is not the worldly consequences of action but the spirit in which they are undertaken. How do they stand in relation to the viewpoint of eternity in which all consequences have ceased to be? What in a mundane sense was simply a well-intentioned blunder now may be seen as an act of supreme generosity by a leader who sacrifices himself on behalf of all. It may not be the wisest course of action by any of the military principles that normally apply, but it could also be seen as guided by a deeper wisdom that mandated more than was possible on a purely human scale. Even sacrifice that in worldly terms seems senseless may serve a higher purpose when it is subsumed within the redemptive axis of history. That is surely the perspective within which Solzhenitsyn is thinking about the Russian Revolution. How else can one contemplate the past except to find the meaning of the catastrophe that has occurred? And when every last particle of blame has been meticulously assigned, there still remains the challenge of surmounting the accumulation of evil. It is one thing to acknowledge the "banality of evil," but has one really been anything more than a guilty bystander if this is all that has been accomplished? Can evil be acknowledged without overcoming it? That requires the unconditional love that sacrifices itself on behalf of all. Redemption as the truth of history is the still point around which *The Red Wheel* revolves. One might even regard Solzhenitsyn's lifelong absorption with the project as itself one great act of redemptive self-giving. No detail was too small, no episode too insignificant for inclusion within the ever-expanding cycle of knots that he sought to comprehend by way of untying them again. To be released from the deadly fatality unleashed by the revolution required not only an analysis of the responsibility for evil but also the spirit of forgiveness that triumphs over it. Samsonov stands for the Russian depth of soul that, despite its evident insufficiency in the moment of its greatest trial, yet remains as the possibility of renewal at some future time. The loss has not been for nothing. This is what *The Red Wheel* proclaims as it dutifully remembers and thereby saves.[14]

Some confirmation of this reading of Samsonov, who is the most consequential figure of *August 1914*, is surely provided by the author's alter ego, the ubiquitous Colonel Vorotyntsev. This is all the more notable given that Vorotyntsev is at this stage still brimming with confidence in his own capacity to turn things around. He is the impatient man of action in contrast to the lumbering general, who, like his army, is about to be no more. Yet it is Vorotyntsev who recognizes the changes that have taken place in the Second Army commander, changes that left him incapable of receiving any further reports or issuing commands: "It was too late, and no use. Samsonov was soaring at such a height that he had no more use for such things, he was no longer surrounded by terrestrial enemies, no longer threatened, he had outsoared all dangers. No, it was not guilt but a sense of unappreciated greatness that had shadowed the commander's brow: perhaps seen from the outside he had done things that contradicted ordinary earthly ideas on strategy and tactics, but from his new point of view every action of his had been profoundly correct."[15] It is almost as if Vorotyntsev-Solzhenitsyn concedes that the redemptive significance of the general outweighs his military incapacity. His piety may have misled him but it underpins his sacrificial role. In submitting to inscrutable divine wisdom, including the premonition that Russian defeat will eventually lead to revolution, Samsonov ceases to play a role within any purely mundane ordering of purpose. On the retreat, he removes the general's insignia from his uniform, and, becoming again the common soldier, he slips away from the group so that he might encounter the death that is their inescapable fate. Only as a man who claims no special privileges for himself can he stand in place of other men. In such an act of expiation, however, he has also ceased to be a part of history, with all the particularities of his time and setting, but has assumed the place of all who must follow after. History, we see, is not just about the actions and events that happen in it, but also about the actions and events that make it possible.

Whatever Russia is to be in the future, it must arise from those individuals who beheld it inwardly in the supreme sacrifice they made on its behalf. By transcending their merely historical situations, they make history possible. This is the meaning of all epic accounts, for they do not so much record the past as transmit it into the future. The exemplars furnish the models that constitute a common way of life. Men and gods engage in the heroic struggle through which the measure of what counts is instituted. In *The Red Wheel* this struggle is largely transacted between those who seek to remake Russia in accordance with their own idea of it and those who submit to the idea of Russia as itself the guiding principle of their action. It is the difference between ideology and truth. The protagonists of ideology are driven by the conviction of the superiority of their conception to all that has existed. The servants of truth subordinate themselves to what is required to bring what is already there more fully into existence. At issue is where reality lies when we are responsible for bringing it about. Are we entirely free to impose our will on reality, as Lenin sought to insist? His whole role and significance turns on a readiness to press this conviction to the limit. It was from his titanic drive, Solzhenitsyn seems to suggest, that his historical success derived. Is history then a field in which the resolute can remake reality at will? For all of his personal foibles and tactical ineptitude, Lenin exemplified the drive that ultimately came to direct the red wheel. What could a Samsonov or even a Stolypin do to oppose the diabolical ruthlessness that would rather destroy Russia than see it slip out of the grasp of Bolshevism? In the face of historical success, what can be said on behalf of truth lost from history? Surely this is the question toward which *The Red Wheel* continually points ever since the original plan of a celebratory exposition was replaced with the mature assessment of its disastrous effect.

It is in this respect that an artistic surpasses a purely historiographic treatment. Art is not limited to presenting the historically significant events and outcomes. It is free to picture what has not been realized along with what has. By entering more deeply into the reality it investigates, art is able to address what must remain silent in the perspective of historiography. Art can include the standpoint that is shared with historiography but which the latter cannot confess, that is, that the subject, in this case the fate of Russia, matters. When every major institution and every level of society fails, when the disease of spiritual disintegration has become so extensive that the nation's fate is sealed, when Russia is doomed, there nevertheless remains a true Russia that is preserved, even if only in the status of the irrevocably lost. But it is not really lost. Even to write the history of Russia's descent into revolutionary madness is to write the history of what is not utterly unreal. The Russia about which such an historical fate can be recounted remains its truth. The true idea of Russia as the community of those who are bound together within their common self-consciousness, not the antagonistic factions that have lost any connection to a common way of life, somehow endures. That endurance is the condition of the possibility of writing its history. At the deepest level, there cannot be a history of Russia's revolutionary self-destruction. Disintegration is premised on integration, even if it exists only in the mind of the historian, who, of necessity, must hold out the promise of what has not happened. Solzhenitsyn's *Red Wheel* is even more deliberately a work of national salvation, an act of imaginative restoration of what history has scattered. The historian too affirms a similar act of faith. Even if he or she no longer holds out hope of a whole to be regained, there is the affirmation that the Russia that has disappeared is worthy of such an effort. It is at least worthy of being remembered. History is in this sense inescapably preservative of what has been lost.

The historical epic, however, can go much further. It looks resolutely toward the future and indeed calls forth the future it makes possible. The epic constitutes a new social order, often explicitly so on the basis of the disintegrated past. *The Red Wheel* is thus not simply a book about the revolutionary upheaval in the Russian past. It is the definitive means of surmounting it in the creation of a Russian future. Just as it was not necessary for Homer to have a concrete picture of the kind of society that would succeed the death struggle of Achaeans and Trojans, so it is not necessary for Solzhenitsyn to hold out a detailed conception of a post-revolutionary Russia or, by extension, of a post-totalitarian modernity. What matters is that *The Red Wheel* carries within it the seeds of that other society. When and where they are capable of bearing fruit is not the decisive aspect. It is enough that they are there embedded within the account of a great disaster as the only perspective from which the true scale of the catastrophe can be contemplated. The other Russia that resists the descent into revolutionary madness is preserved. Perhaps it is nowhere else preserved but within the pages of *The Red Wheel*. That is enough, for it means that Russia remains in its truth. Whenever and wherever Russia regains its historical path, the virtues on which it will be rebuilt will have been made available. No other foundation is possible for a people that wishes to persevere as a community in history than to find within itself the generosity of self-sacrifice, rather than self-absorption, that makes life together possible. It is the slender thread of heroic action in the face of impossible circumstances that ultimately transfigures defeat into triumph. In remembering the irruption of goodness in the midst of evil, *The Red Wheel* itself goes beyond merely remembering. It undertakes the resistance to history by which history is constituted.

CHAPTER THIRTEEN

Art and History in Solzhenitsyn's Red Wheel

How does art illuminate history? This is the question raised by Aleksandr Solzhenitsyn's great historical epic *The Red Wheel*. Even from his teenage years he had been drawn to the project of creating a literary account of the Russian Revolution, as if only literature could deal with the upheaval in its appropriate scale. A mere historical narrative along the lines of George Katkov (*Russia 1917: The February Revolution*) or Richard Pipes (*The Russian Revolution*) would miss the essential. To penetrate the meaning of the events they would have to be heightened through imagination, rather than flattened within the monologue of the professional historian. History would have to be transformed into art. Or art would have to be presented as history. By permitting participants to speak for themselves, Solzhenitsyn would somehow distill the essence of what had transpired. The technique is not a new one, for the ancient historians Herodotus and Thucydides also introduce the speeches of the actors as a means of shedding light on their subsequent actions. Indeed, we may think of the Bible as the ultimate exemplification of this principle, that the meaning of the events is inseparable from the events themselves, for, in that case, the unity is held together by the word of God that simultaneously communicates and creates. Art may not have the power of the divine paradigm, but it is nevertheless guided by it. In the end it is the resolve to effect a historical change that is the driving force behind the recounting of historical convulsion that is *The Red Wheel*.

The artist takes responsibility, not just for reporting what happened, but for seeing it rightly in light of the principles by which historical reality must be judged and thereby reordered. Whether his prophetic call encounters any answering response in his own society and age is not the decisive aspect. What matters is that his witness has borne fruit in the only form that can mediate a future, if there is to be a future. An epic constitutes a common order of existence if not necessarily the order of the society from which it has emanated. The Achaeans and the Trojans exhausted in their mortal conflict ultimately gave rise, only through the art of Homer, to the heroic flowering of Greek civilization. All that was needed was the poet who remembered, who resolved to preserve what would otherwise have been irretrievably lost. This is surely the project of Solzhenitsyn, especially in his two monumental works, *The Gulag Archipelago* and *The Red Wheel*. They originate in that unyielding pledge that arose within him to save the memory of what had happened from the stream of forgetting. He would not let the catastrophe that had overtaken the Russian people fade imperceptibly away. It must be held within the full awareness of its staggering influence. But how could that be conveyed without losing its force in a numbing litany of miseries? Disaster must be held alive in memory by grasping its connection with the memorable. Only art can distill the truth by which it is to be measured. Mere historiographic narrative continually risks overlooking the historic because it treats every event on the same level. It is only when the pretense of neutrality has been dropped that the narration can single out the crucial moments on which it actually turns. There is finally no possibility of avoiding the question of the significance of every consequential action and event.

In that way the historical account reaches toward the horizon exemplified by Homer, for we are always engaged in remembering what is memorable in all that has occurred. Recollection lifts what has happened out of the indifferent flow to hold before us what is worthy of such preservation. When asked for whom this exercise of remembering had been done, Homer responded that it was for the gods. Through the Muses he sang the exploits of the heroes to the gods who beheld them. In this way the passing has been saved from perishing. It has gained the immortality of memory, an immortality that is not simply literary because the deeds have already stepped outside of the ordinary to stand before the gods. The transcendence of the events has made their remembrance possible, rather than the other way around. This is why *The Red Wheel* cannot be regarded as a novel stamped with a particular author's point of view. Instead it must be seen as the voice of a whole society that reaches up to the awareness of whence it has emerged. Within the genre of epic, the question of truth assumes a very different meaning.

It is not so much the question of whether the author has captured the facts of what happened, but whether Russian society would recognize the representation of itself. For this recognition to occur, for the account to acquire authoritative status, the responsibility must be shared between author and readers. It is not simply up to the author to report as accurately and completely as he can, or for the reader to privately ponder the fate of the characters. They must be joined in the common acknowledgment of what has transpired. In contrast to the subjectivity of the novel, the epic can only exist within an openness that is public. The work depends for its very existence on the emergence of a society that is capable of an epic consideration of its history and on an author who is capable of configuring its past along such lines. When the author has ceased to speak in his own voice in becoming the voice of a people, we see how much the mutuality of writer and readers have interpenetrated. Just as there would be no epic without a people, there would be no people without the epic. In defining one another they constitute one another. All other writing can assume a readership already prior to its appearance, the epic alone brings its readership into existence. It is this deeply interwoven relationship that marks the genesis of *The Red Wheel*, thereby making the question of its truth far more profound than the question of its accuracy. The truth of the epic is inseparable from the truth of the events it recalls. Events and actions can be depicted only because they have attained a truth that installs them in memory. Even in the maelstrom into which the Russian Revolution descends there must remain a transparency toward the reality that has been lost.

It is in such epiphanies that the past is illuminated in the only way that it can be overcome. This was the goal of Solzhenitsyn's remembrance of the horrors of the Gulag that was tied to the interior story of his own spiritual growth. Without transcending the suffering along the lines of the redemptive sacrifice suggested to him by the old doctor, Boris Kornfeld, he would scarcely have reached the equanimity of perspective from which the account could be written.[1] Only a soul that has been saved can recount the truth that includes his own salvation. He can finally murmur, "Bless you prison for being in my life."[2] To the extent that it is the purpose of *The Red Wheel* to arrive at a similar transcendence of the catastrophe, it is crucial for the author to find within the events the moments in which the full measure of what has happened can be taken. They are the luminous peaks in the account that, though they may play no role in shaping the course of history, are the indispensable turning points within it. They carry the possibility of a future in whose light the past can be beheld and transcended. It is no accident that such singular moments, by which the historical course as a whole has been grasped, are rooted in the revelatory glimpses that are received by a few privileged persons. They have begun to occupy the perspective of "absolute spirit," as Hegel termed it, in identifying art as an equivalent pathway toward the goal that was shared with philosophy and religion. What is memorable in history are the intersections of the timeless with time that constitute history and that art too can summon forth. It is in this way that Solzhenitsyn can locate within the narrative those flashes of transcendence by which its structure can be comprehended.

One of the most elaborate is the profound meditation that accompanies the death of Stolypin, the "best head of government" that Russia had had in two hundred years.[3] The one man had been assassinated (1911) who might have been able to check the revolutionary descent, who grasped clearly both the imperative for reform and the necessity of anchoring it within the Russian soul, the one man who possessed the capacity and confidence to navigate the treacherous historical moment. Now as he lay dying he still thought deeply about how Russia might be saved, despite the fact that neither the tsar nor any other official saw fit to pay him a visit in the few remaining days. History had marched on and left its hero behind. But in Solzhenitsyn's account the hero retains his grip on history, even if only in the inwardness of his own thoughts. Whether Stolypin succeeds in reversing the course of things, Solzhenitsyn seems to say, is of no matter. What counts is that he has pronounced the word of truth from which any future must arise. No one man, Stolypin reflects, can reverse the course of history. Yet when history begins to reverse itself, he is the one who furnishes its direction. Responsible government in Russia could only arise when Russians had learned to exercise self-responsibility. Nothing could come from the introduction of liberal reforms that removed all external restraints while inculcating none internally. A people that has placed itself above the law is incapable of self-government. Stolypin was, Solzhenitsyn establishes in an accompanying historical survey, the one true friend of liberty. He was the only constitutional thinker who sought simultaneously to free the peasants and to preserve the monarchy: "Stolypin's central idea was that it is impossible to introduce the rule of law until you have independent citizens, and in Russia those citizens would be peasants. 'Citizens first, then civil rights.'"⁴ Self-government would have to be introduced from the bottom up, through local *zemstvos* (assemblies) in which citizens would acquire the traits and experience so essential to responsible governance. In the most acute crisis of Russian history, Stolypin alone knew how to respond to the modernizing demands, without losing the connection with all that had made Russia possible.

He alone, Solzhenitsyn insists, could have steered the red wheel before it careened out of control. Reform rather than revolution would have preserved the two most important institutions of Russian life, the monarchy and the Church. It was through the monarchy that the vastness of Russia had been drawn together, and the tsar had remained the great unifying focus. But it had been the Orthodox Church that had spread Christianity into every corner of Russian life, making the word "peasant" synonymous with the term "Christian." Together, monarchy and Church had been indispensable to the formation of the Russian identity, and they must not now shatter at the moment of their greatest peril. "To reform our way of life, without damage to the vital foundation of our state—the soul of the people," had been Stolypin's guiding principle.⁵ Yet it was not to be. Stolypin knew it as he lay dying, abandoned by all whom he had tried to save. His reflections at this lowest ebb of his own life, and of the prospects for Russia, are particularly significant. Solzhenitsyn does not conceive of him yielding to recrimination or complaint. Knowing the situation is hopeless, Stolypin does not abandon hope. Instead he places it in the only source from which it cannot be disappointed. The fate of Russia rested in the hands of God. The emperor who had not come to the dying man, no more than he would be able to come to the aid of Russia in its mortal hour, was "a weak man" incapable of anything more: "It was God's will to send us such an Emperor at such a time. It is not for us to weigh Thy purposes."⁶ Beyond all that men can do or fail to do there lies the inscrutable divine providence that governs all. Human beings can grasp the principle of that will in fulfilling the duty imposed upon them, but they cannot penetrate to the consequences that follow within the stream of history. In the end we do not make history; we simply act within it. History is the divine judgment unfolding within time. The highest perspective available to us is the recognition of its inscrutability. "It is as Thou hast ordered it,

O Lord, whose designs are beyond our understanding."[7] We know only its unqualified goodness.

The truth that constitutes Russia, preserved now only in the solitary reflections of the dying Stolypin, is at one with the truth of God. He is not alone, for he is united with the unsurpassable divine care extended over all. Stolypin cannot foresee the future, which includes the seventy-year nightmare of Bolshevism and its eventual collapse, but he knows that God is good. This is the goodness from which his own selfless devotion has arisen. His personal witness to the triumph of good over evil is the affirmation of its ultimate historical fulfillment. One cannot pour oneself out in a life of unstinting public service without believing that the sacrifice is worth it. Where or when or how its fulfillment will arise remains impenetrable, but the certainty of its attainment is unshakeable. In the end, historical action is anchored in faith. It is a faith not in history itself but in the God who is beyond history that sustains it all. The collapse of everything in his own life and in the life of the nation does not mean for Stolypin the end of all hope. It is rather the moment for the hope of redemption to dawn. Somehow all that is lost will be restored, even if only in the embrace of God who loves without limit. This is what makes it possible for Stolypin to depart with such equanimity as he contemplates the destruction of everything he has sought so tirelessly to preserve. He knows that ultimately the work is not his, or not his alone. The Russia that he held within his heart had already been contained in the far more expansive embrace of divine love. Its survival was assured more profoundly than his efforts could ever secure. This is the faith that sustained all the steps he had taken and it would bring them to fruition long after he was gone. The providence he had sought to exercise was included within the all-encompassing providence of God.

This acknowledgment by Stolypin that it is God who ultimately is the truth of history is the highest insight attained by *The Red Wheel*. The perspective of the author does not surpass that of the most exemplary historical figure, but even Stolypin does not provide the opportunity for its most extended elaboration. For that Solzhenitsyn uses several minor characters who are insignificant from the point of view of the historical action but are of central importance in probing its meaning. The two most important such figures are surely Sanya Lazhenitsyn, modeled on the author's father, and a young woman known as Zinaida. Sanya is the young searcher who enters into some of the deepest conversations about the meaning of history, particularly by way of underlining Solzhenitsyn's disagreement with Tolstoy. First, in *August 1914*, Sanya, who has already discovered in *Vekhi* (*Landmarks*, the famous anthology from 1909)[8] an antidote to Tolstoyan moralism, enters into conversation with an old Moscow scholar named Varsonofiev. The "Stargazer," as he is nicknamed, reveals to the young students that it is not our task to sit in judgment on history but to respond to the call of justice that comes to us from within it. Sanya has already left his pacifism behind in volunteering to serve in the army and has thereby demonstrated that duty takes precedence over any presumption that we know how history should unfold. That had been the conceit of Tolstoy, who was convinced of his own superior moral vision as one that could be imposed on all things. Instead Sanya learns through hard experience that the outcome is in the hands of God. When he next appears, in *November 1916*, Sanya is in the midst of a deep spiritual crisis in which he tries to come to terms with his own responsibility for the death of Cheverdin, one of the members of his gunnery team. It is in a lengthy conversation with Fr. Severyan, the company chaplain, that he is finally freed from the Tolstoyan moralism that sought "to save man without the aid of God." Only by shedding the last vestige of pride, including pride in our moral superiority, can we become instruments of God, who alone is the one who redeems the evil of existence. The transformation of history is beyond our powers. That had been the mistake, not only of Tolstoy, but much more militantly of Lenin and his followers. Instead the only route is fulfillment of the duty eternal responsibility has imposed on each one of us, while leaving the many threads of consequences in the hands of the One whom we can trust to weave them into goodness as a whole.[9] We are not responsible for history, only for our actions within it. Yet that is enough, so long as we unite our efforts with the will of God who ultimately governs all. The most crucial moment, Sanya discovers, is when we have reached the point of exhausting all our own powers and recognize that we can do nothing without God. Tolstoy, Fr. Severyan reflects, never reached the state of utter helplessness: "When there is no strength left for independent action—with what strength is left we try to pray. We want only to pray, to take in the strength that flows in abundance from the Almighty. And if we succeed in it, it is as though our hearts are flooded with light, and our powers return. And we realize the meaning of the words 'preserve and pardon us with thy grace!' Do you know that state of mind?"[10] To which Sanya replies: "That was my state of mind when I met you today." It is difficult to resist the conclusion that this is a largely autobiographical experience.

The other penetrating spiritual meditation is, by contrast, more symbolic in its significance. It concerns the "Confession" of the young woman, Zinaida, both a name and a character that evokes life in all its irrepressible vitality. The representative significance of this episode is underlined by its placement as the concluding chapter of *November 1916*. Indeed, the appearance of Zinaida seems largely symbolic since she plays no role in the action of the story. She serves only to heighten the meaning of what has transpired. We are prepared for the culminating epiphany of the volume by her earlier introduction as a topic of conversation between Vorotyntsev and the writer, Fyodor Kovynov, who pass the time together on a train journey. Even there Zina Altanskaya works her fascinating influence. She is like a presence that hovers between these two alter egos of the author, the writer who collects samples of the people's language and the indefatigable man of action, as they are joined together around the samovar in their compartment contemplating this unusual young woman while the countryside rushes by in the dark. Even earlier, however, she is mentioned in the notebooks of Kovynov and thus speaks in her own voice before anything else is said of her. It is a remark that situates her significance and proclaims the central principle of the work: "Zina makes no distinction between 'great' and 'small' deeds. Each person, she says, has a certain fund of moral strength and everyone who uses his strength to the full has performed a great deed. All such people are equals, although to the outside world their actions are incommensurate. Can she be right?"[11] The most insignificant individual can disclose the most profound insight because the whole is contained within each one. This is surely what is implied in the conversation between the traveling companions, the writer and the soldier, both of whom have fallen short of their respective ambitions, as they grapple with the mystery of this young woman whose passionate intensity far surpassed their cramped cautiousness. She had been the one who held up the light of truth so compelling to the writer that he could not turn away from her. Yet he could not rise to the responsibility of marriage and, in the end, precipitated the disaster of her recourse to an affair with a married man with all of the unhappiness that followed for Zina, her child, her mother, and the man's wife. The writer failed to be a man. But the colonel too is disturbed by the story, not by the indifference of his companion, but by his own response to the account. He shuddered to think of the attraction such a woman could exercise over a man. "This consuming passion under a humdrum exterior—that was what amazed him. And awakened his envy. And a vague feeling that he had missed something."[12]

Now at the conclusion of *November 1916*, Zina Altanskaya herself appears as the fitting culmination of all that has transpired. She alone seems to rise to the full measure of the catastrophe that has been precipitated. The woman, who had fascinated the writer and the soldier, now steps into the story to evoke the transcendent perspective by which the accumulated disorder might be overcome. Somehow, somewhere, the word must be pronounced that historically has so far not been uttered: repentance. By means of repentance the mindless train of destruction can be arrested or at least opposed in the only way by which a new beginning becomes possible. Zinaida is that new possibility. Bearing no immediate or apparent connection to the events that have unfolded up to that point, she nevertheless carries within her the promise of something quite different. History does not have to be the perpetual round of oppression, revenge, and further oppression. The cycle can be broken only by the one who steps forward to forgive and seek forgiveness. Zinaida, without any overt reference to the larger catastrophe unfolding around her, undertakes just such a reawakening in the equally disastrous chaos of her own life. Russia, Solzhenitsyn seems to say, has lost itself as thoroughly as this besotted young woman who gave herself to a man from whom nothing but unhappiness could follow. Turning aside from her responsibilities she had placed her needs and desires first and in the process lost all that made life precious for her. The Russian Revolution had been a collective loss of reason in the madness of unattainable desires. Sanity could be restored, if it ever is to be, by the painful admission of responsibility for the evil committed. Even if there is nowhere in *November 1916*, or any of the other knots, a historical carrier of that realization, none who is capable of making it socially authoritative, the truth of repentance as the truth of Russia is ineluctable. If Russia is yet incapable of repentance, its necessity must be depicted in the personal recovery of a deluded young woman.

Art surpasses history by penetrating to what history has yet to discover within itself. The truth of art is the truth toward which history converges. That is the achievement of Solzhenitsyn, who does not sit in judgment over what has happened but instead shares in the suffering and self-repentance from which it can be contemplated. He is the voice through which the reawakening of Russia occurs. The "Arduous Confession" of Zinaida is the viewpoint from which the whole work has been written. Like the advice Solzhenitsyn receives from Dr. Boris Kornfeld in the *Gulag Archipelago*, to ponder his past life in order to discover his own responsibility for evil, repentance is the turning point through which goodness is regained within existence.[13] Only through confession do we attain the clarity by which we see things rightly because it eliminates the last remnant of self-distortion from our perspective. It is the perspective of God that can be attained only through the wholehearted prayer for forgiveness. Anything less places us outside of the truth. This is what Solzhenitsyn intuits as he struggles to penetrate the forces that set the red wheel in motion. For all of their brute power, for all of their indisputable historical influence, the forces remain in their core spiritual. The failure of responsibility is their innermost source. How can that be comprehended? Nothing in history is sufficient to explain it, for history can only record its non-occurrence. To reach deeper one must assume the attitude of a penitent, one for whom the betrayal of responsibility is admitted as one's own. Only a penitent can acknowledge the full extent of responsibility for the outcome and only a penitent can reach that absolution by which evil has finally been overcome. In repentance the past has been fully admitted and simultaneously set aside as past. Repentance is the new beginning toward which the project of *The Red Wheel* continually strives. It is the turning point from which the promise of resurrection dawns, even if there are no other signs of its emergence anywhere else in history. Repentance is in this sense the possibility of a future, of a future history. It is the moment outside of time from which time has the possibility of unfolding. This is why the confession of Zinaida is so important, even though it bears no immediate relation to the historical circumstances surrounding it. This purely inward moment contains the heart of Russia.

It is surely for this reason that it is so lovingly elaborated by Solzhenitsyn. There is not a hint of condemnation. Only the healing balm of divine mercy pervades the scene, as Zina contemplates the image of Christ within the church where the office of Our Lady of Tambov is being sung. In Christ she sees not condemnation but the unutterable sadness of the One who has taken all our sinfulness upon himself. She knows, despite the lack of faith with which she began, that her dead son has not been irrevocably lost to her. "She could see now that *somewhere* there was *something*."[14] Prompted by the chant that laments the iniquities that have overwhelmed us, Zina begins to reflect on her own misbegotten life, to tally up the wrongs of which she is guilty. Despite the avowal that she never intended to cause harm, she has nevertheless been responsible for a long trail of misery in her life and in the lives of others. She had seduced a married man, split his family, turned away from her dying mother, abandoned her son, and now come face to face with the realization that she could still not repent of the final sin. She would not give up her lover. It is at this point that the priest invites her confession, to which she accedes, but she knows she is not yet capable of that final act of repentance by which she might overcome the passion for her lover.

The priest pronounces the words of absolution over her but knows that she has not yet yielded up everything to God as he has prompted her. She has held back the deepest source of revolt within her soul, her consuming passion. What is remarkable about the treatment that follows is that it demonstrates Solzhenitsyn's awareness of the difficulty of breaking such an irresistible obsession. Russia too has been in the grips of a passion that blinds it to the reality of the consequences. It would rather stick with the historical train of self-destruction than give up the illusion that has possessed it. The touch of divine forgiveness has come close to piercing the self-will that will brook no opposition to its demands. One might be inclined to conclude that this is the final disclosure of the hopelessness of the fate entangling Zinaida-Russia. But that is not where Solzhenitsyn leaves us.

Instead he turns the ostensible evil into good. He shows us that the mania that had driven the red wheel so relentlessly is not wholly bad. Indeed, it would not have reached so far if it drew only on the energy of hatred. What has really given it its power is that it is rooted in the good, in love itself, albeit a perversion of its true form. The evil of the revolution has been goodness deformed. This is the remarkable conclusion to what is probably the most remarkable chapter within *The Red Wheel*: "In each of us there is a mystery greater than we realize. And it is in communion with God that we are able to catch a glimpse of it." Zina, however, has not yet learned to pray in such a way that the path of God might be disclosed to her. For now there is no answer to the question of how she might overcome a passion she longs passionately to retain. There is only the word of the priest, who declares what she has yet to hear: "The world holds no sufferings worse than those caused by family problems. They leave festering sores on the heart itself. For as long as we live this is our earthly lot. You can rarely decide for another that he or she should or not do this or that. How can anyone forbid you to love when Christ said that there is nothing higher than love? And He made no exceptions, for love of any kind whatsoever."[15] Abandonment of the great obsession that drove the revolution will involve the acknowledgment that it was not wholly evil. It could only succeed as much as it did because it drew on what was good. That is the key to overcoming it. Misdirected love must discover that its true fulfillment consists in finding the right order for its expression. Love demands a setting aside of self that sets aside any suggestion that it knows what is best for the world.

The revolution had put itself before the human beings it had sought to serve. In the name of saving men it had trampled them. But this did not mean that its impulse to serve had been wholly mistaken. It had simply not been purified of the self-inflation that attaches to any great human undertaking. The revolution had not yet learned to place individual human beings ahead of humanity as the only means by which it might advance the cause of the latter. To fulfill its aspiration, the revolution would have to go deeper and more inward than it had anticipated. It would have to become a change of heart. Christianity is not an alternative to the revolution: it is its truth.[16] The formidable appeal of human emancipation, so bitterly betrayed by Lenin and his followers, was not for all of that without spiritual power. It worked to the extent that it did because of the effectiveness of that Christian appeal. But it collapsed because it fell short of, indeed it rejected, the fullness of what was required of it. In place of unconditional love it had imposed the condition of subservience to the party and the leaders of the revolution. Love had been dissolved into hate. What would now be required of it is the movement of repentance for the perversion for which it had become responsible. The revolution must undergo its own inward revolution so that it is no longer the movement that brings history to its close but becomes, rather, the self-giving by which all of history unfolds toward every human being as its irreplaceable center. Rather than sacrificing history for the sake of the revolution, the revolution must sacrifice itself for the sake of history. In its final outcome, revolution is indistinguishable from redemption. The action of man must become one with the action of God. What is perhaps most remarkable of all in the evocation of repentance, with which *November 1916* closes, is that the author too has been brought further than he might have envisaged. To see the revolution not simply as something to be condemned but as already an opening toward self-repentance is a new realization. Repentance as the revolution that brings about the new beginning had eluded Solzhenitsyn the historian, but it had not escaped the artist. In this distillation of *The Red Wheel* into the transformation effected in one young woman we see why art penetrates deeper than history.

CHAPTER FOURTEEN

The Person as the Opening to the Secular World

Benedict and Francis

The call for a new evangelization was issued by Benedict XVI and put into practice by his successor, Pope Francis. They share a powerful sense of the challenge that the secular world represents. How can the Church speak to a world that has not only lost its faith but is no longer even searching for it? Where John Paul II could counter the false faith of communism with the true faith of the gospel, Benedict faced the less dramatic situation of a world from which all forms of faith had ebbed away. One could argue with a false faith, but what could one say to a world that no longer asked the question of faith? The militant atheism of Eastern Europe had called forth the heroic resistance of the dissidents who eventually overcame it. But what is the response when God is not so much rejected as simply ignored? This is the world of Benedict XVI, a world whose traumas lie in a distant past now almost forgotten.[1] How can one reach a society of "last men," as Nietzsche so presciently described it? Something more than marketing is required to meet a crisis that goes to the core of both the Church and the world. A genuine meeting must take place, one in which the deepest in each is fully encountered. The Church must go beyond merely being the Church to really become the bearer of Christ; the world must move beyond the self-satisfaction that seems to enclose it. That is the challenge that at the deepest level has informed the teaching life of Benedict XVI.

Behind all the pastoral and organizational and diplomatic initiatives of his papacy is the purpose by which they are defined. New evangelization is more than a slogan and is certainly not reducible to a program. It is the conviction that the Church must meet the modern world where it is, and at the same time open itself to the vulnerability of rejection. Nothing can be held back if the meeting is to have Jesus in its midst. For such a radical adventure of faith a new theological language would be needed to overcome the stale conventions of the past. In many ways the whole life of Joseph Ratzinger seemed to prepare him for that moment when as Benedict XVI he would pull together all of the possibilities the new evangelization must contain. Far from merely conserving the tradition, Benedict has been on the mission of revivifying it.[2] In many respects he has extended the profound theological renewal that preceded and culminated in Vatican II, and this had become abundantly evident in the philosophical personalism that informed the life and thought of John Paul II. But it was only as pope that Benedict seems to have found the daring to push forward his own theological personalism. As yet the intellectual achievement of his papacy has scarcely been noticed, let alone recognized. But it will become evident as the only viable foundation on which his successors can build. Some sense of its effect can be gained from an examination of the unity that pervades the three encyclicals issued under his own name, and the fourth virtually completed encyclical that was issued by Francis. To anticipate the major point, we may place them in relation to those of his predecessor. Where John Paul II had made the person central to his whole intellectual framework, often quoting the council's remark that the Church is an expert in humanity,[3] Benedict began to work out what this more personalist emphasis would mean for the way Christianity understands itself in the heart of the secular world. The Church would change the world, neither by separating from it nor submitting to it, but by revealing the eschatological secret buried within it. Outwardly nothing is changed, but inwardly all would be different. That would be enough to leaven the whole.

Some sense of what that would entail is evident in the conversation with Jürgen Habermas in which Ratzinger too concedes that the secular world must first be understood on its own terms.[4] Yet both of them converge on the admission formulated by Habermas that we also live in a "postsecular" age. That is, the secular world, they agree, not only has difficulty in finding the spiritual resources for its own survival, but cannot fully comprehend itself in purely immanent terms. The secular world has reached its limits when it concedes that it requires more than its own bounded rationality. Finding an adequate formulation of what might sustain the life of reason within modern civilization, however, is a goal that largely eluded the interlocutors. Progress had been made in identifying the problems, but the path toward a perspicuous solution proved more daunting. What is notable is that Ratzinger concedes that natural law can no longer provide the philosophical foundation on which the exercise of reason in such diverse realms as human rights and empirical science can rest securely.[5] Modern reason, as John Paul II had declared in *Fides et ratio*, had reached a dead end. Incapable of justifying itself and unable to restrain its self-critique, reason seemed to endanger the very achievements its development had made possible. Habermas's concession was a significant and defining moment, but equally Ratzinger's refusal to press the advantage was also crucial. It demonstrated that the Church is ultimately on the side of reason, for it knows that reason cannot be supported fideistically. The life of reason can only be sustained through its own autonomous enlargement. Reason must reach up to the horizon of faith, and faith must include reason within its own unfolding. A more extended reflection on the same topic was provided in the first year of Benedict's pontificate in the famous Regensburg Address (2006). There he emphasized his agreement with the Byzantine emperor that to go against reason is to go against God.[6] The Greek discovery of reason, Benedict insisted, was not a culturally relative event but of universal significance. The biblical encounter with the Greek world, as reflected in the Septuagint translation and the wisdom literature of the Old Testament, was not just incidental. It formed part of the unfolding of revelation.

The occasion of other addresses to parliaments and assemblies provided the opportunity for the political elaboration of this point. Within the context of contemporary human rights discourse, Benedict drew attention to the most critical issue of their foundations. In the absence of any philosophical or rational justification, human rights have most commonly been derived from the irresolvable plurality of viewpoints. In a world without truth, everyone is entitled to pursue his or her own conception of truth. But as most observers sense, and many openly admit, agnosticism provides an uncertain basis for the protection of inviolable dignity and respect. If everything is relative, then it is difficult to maintain an exception for human rights. Tolerance may undermine itself if it is extended to the intolerant. Again, Benedict never attempted to score points or highlight the confusion that overwhelms liberal self-interpretation. He sought to remedy and repair as best he could. This, he knew, would entail finding a solution within the liberal political framework itself. His political addresses are notable for the extent to which they rigorously eschew any theological or philosophical presuppositions not universally shared. The identification of the right to religious liberty as the point of access to the system of rights served the important practical function of calling attention to the numerous abrogations of it on the contemporary scene. The pope most of all has a primary responsibility to speak out on behalf of persecuted Christians, and of believers of all faiths, wherever they may be. His interventions in such arenas were not, however, limited simply to defending the defenseless. They also served the larger purpose of grounding a regime of rights on the only philosophical foundation on which they can be rendered coherent. Human rights cry out for a transcendent basis, for they express the unconditional right of every human being in the world. If everything in existence has only a finite value, how can human beings turn out to be of infinite worth? How can a person outweigh the whole world?

Even the UN Universal Declaration of Human Rights cannot say why it must be so. But that does not mean that it does not indicate what it fails to explicate. Benedict homes in on the right to religious liberty as the most crucial such point where a regime of rights says more than it can say. In addressing the UN General Assembly (2008), he highlights the centrality of religious liberty, which, far from being an incidental right, is crucial to the entire conception of rights: "When presented purely in terms of legality, rights risk becoming weak propositions divorced from the ethical and rational dimension which is their foundation and their goal. The *Universal Declaration*, rather, has reinforced the conviction that respect for human rights is principally rooted in unchanging justice, on which the binding force of international proclamations is also based."[7] This is why it is "inconceivable" that the full exercise of rights might be conditioned on the suppression of religious liberty. The argument Benedict mounts is not simply directed at protecting believers from persecution, but also at establishing the primacy of religious liberty within the order of rights. He grasps, even if he does not always highlight it, that it is the acknowledgment of religious liberty that establishes rights as a more than secular regime. The acknowledgment of the right to religious liberty is the acknowledgment of the transcendent destiny of the human person. The secular world may not be capable of comprehending the purpose of such a right but it is capable of intuiting its significance. It is the point at which secular reason affirms its own limit. The confession of mystery is already an opening toward it. A poignant illustration of that connection is adduced by Benedict in his address to the German Reichstag (2011). There he singles out the change of heart evinced by the famous legal positivist, Hans Kelsen, whose pure theory of law seemed to disavow any principle beyond it. Toward the end of his life, Kelsen seemed to modulate away from the notion of law as mere legality to consider that it may be grounded in the will of a creator. Benedict welcomed the concession, which, even if it was not conclusive, suggested a softening of what had previously seemed so inflexible.[8]

The incident is indicative of the overall approach. Unwilling to crush a bruised reed, Benedict was ever ready to invite the enlargement of the heart by which the invisible foundations might be glimpsed. Even the most hardened relativists can begin to see that there is more to the convictions that underpin rights than arbitrary choice. The problem is that the traditional language of a human essence, the immortality of the soul, and natural law served only to obscure what should be made transparent within them. Human rights is a discourse we cannot explain. What is needed is the willingness to revisit the genesis of our philosophical and theological language with a view to rendering it more transparent. This is a task on which Benedict, along with many others, has been engaged for quite a long time. Without tackling the issue centrally, Joseph Ratzinger had consistently remarked on the defectiveness of the language of substance, including its introduction through the Trinitarian formulation of three hypostases, for the relations that define what it means to be a person. In his *Introduction to Christianity* he takes note of the challenge:

> Therein lies concealed a revolution in man's view of the world: the sole dominion of thinking in terms of substance is ended; relation is discovered as an equally valid primordial mode of reality. It becomes possible to surmount what we call today "objectifying thought"; a new plane of being comes into view. It is probably true to say that the task imposed on philosophy as a result of these facts is far from being completed—so much does modern thought depend on the possibilities thus disclosed, without which it would be inconceivable.[9]

It may well be that it was his elevation to the papacy that gave Ratzinger the boldness to attempt that massive reorientation of Greek and Christian thought he had pronounced as a desideratum. What is clear is that the encyclicals soar with a new-found freedom that could well be attributed to a spiritual breakthrough. Generally missed in the public dissection, typically confined to the policy adumbrations, is the far more consequential shift of theoretical perspective underway within his encyclicals. Not only do they build on the person-centered philosophy of his predecessor, but they advance it by installing it as the viewpoint from which they are written. Instead of simply talking about the primacy and inexhaustibility of persons, Benedict has carried out his own suggestion of thinking within the category of relation. In many respects they fulfill the promise, contained in the development of the Church's social teaching, to find a way of speaking to the world while looking toward the movement beyond it.

Even discourse about transcendence can assume an objectifying quality if it is not located within the interiority of the person. This is the breakthrough Benedict achieves in these luminous reflections. He goes beyond merely talking about the relationship with God, to focus on the inner life within which it is disclosed. There is no relationship with God but the one that is accessed in interiority. Indeed, it is the relationship with God that discloses our interior life. We are called back from the rush of external preoccupations to discover what really counts, the still point of the turning world in which the encounter takes place. Without the meeting there would hardly be the place of its possibility or it would scarcely be intuited, except as the possibility of meeting. Within that meeting of persons we discover that interiority is what persons are. It is where we exist. But even more it is where God is, for God too holds everything inwardly. It is love that is the juncture, as Benedict marvelously explains in *Deus caritas est*. God does not first exist and then decide to love, for love is his being, and all that is in being exists within that love. To share in the being of God is to share in love. Theological personalism has reached its goal when it has found the horizon for its thought. There is no higher viewpoint than love; love is the life of God. To be a person is to love, for we are scarcely persons except to the extent that we love. There is no life beyond the life of love. Our love is not as limitless as the love of God but we are similarly defined by it. To the extent that we have failed to love we have failed to become what we are. We have fallen short of what it means to be a person. This is why all love points toward God.

Even *eros*, Benedict recalls, was "celebrated as divine power" (*Deus caritas est*, para. 4). Starting from that beginning he builds toward the realization that God is love and that all love is a participation in the life of God. Eros finds its fulfillment in *agāpe*, the New Testament term for the utterly selfless love that was to characterize the Christian community. The transition takes us by surprise since they are conventionally juxtaposed,[10] but Benedict's intention is not so much to discourse about love as to find the path to its inner reality. Eros brings us into that immediate realm of experience because it is the love that simply overwhelms us. We have no choice but to love the one with whom we are in love. His point is to emphasize that Christian love is like that, a love we cannot help and a love that aims at the heart of the other. We are seized by love because we know it is not ours and does not come from us. It befalls us from beyond ourselves. We cannot help but love. Christian charity is thus not a duty but an invitation we rush to accept. It is only in this way that the neighbor whom we serve knows that it is undertaken, not for the sake of duty, but for his or her own sake. We can love only if we love the other person and the other knows it as a love destined solely and uniquely for him or her. It is no accident that the Church, as Benedict suggests, has always looked to the Song of Solomon to capture the relationship between God and the soul. Lover and beloved turn a gaze of love toward one another from which all others are excluded. Each one must be for us the whole world. The mystery of *agāpe* is that, although it is impossible for us to look upon every person with that gaze of total love, it is possible for God who is love. This is why Christian charity is an opening toward a universal love that reaches each one in his or her singularity. It is a love beyond the human to which we are called. Eros points the way, but only the gift of divine *agāpe* makes it possible.

In this way Benedict feels he has answered the complaint of Nietzsche that "Christianity had poisoned eros" (*Deus caritas est*, para. 3)," for it has shown the way to save eros from its debasement into merely physical passion. Eros finds its fulfillment when it discovers that its passion is the invitation to discover the other as lovable without limit or end (para. 6). In words that echo Nietzsche's own aspiration for the "eternal return," Benedict insists that "love looks to the eternal." It can never remain a merely human love. That is the great flash of transcendence the Church brings into the world. The humanitarian impulse of service to others, especially as it is organized by the great modern states, is never sufficient for the human heart. Service without love is hardly even a service. What matters to each of us in need is the healing touch of the other who reassures us that we alone are what counts in the whole world. To be loved is to be loved as only God can love us. The second half of *Deus caritas est* is dedicated to following out the practical implications of this discovery. He notes that the distribution of goods to the poor was seized upon in the early Church as one of its primary obligations. Its centrality was noted by the emperor Julian the Apostate, who regarded it as the only aspect worth retaining, a perception that is often repeated within our secular humanitarianism. But true love cannot be merely copied. It is love only if it is true to the truth most deeply held within it, namely, that it is from God who is love. The self-outpouring of Christ is that definitive revelation of love. This is what the Church brings to the contemporary world in the form of its social teaching: "Love—caritas—will always prove necessary, even in the most just society" (para. 28). It is only love, according to Benedict, if it follows that path of Christ in giving all. Giving what is needed is good but it is not enough, unless it is given in love. We must give our very selves to those we serve. "I must be personally present in the gift" (para. 34).

Externally perhaps nothing very different occurs, but the inner reality is transformed. What is given carries the meaning of a transcendent love. Meditating on how that is possible is the burden of Benedict's next encyclical, *Spe salvi* (2007). In hope we are saved. It is through hope that what we do not yet possess and, for that reason, cannot really give is nevertheless received and given. Hope is the eschatological dimension within which our lives are lived. This is what the Church brings to a world often imprisoned within the finitude of its own self-definition. The love that transcends all that is given is glimpsed as the hope that makes it possible. What is impossible for us is made possible by hope, not as an expectation of a future that never arrives, but as the present possession of that for which we long. This is no idle dream of utopia but the fulfillment already present. The self-giving of Christ, nowhere more lovingly expressed than in the Eucharist, has completed the journey of time. Benedict does not explicitly refer to the convergence of this fulfillment with the deepest aspirations of the secular world, but he might well have presented his reflections on hope in this way. The Church brings the message of true hope to a world that has sought to incorporate hope within its structure. It has failed to see that hope is what makes its structure possible and therefore always remains beyond it. If we think of the energy our modern civilization pours into the progress of human society, then it is only natural to assume that the aspiration will reach its fulfillment within time. But this is to overlook the difference between the condition and what it conditions. The truth of our dynamic civilization, with all of its successes and disappointments, is that it is driven by a longing that cannot finally be satisfied within it. Far from dooming it to futility, that perpetual postponement is what guarantees its vitality. Satisfaction would rob it of life. The great modern thinkers had intimations of this but they could never quite express them. What they lacked was the account of hope as Benedict unfolded it, a way of seeing the irresolvable tension of existence as their own best hope. They would have to discover that persons are not the source of hope, but rather hope is what constitutes the life of persons. To be a person is to live within the eschatological tension of the already and the not yet.

Clarification of the meaning of eschatology had been a long-standing occupation of Ratzinger the theologian.[11] Now as Benedict he would find the words to evoke what he sought. In *Spe salvi* he affirms that hope is eschatology. We do not hope for the eschaton but live within its assurance. That is the meaning of the famous definition of faith in Hebrews 11:1. "Faith is the substance [*hypostasis*] of things hoped for; the proof of things not seen." Benedict devotes considerable attention to the way the meaning of the formula has been handled over the course of the tradition. The presence of the term "substance/hypostasis" seems to alert him to the core difficulty. That is, that we are dealing with what is constitutive of the interior life in language derived from the world of things. This had been a fateful move in the Trinitarian and Christological dogmas where "hypostasis" had acquired the status of a technical term. Benedict reminds us that the result has been our inability to access the interior life in any language other than that of subjectivity. If truth is assigned to things, entities, substances, or objects, then our grasp of it must be from a wholly private perspective. We cannot understand ourselves as continuous with the movement of reality itself. That is the problem in Luther's heavily subjective interpretation of Hebrews 11:1, where "proof" has now been replaced with "the conviction of things not seen." This is no longer tenable in the view of later exegetes: "Faith is not merely a personal reaching out towards things to come that are still totally absent: it gives us something" (*Spe salvi*, para. 7). Benedict goes on to examine the rich terminology of the Letter to the Hebrews in which it is this sense of already possessing what we await that is the central point. Just as in the story of the Prodigal Son where "substance" is the usual translation of *ousia*, we see that substance is that from which we live.[12] It cannot therefore be the same as life itself, which has already gone beyond what sustains it. Hope lays hold of its goal. It has already, Benedict explains, gone beyond this life. That is why we do not hope for endless life.[13] Even death can be seen as a blessed release by which we finally apprehend our true end. Death, as St. Ambrose suggested, is a remedy by which we gain eternity rather than mere endlessness.

This is the answer to the modern world that has looked toward the future, whether reached through progress or revolution, as its defining feature. For too long the Christian churches, including the Catholic, have thought they must serve the world by assisting in its project of civilizational advance. But the contribution of Christian social teaching is to hold forth the true goal of the modern aspiration, so that it neither pursues an illusion nor lapses into despair. Like St. John Paul II, Benedict made the Church the guarantor of all that is good in the contemporary world. That requires the clarification of hope as eschatological rather than merely temporal. Making the world a better place is still making a world that also passes away. The goal of our hope must be eternal, not merely endless. This is the subject of the second main section of *Spe salvi*, titled "Action and suffering as settings for learning hope." It begins with prayer, especially the prayer of the contemplatives who have withdrawn completely from the world and yet hold it more deeply within. In the same way, suffering can be the way we unite ourselves with others, whether suffering with them or bearing our own suffering for them. Consolation (*con-solatio*), "suggests *being with* the other in his solitude, so that it ceases to be solitude" (para. 38). But it is in the demand for justice, for a redress of all the shocking assaults on humanity requiring an absolute redress, that the meaning of eschatological hope is most fully displayed. Rather than put ourselves in place of God, we must yield ever-more fully to the divine judgment that includes the divine grace. What is interesting is that Benedict, after referencing Dostoevsky and Plato on judgment, dwells on the story of the rich man and Lazarus. There he emphasizes that this is not an account of the final judgment but only of the intermediate stage before it has taken place. We pass through a fire in which all that is evil in us is burned away. That fire is the love of Christ. "The judgment of God is hope, both because it is justice and because it is grace" (para. 47). It is in that eschatological event that the contradictions of existence are resolved, the unrequited demand for justice is requited in divine love. Earthly justice cannot compensate for all that is lost in the damage inflicted on human beings; it can only agree that reparation is owed in whatever paltry form we happen to have available. Nowhere in this world is justice finally done. Yet we cannot abdicate our responsibility for justice without yielding to an even greater abyss of injustice. Fidelity to the path of justice requires a perseverance, in the face of its worldly incompleteness, that is only possible through faith in judgment as such. The eschatological hope underpins temporal existence.

What is decisive is that the eschatological horizon is not a mere spiritual ideal. Benedict does not engage in wishful thinking in suggesting that the final judgment is the truth of all judgment. Rather he is saying that God's judgment is the reality sought in every human judgment. We cannot even begin to exercise our human judgment if we are not convinced that its requirement outweighs every other consideration, including our ability or inability to realize it. Inexorable judgment matters more than the frailty of the judges. The truth is, as Dostoevsky noted, we cannot judge one another, because we cannot see into the innermost self of the other.[14] Even the person does not have definitive access to who he or she is. All judgment therefore is a participation in the eschatological moment in which justice and grace intersect. We affirm that final transparence while recognizing our distance from it. But this means that no person has yet determined him or herself completely. There always remains the possibility of bringing about a change that has so far eluded us: "It is never too late to touch the heart of another, nor is it ever in vain" (*Spe salvi*, para. 48). To the extent that we recognize the truth of that observation we acknowledge the extent to which we live within eschatological hope. What a human being is is revealed not in what they have said or done but in the undisclosed possibility that can never be fully contained within this life. The flash of transcendence in every person is glimpsed, not in what is manifest, but in what always exceeds manifestation. This is why even death is not an impermeable barrier to their communication: "The belief that love can reach into the afterlife," Benedict notes, has been a part of Christianity from its beginning (para. 48). It is in hope that the eschatological structure of existence is opened. Hope does not disappoint, because the end is present in the beginning. This, Benedict concludes, was true preeminently of Mary, who said yes to the message of the angel and brought forth all that was contained in that promise. The invitation made possible the response, but it could only be laid hold of in the event of response: "Who more than Mary could be a star of hope for us?" (para. 49).

It is the capacity to become more than we are that is the truth of the person. That is what Benedict comprehensively unfolds in the final encyclical under his own name, *Caritas in veritate* (2009), where it is the full development of the person that is held before us as "the truth-filled love, caritas in veritate, from which authentic development proceeds" (para. 79). Resuming the theme of integral human development that has been at the heart of the Church's social teaching, notably in Paul VI's *Populorum progressio*, Benedict goes beyond the customary admonition that material development is not enough. He agrees that it is the development of the person, reaching full stature as a sharer of the divine life, that structures all talk of the distribution of the benefits of modern civilization. Innovations that diminish the inexhaustible mystery that each human being is can hardly be considered a gain to humanity. Yet how to resist them has proven to be a considerable challenge. It is not enough merely to call for "integral humanism," for it must be shown to be the only humanism worthy of the name.[15] This is the truth that Benedict articulates in his last encyclical. It is a truth centered on what it means to be a person. He evokes the reality of self-transcendence as the authentic meaning of progress. In this way Benedict has provided a vision of what a person-centered civilization would look like. The call for a civilization of love is fulfilled when it is understood to be the only appropriate way of addressing persons, who are always more than all they have said or done. Human development entails the recognition that it is sustained and directed by persons who from the beginning exceed their role in the process. Persons as the only genuine ends-in-themselves are, thus, the only adequate end of civilization itself. This may not be a departure from what the Church has always taught, indeed it is the good news of God's love for each one of us that Jesus announced, but the discovery of a language that renders it transparent for the contemporary world is a signal achievement. That is what Benedict accomplished in bringing his theological personalism to bear on the larger tradition of Catholic social thought.

"*A humanism which excludes God is an inhuman humanism*" (*Caritas in veritate*, para. 78). This italicized sentence may state the conclusion, but it is the path toward it that is decisive. After two introductory chapters in which the effect of globalization on development, with its own attendant challenges, has been noted, Benedict turns to the more theoretically profound reflection on economics itself. Not only is an economy sustained by virtues of honesty and responsibility, but it is itself an instance of the self-transcendence that marks a community of persons. Over and above the economy, the exchange of things, there is the mutual self-giving of persons. This is why "in *commercial relationships* the *principle of gratuitousness* and the logic of gift as an expression of fraternity can and must *find their place within normal economic activity*" (para. 36). John Paul II had aimed at the same thought in elevating civil society to the level where fraternal solidarity is exercised. But Benedict insists that gratuitousness, the generosity that sustains an order beyond the interests of the parts, is the basis also of the market and the state. He suggests that "today it is clear that without gratuitousness, there can be no justice in the first place" (para. 38). He is aware that this involves a new way of understanding business enterprise, but the suspicion that few businessmen had glimpsed the human reality of what they do is perhaps a bit overstated. When he considers the different kinds of businesses, not only for-profit and nonprofit, but also the hybrid type that pursues profit in light of social responsibility, the misperception is corrected. A high point is reached in the acknowledgment that each generation is only a steward rather than the owner of the Earth's resources and that we bear a responsibility for their preservation for the human beings of the future. Benedict seems to take particular satisfaction in declaring that "when 'human ecology' is respected within society, environmental ecology also benefits" (para. 51).

The crucial connection is underlined by Benedict in "Chapter Five: The Cooperation of the Human Family" of *Caritas in veritate*. He does not merely exhort a more selfless concern but shows that it is inherent in who we are. The recognition that we are all members of one human family requires a new way of thinking that he locates in "the category of relation." Over and above concrete proposals, development requires a metaphysical understanding of the relation between the individual and the community by which they are seen as "the relation of one totality to another."[16] This is the way the individual is valued in the family and the Church, which exist for no other purpose than to succor their members: "The theme of development can be identified with the inclusion-in-relation of all individuals and peoples within the community of the human family" (para. 54). Its analogue is "the relationship between the Persons of the Trinity within the one divine Substance." A community of persons is one in which each, far from losing his or her identity, finds it enhanced immeasurably. "The Christian revelation of the unity of the human race presupposes a metaphysical interpretation of the 'humanum' in which relationality is an essential element" (para. 55). That sentence is surely the theoretical highpoint of the document. It grounds solidarity and subsidiarity in a wholly novel way that encourages Benedict to think about their practical elaboration. He even suggests that "fiscal subsidiarity" might take the form of allowing us to individually allocate how our taxes are expended, thereby creating a form of "welfare solidarity" with those whom they benefit. The impracticality of such a proposal is hardly a barrier to its truth, for, in a sense, that is what we do in authorizing the state to support the neediest. Even the concluding assertion of an "urgent need of a true world political authority" (para. 67) may be taken in the sense that we already form such a moral community inclining us toward collective action. How such persons might transmit their consent to a world government is one of the limitations of a teaching that focuses only on the social while neglecting the properly political. The oversight is not, however, insuperable since the emphasis on the person already guards the central political principle.

It may not be a fully developed political theory, but Benedict and the wider social teaching do aim at defending the person from the devaluation that technological mastery poses. This is the final chapter of *Caritas in veritate*. Development requires the acknowledgment that "we all build our own 'I' on the basis of a 'self' which is given to us" (para. 68). We create and we do not create ourselves. That is why technology, with its dream of extending control limitlessly, is such a seductive blind alley, for it easily suggests that we are free to make ourselves in any way we choose. We are the supreme masters of our fate. But this is to overlook the extent to which the masters are themselves mastered from somewhere else. There is no mastery; there is only acceptance or rejection of responsibility. Technology is wielded within a web of mutual responsibility. What makes it possible for us to enjoy its power is that we have been given such a possibility. The problem Benedict confronts is that under the reign of technology there seems to be no realm immune to its invasion. We know that an absolute limit to control must be the interiority of the person in him- or herself. The problem is that we have difficulty defending the notion of the soul when even consciousness is reduced to its neurological substratum. What do freedom and dignity mean when the words have no tangible referent? We are left with the moral intimations that restrain us from the worst aspects of dehumanization and, Benedict suggests, this is how faith works to save reason from its own excesses. But we still need some means of explaining this to a world consumed with the allure of technological reason. In a coda to the discussion, Benedict points to a way that might yet loosen the constraints that instrumental reason imposes on us. He reminds us that even reason has something mysterious and inexplicable about it: "All our knowledge, even the most simple, is always a minor miracle, since it can never be fully explained by the material instruments that we apply to it" (para. 77). In the end it is the mystery of the person that encompasses the mystery of knowledge and of love. There is no higher reality than the person for there is nothing higher than God.

The only difficulty is that we still talk about persons as if they are part of the order of things. In Benedict's perceptive formulation we use the language of substance to identify persons who have already sacrificed their substance. Knowledge and love is a movement of pure relation where the person has forgotten him- or herself. It is thus difficult to say what the person is who has always disappeared in what each has said or done. The development of an adequately personalist language sought by Benedict and others cannot be attained through their solitary efforts. It requires a recognition of the modern philosophical convergence with it. A proper humility would even entail the admission that the language of human rights, by which each person is acknowledged as an inexhaustible center of the universe, developed largely outside of the influence of the Church. It is enough that the Church came eventually to recognize it as coincident with its own deepest intuition of the person.[17] But some such admission is required if the Church is to take the best of the modern philosophical developments and make them flower within the evocative theology of the person.

Benedict's instincts have led him to pay attention to the great modern thinkers, but he has usually ended by accepting conventional characterizations of them as falling short of the Christian horizon. As a consequence, neither he nor his predecessor has been able to exploit the full potential of the modern philosophical revolution. Tantalizing suggestions as to what might be possible, however, do become visible. It is remarkable, for example, how frequently Benedict returned to Kant to probe the Christian core of the "rational" faith the latter puts in place of "ecclesiastical" faith. Yet Benedict does not quite see that this implies, whatever Kant's mischaracterization of historical Christianity, that Kant nevertheless sought its purer, more interior, affirmation.

Something similar applies to the intriguing references to the Frankfurt School in *Spe salvi* (para. 42). Max Horkheimer and Theodor Adorno in different ways engage in a "negative dialectic," which denies them the possibility of finding God in anything within the world. At the same time they cannot affirm any image of God beyond it. The result may be a strange ambivalence whereby they insist on the need for a transcendence they can never attain. But is this not a mode of transcendence? Benedict seems unwilling to push the meditation to that next step that would suggest that the longing for an unattainable God is itself a mode of attainment. There is a reluctance to grasp the potential of the personalist language that has been introduced. Instead he is content to rest with the conventional espousal of positions that, in truth, are no longer as fixed as they appear to be. The loss of God may be stated, but it can only be stated because God has not been lost. This is the great drama of modern atheism that the Church has often come achingly close to grasping.[18] What is needed to overcome the tendency to dismiss it as mere artifice is the realization that it arises from within the Christian experience itself. The God who is absent is the one who is held with the deepest inwardness. "My God, my God, why have you forsaken me?" is not only the cry in which God is lost most completely. It is also the one in which God is loved most completely. Can the transcendent be held in any other way than through transcendence? This is the opening that Benedict finally lays before us in *The Light of Faith* (*Lumen fidei*), the encyclical he had virtually completed when he stepped down from the papacy and that was subsequently issued by Francis in 2013.

Within that bridge encyclical, Benedict/Francis no longer talk about the person and the imperative of conceiving human life within the category of relation. Now that perspective is implemented as a meditation on the light of faith that makes all faith possible. The circuit that had begun with the opening reflection on God, *Deus caritas est*, and then taught us we are saved by hope, *Spe salvi*, reaching what seemed a conclusion in locating charity within truth, *Caritas in veritate*, now looks back on what has made the whole reflection possible. *Lumen fidei* thereby gains a higher viewpoint on the whole meditation, for it not only completes the trilogy of theological virtues, but discloses the movement of knowledge through love from which they arise. Faith formed by love, and the hope that love sustains, now emerges as the very structure of the relationship in which God and man are united. Rather than beginning with faith as the conventional starting point, Benedict has made it the end point. His strategy must surely have something to do with the suspicion under which any profession of faith falls in a secular age. Love and hope are far less burdened, for even in the absence of God they remain viable features of human life. Faith, because it emerges as a truth claim, already strains against the presumption that there is no truth. Here at last Benedict reaches the target of his lifelong struggle against relativism. The question of truth on which all else ultimately turns is confronted. The great breakthrough is that where previously Ratzinger-Benedict had felt compelled to defend truth, even faith in truth, now he could unfold truth as its own movement of faith. The shift to the relational perspective of the person had been completed. And that meant that faith could be contemplated entirely from within the movement by which it is constituted, without the slightest concession to the subjective character of its conviction. Interiority had been banished when the transition has been made to the reality within which it is located. We do not keep faith, for faith is what keeps us.

The light of faith is not our light but the light by which faith itself is reached. It is a gift that, contrary to Nietzsche's admonition, does not preclude seeking, for it is what sustains it.[19] An age that has begun to concede the limits of autonomous reason is already opening toward "a luminous vision of existence" (*Lumen fidei*, para. 5) as its deepest condition of possibility. The light by which we see all things cannot itself be seen, but it can be apprehended as we enter upon the path of faith. The sequence of steps is not laid out in advance. Yet in looking back from its end point we can see the journey that has been undertaken. It consists of taking the search for truth as a quest that carries its own dimension of faith within it from the very start. Truth cannot be declared impossible if it is to be sought. But that faith in truth must be derived from something more than a longing that may prove to be groundless. If faith is to be relied upon, then it must arise from a source that is utterly faithful. Initially it is only a faith in the trustworthiness of the call that draws us into the search for truth. Only gradually does it become apparent that that trust is most appropriately placed in a person who is trustworthy, who is trustworthiness as such. Then the searcher begins to discern the full dimension of the quest on which he or she has been launched. Even its beginning, we see more clearly, is not our own. There would be no search unless we had first been called to enter upon it. The question, or what stirs the question to life within us, must come from beyond ourselves. It is the self-revelation of that source that is the pivotal moment in the unfolding of the quest. Faith is confirmed in the encounter with the Other who thereby assures us of his faithfulness. The quest of faith heads toward the One who has all along been the source of its call. Benedict intuits his way toward this conclusion that the reality in which we find ourselves is inescapably personal, rather than explicating the steps through which he passes. For him it is the disclosive character of existence that stands out most prominently. We are at every point drawn toward the One who continually draws us through the materiality of things. Meaning points ultimately toward the person who comprehensively reveals it. If reality is a love letter, then the love it discloses is always just about to surprise us.

Chapter One of *Lumen fidei*, "We have believed in love" (1 John 4:16), begins with the call of Abraham. Faith is thus not a general possibility but the possibility for a specific individual. It is the call of each person by God, who reveals himself as a person. The call of Abraham consists of hearing the word of God, while the vision of the future is seen only by the response of believing it. Call and response unfold through the bond of fidelity (*fidelitas*), by which the man of faith is drawn into relationship with the God who is faithful. The promise is what opens time as its underlying relationship. Idolatry is the arresting of the moment into the present that scatters time into a multiplicity without coherence. By contrast, faith opens into the We of the community that is constituted for the journey of faith in time. Moses mediates his faith to the community that participates in his encounter with God. Everything in the Old Testament points toward that culminating moment when the perfect mediator becomes present in Christ. His perfect love extends beyond the natural limit of death to confirm the utter reliability of God. It is the Resurrection that reveals the fidelity of God's love, who is now seen through the eyes of Jesus. Faith is thus the eye of love. It is the moment in which the primacy of God's gift comes into view. Drawing on the Pauline formulation that it is not I who live but Christ who lives within me (Eph. 3:17), Benedict shows the full relational character of that understanding: "The self-awareness of the believer now expands because of the presence of another; it now lives in this other, and thus, in love, life takes on a whole new breadth. Here we see the Holy Spirit at work" (*Lumen fidei*, para. 21). As such a personal relationship, faith is necessarily an opening to all other persons, especially in the ecclesial setting of those who are united in Christ.

In Chapter Five of *Lumen fidei*, Benedict broadens the relationship of love to show how faith apprehends the truth that it thereby understands. The title of the chapter is taken from his preferred rendering of Isaiah 7:9 as "Unless you believe, you will not understand." In a fascinating aside he lays out the alternative versions of the verse in the Septuagint and the Hebrew text. The latter has "be established," whereas the Greek emphasizes the more intellectual "understand." The apparent difference in formulations, Benedict explains, disappears when we realize that "established" derives from the understanding of God's fidelity. Faith is therefore not a projection of our yearning or a lofty sentiment. If it were a merely subjective event, King Ahaz would have been right to dismiss the prophet's admonition to trust only in God rather than in his own rational calculation of the safety of an alliance. The superiority of faith lies not in its subjective conviction but in the connection with truth that is built into it. As a relation to God faith is a participation in the certainty that is the reality of God. It is this "intrinsic link to truth" (para. 24) that makes faith of such signal importance in a world that has lost faith in truth. "The question of truth is really a question of memory, deep memory, for it deals with something prior to ourselves and can succeed in uniting us in a way that transcends our petty and limited individual consciousness. It is a question about the origin of all that is, in whose light we can glimpse the goal and thus the meaning of our common path" (para. 25). We do not simply think about the whole order of things, Benedict seems to be trying to say, but find ourselves already a part of it. Our mind is a part of the reality it contemplates. We thus know it from within, and, like all that is known within relationship, it is glimpsed more fully the more we open toward it in love. As a personal relationship, the relationship to truth is one that derives from a personal response. The truth we seek is already there before we begin, for it is the condition of our seeking it. We must have faith in truth if we are to arrive at truth.

Faith is prior and more certain than knowledge because it is a knowledge of what is sought. It is the knowledge born of love. Benedict quotes the observation of Wittgenstein that believing is like falling in love and therefore something entirely subjective. But that on Benedict's reading is to deny the nature of love that aims at union with the beloved. Contrary to a merely subjective apprehension of the other, it aims at the truth of the other: "One who loves realizes that love is an experience of truth, that it opens our eyes to see reality in a new way, in union with the beloved" (*Lumen fidei*, para. 27). It is a relational form of knowledge, for it sees with the eyes of the other. In the biblical setting this means seeing through the mind of God whose covenantal love is what opens up the path of history. The truth of God's love, conclusively revealed in the complete self-giving of Christ, is finally recognized as the culmination of love itself. All our loves are seen as a sharing in its inexhaustibility. The personal encounter with the Other opens to all others who are loved in the same way, without limit or condition, and thereby moves definitively away from anything merely singular or private. The truth of love and the love of truth underpin the common good. It unites all who are seeking, whether in science or other religions or in theology itself, for it is a subordination to the call of truth that each has heard in his or her own uniquely personal way. The search that each must personally undertake now reaches its goal in the disclosure of God as a person who has all along been present in the call. Interpersonal knowledge as the culmination of faith affirms the validity of knowledge. "God cannot be reduced to an object. He is a subject who makes himself known and perceived in an interpersonal relationship" (para. 36). The prompting that had all along sustained the movement toward its goal is now reached in the person who stands as its overarching warrant. Like the woman who suffered from a hemorrhage in the gospel, we can only truly touch Christ if we do so with our whole being. Faith is the personal encounter with the Lord (para. 31).

It very much depends on the readiness to open oneself fully to the One who calls, for the revelation cannot be received by anything less than the whole person: "Faith transforms the whole person precisely to the extent that he becomes open to love" (*Lumen fidei*, para. 26). Quoting

Paul, "One believes with the heart" (Rom. 10:10), Benedict links all of our searching, including the rational path opened through Greek philosophy, with the ultimate horizon of the person in whom it is located. The path of faith that Isaiah opens for Ahaz, "Unless you believe, you will not understand," is the invitation available to every man, for each carries the capacity for a personal opening within. Even when they do not know for whom they search, they still attest to the ineradicable openness out of which their seeking comes. It is the inherently personal dimension of questioning that Benedict wishes to highlight in his ever-deepening meditation on faith: "This discovery of love as a source of knowledge, which is part of the primordial experience of every man, finds authoritative expression in the biblical understanding of faith" (para. 28). He is convinced that the opening to love through faith is the answer to the crisis of truth in our time, for he repeatedly references the dismissal of the claim to truth as either a totalitarian imposition or a retreat into subjectivism (para. 34). The location of truth within a reality that "establishes" it depends on contact with that which is enduring beyond all possibility of decline. But where is that to be found? Only one who searches with the whole self will open to the encounter with another self that has already given all. It culminates in the encounter with the God who is love and who loves to the point of his own extinction. There may be a certain dissatisfaction that this does not provide a sufficient answer to those who, like Ahaz, are not quite prepared for the complete self-surrender to God. Benedict seems aware of this hesitation, but he does not explicitly address it, even by way of explaining why the encounter with God cannot take place with anything less than our whole being. Intuitively, however, he knows that the meeting of persons entails a complete self-giving. "I and Thou" cannot be said in half measures.

We begin to see this when we include the role of the Church in transmitting the life of faith. Benedict is careful to avoid the implication that this is a solitary enterprise. It is through the Church that we encounter the chain of witnesses that go all the way back to the apostles who first encountered Christ and who resolved to devote themselves to handing it on to us: "Persons always live in relationship. We come from others, we belong to others, and our lives are enlarged by our encounter with others" (*Lumen fidei*, para. 38). In Chapter Three, "I delivered to you what I also received (1 Cor. 15:3)," Benedict describes how it is through the Church that we become contemporaries with Christ meeting him today. He goes on to detail the way this occurs through the teaching and sacraments of the Church, emphasizing the extent of our dependence on others for hearing the Word and for receiving the material signs of its transformative effect. In this way faith is broadened to include the whole community of the faithful. It is through others that we enter upon the dialogue with God that culminates in love, and we in turn play our part in building the unity that assumes visible form in the concrete reality of the Church. Even here, Benedict returns to his theme of the compatibility of a communitarian vision with individual autonomy. Far from a conflict between them, he sees the unity of truth as their mutual confirmation: "We tend to think that a unity of this sort is incompatible with freedom of thought and personal autonomy. Yet the experience of love shows us that a common vision is possible, for through love we learn how to see reality through the eyes of others, as something that does not impoverish but enriches our vision" (para. 47). It is resort to private viewpoints that ruptures the unity of the Church and thereby invalidates the claim to truth that is asserted. Departure from the universality of the Church's vision of the Lord attests to the distorting effect of individual perspectives. Faith, Benedict emphasizes, rests on the unity and universality of the community that transmits it: "For this reason, the magisterium always speaks in obedience to the prior word on which faith is based; it is reliable because of its trust in the word which it hears, preserves, and expounds" (para. 49).

That theme of the broadening of faith to the community that sustains it provides the opening to the final chapter, on the city: Chapter Four, "God prepares a city for them (cf. Heb. 11:16)." Faith calls forth the community that journeys toward God through history, but it also provides the basis for the building up of community within history. Benedict connects his meditation with the social teaching of his public addresses and of the preceding encyclicals. He continues the personalist shift in his reflection on how the community of faith underpins the temporal community: "Precisely because it is linked to love (cf. Gal. 5:6), the light of faith is concretely placed at the service of justice, law, and peace" (*Lumen fidei*, para. 51). Faith grounded in love is a disclosure of the deepest bond of all human relationships, which must now be seen in a new light. The justice that underpins the publicly common good may not reach the full amplitude of divine love, even though that remains its foundation. "Without a love which is trustworthy, nothing could truly keep men united" (para. 51). This is seen most clearly in the family where the upbuilding of faith is most needed. There we are called to make a pledge of fidelity that our finite resources seem ill-equipped to bear. It is only possible, Benedict explains, if we see our pledge of mutual love as sustained by a pledge that derives from beyond us. In this way faith also enables us to glimpse the meaning of the begetting of children, "as a sign of the love of the Creator who entrusts us with the mystery of a new person" (para. 52). Through faith our horizons are enlarged and we become aware of "the vocation of love" as the calling for each of us. From there love broadens into the brotherhood of all human beings. The gaze of Christian faith illumines the unique dignity of every person, as opposed to the reductionist perspectives that were present in the ancient world as much as in our own. In this light, nature is no longer material, appearing only in the framework of utility, but a gift from God to be reverenced and preserved. Even forms of government come to reflect their divine authorization and are sustained by a willingness to forgive that attests to the priority of goodness over evil. That requirement might even entail, Benedict suggests, acknowledgment of God in a world that is no longer comfortable with such public affirmation. In the end, it is the light that faith brings in the hour of trial that is its most convincing witness. Just as Mother Teresa did not eliminate the suffering of the dying whom she lifted off the streets of Calcutta, so faith does not change the condition in which we find ourselves. But it does offer an accompanying presence: "In Christ, God himself wishes to share this path with us and to offer us his gaze so that we might see the light within it" (para. 57). This is preeminently presented to us in the gaze of Mary, who unites herself with Jesus in a prayer that joins Benedict and Francis.

CHAPTER FIFTEEN

Science Is Not Scientific

The chapter title is intentionally provocative. It takes aim at the unquestioned authority in our world and asks it to explain itself. Can science be scientifically justified? One can almost hear the howls of dismissal. Science is what justifies all other claims to knowledge. It itself requires none. How could we have the temerity to suggest that it demonstrate its validity? What could be more reliable than that which tests all reliability? The supremacy of science arises from the invincibility of its method. For most purposes that is enough. The success of science is demonstrated in the ever-more comprehensive access to reality it provides. We simply know the universe around us in more compelling ways. Yet we cannot quite eliminate a flickering awareness of the partiality of its perspective. To comprehend science we must, first, be prepared to go beyond it, since science is incapable of understanding itself. The breakthrough occurs, second, when we realize that science is a reaching up toward the mind of God. Our conclusion, third, is that science is itself a spiritual reality, a transcending of all that merely is. It is the love of God even when it does not know God.

Science Cannot Know Itself

Science is not all of knowledge. We know this most of all when we notice its inability to ground its own first principles.[1] They can only be assumed. No one can demonstrate that scientific method provides a true access to reality. Even the fact that it has yielded a probably true account is no more than the accumulation of evidence. The leap of judgment by which we assert that the evidence is sufficient is not itself something based on evidence. It is the point at which we stand outside of evidence to render judgment upon it, for evidence cannot compel this assent. We must freely reach it in our capacity to transcend what is merely given. All working scientists know this interplay of thought and the material on which it works. They know the pull of competing theories and approaches; they know that they already soar far above them. It is the romance of uncovering hitherto unknown vistas that draws them on, refusing to remain within the limits of the routinely known. In many respects they are less interested in knowledge than in the quest for it. It is wonder, Aristotle remarked, that is the great opening of the mind upon reality.

We forget, in other words, what makes science possible. It is only occasionally that our somnolence is ruptured by the thought of the strangeness of science itself. We sense that we are at the heart of a mystery. How can science be possible? How is it that at one point in the universe there exist small creatures, human beings, capable of contemplating it all? We are a part of the cosmic vastness and yet we can think of it as if we were not. A thinking reed, as Pascal called us, is simultaneously permanent and impermanent. Not only is it a wonder that we arrive at insights and judgments that form the building blocks of scientific theory, but its possibility is something that utterly escapes us. We know that the process of discovery involves creative events beyond our control. All our investigations of the universe depend on those flashes of genius we cannot summon and must accept in gratitude. Where our thoughts come from we do not know. But when we think about thinking as such we seem incapable of plumbing its mystery. Even Aristotle, who gave us the formulation "thought thinking itself" (*noêsis noêseôs noêsis*) (*Metaphysics* 1074b34), could only lead us to the boundary of the mystery. Its veil could not be removed. We are left with the admission of unsurpassability proclaimed by Einstein two millennia later: "The most incomprehensible thing about the universe is that it is comprehensible."[2]

That demarcation of a limit, however, must not be taken as the final word on the matter. Science may carry on without examining what it can never fully investigate, but philosophers have a calling to probe it as far as thought will allow. In an age dominated by science and the forgetfulness of its foundations, that responsibility assumes even greater importance. The present reflection is offered as just such a modest pondering of the imponderable. As such it lays claim to no greater insight or information but only to fidelity to the question that the existence of science itself calls forth. Like Socrates we concede that we have no greater wisdom, but like him we realize that that concession is already the beginning of wisdom. Admitting a boundary to thought is not quite the same as reaching a wall that blocks our path, for it is already the beginning of a glimpse beyond it. In knowing the limit we have begun to see it as limit, that is, as what does not just limit us. Even if we have not moved much beyond it, we have in a small way grasped that possibility. We have not remained silent about what cannot be said, but have said more than can be said.

We have seen further than science itself can see, for we have glimpsed what remains invisible within its perspective. Too preoccupied with what it investigates, science scarcely gives a thought to itself. It does not see how extraordinarily different it is from everything it examines. This is the blind spot of every observer who cannot include the self within the field of vision. Yet even this analogy is not quite accurate, for we have just defeated it. We have noticed what cannot be seen or known. Science can ask about the condition of its own possibility and in this way is fundamentally different from every other reality that simply is. The mind is present by way of never being fully present. Its capacity to know things contains both itself and what it knows. Self-consciousness is its deepest reality. The incomprehensibility, that so struck Einstein, has begun to diminish slightly. We begin to see that science rests, not on a method that infallibly guarantees its success, but on the capacity to stand outside of the whole including the self that undertakes the contemplation. No artificial intelligence (a contradiction in terms) could ever raise the question of its own capacity, as Einstein did. Comprehension, it turns out, includes marveling at itself even if that reflection yields up the confession of its incomprehensibility. We do not know how it is possible for us to know the universe, the process that science accomplishes every day, but we do intuit the mystery by which it occurs. Science is contained in the mystery of its possibility. It is not a sheer mystery but one that, in being contemplated, discloses its presence.

Prior to the method of empirical verification is the readiness to embrace it as method. Like the rule of law, following scientific method is not included within its rules. It is the possibility of a rule as such. This means that the validity of science does not derive from its method but from the openness that embraces a methodical approach to the analysis of reality. Whence does the openness originate? That is what is mysterious. We cannot get behind it, but we can say something about it. We know that it is something given to us, an invitation we willingly and readily take up. In responding to the call of reality we discover our own capacity to set everything aside, even our own biological needs, for the brief moment in which we put ourselves in the position of what is not ourselves. We know by setting ourselves aside for the sake of knowing the other. Scientific method is no more than the formalization of that generosity. We become nothing so that the reality we investigate may occupy the whole of our attention. Objectivity is possible because subjectivity can be overcome. We do not live in ourselves but in the whole universe. While occupying a particular place and time we disclose our capacity to embrace every place and time. Nothing lies beyond the reach of our minds. Nothing is so alien that it cannot be comprehended. The inwardness that reaches everything outside of us demonstrates that we are utterly different from all that we consider. It is that unlimited openness that makes it possible for us to follow the canons of scientific method without imposing any preconditions. Wanting nothing in return we can come to know reality as it is. We have transcended it. That is the perspective of science that can with difficulty be glimpsed from within its practice but never encountered in any reality other than the scientist.

Science Seeks the Mind of God

Science can in other words understand everything except science itself. This is a revision of Einstein's observation, but one that calls attention to the great intellectual challenge science confronts today. For most of its modern development science could safely ignore itself as it explored the nature of the universe around it. But gradually as the scope of its mathematical penetration became ever-more comprehensive it could not avoid pronouncing on the nature of the whole. The theory of everything that Einstein proposed as the goal of physics would have to include the genesis of reality itself. Stephen Hawking, for example, could not resist pronouncing on the question of creation. His 2010 book attempts to establish the possibility that the universe may be one of many universes that are capable of coming spontaneously into existence.[3] God is rendered obsolete. Other scientists, notably Richard Dawkins and Daniel Dennett, undertake a more aggressive critique of the notion of God.[4] He has become an outdated delusion to be discarded by a scientific worldview that can now stand on its own feet. What is the value of a God hypothesis that can play no role within our comprehension of the world? One would almost be inclined to agree with them, except that their protest against God suggests that he cannot be so easily set aside. Even the atheists are curiously absorbed with him. They constantly recall what they wish to reject. Perhaps the whole imbroglio arises from a deeper unease that cannot quite be acknowledged. Could it be that the place of science itself cannot be assured without a mind that transcends it? If the physicist is no more than a thinking speck of matter, perhaps what he or she thinks is equally insignificant.

Dependence and rivalry with a divine creator seem inherent to the scientific enterprise. We are, after all, aiming to comprehend reality from a God-like point of view. But this presupposes that such a viewpoint is possible, for we cannot even approach it if it is not real. This is the great crisis that rumbles beneath the surface of contemporary science. Talk of a "God particle" or of a theory that explains everything carries something of the bravado that dares not confront the most troubling implication. That is, that such a perspective would have to include itself or risk the incompleteness that would overturn it. If science is as contingent as everything it studies, then its knowledge is also contingent. It is ephemeral. Probability may be the closest that science approaches in making its truth claims, but it cannot afford to regard that assertion as itself merely probable. Somehow, somewhere it must be anchored in the more than probable. Science is the absolute assertion of probability. As with the weather forecasts, the employment of percentages allows them to claim 100 percent accuracy. The premise of probability is certainty. Statistics as a discipline is not statistically true. Ancient science did not suffer from the same impediment since it knew that it stood within the arc of the first principle or ground of all things, from which it sought to derive the order of the cosmos. Modern science with its shift to the empirically verifiable could long overlook its own derivation from a lingering absolute. It could discourse in probabilities without attending to the nature of that discourse itself. But now that it aims at a comprehensive worldview, it cannot simply bypass itself. It has no choice but to provide its own grounds by displacing God in reaching for God-like comprehensiveness.

The curious character of an independence that underlines its dependence can now be understood. The spectacle of a science that seeks to eradicate God, and thereby proclaims his ineradicability, is puzzling until we understand its source. A science of contingency cannot itself be contingent. It must arise from a necessity that insists that, even though the universe is not necessary, science itself is. The cosmos can only be comprehended from the perspective of that which escapes its contingency. It is by accounting for the whole that the authority of science is established, for then it has comprehended the condition of its own possibility. By contrast, invocation of a creator would constitute an affront to the unsurpassability of science. It would be to appeal to an extrinsic explanation for what can only be compelling if it arises from within the intrinsic realm. Needing nothing beyond itself, science can now enjoy the absoluteness of that which exists in undiminished supremacy. Ancient science understood that contemplation was participation in the life of the gods, but modern science has vaulted directly into that highest attainment of autarky. Science is no longer reading the mind of God—it has identified itself with the mind of God. Its ambition must outstrip its character as a science of contingency because it intuits its untenability as science on any other basis. Like Nietzsche, science has no choice but to become God because it knows that only God's knowledge is true.

The impossibility of the aspiration only becomes explicit when science turns its focus toward human origins. Then it becomes evident that human beings are reducible to the biochemical ingredients that constitute them. Their emergence is sufficiently accounted for in some version of Darwinian natural selection. Evolutionary emergence becomes the comprehensive theory of life, including human life. The shock wave that assaults religion is only the most notorious effect of the theory of evolution. Less noticed are the disturbances that ripple across the self-understanding of science. Darwin himself confessed to the unease that troubled him when he thought of the status of his own theory. Was it any more than the convictions a monkey might harbor, supposing there were convictions in a monkey brain?[5] It was clear that the prospect that his own science might be no more than the feverish working of a particular organism had unnerved him. He had begun to contemplate what has become a commonplace of neuroscience in our own day, namely, that thought, including the thought of neuroscientists themselves, is nothing more than electrochemical events within the brain. The difference is that we no longer even voice the hesitations that Darwin admitted. We are too awed by the prestige of science to point out any contradiction in its view of the universe, especially when the conflict involves its basic presuppositions. There cannot be anything in the universe that cannot be analyzed into its material constituents. Not even science itself can be permitted to stand in the way of science.

Naturally, the suppression of inconsistency must involve a range of defense mechanisms. The simplest is avoidance of the questions that might trouble it, or, when they do occur, a flat rejection of their relevance, or, in the last resort, denunciation of the questioners as deluded. The vehemence with which any murmuring against the monopoly of materialistic explanations is greeted confirms the discomfort. As a consequence it takes a brave soul to publicly critique the regnant naturalistic worldview. Scientists themselves can only do so by strictly separating their spiritual convictions from what is scientifically authorized. No right-thinking person could dispute the materialist paradigm, but, occasionally, a gadfly will suggest that it is badly in need of an overhaul.[6] The scorn heaped on such a suggestion is proof of materialism's status as unquestioned orthodoxy. Allegiance is socially enforced rather than reached through mutual agreement. We are in the curious situation where science itself, in the sense of the rigid requirements of professional conformity, is the principal obstacle to the openness of inquiry. One is simply prohibited from pursuing certain lines of questioning. Scientism is in danger of supplanting science. Defensiveness may have arisen from the clashes between science and religion that have periodically erupted, but resistance to the possibility of a paradigm shift is surely the point at which science moves furthest away from science. This is the big insight of Thomas Kuhn's famous book *The Structure of Scientific Revolutions*. He narrates the history of science as a series of disjunctive leaps that establish a sequence of new stabilizations. At each of those decisive turning points it is the validity of science itself that is at stake, as it struggles to choose between loyalty to the dominant paradigm or the intellectual expansiveness required to build a new one.

It is hardly too dramatic to suggest that we are at just such a juncture today. The steady accumulation of inconsistencies within the prevailing model has become unsustainable. An intellectual breakthrough is conceivable once we have begun to discern the outlines of an alternate worldview. This prospect does not, despite the gloomy forebodings often broached, entail any return to premodern patterns of discourse. One does not have to be a fundamentalist to concede the limits of a materialist outlook. Nor does one have to jettison the enlargement of rationality that the advent of modern science has introduced into our understanding of the universe. What is needed is a willingness to follow the thread of reason more deeply. The courage to entrust ourselves to the sustaining power of science itself can carry us beyond the impasse into which it has temporarily led us. A science that yields a view of the world that has no place for science itself is stunningly at odds with all that we know. Nothing is to be gained from refusing to concede the contradiction. However we begin to reconcile the activity of mind with a world that is explained largely in terms of its material components, nothing is to be gained by persisting in the attitude of denial. Obstinacy cannot disclose the way forward. Only a readiness to expand the horizon of our thought can accommodate the divergent implications within it. Somehow they must be compatible within a whole. It was that faith that has sustained the great enlargement of understanding that modern science has made possible. This is hardly the moment to renege on it for the sake of preserving an orthodoxy that daily becomes more threadbare. We must be willing to admit that science itself is at odds with the worldview it has constructed.

Science Is a Spiritual Reality

That concession is sufficient to inaugurate a turn away from the regnant paradigm. Far from betraying the scientific advance, this entails a fuller commitment to its unfolding. Science must now begin to include itself within its purview. It can no longer limit itself to the material universe in order to find a basis for itself. The model of physical causation is simply not adequate to the thought world of science itself. Even if neuroscience were to comprehensively map consciousness within the brain, that would still not provide any access to what consciousness contains. It would be like looking at a house from the outside without having any intimation of what is going on within it. No doubt much useful information could be accumulated by such an enterprise. We might even be able to formulate general patterns of activity. But their meaning would entirely escape us. For that we would have to enter into the life world of the residents, questioning them as to their intentions and in the process revealing ours to them. Human society can only be known from within it. The same is true of the great enterprise of science it has generated. Science can only be understood in its own terms. Not even neurophysiologists communicate their thoughts in the form of brain events. They know their theories are intelligible only as thoughts. Of course, there are physical correlates to what occurs in the mind, but that is very different from the assertion of an identity. Science, we must admit, is essentially a nonphysical event in the sense that it can be accessed only in terms of thinking it. Just as science is not reducible to neurological phenomena, so it is not containable within the physical means of its communication. Science is no more in brains than it is in books. The marks or traces that scientific inquiry leaves behind are intelligible only within the minds that created them. Its collaborative aspect is primarily a meeting of minds.

That is an event that can occur anywhere and anytime because it occurs nowhere and in no time. While exploring the events of space and time, science itself is definitively outside of both. There is no analogue in the external world. Science is contained nowhere but within itself. Simply because scientists occupy space and consume food does not mean that their work can be identified with the evidence of their physical presence. From a biological perspective, endless hours of attending to test tubes, dials, and texts is well-nigh incomprehensible. It is only because we too know something of its interior dynamic that it becomes intelligible. Strictly speaking, science exists only within the minds of scientists. They do not even have to be in proximity to one another in space or time for that event to occur. Understanding leaps across the boundaries that confine us and endures forever. Even death does not destroy it, for it can be accessed by all who come upon the record much later. What is preserved are not the marks on paper or a screen but the meaning by which they can be comprehended. A physical means of communication indeed is indispensable. Science does not work through telepathy. But its most decisive aspect is not the physical remainder but the meaning that lies utterly beyond it. If we did not know any better, we would be inclined to say that science is essentially a spiritual reality and that scientists are spiritual beings. Even the term "spirit," however, derives from the physiology of breathing. It suggests another kind of physical reality rather than another reality altogether. When pressed to name it, we can only say it is within us. Yet even that is not quite accurate since we are just as much within *it*.

The tropes of subjective and objective defeat us, as they must, when talk about them underlines their failure to encompass the real. All our thinking occurs outside the boundaries that might be assigned to it. The world of thought is certainly not subjective, but it is also clearly not in any way an objective reality. It is definitively within itself. We do not create it but find ourselves within it. The whole possibility of thinking arises from its primordiality that we can apprehend but not penetrate. We cannot think beyond the possibility of thought. It simply is, neither coming into existence nor departing from it. To think is to move within its eternity, but that does not mean that we become or comprehend the eternal. The mystery of thought is its transcendence of temporality. How that is possible we cannot really know because to do so would be to engage in the same transcendence. All that we can say is that it is the condition of the possibility of thought, just as it is the condition of the possibility of the person. The process is slightly more familiar in the case of the latter and may provide the best avenue on what thinking is. We know that persons present a persona, as the Greek origin of the word as mask (*prosōpon*) indicates. The actor who holds a mask is not in the mask but has clearly gone beyond it. The whole of a person's life, all that he does or says, is not sufficient to disclose who he is, even to himself. In every revelation the person escapes revelation, as the inexhaustibility from which it derives. Yet we know him or her as such. The infinity that the person is cannot be named, but it can be glimpsed, for that is the horizon within which all communication occurs. The person always says more than is said and reveals more than can be revealed. The uncontainable is contained, for we encounter the other. Transcendence is the medium of communication. Science that moves within the same transparence is no stranger to the inaccessible. It can apprehend the order of things because it knows its own derivation from beyond it. This has nothing to do with belief in a divine origin or even with the aspiration for God-like comprehension we noted above. It is simply the transcendence of every limit that is the reality of thought. Even its own thinking is not outside of its purview, but it can glimpse that transcendence only obliquely.

Science arises from we know not where. Its beginning can be dated historically but not what provides the possibility of its beginning. That is the arc of the unsurpassable that Immanuel Kant was the first to clearly acknowledge. He saw that the epistemological quest for certainty was a dead end. Knowledge cannot secure itself without appealing to the same test of validity. Empirical verification cannot be empirically verified. What Kant did not discern so clearly is that his own insight is not so similarly afflicted. It is a grasp of the inexorability by which knowledge itself is grasped. Somehow his insight has managed to embrace its own ground. That is what the opening of knowledge always entails. It arises from the conviction that it must incorporate the means of its own success within its movement. Just as moral action includes the postulate of freedom, so scientific inquiry must include the postulate of intelligibility. The mind can understand and the universe can be understood. Nothing can empirically justify such faith, which is both undeniable and indemonstrable. It is abyssal in the sense that it arises from a depth that cannot be plumbed. To call it a leap would be inaccurate, for it is incapable of departing from its beginning, the intuition that it is in contact with the whole of being it inchoately contains. How could the mind sever itself from what is innermost within it? The reliability of knowledge is not a conclusion to be reached but the basis by which it reaches out to the world. Nothing can confirm faith but faith itself. It is the movement by which all subsequent movement is sustained. Before it believes in anything, faith believes in itself. It is faith in faith. To say it is the horizon of thought is to create the impression that we know what it is. We are incapable of mastering it and stand instead within its radiance. The apprehension of truth, even a probable truth, cannot but acknowledge truth as such. We may, like Kant, be able to talk about categories of understanding, but we cannot talk about the category of that discourse. We simply move within it.

In the same way, there is no science of science. There is only the transparence of the movement toward the truth and reality of things, a movement that exceeds any of the things to which it leads. Science, as Einstein so evocatively observed, is a bigger mystery to itself than any of the mysteries it seeks to probe. It is the comprehending mystery. That is why it resists scientific analysis, especially of the reductionistic variety that remains the contemporary default model. Not only is there no branch of science that operates as a form of mechanical causation, but science itself is the definitive refutation of the materialistic explanations it applies everywhere else. The "selfish gene" may be a scientific explanation, but it is not an explanation of science. Nietzsche suggested that religious asceticism had migrated into the scientific asceticism of truth.[7] His point is commonly seen as an aspersion on the spirit of asceticism, but it could just as easily be taken as a more positive evaluation of science. For us science is the modern form of spirituality. It arises from an awesome dedication to truth, one that is willing to cast aside all that might provide comfort, including the comfort of illusion, for the sake of unwavering fidelity to truth. Even if science can find no higher meaning, it can still persevere in its unyielding commitment to truth. It would rather die without consolation than accept a consolation it knew to be false. Preservation of its integrity is sufficient reward for its struggle. When one thinks over Nietzsche's own commitment to the same struggle it is not clear that his remark is so disdainful. It may well be that he had hit upon the secret of modern science.

The resolute refusal of all consolation but truth may be its deepest impulse. When we ask whence this guiding conviction arises, we must concede that it seems to come from far below the surface we normally inhabit. In many respects it emerges only from within its own logic. We know it cannot derive from scientific method since no method can be the source of its own initiation. A method is always adopted from outside of it. There must be something beyond the method that prompts its embrace. Faith in the method begins in faith itself. Nothing grounds it since nothing is prior to it. Faith is the sustaining movement that is the continuous unfolding of a beginning we cannot entirely fathom since we are borne along by it. All that we know is that it puts us in touch with a higher imperative than the merely biological. Life itself must be subordinated to its inexorability. Science in this sense is not only a transcendence of the spatio-temporal limits of our existence but arises from the same transcendence. Stephen Hawking's endeavor to supplant God within a theory of everything, including how everything came into being, is not so wide of the mark as its Promethean echo would suggest. It resonates with the very core of the scientific drive. Even God cannot be permitted to block the path by which we open toward the truth of all things. Like several modern mystics, Hawking's theory of everything represents the determination to let nothing stand in the way of God, not even God himself.[8] The very intensity of this imperative discloses how far beyond science its interior impulse lies. Transcendence of all that might only satisfy, but not fulfill, attests to the unlimited openness from which it springs. Science at its deepest is the love of God. The challenge is to maintain the purity of heart required to put away the last vestige of ambition in the process. No hint of self-aggrandizement can taint it. The self itself is finally transcended in its acknowledgment that its self-transcendence is not its own. Only that which is transcendence can provide the condition of its possibility. Even the freedom of response is not properly its own, for it arises from it knows not where. Science with its soaring trajectory of all that *is* is ultimately a gift that, like all gifts, can neither be claimed nor deserved. Perhaps it is in Hawkings's own life that the life of the gift is most fully exemplified.

CHAPTER SIXTEEN

Hope Does Not Disappoint

When hope is lost it is needed most of all. It is only when the situation has become hopeless that hope comes into its own, for we cannot lose hope. The very meaning of hope is bound up with this paradox by which the more it is lost the more deeply it is retained. This is evident in the ordinary meaning of the word, for we would hardly consider it a mark of hope if it was present merely when everything was going well. On the contrary, we are inclined to think, it is precisely when the whole world has fallen apart that hope rises to sustain us. It is in this sense that hope does not disappoint. Everything else may disappoint but hope cannot, because it has already reached its goal. This is what it means to hope, that we cannot be disappointed. Nothing that happens can dislodge us from our hope because that is precisely what hope is, a warrant against disappointment. That is not the same as success. Hope does not carry a guarantee that we will accomplish or reach the objectives we set for ourselves. But it does immunize us against abandonment of the struggle. Without giving us the sure possession of our goal, hope provides us with the only sure pathway toward it. Through hope we lay hold of our goal and thereby become capable of reaching it. Put another way, we might say that we have already arrived at the goal at which we still have yet to arrive. Hope is what spans the work of life. We may think that it is up to us to hold onto hope, but it is really hope that holds onto us. In the end this is why hope cannot disappoint. We may disappoint, but hope, by definition, is what cannot disappoint. Hopelessness is only our failure to hope. It is not a failure of hope itself.

All of this dynamic comes vividly into view at times when hope itself is under strain, when we can discern few reasons for hope. In the absence of hope we become aware of its deeper undertow. We realize that not only does hope not depend on reasons, but that it is most manifest when the reasons for hope have disappeared. The crisis of confidence that gripped the world financial markets in 2008 and pervaded the global economy is such an instance. Hope in the ordinary reliability of contracts had evaporated and the clothes of optimism were in tatters. Acceptance of the normal ups and downs of business transactions was replaced by the paralysis of a globalized distrust of exchange. Metaphors of machines seizing up hardly captured the sheer panic of the prospect that cash would no longer be available when we sought to withdraw it from our ATMs. The terror that induced money managers to accept, even for a short while, a negative return on U.S. Treasury bills was a more telling indication. When no repository can be relied on, funds must be parked in the only repository that can be relied on. It was a moment of acute awareness of the insubstantiality of all of the arrangements so routinely taken for granted. The world economy rested, we saw, on evanescence. Collectively we experienced that unmistakable jolt with which our feet pound the floor when we thought we still have one more step to descend. Instantaneously we were alert to what we had scarcely been aware of only moments before. We saw with searing clarity that the whole vast network of interlocking transactions was in reality nothing more than a web of hope. Would it endure?

The global shudder that pervaded world financial markets, and perhaps still ripples through the real economic relationships of our lives, has yet to encounter an answer to that question. Recession is merely recognition of the absence of an answer. That is, the cascading effect of myriad individual choices to withdraw from circles of exchange in order to hoard all that is of value. Without hope our global economy can spiral downward without a break against its descent. This is what was striking about that epic crisis. We could see that there is no source of a counterthrust. All are caught in the same downward inexorability. Yet even this global character of the decline seems less a cause than a symptom of an underlying deficit that is more than economic. The mere absence of money does not betoken a lack of it, only an extreme aversion to circulating it. Everything remains as it was in the real world of those tangibles on which human existence and flourishing depends while, at the same time, everything has changed in the way we regard them. Value declined because demand dried up. Now, such corrections, we know, are normal in the course of any economy in which supply and demand get out of balance. Indeed, price changes are the main signal and mechanism by which such adjustments are effected. Here, however, we seemed to have entered onto a persistent preference for withdrawal that, if it were to continue, would have had catastrophic consequences. Whatever the hazards contemplated from global warming, the effects of prolonged recession would be far more detrimental to the billions sustained by systems of global exchange. It is the possibility of a world economic collapse on top of the narrowly avoided financial meltdown that concentrated our attention. We begin to see the real scope of the danger if our postrecession world extends beyond a temporary readjustment to become a continuing aversion to the very dynamism of economic growth through which our world has been built. Such a turn can become more than an economic downturn. It carries within it the darkest possibility of a turn against life itself.

We are no longer at that point, but the sharp reversal of our fortunes in 2008 and after brought into view the extent to which we have lived on hope. A self-fulfilling prophecy that the future will be better than the past has no other basis for its fulfillment than the prophecy itself. Once alerted to the insupportability of such a faith, the headlong pace of descent accelerates. It is only if we can somehow regain the anchor of hope that there is any possibility of arresting the acceleration. We know that all we have achieved has been made possible by the powerful dynamic of hope, and yet we also know that such achievements can hardly underpin the hope that has made them possible. Somehow hope must be rediscovered as the momentum that enables us to stay aloft so long as it is not questioned too closely. Our situation has been reminiscent of the bumblebee whose flight is predicated on its unwillingness to listen to the notice that its wings are too slight to support it. Everything works out fine for the bumblebee so long as it eschews such self-doubt. Abrupt economic descent seems to originate in a similar moment of self-debilitation. Yielding to the proliferating uncertainties that afflict every possible transaction, we reflexively turn aside from the imponderables of risk through which action takes place. Instead, we hold back from existence thinking we can thereby regain the mastery we have lost. Such a step is fatal. It is the deliberate turning away from the dynamic of life by which we are drawn beyond ourselves to forge bonds of mutual responsibility. The fatality is made evident by its impossibility, for, far from achieving a new position of mastery over the whole in which we find ourselves, we have only thereby managed to shrink existence into a nullity. Withdrawal is not an alternate form of existence but merely the definitive form of nonexistence. No more than any living thing can we choose to enter a state of suspended animation, the economy cannot opt to freeze the dynamic of growth by which it is sustained.

Political Infusions of Hope

What was instructive in the financial crisis is that even when economic institutions were inclined to effect such an interruption, they were not permitted to do so. Much was made of the parallels to the Great Depression of the 1930s and no doubt there were such. But the one decisive difference was in the political responses. In contrast to the aversion against energetic economic intervention in the earlier era, now we are more likely to suffer from an excess of political intrusion. The one thing that policymakers could not be accused of was inaction. Governments around the world have been highly solicitous of the capital requirements of the financial markets and of the stimulative spending mandated for economic recovery. All have pursued the same policy directions, while diverging only on the levels of commitment indicated. Governments, too, displayed a remarkable degree of coordination, extending even to the need for revitalization of the developing world. At that point no one could tell what the outcome of such abundant ministrations would be, whether they would have the intended benefits or would lead to yet unexpected consequences. What became clear, however, was the principle of the priority of politics over economics that remained in doubt during the 1930s. This was indeed the outcome of that bitter experience of the Depression and its unfolding into the great totalitarian convulsion of World War II. Now no government is prepared to stand aside while its economy spirals downward, and, to the extent that all national economies have become interdependent, that predetermination has become universal. Taken as a whole, such initiatives constitute an impressive affirmation of the shared social reality that, though normally unnoticed, nevertheless undergirds a system of free economic exchanges.

Private property that is communally produced, Marx declared, cannot simply be owned by individuals. All have a share in its production and therefore a claim on its benefits. But Marx's is still an excessively materialist perspective, suggesting that wealth is a physically fixed quantity. In reality, as we saw in the asset deflation, the very meaning of wealth is socially constituted. Diamonds and houses remained what they were, as useful or as useless as previously, only they declined in value because demand for them shrunk. What we thought was owned separately turned out to have a very significant component of social recognition built into it. Not only is the very idea of property socially constituted, for ownership is primarily how other people regard as my possessions, but much of the value of such commodities is inextricably tied to the estimates and exchanges that take place in the minds of others. Use value is constant, but that is by far the least significant component of value. It has been the precipitous decline in socially constituted wealth that had such depressive effects in prompting a flight from leverage and risk. Who wanted to buy or borrow when the same things might be had more cheaply in the future? Why assume risk when everyone was heading for safety? Such were concerns not just of individual decision-makers but of the social whole from which individuals took the cues to which they responded. An economy is made up of multiple independent centers of decision, but its dynamism derives from the mutuality of interconnection that is more than a product of separate wills. For better or worse we are bound together for better or worse. Even our individual calculations are premised on the sustaining dynamism of the whole that is nowhere reducible to the sum of its separate constituents. When pressed to identify the source of that overarching confidence or hope, we can only suggest that it comes from outside ourselves. We are not simply individuals; we are members of a social whole. That is why the collapse of confidence must be socially or, more precisely, politically addressed, since it is through political organization that societies take action.

The interesting question that follows is this: What gave the political community the confidence that it could recapture the hope that was lost at the economic level? How is it possible for governments to inject the trust that must be present before the cycle of exchange, buying and selling, can even begin? Can political action compel what cannot be compelled? What was noteworthy about the energetic interventions from the political side in 2008/2009 is that they were undertaken only reluctantly, with full recognition that they must also recede at the earliest signs of economic reawakening. Government knows that it cannot substitute its direction for the initiatives of the free market. We were not in any danger of a political overreach that would supplant the vitality of private enterprise. Consensus revolves around the recognition that free markets are the prodigious generators of wealth; government can only offer a pale substitute for their dynamism. Even countries, like China, with the institutional capacity to return to a command economy show not the slightest inclination to do so. They seek only to restore the market to its full vigor, albeit with whatever regulatory mechanisms might be indicated for its future enhancement. Interventions are, in other words, largely premised on the necessity of making markets work better. Government aims at restoring, not abolishing, economic liberty. No doubt there was to be some resistance to the devolution of political powers assumed within the crisis, but the temptation would have had to overcome the long-standing objection of the unsuitability of government to the generation of wealth. So what then was the nature of the interventions undertaken by political communities? They were nothing less than a redirection of the markets toward their own social nature. There is no incompatibility between the political and the economic because the economic already points toward the political. Markets are only apparently constituted by a privileging of private decisions. Their reality is that they constitute a public order. Participants may generally ignore that larger good that sustains their pursuit of private profits, but they cannot, as we saw, utterly disregard the consequences of their actions on the system as a whole except at their peril. The logic of markets is that they are sustained by what is not reducible to the terms of the market.

Profit and loss may seem to be defined by the perspectives of the particular entities involved, but the possibility of their interrelationship derives from considerations that are beyond measurement in terms of profit and loss. It is well known that there are many factors that make market exchanges possible that are not susceptible to being bought and sold in the same way. Honesty and reliability, along with the rule of law and the enforcement of contracts, cannot simply be priced. They are not for sale. Buying and selling are possible only because of the presence of such abiding commitments. This is also why we cannot buy and sell human beings, or in any way discount the dignity of their humanity, because their engagement in commercial exchange is possible only by virtue of their full spiritual reality. Markets, far from diminishing the stature of human beings, imply their nonreducibility to the finite terms of their transactions. This elevation of human dignity was entirely overlooked by Aristotle and much of the traditional disdain of commercial grubbiness, a prejudice refuted in the sheer human exuberance that exceeds the boundaries of virtually all economic transactions. But over and above such individual transcendence of the marketplace there is also the living dynamism of the systems of exchange as a whole. It is not just that individuals and their virtues are beyond negotiations of the market, but that markets themselves are somehow more than they appear to be. In themselves markets are a testament to hope in a future that does not arise from any particular contract. Nothing in what has happened fully justifies the virtually limitless confidence with which they confront the future. Even risk assessment seems to be premised on the faith that risk might be defeated. However dubious such an effort of containing what cannot be contained is, we nevertheless persevere within hope, because we know that without such hope there would be no possibility of overcoming the unpredictabilities that can be overcome. The difficulty is that the economy has no way of recollecting what it had never made articulate to itself. Hope does not disappoint, but it can be forgotten.

Politics Constituted by Hope

Recollection of hope is the function of the political community. We might say, along the lines of Hegel, that the community that is implicitly present between participants in the marketplace becomes explicit in the mutual recognition that constitutes the political community. It is at that point that hope comes into view since the political community is its historical invocation. No one asks whether there will be a market, it is simply taken for granted, except on those occasions when its collapse raises the question. But the political community stakes its existence on a promise toward the future that cannot occur without express acknowledgment of the order of time in which it finds itself. When the political community comes to the aid of the beleaguered economy, it makes explicit what is merely implicit in the latter. Politics is the truth of economics. Hegel understood this rather well, for he was probably the first thinker to recognize that the economic system, although it follows its own autonomous dynamic, subsists within the political whole. As a system of mutual cooperation, albeit operating through the invisible hand of self-interest, the economy could not be sustained without acknowledgment of its political culmination. That is, that the pursuit of private profit is only one side of economic reality and not by any means its most significant aspect. Deeper even than the participants are aware is the community that makes the rounds of exchange possible and that in turn is sustained by them. Politics too may lack the full evocation of the priority of hope, but it cannot evade the awareness that it is more than the sum of its parts. Individual citizens are bearers of responsibility toward a good greater than their individual well-being, and that fidelity is itself the product of a faith without which their individual efforts could neither be initiated nor sustained. It is in the political community that the spiritual reality of human life is finally acknowledged. We are not the source of that larger dynamic of existence by which we are lifted beyond ourselves. It is rather the case that our self-transcendence is merely the point at which the spirit of hope is apprehended. Hope in this sense is not ours, for, strictly speaking, we belong to it.

This may seem a rather elevated conception of politics, and indeed it is, but it leads directly to some crucial practical consequences. Governments, it turns out, can raise almost unlimited money on the world capital markets. It has been through this recourse that governments were able to undertake such vigorous measures to arrest financial and economic declines. When great multinational companies that had for years bestrode the globe either could not access or could not afford the terms of credit markets, mere governments have been able to raise as much as they desired on extremely favorable terms. Although bankruptcy had been mentioned in reference to some governments, none came anywhere near the precipice over which the great investment banks and other corporations fell. To date, at any rate, no government entities have found the capital markets irrevocably closed to them. Besides, what would it mean for a country to go bankrupt? Insolvency is a condition that attaches only to those organizations that are reducible to their parts. Bankruptcy proceeding is merely the legal process by which that dismantling is effected. For a political community, that is not just unthinkable, it is impossible. The political community is so elusive, as Aristotle discovered, that it cannot even be identified with its constitutional form. Its invisible substance remains over and above every change through which it passes. There are no parts to be sold off because the political community scarcely exists in such transient expressions of its reality. Indeed, it cannot go bankrupt because it is never truly and fully present at any time in its history. It is this historical nature that at once insulates the political community from the mortality of all mere enterprise associations and at the same time ensures its capacity to call on almost limitless resources. To the extent that the civil association exists in an indeterminate time horizon, it is not shackled by the finite commitments within which all other entities must live. The state can mortgage not just the present, but its pledges can include the future. Just as the present generation has honored the debts incurred by the past, so it can, in turn, make commitments that entail future generations. That does not mean that the political community can draw on truly unlimited resources or presume on the forbearance of its successors, but it does mean that the limits are more elastic than those of all other corporations. States alone do not have to amortize their debt since they are more than mortal.

States do go into and out of existence, but even when they are no longer present they seem to retain an attenuated presence. Despite the solidity of the instruments of state power and the firmness of the trappings attached to it, we know that this fierce reality is in many ways the least substantial aspect. Expressions of political might are only the temporary manifestations of a vitality that reaches back into a time beyond memory and stretches toward a future that is all but imperceptible. Swords and tanks eventually rust, nuclear warheads decay, and all the accumulated economic might drains away, but the community from which they spring endures through generational renewal. The inexorability of death is defeated, not just through the miracle of biology, but through the even greater miracle of the spiritual bond of union. A state cannot die because it literally does not exist, at least not in the sense of any physical entity in space and time. Its real existence is through the community that spans space and time and therefore escapes their vicissitudes, to a very considerable extent. The language of a contract has been invoked to denote this spiritual condition through which the political society exists. But there has always been something too specific in such a notion, as contract theorists themselves always conceded. Edmund Burke perhaps came closest to the core when he described it as an "eternal contract" between the ages and the generations. In other words, the state is founded not through the actions of its founders but through the founding that has already occurred before they or any of their successors come on the scene. Perhaps it would be more accurate to say that founding is made possible by the prefounding that happened before they began. We do not make contracts, contracts make us. It is this constitution outside of space and time that is the source of the formidable power of the political community both to maintain itself and to shelter us from the disasters that befall us.

The resources on which the political community can draw are beyond the limits of all other entities because the political community emerges from beyond those limits. In this sense we may say that the political community is the pure sign of hope, the hope that does not disappoint because it has already reached its goal. If the contract that constitutes it is eternal, then it has already surpassed the uncertainties of existence. The ups and downs through which the state may pass cannot erase what is there as the condition of possibility for the unending struggle of its existence. In each generation we play our part in transmitting the community in which we find ourselves before we even begin. At one level this imposes an awesome responsibility on us to preserve and pass on all that we have received; at another level we have nothing to pass on but what can never be passed on because it always remains untouched. We are bound together in mutual responsibility within and across the generations, but there would be no possibility of being bound if we were not already in a community of mutual responsibility. It is up to us to build up and provide for the future as an act of homage to those who cared for us from the past. But there would be no possibility of such an undertaking if we were not from eternity already related across and within time. Responsibility is ours, but the condition of responsibility does not depend on us. It has already been given, and it cannot be taken away. A political community can only be built up by those who are already in community with one another even though they may not even know it yet. This is precisely the relationship we have with those who came before us and who follow after us. We do not know one another, yet we are known to one another. It is possible for us to join together because we have already been joined together before our lives have begun or ended. Not only is failure not an option, it is not even possible.

All of this was no doubt only dimly intuited in Burke's striking formulation of an "eternal contract," but such intimations identify the source of its evocative power. His formulation perfectly captures the faith that is needed for a political community to persevere through the vicissitudes of history because the faith itself is not exposed to the same deviations. Nothing about this faith guarantees that it will reach its worldly goal, but it does inure it against abandonment of the effort. States will still disappear from history, but even when they do their idea, that which sustained them from eternity, remains unimpaired. Burke himself was familiar with lost causes, having backed more than his fair share over the course of his public career. But he also knew that practical defeat affected the moral principle that was at stake not one whit. He was very much like Plato, who knew that the actual Athens with its corrupt self-destructiveness did not in the slightest impair the true Athens he beheld within himself. Unfortunately, the association of this true city with the term "idea" has proved to be a major obstacle to apprehending its real status. Western political thought has struggled to overcome the association of what is known inwardly with all forms of private, imaginary, and subjective connotations. Largely overlooked in the discussion has been the derivation of all real cities from this ideal reality. It has been difficult to unravel the paradox of the Platonic heritage in which the ideal city is the most real, while the real city is the least real. It is only with Hegel that the issue begins to be resolved, but even he has far from won universal assent to his claim that the opposition is entirely redundant. The exhortation, he explained, by which the actual city is pressed to conform to the ideal makes no sense unless the latter is somehow contained in the former. There may of course be a tension between the two, but it is premised on their deeper affinity, for we cannot be exhorted to become what we are unless we are somehow what we are to become. It is within that irremovable tension that history unfolds.

The formidable power by which states make history, nowhere more vividly than in the moment when governments became debtors and creditors of last resort, arises directly from their historical existence. When credit markets had suddenly closed to all other entities, governments had little difficulty in raising capital that they in turn loaned back to all the recently rebuffed borrowers. Overnight, governments had been entrusted with the wealth of the world, not because they were judged to be better managers of it, but simply because they could not disappear. General Motors or Citigroup had revenues larger than many states, but they could only call on the finite resources of their current shareholders. There are no future generations ready to honor the debt incurred for the sake of the corporation's survival. Yet even the smallest state can summon the loyalty of citizens not yet present in time. There will always be an Iceland, but the same could not be said for Lehman Brothers. The relationship of the participants to the larger enterprise is markedly different. Owners of joint-stock companies are by definition willing to put a limited amount of capital at risk for the sake of their projected gains, but citizens find themselves under a limitless obligation only remotely connected to the benefits they may expect to receive. The first can calculate the limit of his indebtedness in advance; the second may not know when they will be called to exceed the full measure of devotion. The reason for the astounding durability of associations of the latter sort is not hard to see. They are formed on the basis of a debt that cannot be fully repaid, so that it is not surprising that they are prepared to shoulder burdens whose limits cannot be known in advance. This is the very meaning of the historical existence of political communities. They are constituted by a readiness to sacrifice that, because it is indeterminate, is prepared for every eventuality.

Obligation as Hope

An eternal contract is one to which our name has been affixed even before we have been named. Far from being a mere aspiration or ideal to which we might choose to lend our support, the obligatory force of the political community is of a primordiality that outweighs all else within our existence. It is for this reason that the unreal, that which is not yet, is the most real, that which underpins everything else. Before there is political action there is the obligation that propels it. Our moral language, like our political language, has suffered from an excessive individualism, beginning with the Greek discovery of mind as the seat of decision-making. As autonomous, as self-legislating, we seem to be always there before the decision has to be made and therefore enjoy a distance stretching infinitely away from us. But this is completely the opposite of the concrete moral life where duty imposes itself upon us with a brutality that is far from welcome. Obligation leaves us with no choice. That is its very meaning. Our freedom has been abolished once we find ourselves under obligation. That of course does not mean that we ever lose our freedom to walk away, to reject our responsibility, but it does mean that such freedom is tantamount to the abandonment of its highest calling. What does freedom mean when it has been turned against itself? This is a familiar question within the kind of liberal discourse that marks our modern moral reflection. We may not have unraveled the conundrum of freedom, but we have not by any means despaired of the attempt. The crucial insight we have yet to absorb is that freedom is not something we can comprehend, for it comprehends us in our entire existence. Only the freedom inextricably woven into our prior obligations is worthy of the name. The force of such obligations may initially strike us as a diminished reality—they are after all still to be determined by our free choice—but in hindsight we realize that they encompass the whole reality of our being. Obligations are not an unreal possibility but the very real ground of all possibility. It is we who are in danger of becoming unreal if we fail to live up to them.

Despite his reputation as an idealist, Kant is the point at which this primordiality of the moral life begins to find its appropriate formulation. His elevation of duty to a primacy that supersedes all other considerations is, however, only a beginning, because he still did not manage to identify the full existential import of that prioritization. For Kant, it is still we who make duty possible, rather than the other way around. It is only when attention is shifted to the political level that the generative and regenerative force of duty becomes fully apparent. Duty makes historical existence possible, to wit, the persistence of political communities bound together over time by nothing more substantial than that transcendent imperative. This is what has been in evidence in the impressively elastic borrowing capacity of governments of our recent past. Over and above the daily gyrations of markets is a readiness for responsibility that arises from depths hitherto unsuspected. It is that possibility of shouldering responsibilities beyond pragmatic calculations that impresses us with the reality in depth from which our lives have always emanated. The pull of obligation is deeper than we are ourselves. It is almost as if we are the latecomers who must take up the call of duty that has preceded us. In this regard, exhortation is beside the point, for there would be no point in exhorting us to step up to the call of duty if we had not already heard it. Those who cannot sense its imperious pull can hardly even be candidates for such homiletics. By contrast, those who hear such an appeal have already heard it as the very condition of their hearing. The moral undertow of existence is so close to us that it is nearer to us than we are ourselves. It is this closeness that has been the reason we have so often overlooked it, for we can scarcely gain the distance needed to see it apart from ourselves. A rupture is required to open us up to the glimpse of what it is that makes our moral existence possible. In sacrificing ourselves, we see that we are not our own but are rather carried along by a goodness that is greater. All moral action is an enlargement of the self, but its possibility is rooted in the transcendence of the self that is prior to even being a self. It is what we are *not* that enables us to become what we are.

The eternal dimension is what makes time possible. History is a possibility only for beings that are not historical, at least not in the sense that their reality is wholly contained within history. With us it is precisely the impossibility of encapsulation within finite expression that makes the unfolding of all conversation possible. There is something inexhaustible, we know, about every human being, an unfathomability that makes it impossible to finally know him or her, or even ourselves. No matter what is said or done, the sayer or the doer escapes all tangibility. This mystery at the core of the person is not something incidental but the central possibility of our existence. Only occasionally do we brush up against the abyss of unattainability, yet it is palpable in every moment through which we pass. When pressed to name it, we are incapable of giving it a definition, for all definitions arise out of the indefinable. But we do know that it is the mystery of the beyond in which we participate without ever knowing what it is. Even more than what is accomplished inexhaustibility is who we are.

It is this possibility of communication beyond all that is said that makes it possible for us to join with one another in the formation of political communities bound together through time. We know one another before we even know one another because we have already responded to the call of the other before we have even met. Responsibility, that by which we are connected with those we do not know, is what makes it possible for us to bridge the separations of space and time. History is merely the path along which responsibility is enacted. The capacity of political communities to undertake commitments indefinitely into the future is testament to their transcendence of all purely temporal origins.

They aim, not at success, but at the eternal principles from which all action springs. In this sense they have always already reached the goal that still has to be attained through the struggle with the vicissitudes of time. Whether the target is hit or missed is not the most crucial aspect, for there would be no possibility of action unless it were first kept in mind. Already our minds have leapt ahead to that goal as the very condition of the whole uncertain undertaking. The possibility of reaching it lies in the priority of having reached it. Failure appears incidental to the trial. What counts is fidelity to the beginning that can be lost, not by the inabilities and adversities that block our way, but by deviation from the principle itself. It is the possibility that we might fail to hold onto the principle by which we are held that is the great danger. Even when the exercise of responsibility is prevented from reaching the intended beneficiaries, the very fact of its having been undertaken already means that it has been exercised. The others know it too, for they do not hold an unpreventable failure against us. Only the refusal to undertake the effort is culpable. Those who have expended their best have been absolved of blame by those who are joined with them in a community built on the supererogatory. Historically there is nothing to be accomplished because it is already there in the beginning. All that remains is the adventure of discovering the degree to which our efforts bear temporary fruit, since nothing remains within history except the witness to impassable goodness from which all good action springs. Eternal truth cannot be wiped away by the mere passage of time.

This is what is meant by the phrase "hope does not disappoint." It appears in Romans 5:5 with an all-important ground of explanation, "because the love of God has been poured into our hearts through the Holy Spirit who has been given to us." Within the context of St. Paul's letter, the principle and its justification flow seamlessly into one another. Yet their connection can also be separated or, perhaps, so deepened that they silently include one another. Then "hope does not disappoint" stands on its own. The "because," we discover, was already embedded in hope as that which cannot fail. We may disappoint hope but hope cannot disappoint us. We may lose hope but hope can never lose us. We may become hopeless but hope cannot. Hope abides because it is hope. Not only does hope spring eternal but it is eternal as that which cannot turn away from itself. It is for this reason that we live in hope and from hope, as the vital wellspring of all our actions. Hope never ceases, not only in the conceptual sense that it is fixed, but in the preconceptual opening that includes our whole existence. We live in hope as the very possibility of living. There is nothing prior to hope or, more accurately, there is nothing for which we have to hope before we arrive at hope. We cannot get back to what is there before there is hope, for then we would need hope for that. There is nothing more hopeful than hope. We are contained and embraced by hope.

To speak of hope as a virtue is not inaccurate, but it still suggests that we are the bearers of hope, as a quality that resides within us. Absent from this traditional formulation is the existential priority of hope that is better captured by its acknowledgment as a gift. We do not, indeed cannot, make any special efforts to obtain hope, for the whole possibility of making efforts cannot depend on a prior effort. A beginning must always be found in what is purely and simply given, behind which we cannot go. Hope is in that sense the gift of being that makes all existence possible. Again contrary to a traditional notion, we do not move from existence toward being, to that which is more fully than ourselves, but from preeminent being to the transitory unfolding of existence. The Platonic idea of recollection defines our orientation toward a fullness we have lost, but the truth is that we could only seek that which we have never really lost. All seeking is within the horizon of finding. Not only do we know that for which we search, but, more importantly, the possibility of searching is provided by that for which we search. From our perspective we move from potency to act, but from the perspective of potency there is only act. Nothing more remains to be accomplished since all possibility of accomplishment is contained within it. The finitude of the language of potency and act in this sense is already well highlighted by St. Thomas's observation that God is all act and no potency. There is nothing that remains to be actualized in God. Now we begin to see how such a glimpse of God might be possible, from within our own movement from potency to act that is already transparent for the condition of its own possibility. Only by virtue of that which fully *is* do we gain the possibility of attempting to be. Hope is the thread by which we are held. Its durability surpasses all our expectations.

Optimism may be lost but hope cannot be lost, for it is most manifest when the situation has become hopeless. Expectations of success or failure closely track the oscillations between optimism and pessimism. Hope floats serenely above such vacillations or, more accurately, below them as the anchor that is its artistic symbol. Optimism and pessimism are sentiments blown about on the surface that provide no basis for human action. They are more like the attitudes we take up when we have distanced ourselves from the imperative of action. We ask about how we feel in regard to the future, a question that is utterly irrelevant when we are called upon to assume responsibility for it. Action cannot be held hostage to speculation on its prospects for success, most of which involve a myriad of factors beyond our control. All that we know is that the likelihood of success is zero unless we undertake the effort. That is under our control, or at least the beginning of action is. What provides the possibility of beginning cannot be provided by us for it is the gift of hope that itself has no beginning, for every beginning presupposes hope. A baby is not a sign of optimism but of hope. No one can know what the future will hold, but we do know that there will be no future without hope. Quite apart from success or failure, or even how we measure them, there is the guarantee of a future that is life itself. Optimism and pessimism are each divergences from hope that tilt dangerously toward despair. Postponement of life for the sake of something more is already a turning away from life. The complete withdrawal from action, the fall into depression is not an option, least of all for a whole society. It has been this refusal to commit what Kierkegaard termed the only original sin, the turn away from existence, that has been on display in the impressive political initiatives of the crisis years. Economic life may have declined, but political life has reasserted itself. No one knew what the outcome would be, and there were good reasons to be dubious about the merit of various initiatives, but we cannot doubt the determination to do something. Even in the Great Depression this was really all that was achieved.

Persons as Opening of Hope

Whether the political realm preserves the economic is never the most decisive point. What counts is that it preserves hope. That was in the end its signal contribution to an economy that had seemed to lose hope. But more than that it brought hope into view as the horizon of our existence. This may in turn bring about a deeper account of what the political itself is. As the community that is constituted by hope, it exists in the point of intersection of the timeless with time, not in the seemingly solid embodiments of power and presence with which it is readily identified. This is something we have always known. Certainly it is familiar to the wielders of public power, who cannot quite eliminate the nagging possibility that their writ might one day go unheard and unaccomplished. Perhaps now we can admit the fragility of power without the heightened anxiety that usually accompanies it. For we have seen that it is precisely this fragility, its eruption from depths immune from evanescence, that is the source of the prodigious strength and durability of political communities. Mere changes of government, even extraconstitutional ones, do not touch its underlying dynamic, for the political community is already present in the hope that precedes its formation. All that is needed is the assent by which possibility is affirmed. Free government is merely its most explicit realization, but all governments are based on consent. It is simply that the less free varieties cannot be certain of their foundation and thereby must resort or be ready to resort to the uncertainty of coercion. A genuinely free polity is an awesome expression of strength. It is the most compelling testament to the power of hope that bridges the separation between human beings. Assent may be the means by which they are united, but its possibility is provided by the hope in which they are already united before they begin.

There is no foundation before hope, nor is there historical access to any point before it. This is why the formation of states is a mysteriously impenetrable process. It is not defined by constitutional conventions or ratifications because they already presuppose a community for which such events are authoritative. What is crucial is perhaps most noticed through its absence, when trust has suddenly collapsed, as it did in the great financial crisis. No one knows whether the other party is truthful or reliable; suspicion distances each from engagement with the other. How, Thomas Hobbes asked in the midst of the English Civil War, is it possibly for such mutually suspicious individuals to come together in the formation of a civil society? The answer that he gave of an agreement or covenant has colored our perception of political community ever since. Its individualistic premise avoids the most decisive aspect, namely, that individuals could never come together by way of an agreement if they were not already within a relationship of readiness to form agreements with one another. Hobbes knew this and for that reason invoked the priority of natural and divine law, but his formulation placed all of its weight on the necessity of individual decision. That precarious commitment of individuals to the formation of a commonwealth is precisely what leaves modern societies prone to periodic collapses of trust and confidence, until they discover that what they thought they had lost has never really been lost because it was never simply there. How can we lose what furnishes the condition of our existence? Or how is it possible for what provides the dynamic of our lives to become completely present within them? Crises of confidence are themselves only a possibility for beings that can never so fully incorporate the hope from which they live nor ever so fully lose it that they cannot even remember it. Hope does not disappoint because it is what we live within.

The problem has been that we have lacked a model or metaphor that would enable us to grasp this about ourselves. That in turn has made hope that much more inaccessible. We may be held by hope, but we cannot hold onto hope without knowing that we are held by it. This is the big philosophical revolution underway since the time of Hobbes as we discover that the language of entities and fixed quantities does not apply to human beings. A very different mode of discourse was needed to break the hold of objectification. The breakthrough occurred in the realization that the model or metaphor we had been searching for has literally been under our noses all along, for it is as persons that we are capable of becoming what we are not and of discovering that we are more than we thought we were. It is not that this awareness of persons has failed to inform our whole liberal political tradition. We might even point out that the centrality of persons, entitled to limitless concern and respect, at the core of liberal political thought, arises from just such awareness. A person, we know, is a source of inexhaustibility in the universe, each one incapable of reaching the limit of what he or she is. Most of all we know this about the people we know and love. Our political practice has been built around this elevation of persons as ends-in-themselves, never to be used, as Kant insisted, as a mere means. The problem is that we have lacked the adequate linguistic means of conveying this because all our language references entities of a relatively fixed nature. How can we talk about persons who are distinguished by the impossibility of fixing them in any particular status? The answer must begin from the recognition that such a question can only arise from persons and that we are capable of answering it only because we ourselves are persons. Not only do we not have to abstract from our own existence as persons, but we must not if we are to have any possibility of grasping the reality of persons. Indeed, it is only through the horizon of the personal that we have any chance of grasping what can be known about the whole within which we find ourselves.

We discover that we are not isolated monads wandering aimlessly through the universe, but are borne along by a trust in what is trustworthy before we even become aware of ourselves. Even Hobbes's solitary individuals eventually yield to that predisposition as the possibility of creating a Leviathan. The loss of trust only comes later in response to bitter experience, but it cannot eliminate the priority from which it recedes. Our collapse of financial confidence in 2008 was just such a moment and it was, interestingly, followed by a robust reaffirmation from the political level, but a reaffirmation that could not fully account for the source of its own confidence. That more delicate reflection entails an enlargement of perspective to include the condition of the possibility of political community that only becomes visible in the mutuality of persons. It is only possible for persons to form such enduring associations across space and time because that is what persons are. Not simply confined to what they are, persons are the movement out of nonexistence that is never exhausted in existence. The possibility of forming community has in principle no limits because there is never a point where responsibility for the other has reached its limit. I carry every other human being within me, including all who have ever lived or will live. This is what underpins the possibility of communication between us. Barriers of language and circumstance are only incidental. I can know each other as a unique other, that is, as a person. Indeed, there is a sense in which we have not really met until we have met in person. All other forms of communication, including mass communication and the myriad possibilities of contact available to us, are all derivative from that primacy of persons to one another. The hope through which we reach out to one another is what it means to be a person.

The mistake within political thought was to think we could comprehend it, to render it intelligible in terms of some more elemental factors of need or interest. Overlooked in this assumption of an easy mastery over the conditions of our own existence is the degree to which we have ourselves already eluded them. Calculations about need and interest are only possible because we are not simply reducible to need and interest. Indeed, the political arrangement by which such elemental imperatives are served is viable because we are already joined within a community beyond need and interest. A community of persons exceeds a community of drives. Persons in community become capable of considering and cooperating in the satisfaction of their desires through the freedom in which they are already related to one another. The whole premise of the contemplation of necessities is that we are not captured by them. If we were simply the sum total of our impulses, there would never be any need to name and reflect upon them; their imperious demands would render any self-reflection irrelevant. The cooperation of an anthill does not have a theoretical underpinning. For us, by contrast, the whole point of the acknowledgment of our primary drives is to construct a mode of satisfaction that attests to our transcendence of them. A political community is by definition a free community, for it exists, as Aristotle insisted, not merely for the sake of life but for the good life. Strictly speaking we might say that there are no untranscended drives within human existence, that is, none that have not already been seen through the eye of the other whose needs come before my own. The moral community of persons is always prior to the urges of animal life. We cannot understand the former in terms of the latter without defeating the very possibility of a free community and rendering the very idea of understanding impossible. Hope is not just the horizon within which the political unfolds but is also the horizon in which all thinking about it is possible.

Reductive thinking is itself a forgetting of thought. Only those who are not reducible to their elementary impulses can ponder the possibility of such thinking, but only so long as they fail to recall the impossibility of their pondering it if it were so. To understand hope, therefore, requires us to concede that it is itself the horizon of our thinking. We cannot understand hope in terms of anything else, but rather everything else within the light of hope. We cannot think outside of hope. This is what it means to say that hope does not disappoint. Not only can we not live without hope, but we cannot even think about it without hope. The movement of thought toward its object is a movement that is sustained by the hope in the possibility of reaching it. To the extent that everything is understood in relation to hope we cannot, for that reason, understand hope. All that we can do is stand within hope, thereby gaining the only perspective that is possible for us. Through hope we glimpse hope. To stand outside of hope is to lose hope or at least our connection with hope. We cannot reduce hope to something else without eliminating hope from the frame of our thought. If it were possible for us to do that, then we might be seriously in trouble. The truth is that we can only forget about hope, a hope that now endures by way of forgetting. Even when it is forgotten, hope is present in the mode of its absence. We can even question the possibility of hope, but the questioning itself occurs within hope. It is by means of hope that we can ask about hope. How is it possible to understand such a vertiginal dynamic? We seem to be at the limit of thinking, a limit that early modern political thought assumed it could surmount, but we now realize that it is through such limits that the unlimited is glimpsed. Even the effort to find a way of rendering hope more certain, to include it within what we control, cannot dispense with hope itself. There is no stepping outside of hope. Not even by losing hope do we lose hope, for hope does not lose us. Hope remains. To say that hope does not disappoint is appropriately redundant, for that is the very meaning of hope.

NOTES

Chapter 1

1. That is the path I sought to sketch in David Walsh, *The Modern Philosophical Revolution* (Cambridge: Cambridge University Press, 2008).
2. Bruno Snell, *The Discovery of the Mind* (New York: Harper, 1960); Karl Jaspers, *The Origin and Goal of History*, trans. Michael Bullock (London: Routledge and Kegan Paul, 1953); S. N. Eisenstadt, ed., *The Origins and Diversity of Axial Age Civilizations* (Albany: State University of New York Press, 1983); Eric Voegelin, *Order and History*, Vols. 1–3, in *Collected Works of Eric Voegelin*, Vols. 14, 15, and 16 (Columbia: University of Missouri Press, 2000–2001); Brendan Purcell, *From Big Bang to Big Mystery: Human Origins in Light of Creation and Evolution* (Hyde Park, NY: New City Press, 2012).
3. It is that capacity that is exhibited in the famous "Dialogue of a Man with His Soul" while it is simultaneously overlooked by the man himself. He had not yet discovered that he had a mind; see Anonymous, "A Dispute over Suicide," in *Ancient Near Eastern Texts Relating to the Old Testament*, ed. James B. Pritchard, trans. John A. Wilson (Princeton, NJ: Princeton University Press, 1950), 405–7.
4. Aristotle, *Politics* 1253a14.
5. Ibid., 1253a15. All emphasis in quoted material is in the original unless otherwise indicated.
6. Thomas Aquinas, III *Sentences* d. 5, q. 3, a. 2.
7. Aquinas, *Summa theologiae* I-II, Q.21, a. 4, ad 3.
8. Jacques Maritain, *The Person and the Common Good*, trans. John J. Fitzgerald (Notre Dame, IN: University of Notre Dame Press, 1966; original 1946).

9. Georg Wilhelm Friedrich Hegel, *The Philosophy of Right*, trans. T. M. Knox (New York: Oxford University Press, 1967), pt. III, sec. 1.

10. David Walsh, *The Growth of the Liberal Soul* (Columbia: University of Missouri Press, 1997); and Michael Oakeshott, *Rationalism and Politics*, rev. ed. (Indianapolis: Liberty Fund, 1991), and Oakeshott, *On Human Conduct* (Oxford: Clarendon, 1975).

11. Alasdair MacIntyre, *After Virtue* (Notre Dame, IN: University of Notre Dame Press, 1984); Richard Rorty, *Contingency, Irony, and Solidarity* (New York: Cambridge University Press, 1989); and, more recently, Patrick Deneen, *Why Liberalism Failed* (New Haven, CT: Yale University Press, 2018); and Rod Dreher, *The Benedict Option* (New York: Sentinel, 2017).

12. See "Rights as an Epiphany of the Person," in David Walsh, *Politics of the Person as the Politics of Being* (Notre Dame, IN: University of Notre Dame Press, 2016), 246–56.

13. Walt Whitman was among the first to grasp this dimension, one that he sought to identify through his coinage of the term "personalism." The relevance for our understanding of human dignity is well explored in George Kateb, *Human Dignity* (Cambridge, MA: Belknap, 2011), and Kateb, *The Inner Ocean* (Ithaca, NY: Cornell University Press, 1994).

14. The title of John McNerney, *Wealth of Persons* (Eugene, OR: Cascade, 2017), is an indication of the extent to which Adam Smith saw more than he realized in his *Wealth of Nations*.

15. See Jeremy Waldron, ed., *Nonsense upon Stilts: Bentham, Burke and Marx on the Rights of Man* (New York: Methuen, 1987).

16. The contemporary pattern was established in the Charter 77 movement in Czechoslovakia that sought to compel their government to respect the human rights requirements to which they had been pledged by treaty; see Václav Havel, *Open Letters: Selected Writings, 1965–1990* (New York: Vintage, 1992). This example was followed by the Chinese dissident Liu Xiaobo in his Charter 08 initiative; see Xiaobo, *No Enemies, No Hatred: Selected Essays and Poems*, ed. Perry Link (Cambridge, MA: Belknap, 2012).

17. The difficulties arising from the standard definition of a person provided by Boethius, "an individual substance of a rational nature," are well explored by Hans Urs von Balthasar, "On the Concept of Person," *Communio* 13 (Spring 1986): 18–26; and also Joseph Ratzinger, "Retrieving the Tradition: Concerning the Notion of Person in Theology," *Communio* 17 (Fall 1990): 439–54.

18. The pattern is familiar from the presentation in MacIntyre, *After Virtue*.

19. Thomas Hobbes, *Leviathan*, ed. C. B. Macpherson (Harmondsworth: Penguin, 1968) chap. 14.

20. Ibid., chap. 20.

21. Ibid., chap. 18.

22. "Just the same [as mathematics] is it in moral knowledge: let a man have the idea of taking from others, without their consent, what their honest industry has possessed them of, and call this *justice* if he please, . . . But yet for all this, the miscalling of these ideas, contrary to the usual signification of the words of that

language, hinders not but that we may have certain and demonstrative knowledge of their several agreements and disagreements, if we will as in mathematics, keep to the same precise ideas, and trace them in their several relations one to another, without being led away by their names"; John Locke, *Essay Concerning Human Understanding*, ed. P. H. Nidditch (Oxford: Clarendon, 1979), bk. 4, chap. 4, para. 9.

23. John Locke, *The Political Writings of John Locke*, ed. David Wooten (New York: Mentor, 1993).

24. Benedict XVI, Address to the General Assembly of the United Nations, April 18, 2008, http://w2.vatican.va/content/benedict-xvi/en/speeches/2008/april/documents/hf_ben-xvi_spe_20080418_un-visit.html.

25. "From this one may learn that they are mistaken who think agreement on divine matters is necessary in a friendship. For even though Justice, one of the finest virtues, and the good faith between men in society which arises from it, scarcely seem able to exist without religion or dread of some divine power; nevertheless, the strength and goodness of men's natures are sometimes so great that they are able to draw together into mutual affection men who are unwilling and quarrelsome"; Jean Bodin, "Letter to Jean Bautru," in *Jean Bodin: Selected Writings on Philosophy, Religion and Politics*, ed. Paul Lawrence Rose (Geneva: Droz, 1980), 79–81.

26. Eric Voegelin, "Equivalences of Experience and Symbolization in History," in *Published Essays: 1966–1985*, Vol. 12 of *Collected Works*, ed. Ellis Sandoz (Baton Rouge: Louisiana State University Press, 1990), 115–33.

27. The theme of "pure giving," that which comes from outside of being, is strongly announced by Jean-Luc Marion, beginning with Marion, *God without Being*, trans. Thomas A. Carlson (Chicago: University of Chicago Press, 1991).

28. See, for example, Andrew Sabl, *Hume's Politics: Coordination and Crisis in the "History of England"* (Princeton, NJ: Princeton University Press, 2015).

29. Thomas Pfau, *Minding the Modern: Human Agency, Intellectual Traditions, and Responsible Knowledge* (Notre Dame, IN: University of Notre Dame Press, 2015).

30. See, for example, Andrew Bowie, *Schelling and Modern European Philosophy* (London: Routledge, 1993).

31. Walsh, *Modern Philosophical Revolution*, chap. 1.

32. See the overview essay, Thomas D. Williams and Jan Olof Bengtsson, "Personalism," in *The Stanford Encyclopedia of Philosophy*, http://plato.stanford.edu/archives/spr2014/entries/personalism.

33. In a sentence that echoes the Aristotelian awareness of thought as an activity rather than a result, Hegel observes: "Neither the one nor the other has truth; the truth is just their movement in which simple sameness is an abstraction and hence absolute difference, but this, as difference in itself, is distinguished from itself and is therefore absolute self-sameness"; Georg Wilhelm Friedrich Hegel, *Phenomenology of Spirit*, trans. A. V. Miller (Oxford: Oxford University Press, 1977), 472–73. See Walsh, *Modern Philosophical Revolution*, chap. 2.

34. Georg Wilhelm Friedrich Hegel, *Lectures on the Proofs of the Existence of God*, ed. and trans. Peter C. Hodgson (Oxford: Clarendon, 2007).

35. "The 'I think,' 'I am,' is since Descartes the fundamental error of all knowledge. Thinking is not my thinking, and being is not my being, for everything is only of God, or of the All"; F. W. J. Schelling, "Schelling's Aphorisms of 1805," in *Idealism and the Endgame of Theory: Three Essays by F. W. J. Schelling* (Albany: State University of New York Press, 1966), §44.

36. "Goethe, like Schelling, believes that Kant posed himself to discuss the metaphysical realm but held back from doing so. 'Kant resolutely limits himself to a certain circle, and constantly points ironically beyond it,' Goethe writes in one aphorism"; Richard Velkley, *Being after Rousseau* (Chicago: University of Chicago Press, 2002), 133.

37. Parmenides, Fragment B3, in *Early Greek Philosophy*, ed. and trans. Jonathan Barnes (New York: Penguin, 2002).

38. F. W. J. Schelling, *Schelling's Philosophy of Mythology and Revelation*, ed. and trans. Victor C. Hayes (Armidale: Australian Association for the Study of Religion), 216.

39. "An *immediate* relationship to a personal being can, though, *also* be a personal one: I must deal with Him, being in truly empirical relationship with Him; but such an empirical relationship is just as excluded from reason as *everything* personal is excluded from it; *it is supposed* precisely to be that which is impersonal"; F. W. J. Schelling, *On the History of Modern Philosophy*, trans. Andrew Bowie (Cambridge: Cambridge University Press, 1994), 170.

40. Pfau, *Minding the Modern*, 552.

41. John Rawls, *A Brief Inquiry into the Meaning of Sin and Faith: With "On My Religion,"* ed. Thomas Nagel (Cambridge, MA: Harvard University Press, 2009).

42. Robert Spaemann, *Persons: The Difference between "Someone" and "Something,"* trans. Oliver O'Donovan (Oxford: Oxford University Press, 1996).

43. See, for example, Sebastião Salgado, *Sahel: The End of the Road* (Berkeley: University of California Press, 2004).

44. Antoine de Saint-Exupéry, *The Little Prince* (New York: Harcourt, 1943).

45. Thomas Nagel, "What Is It Like to Be a Bat?," *Philosophical Review* 83, no. 4 (1974): 435–50.

46. Aquinas, *Summa theologiae* I, q. 50, a. 5.

47. Plato, *Symposium* 175c.

48. Jaroslav Pelikan, *Christianity and Classical Culture* (New Haven, CT: Yale University Press, 1993), chap. 15.

49. Søren Kierkegaard, *Philosophical Fragments*, ed. and trans. Howard V. Hong and Edna H. Hong (Princeton, NJ: Princeton University Press, 1985), especially III, "The Absolute Paradox (a Metaphysical Caprice)."

50. This was evidently not the case in the outstanding illustration of the problem in Thomas Nagel, *Mind and Cosmos: Why the Materialist Neo-Darwinian Conception of Nature Is Almost Certainly False* (Oxford: Oxford University Press, 2012).

51. Václav Havel, *To the Castle and Back*, trans. Paul Wilson (New York: Knopf, 2007), 329–30.

Chapter 2

1. Michael Oakeshott, *Rationalism and Politics*, rev. ed. (Indianapolis: Liberty Press, 1991), and also his neglected masterpiece, Oakeshott, *On Human Conduct* (Oxford: Clarendon, 1975).

2. A good example of this shift toward a more radical questioning of the liberal democratic tradition was the excitement generated by the *First Things* symposium of November 1996. See *The End of Democracy? The Celebrated First Things Debate*, ed. Mitchell Muncy (Dallas: Spence, 1997). The taint of suspicion attaching to the whole liberal tradition is, however, not far from the surface even in such reformist critiques as Mary Ann Glendon, *Rights Talk: The Impoverishment of Political Discourse* (New York; Free Press, 1991), or Michael Sandel, *Democracy's Discontent* (Cambridge, MA: Harvard University Press, 1997). The approach is continued in Patrick Deneen, *Why Liberalism Failed* (New Haven, CT: Yale University Press, 2018).

3. The transition is exemplified by the distance traveled between Rawls, *Theory of Justice* (Cambridge, MA: Harvard University Press, 1971) and Rawls, *Political Liberalism* (New York: Columbia University Press, 1993). See also Richard Rorty, *Contingency, Irony and Solidarity* (New York: Cambridge University Press, 1989), and Rorty, "The Priority of Democracy to Philosophy," in *The Virginia Statute of Religious Freedom*, ed. Merrill Peterson and Robert C. Vaughan (New York: Cambridge University Press, 1988), 257–82. For an overview, see William Galston, *Liberal Purposes* (New York: Cambridge University Press, 1991).

4. "From this one may learn," he wrote to his friend, Jean Bautru, "that they are mistaken who think agreement on divine matters is necessary in a friendship. For even though Justice, one of the finest virtues, and the good faith between men in society which arises from it, scarcely seem able to exist without religion or dread of some divine powers, nevertheless, the strength and goodness of men's natures are sometimes so great that they are able to draw together in mutual affection men who are unwilling and quarrelsome. . . . I had written to you in prior letters to this effect: do not allow conflicting opinions about religion to carry you away; only bear in mind this fact: genuine religion is nothing other than the sincere direction of a cleansed mind toward God"; see Jean Bodin, *Jean Bodin: Selected Writings on Philosophy, Religion and Politics*, ed. Paul Lawrence Rose (Geneva: Droz, 1980), 79–81.

5. One of the most effective brief statements of this principle is contained in Jacques Maritain, *The Person and the Common Good*, trans. John J. Fitzgerald (Notre Dame, IN: University of Notre Dame Press, 1966).

6. Immanuel Kant, *Groundwork of the Metaphysics of Morals*, trans. H. J. Paton (London: Hutchinson, 1948).

7. It is noteworthy that even thinkers who are not particularly sympathetic to religion find themselves compelled to reach back to the language of the sacred when they wish to convey the unsurpassable dignity that attaches to each human being. Adam Smith, for example, reflecting on the fate of slaves and workers,

insists that "the property which each man has in his own labor as it is the original foundation of all other property, so it is the most sacred and inviolable"; Smith, *The Wealth of Nations* (Indianapolis: Liberty Fund, 2009), Ix.c.12.

8. Edmund Burke, *Reflections on the Revolution in France* (Indianapolis: Bobbs-Merrill, 1955), is a powerful critique of the abstraction of the Rights of Man. But it is also a powerful re-evocation of the more substantive historical community that underpins an order of liberty. Interesting parallel critiques of liberal abstractness are provided by Jeremy Bentham and Karl Marx. See the anthology, Jeremy Waldron, ed., *Nonsense upon Stilts: Bentham, Burke, and Marx on the Rights of Man* (New York: Methuen, 1987).

9. Locke wrote his famous *Essay Concerning Human Understanding* in large part in response to the difficulty of resolving the moral and religious questions that underlay his conception of civil society. In light of the inconclusiveness of his efforts at philosophic justification, he subsequently undertook a reapplication of Christianity that would fulfill the same foundational role in his *On the Reasonableness of Christianity* and his later commentaries and paraphrases of the Epistles of St. Paul.

10. This nostrum of Joseph Schumpeter is quoted by Isaiah Berlin in his widely influential essay "Two Concepts of Liberty" as its central thesis; see Berlin, *Four Essays on Liberty* (New York: Oxford University Press, 1969), 172.

11. Alexis de Tocqueville, *Democracy in America*, trans. Henry Reeve (New York: Vintage, 1956–58), 2:127.

12. Alasdair MacIntyre, *After Virtue* (Notre Dame, IN: University of Notre Dame Press, 1984).

13. *On Liberty*, *Utilitarianism*, and *Considerations on Representative Government* are contained in John Stuart Mill, *On Liberty and Other Essays*, ed. John Gray (New York: Oxford University Press, 1991); Mill, *Principles of Political Economy*, ed. Donald Winch (London: Penguin, 1970); Mill, *Three Essays on Religion* (Amherst, NY: Prometheus Books, 1998).

14. This is essentially Hegel's critique and development of Kantian morality in Hegel, *The Philosophy of Right*, trans. T. M. Knox (New York: Oxford University Press, 1967). For a contemporary version of the argument, see Charles Taylor, *The Ethics of Authenticity* (Cambridge, MA: Harvard University Press, 1992), or the more extended account in Taylor, *Sources of the Self* (Cambridge, MA: Harvard University Press, 1989).

15. Virtually any of the Lincoln anthologies contain the key selections; see, for example, *Lincoln on Democracy*, ed. Mario Cuomo and Harold Holzer (New York: Harper, 1991).

16. This insight is the centerpiece of the argument I have explored at greater length in David Walsh, *The Growth of the Liberal Soul* (Columbia: University of Missouri Press, 1997), esp. chaps. 6–8.

17. John Paul II made the dignity of the human person the centerpiece of his social teaching and sought to underpin the language of rights with the more expansive truth of Christ. See, especially, *Veritatis splendor* (1993) and

Evangelium vitae (1995). I cover the continuity in the pontificates of Benedict XVI and Francis in chapter 14.

Chapter 3

1. John Locke, *An Essay Concerning Human Understanding*, ed. P. H. Nidditch (Oxford: Clarendon, 1979); Locke, *Political Writings of John Locke*, ed. David Wooten (New York: Mentor, 1993); Locke, *The Reasonableness of Christianity*, ed. George W. Ewing (Washington: Regnery, 1965); Locke, *A Paraphrase and Notes on the Epistles of St. Paul*, ed. Arthur Wainwright (Oxford: Clarendon, 1987).

2. For a fascinating exploration of the question, see the exchange in Jürgen Habermas and Joseph Ratzinger, *The Dialectic of Secularization: On Reason and Religion* (San Francisco: Ignatius, 2007). Or we might contrast the diminished enthusiasm for liberal democracy in Ryszard Legutko, *The Demon in Democracy: Totalitarian Temptations in Free Societies* (New York: Encounter, 2018), with the desire for withdrawal from it in Ron Dreher, *The Benedict Option: A Strategy for Christians in a Post-Christian Nation* (New York: Sentinel, 2017).

3. Søren Kierkegaard, *The Concept of Irony with Continual Reference to Socrates*, trans. Howard V. and Edna H. Hong (Princeton, NJ: Princeton University Press, 1989). Contrast this with Richard Rorty, *Contingency, Irony, and Solidarity* (New York: Cambridge University Press, 1989).

4. Michael Zantovsky, *Havel: A Life* (New York: Grove Press, 2014).

5. Nietzsche, *Human, All Too Human: A Book for Free Spirits*, trans. R. J. Hollingdale (New York: Cambridge University Press, 1986), 172.

6. Søren Kierkegaard, *Philosophical Fragments*, trans. Howard V. Hong and Edna H. Hong (Princeton, NJ: Princeton University Press, 1985), see pt. 3, "The Absolute Paradox."

7. Emmanuel Levinas, *Totality and Infinity*, trans. Alphonso Lingis (Pittsburgh: Duquesne University Press, 1969), sec. III, C, "The Ethical Relation and Time."

8. "Tantamne profunditatem creditis esse in homine, quae lateat ipsum hominem in quo est?"; Augustine, *Enarrationes in Psalmos*, 41, para. 13, in *Corpus Christianorum*, ed. D. Dekkers and J. Fraipont (Turnhout: Brepols, 1956), 38:470. This is from St. Augustine's commentary on the lines "Deep calls to deep at the roar of thy waterfalls" (Ps. 42:7 RSV).

9. "Rather, it is important finally to realize that precisely through the characterization of something as a 'value' what is so valued is robbed of its worth"; Martin Heidegger, "Letter on Humanism," in *Basic Writings*, trans. David Farrell Krell (San Francisco: HarperSanFrancisco, 1977), 228.

10. Jacques Derrida, "Différance," in *Margins of Philosophy*, trans. Alan Bass (Chicago: University of Chicago Press, 1982), 1–27.

11. Søren Kierkegaard, *Either/Or*, trans. Howard V. Hong and Edna H. Hong (Princeton, NJ: Princeton University Press, 1987), "The Esthetic Validity of

Marriage"; Kierkegaard, *Stages on Life's Way* (Princeton, NJ: Princeton University Press, 1988), "Some Reflections on Marriage in Answer to Objections by a Married Man."

12. Jacques Derrida, *Given Time: I. Counterfeit Money*, trans. Peggy Kamuf (Chicago: University of Chicago Press, 1992), and Derrida, *The Gift of Death*, trans. David Wills (Chicago: University of Chicago Press, 1995).

13. The convenience of the term "contract" leads us to overlook Hobbes's insistence on "covenant," Locke's preference for "compact," Rousseau's conception of a moral contract, and Burke's adoption of "eternal contract."

14. Emmanuel Levinas, *Of God Who Comes to Mind*, trans. Bettina Bergo (Stanford, CA: Stanford University Press, 1998); John Paul II, *Splendor veritatis* (1993).

15. A Spanish party in 1810 styled themselves the *liberales*, thereby introducing the specifically political application of the term.

16. See Jürgen Habermas, *The Future of Human Nature* (London: Polity Press, 2003), for a good example of such reflection on the biotechnology questions. A very different but convergent approach is developed in Leon Kass, *Life, Liberty and the Defense of Dignity: The Challenge for Bioethics* (San Francisco: Encounter, 2002); and Robert George and Christopher Tollefsen, *Embryo: A Defense of Human Life* (New York: Doubleday, 2008).

17. Søren Kierkegaard, *Fear and Trembling*, trans. Howard V. Hong and Edna H. Hong (Princeton, NJ: Princeton University Press, 1983).

18. Jacques Maritain, *The Person and the Common Good*, trans. John J. Fitzgerald (Notre Dame, IN: University of Notre Dame Press, 1966).

19. Hannah Arendt, *On Revolution* (New York: Viking, 1963), grappled with this.

20. Alexander Solzhenitsyn, "Matryona's House," in *Stories and Prose Poems*, trans. Michael Glenny (Harmondsworth: Penguin, 1973).

21. David Walsh, *The Growth of the Liberal Soul* (Columbia: University of Missouri Press, 1997), chap. 4.

22. Derrida has sought to articulate this notion of "democracy to come," beginning with Jacques Derrida, *Specters of Marx*, trans. Peggy Kamuf (New York: Routledge, 1994); then Derrida, *On Cosmopolitanism and Forgiveness*, trans. Mark Dooley and Michael Hughes (New York: Routledge, 2001), and most recently in Derrida, *Rogues*, trans. Pascale-Anne Brault and Michael Naas (Stanford, CA: Stanford University Press, 2005).

23. See, for example, Liu Xiaobo, *No Enemies, No Hatred: Selected Essays and Poems*, ed. Perry Link, Tienchi Martin-Liao, and Liu Xia (Cambridge, MA: Belknap, 2012).

24. The position of Christ in "The Legend of the Grand Inquisitor" has long been sensed as just such an ultimate affirmation of liberty, but it is only now we begin to understand why; see Dostoevsky, *The Brothers Karamazov*.

25. A still insufficiently absorbed resource in this regard is the powerfully compressed metaphysics of freedom in Schelling's last published work, F. W. J.

Schelling, *Philosophical Inquiries into the Nature of Human Freedom* (1809), trans. James Gutman (La Salle, IL: Open Court, 1936).

26. The phrase is John Stuart Mill's characterization of the American approach to government; see Mill, *On Liberty* (Indianapolis: Bobbs-Merrill, 1956), 137.

Chapter 4

1. Jacques Maritain, *The Person and the Common Good*, trans. John J. Fitzgerald (Notre Dame, IN: University of Notre Dame Press, 1966).
2. Ibid., 56–57.
3. See Max Scheler, *The Nature of Sympathy*, trans. Peter Heath (Hamden, CT: Archon, 1970); Emmanuel Mounier, *Personalism*, trans. Philip Mairet (New York: Grove, 1952).
4. Karol Wojtyla, *The Acting Person*, trans. Andrej Potocki (Dordrecht: Reidel, 1979); Wojtyla, *Person and Community: Selected Essays*, 2nd ed., trans. Theresa Sandok (New York: Peter Lang, 2007).
5. "Thou art *thyself*," says Juliet, "though not a Montague . . . Romeo, doff thy name, and for thy name, which is not part of thee, take all myself"; Shakespeare, *Romeo and Juliet*, 2.1 (emphasis original); quoted in Maritain, *The Person and the Common Good*, 39.
6. Emmanuel Levinas, *Totality and Infinity*, trans. Alphonso Lingis (Pittsburgh: Duquesne University Press, 1969).
7. "If we accept," Mother Teresa asked at a prayer breakfast in Washington attended by President Clinton and cabinet secretaries, "that a mother can kill even her own child, how can we tell other people not to kill one another?" "Mother Teresa's Address to the National Prayer Breakfast," *Crisis*, March 1994, 18.
8. Jacques Derrida, *On the Name*, ed. Thomas Dutoit (Stanford, CA: Stanford University Press, 1995).
9. Kant's formulation of a kingdom of ends arises from the recognition that "all rational beings stand under the law that each of them should treat himself and all others never merely as means but always at the same time as an end in himself"; Immanuel Kant, *Groundwork of the Metaphysics of Morals*, trans. James Ellington (Indianapolis: Hackett, 1981), 39.
10. John Rawls formulates the principle in Rawls, *Theory of Justice* (Cambridge, MA: Harvard University Press, 1971), 3: "Each person possesses an inviolability founded on justice that even the welfare of society as a whole cannot override."
11. "As a person, man is therefore the subject of work" (John Paul II, *Laborem exercens*, par. 6).
12. Brian Tierney, *The Idea of Natural Rights: Studies on Natural Rights, Natural Law, and Church Law, 1150–1625* (Atlanta: Scholars 1997).
13. Michael Oakeshott, *On Human Conduct* (Oxford: Clarendon, 1976).

14. "Thus it is by the enjoyment of a dangerous freedom that the Americans learn the art of rendering the dangers of freedom less formidable"; Alexis de Tocqueville, *Democracy in America*, trans. Henry Reeve (New York: Vintage, 1956–58), 2:127.

15. On this, see Søren Kierkegaard, *Philosophical Fragments*, trans. Howard V. Hong and Edna H. Hong (Princeton, NJ: Princeton University Press, 1985), 111.

16. An often quoted passage from Chesterton puts this best while also illustrating how the thoroughly personalist cast of his thought gave it its peculiar vigor. "In short, the democratic faith is this: that the most terribly important things must be left to ordinary men themselves—the mating of the sexes, the rearing of the young, the laws of the state. This is democracy; and in this I have always believed"; G. K. Chesterton, *Orthodoxy* (London: Fontana, 1961), 46.

17. This was the criticism that Francisco Suarez mounted against the social contract theorists. See Quentin Skinner, *Foundations of Modern Political Thought* (Cambridge: Cambridge University Press, 1978), 2:155–61.

Chapter 5

1. John Rawls, *A Brief Inquiry into the Meaning of Sin and Faith: With "On My Religion,"* ed. Thomas Nagel (Cambridge, MA: Harvard University Press, 2009).

2. Eric Gregory has written his own considerable reflection on the event in Gregory, "Before the Original Position: The Neo-Orthodox Theology of the Young John Rawls," *Journal of Religious Ethics* 35, no. 2 (2007): 179–206.

3. Cohen and Nagel concede as much in Joshua Cohen and Thomas Nagel, introduction to *A Brief Inquiry*, by John Rawls, 5. I take a minor satisfaction in finding my own earlier reading of the deeply spiritual strain of Rawls confirmed. See David Walsh, *The Growth of the Liberal Soul* (Columbia: University of Missouri Press, 1997), esp. 51–53.

4. Marx's preface to his dissertation opened with this ringing declaration: "Philosophy does not make a secret of it. The confession of Prometheus: 'In one word, I hate all the gods,' is its very own confession, its own sentence against all heavenly and earthly gods who refuse to recognize human self-consciousness as the supreme divinity. And none shall be held beside it"; see Karl Marx and Friedrich Engels, *Werke*, Ergänzungsband, Teil 1 (Berlin: Dietz, 1973), 262.

5. One thinks of Heidegger's erasure of the original dedication of *Being and Time* to Husserl in subsequent editions.

6. Cohen and Nagel, introduction to *A Brief Inquiry*, 1–23.

7. This is, of course, very different from asserting that public reason is secular, since that too would be to insist on a comprehensive doctrine that political liberalism must do without. When asked whether he was making "a veiled argument for secularism," Rawls responded with emphatic denial. "I make a point in *Political Liberalism* of really not discussing anything, as far as I can help it, that will put me at odds with any theologian, or any philosopher"; see *"Commonweal*

Interview with John Rawls (1998)," in John Rawls, *Collected Papers*, ed. Samuel Freeman (Cambridge, MA: Harvard University Press, 1999), 622.

8. See Peter Berkowitz, "God and John Rawls," *Policy Review*, no. 155 (June & July 2009); Gilbert Meilaender, "We Were Believers Once, and Young," *First Things*, October 2009.

9. Jürgen Habermas et al., *An Awareness of What Is Missing: Faith and Reason in a Post-Secular Age*, trans. Ciaran Cronin (Cambridge: Polity Press, 2010); William Connolly, *Why I Am Not a Secularist* (Minneapolis: University of Minnesota Press, 1999).

10. See John Rawls, "Reply to Habermas," in Rawls, *Political Liberalism*, exp. ed. (New York: Columbia University Press, 2005), 372–434. For a broader discussion, see Todd Hedrick, *Rawls and Habermas: Reason, Pluralism, and the Claims of Political Philosophy* (Stanford, CA: Stanford University Press, 2010).

11. Letter to Rawls's editor at Columbia University Press, July 14, 1998, reprinted in Rawls, *Political Liberalism*, 438.

12. John Rawls, "The Idea of Public Reason Revisited," *Chicago Law Review* (1997), reprinted in Rawls, *Political Liberalism*, 611.

13. Rawls, *Political Liberalism*, 113.

14. See several essays in Samuel Freeman, ed., *The Cambridge Companion to Rawls* (New York: Cambridge University Press, 2003), esp. Thomas Nagel, "Rawls and Liberalism," 62–85. Also useful on this and many other aspects of Rawls is Samuel Freeman, *Rawls* (New York: Routledge, 2007).

15. "We should not attempt to give form to our life by first looking to the good independently defined. It is not our aims that primarily reveal our nature but rather the principles that we would acknowledge to govern the background conditions under which these aims are to be formed and the manner in which they are to be pursued. For the self is prior to the ends which are affirmed by it; even a dominant end must be chosen from among numerous possibilities. There is no way to get beyond deliberative rationality. We should therefore reverse the relation between the right and the good proposed by teleological doctrines and view the right as prior"; see John Rawls, *A Theory of Justice* (Cambridge, MA: Belknap Press, 1971), 560. This principle is given a more nuanced formulation in Rawls, "The Priority of Right and Ideas of the Good," in *Political Liberalism*, exp. ed. (New York: Columbia University Press, 2005), 173–211, where he explains that "the priority of right means (in its general meaning) that the ideas of the good used must be political ideas, so that we need not rely on comprehensive conceptions of the good but only on ideas tailored to fit within the political conception" (209).

16. "The social union is no longer founded on a conception of the good as given by a common religious faith or philosophical doctrine, but on a shared public conception of justice appropriate to the conception of citizens in a democratic state as free and equal persons" (Rawls, *Political Liberalism*, 304).

17. Michael Sandel first made a name for himself by forcefully mounting this charge in Sandel, *Liberalism and the Limits of Justice* (New York: Cambridge University Press, 1982).

18. This is in marked contrast to the abandonment of any defense of liberal principles other than their historical emergence in Richard Rorty, "The Priority of Democracy to Philosophy," in *The Virginia Statute for Religious Freedom*, ed. Merrill Peterson and Robert C. Vaughan (New York: Cambridge University Press, 1988), 257–82.

19. Max Scheler, *Formalism in Ethics and Non-Formal Ethics of Values: A New Attempt toward the Foundation of an Ethical Personalism*, trans. Manfred S. Frings and Roger L. Funk (Evanston, IL: Northwestern University Press, 1973); and Edith Stein, *Finite and Eternal Being*, trans. Kurt Reinhardt (Washington, DC: Institute of Carmelite Studies, 2002).

20. That historical unfolding is well summarized in Robert Spaemann, *Persons: The Difference between "Someone" and "Something,"* trans. Oliver O'Donovan (Oxford: Oxford University Press, 2006).

21. For this insight I am indebted to Angelo Valente, "Remarks at Rawls Roundtable," at the American Political Science Association Meeting, Washington, DC, September, 4, 2010.

22. "Personal knowledge is revealed knowledge. It comes about through communication in community. Natural objects immediately disclose their nature; but persons must consent to communicate knowledge of themselves. Therefore by reason man can know very little about God" (Rawls, *A Brief Inquiry*, 224).

23. Emmanuel Levinas, *Totality and Infinity*, trans. Alphonso Lingis (Pittsburgh: Duquesne University Press, 1987).

24. "Each person possesses an inviolability founded on justice that even the welfare of society as a whole cannot override" (Rawls, *Theory of Justice*, 3).

25. The whole project of "political liberalism" that concedes the irreducible plurality of worldviews sets out, not to recapture a common ground within or beyond them, but to affirm the priority of persons before all such discourse about the good. "As free persons, citizens claim the right to view their persons as independent from and not identified with any particular such conception with its scheme of final ends. Given their moral power to form, revise, and rationally pursue a conception of the good, their public identity as free persons is not affected by changes over time in their determinate conception of it" (Rawls, *Political Liberalism*, 30). Rawls correctly insists that this entails "no specific metaphysical implications concerning the nature of the self" (ibid., 27), by which he means that the priority of persons is a condition of liberal speech and not its presupposition. We know it without being able to explain how.

26. John Rawls, *Lectures on the History of Moral Philosophy*, ed. Barbara Herman (Cambridge, MA: Harvard University Press, 2000), xvii.

27. My own account of this is available in David Walsh, *The Modern Philosophical Revolution: The Luminosity of Existence* (New York: Cambridge University Press, 2008).

28. Rawls, *Lectures on the History of Moral Philosophy*, 227.

29. Quoted by Rawls in ibid., 230.

30. Ibid., 301.

31. Rawls, *Political Liberalism*, 19.

32. Rawls, *Lectures on the History of Moral Philosophy*, 322.

33. Ibid.

34. "With these remarks as a preface, we can now see how the principles of justice are related to human sociability. The main idea is simply that a well-ordered society (corresponding to justice as fairness) is itself a form of social union. Indeed, it is a social union of social unions" (Rawls, *Theory of Justice*, 527).

35. "What makes an intelligible world is not our being in another world ontologically distinct from this world, one not in space and time, but all of us, here and now, acting from the moral law under the idea of freedom. The realm of ends is a secular ideal" (Rawls, *Lectures on the History of Moral Philosophy*, 312).

36. This is surely why he abandons even the limited comprehensive doctrine of justice developed in *A Theory of Justice* because it "relies on a premise the realization of which its principles of justice rule out" (Rawls, *Political Liberalism*, xl). The justice that guarantees personal liberty, he now sees, will lead to reasonable pluralism. The imperative is to derive respect for persons from what is prior to the differences in "comprehensive doctrines" that separate them. In the final expanded edition of *Political Liberalism*, Rawls finds a term for this requirement that had eluded him up to this point. It is the imperative of "reciprocity" (xliv). The mutuality of persons precedes their individuality. They are persons in community even, and especially, when it is the thin community of the liberal polity.

37. *Political Liberalism*, 324, where Rawls references the *Critique of Practical Reason* on this point.

38. Ibid., 323.

39. See Eric Voegelin, "On Debate and Existence," in *Published Essays, 1966–1985*, Vol. 12 of *Collected Works*, ed. Ellis Sandoz (Baton Rouge: Louisiana State University Press, 1990), 36–51.

Chapter 6

1. George Kateb takes up a similar challenge in his *Human Dignity* by insisting that we must be able to ground the conviction in wholly secular terms. The project is admirable, but its completion would require a more expansive language than seems to be available, yet he does approach it in invoking Emerson's characterization of every person as an "infinitude." The difficulty is that he immediately dismisses the notion of immortality as a subjective longing for endless life, rather than a glimpse of the true infinite that exceeds the mere extension of temporality. But is not that glimpse itself the proof of immortality? Kateb can, in other words, account for everything but his own convictions: "We need to stay true to what we know—the immensity beyond immensity of space and time and the universe's purposeless waste—because that knowledge is an incomparably superior encouragement to wonder." In light of that true immortality, we disdain the false immortality of mere endless life. See Kateb, *Human Dignity* (Cambridge, MA: Belknap, 2011), 125, 215. As with so many "secular" accounts, Kateb's explains everything except the source of his own perspective. Only infinity can apprehend the finite.

2. This is the famous observation with which Wittgenstein opens and closes his *Tractatus Logico-Philosophicus* by insisting that "what we cannot talk about we must pass over in silence." Unfortunately, most of his readers fail to notice that this nonsaying is in effect a saying. Certainly he has not passed over in silence.

3. Jürgen Habermas, *The Theory of Communicative Action*, Vols. 1–2, trans. Thomas McCarthy (Boston: Beacon, 1984, 1989).

4. The prioritization of practice over theory, and the characterization of political principles as abbreviations, has long been associated with the thought of Michael Oakeshott, especially in Oakeshott, *Rationalism and Politics*, rev. ed. (Indianapolis: Liberty Fund, 1991). It is doubtful, however, that Oakeshott would have applied his notion to the language of rights, even though, I would argue, a more thorough application of the primacy of practice would have required it. His closest approach is in the notion of a "civil association," which he distinguishes sharply from an "enterprise association" in Oakeshott, *On Human Conduct* (Oxford: Clarendon, 1975).

5. Brian Tierney, *The Idea of Natural Rights* (Atlanta: Scholars Press, 1997), provides the historical account, but we can also see Rawls's principle that "the right is prior to the good" as its philosophical counterpart; see John Rawls, *A Theory of Justice* (Cambridge: Belknap, 1971).

6. See the very fine overview in Christopher McCrudden, "Human Dignity and Judicial Interpretation of Rights," *The European Journal of International Law* 19 (2008): 655–724.

7. This is an insight that has remained latent from the beginning in the Greek word *prosōpon*, from which our word "person" is derived. Originally it meant the mask that the actor wore, so it already called attention to the invisible one who was always there behind the mask, but could not be presented as such. We have yet to develop a philosophical account of the person that is adequate to this paradoxical reality. Some first steps in that direction were offered in David Walsh, *Politics of the Person as the Politics of Being* (Notre Dame, IN: University of Notre Dame Press, 2016).

8. Something similar may be said about the heroic resistance against the devaluation of liberty undertaken by Tocqueville in the name of liberty: "It is easy to see that what is lacking in such nations [who have chosen a comfortable slavery] is a genuine love of freedom, that lofty aspiration which (I confess) defies analysis. For it is something one must *feel* and logic has no part in it. It is a privilege of noble minds which God has fitted to receive it, and it inspires them with a generous fervor. But to meaner souls, untouched by the sacred flame, it may well seem incomprehensible"; Alexis de Tocqueville, *The Old Regime and the French Revolution*, trans. Stuart Gilbert (Garden City, NY: Doubleday, 1955), 169.

9. Kant, *The Metaphysics of Morals*, trans. Mary Gregor (Cambridge: Cambridge University Press, 1997), §24–27.

10. Michael Rosen, *Dignity: Its History and Meaning* (Cambridge, MA: Harvard University Press, 2012), covers this and other relevant cases in chap. 2.

11. Primo Levi, *If This Is A Man* and *The Truce*, trans. Stuart Woolf (Boston: Little, Brown, 1991); and the discussion by Dustin Howes, "'Consider If This Is

a Person'": Primo Levi, Hannah Arendt, and the Political Significance of Auschwitz," *Holocaust and Genocide Studies* 22 (2008): 266–92.

12. This idea is well developed in the theological personalism of Benedict XVI: "Faith is not simply a personal reaching out towards things to come that are still totally absent: it gives us something"; see *Spe salvi* (2007), §7.

13. "The cross is the giant leap toward the radical internalizing of the concept of dignity, toward the awareness of something in the phenomenon of dignity at once veiled and unveiled"; Robert Spaemann, *Love and the Dignity of Human Life* (Grand Rapids, MI: Eerdmans, 2012), 31.

Chapter 7

1. Eric Voegelin, *Science, Politics, and Gnosticism*, in *Modernity without Restraint*, Vol 5. of *Collected Works of Eric Voegelin*, ed. Manfred Henningsen (Columbia: University of Missouri Press, 2000), 5:275f.

2. My own effort to address this is David Walsh, *The Growth of the Liberal Soul* (Columbia: University of Missouri Press, 1997).

3. Eric Voegelin, "A Letter to Alfred Schütz concerning Edmund Husserl," in *Anamnesis: On the Theory of History and Politics*, Vol. 6 of *Collected Works*, ed. David Walsh (Columbia: University of Missouri Press, 2002).

4. Derrida observed that the fate of his writing was to be "almost with every letter, to be bound better and better but be read less and less well over almost twenty years, like my religion about which nobody understands anything"; Jacques Derrida, *Circumfession*, trans. Geoffrey Bennington (Chicago: University of Chicago Press, 1993), 154.

5. "Thou art *thyself*," says Juliet, "though not a Montague . . . . Romeo, doff thy name, and for thy name, which is not part of thee, take all myself" (Shakespeare, *Romeo and Juliet*, 2.1).

6. Ratzinger has a far more generous assessment in noting the centrality of the person in relation to others. "Therein lies concealed a revolution in man's view of the world: the sole dominion of thinking in terms of substance is ended; relation is discovered as an equally valid primordial mode of reality. It becomes possible to surmount what we call today 'objectifying thought'; a new plane of being comes into view. It is probably true to say that the task imposed on philosophy as a result of these facts is far from being completed—so much does modern thought depend on the possibilities thus disclosed, without which it would be inconceivable"; Joseph Cardinal Ratzinger, *Introduction to Christianity*, trans. J. R. Foster (San Francisco: Ignatius, 2004), 184.

7. See Peter Gordon, *Continental Divide: Heidegger, Cassirer, Davos* (Cambridge, MA: Harvard University Press, 2012), for an account of the famous encounter.

8. Immanuel Kant, "Idea for a Universal History with a Cosmopolitan Purpose," in *Political Writings*, ed. Hans Reiss (Cambridge: Cambridge University Press,1991), Third Proposition.

Chapter 9

1. See Frederick Beiser, *The Early Political Writings of the German Romantics* (Cambridge: Cambridge University Press, 1996).
2. Immanuel Kant, *Groundwork of the Metaphysics of Morals*, trans. Mary Gregor (Cambridge: Cambridge University Press, 1996), chap. 2.
3. Immanuel Kant, *Religion within the Boundaries of Mere Reason*, trans. Allen Wood (Cambridge: Cambridge University Press, 1998).

Chapter 10

1. William Kneale and Martha Kneale, *The Development of Logic* (Oxford: Oxford University Press, 1962).
2. Jacques Maritain, "The Dialectic of Anthropocentric Humanism," in *Integral Humanism*, trans. Joseph W. Evans (Notre Dame, IN: University of Notre Dame Press, 1973), 28–34.
3. Neither Voegelin nor Strauss, for example, dwells on the notion of form or forms despite its centrality to the classical framework they invoke.
4. Perhaps the most notable feature of our philosophical reclaimers is that they function outside of the field of professional philosophy. Like Kierkegaard or Nietzsche, they were aware of the difficulty of subscribing to membership in the guild while seeking to recover its existential origins.
5. *Faith and Political Philosophy: The Voegelin–Strauss Correspondence*, trans. and ed. Peter Emberley and Barry Cooper (University Park: Pennsylvania State University Press, 1993).
6. "The consciousness of questioning unrest in a state of ignorance becomes luminous to itself as a movement in the psyche toward the ground that is present in the psyche as its mover"; Eric Voegelin, *Published Essays, 1966–1985*, Vol. 12 of *Collected Works*, ed. Ellis Sandoz (Baton Rouge: Louisiana State University Press, 1990), 272.
7. Bernard Lonergan, *Method in Theology* (London: Darton, Longman and Todd, 1972), 20; Lonergan, *Insight: A Study of Human Understanding* (New York: Longmans, 1957).
8. Voegelin, *Published Essays, 1966–1985*, 44.
9. "Now, however, we have the further problem that the subject belongs to the same reality that is to be known as its object—and this subject-object relation is a further type of this complex. It is an event in another reality. It is neither the subject nor the object reality in its thing-ness but a reality that encompasses both, a comprehensive reality. For this encompassing reality, as far as I know, we have no generally accepted philosophical term. Nietzsche dealt with it often and called it the "It," and I will stick to that"; Eric Voegelin, "The Meditative Origin of the Philosophical Knowledge of Order," in *The Drama of Humanity and Other Miscellaneous Papers, 1939–1985*, Vol. 33 of *Collected Works*, ed. William Petropulos and Gilbert Weiss (Columbia: University of Missouri Press, 2004), 392.

10. "The fact that every science as such, being the specific science it is, gains no access to its fundamental concepts and to what those concepts grasp, goes hand in hand with the fact that no science can assert something about itself with the help of its own scientific resources"; Martin Heidegger, *Nietzsche II: The Eternal Recurrence of the Same*, ed. and trans. David F. Krell (New York: Harper, 1987), 112.

11. "What is decisive is not that humanity frees itself from previous bonds but, rather, that the essence of humanity altogether transforms itself in that man becomes the subject. To be sure, this word 'subject' must be understood as the translation of the Greek *hypokeimenon*. The word names that-which-lies-before, that which, as ground, gathers everything into itself. This metaphysical meaning of the concept of the subject has, in the first instance, no special relationship to man, and hence none at all to the I"; Martin Heidegger, "The Age of the World Picture," *Off the Beaten Path*, ed. and trans. Julian Young and Kenneth Haynes (Cambridge: Cambridge University Press, 2002), 66. Robert Pippin published a book whose main thesis is indicated by its title: Pippin, *The Persistence of Subjectivity* (Cambridge: Cambridge University Press, 2005).

12. Michael Oakeshott has all of this conception of self-enactment without rooting it in the notion of the person; see Oakeshott, *Of Human Conduct* (Oxford: Clarendon, 1975).

13. The pattern is exemplified in Charles Taylor, *Sources of the Self* (Cambridge, MA: Harvard University Press, 1989).

14. See Derek Parfit, *Reasons and Persons* (Oxford: Oxford University Press, 1986), and Paul Ricoeur, *Oneself as Another*, trans. Kathleen Blamey (Chicago: University of Chicago Press, 1995).

15. Eric Voegelin, "On the Theory of Consciousness," in *Anamnesis*, Vol. 6 of *Collected Works*, trans. M. J. Hanak and Gerhart Niemeyer, ed. David Walsh (Columbia: University of Missouri Press, 2003), 62–83.

16. Aristotle could not find an adequate explanation for the transmission of reason in our offspring. He concedes "it is a very great puzzle to answer another question concerning reason. At what moment, and in what manner, do those creatures which have this principle of reason acquire their share in it, and where does it come from?"; Aristotle, *On the Generation of Animals* 736b5, quoted in Purcell, *From Big Bang to Big Mystery* (Hyde Park, NY: New City Press, 2012), 314. The purely biological explanation could not suffice.

17. Robert Sokolowski approaches this acknowledgment in his exemplary study of the person as "an agent of truth"; see Sokolowski, *Phenomenology of the Human Person* (Cambridge: Cambridge University Press, 2008).

18. Martin Heidegger, *The Basic Problems of Phenomenology*, trans. Albert Hofstadter (Bloomington: Indiana University Press, 1988).

19. "However, the aim we take for the end is not determined by the choice of the individual himself, but by a natural gift of vision, as it were, which enables him to make correct judgments and to choose what is truly good: to be well endowed by nature means to have this natural gift. . . . But if this theory is true, how will virtue be any more voluntary than vice?" (Aristotle, *Nicomachean Ethics* 114b5–15).

20. Much of the thought of Fernando Pessoa moves within this movement beyond itself. "The search for truth—be it the subjective truth of belief, the objective truth of reality, or the social truth of money or power—always confers on the person who merits a prize, the ultimate knowledge of its non-existence. The grand prize of life goes only to those who bought tickets by chance. / The value of art is that it takes us away from here" (Pessoa, *The Book of Disquiet*, ed. and trans. Richard Zenith (New York: Penguin, 2001), §361).

21. F. W. J. Schelling, *Philosophical Inquiries into the Nature of Human Freedom*, trans. James Gutmann (La Salle, IL: Open Court, 1989).

22. Immanuel Kant, *The Metaphysics of Morals*, trans. Mary Gregor (Cambridge: Cambridge University Press, 1996), 278n.

23. On St. Thomas's notion that every being seeks to communicate itself, see Norris Clarke, *Person and Being* (Marquette, WI: Marquette University Press, 1993).

24. The famous line from Terence (195–159 BC), *Heauton Timorumenos* (*The Self-Tormentor*).

25. "And my heart is a little larger than the entire universe." This line became the title for the selected poems of Fernando Pessoa, *A Little Larger Than the Entire Universe*, ed. and trans. Richard Zenith (New York: Penguin, 2006), 253. The line is in "Original Sin" (1934) by Alvaro de Campos, one of Pessoa's most significant heteronyms.

Chapter 11

1. David Walsh, *The Modern Philosophical Revolution: The Luminosity of Existence* (Cambridge: Cambridge University Press, 2008).

2. It was gratifying to discover that no less a figure than John Paul II had struggled on the eve of his papacy to find the right formulation for the profound philosophical shift that has occurred. He too conceded that it was a "revolution" in relation to the preceding tradition, and also one that was ultimately a deepening rather than a rejection of the form that philosophy had taken. "In that sense one may, and even must, speak about *some kind of revolution* which has occurred in the ethics of modern times. The substantive subordination of practicality to normativity had to bring with it, not so much (as in the case of Kant) the rejection of the entire teleological structure which had hitherto been dominant, but its demotion"; Karol Wojtyla, *Man in the Field of Responsibility*, trans. Kenneth W. Kemp and Zuzanna Maślanka Kieroń (South Bend, IN: St. Augustine's Press, 2011; Polish original 1991), 54 (italics in original).

3. Søren Kierkegaard, *Fear and Trembling*, trans. Howard V. Hong and Edna H. Hong (Princeton, NJ: Princeton University Press, 1983), 70.

4. This was the narrative of Walsh, *The Modern Philosophical Revolution*. For a looser confirmation, see the anthology of Chris Firestone and Nathan Jacobs, eds., *The Persistence of the Sacred in Modern Thought* (Notre Dame, IN: University of Notre Dame Press, 2012).

5. Steven Crowell and Jeff Malpas, eds. *Transcendental Heidegger*, (Stanford, CA: Stanford University Press, 2007).

6. Martin Heidegger, *Contributions to Philosophy (from Enowning)*, trans. Parvis Emad and Kenneth Maly (Bloomington: Indiana University Press, 1999).

7. Martin Heidegger, "Letter on Humanism," in *Basic Writings*, ed. David Krell (San Francisco: HarperSanFrancisco, 1977), 189–242.

8. Emanuel Levinas, *Otherwise than Being*, trans. Alphonso Lingis (The Hague: Nijhof, 1981).

9. Jacques Derrida, *Sauf le nom* (Paris: Galilée, 1993).

10. Jacques Derrida, *The Gift of Death*, trans. David Wills (Chicago: University of Chicago Press, 1995).

11. Jacques Derrida, "Force of Law: The 'Mystical Foundation of Authority,'" in *Acts of Religion*, (New York: Routledge, 2002).

12. Immanuel Kant, *Critique of Practical Reason*, trans. Mary Gregor (Cambridge: Cambridge University Press, 1997), 82.

13. Søren Kierkegaard, *Stages on Life's Way*, trans. Howard V. Hong and Edna H. Hong (Princeton, NJ: Princeton University Press, 1988), 112. See also Kierkegaard, "The Esthetic Validity of Marriage," in *Either/Or*, Vol. 2, trans. Howard V. Hong and Edna H. Hong (Princeton, NJ: Princeton University Press, 1987).

14. "The metaphysical is abstraction, and there is no human being who exists metaphysically" (Kierkegaard, *Stages on Life's Way*, 476).

15. Jacques Maritain, *The Person and the Common Good*, trans. John J. Fitzgerald (Notre Dame, IN: University of Notre Dame Press, 1966), chap. 3, "Individuality and Personality."

16. This is the upbuilding thought that forms the concluding "Ultimatum" of *Either/Or*, pt. II.

17. Kant's categorical imperative is addressed to each one personally: "*Act only on that maxim through which you can at the same time will that it should become a universal law.*"

18. This is why a man who goes through life on the assumption "that he is not a criminal but not faultless, either, is of course comic" (Kierkegaard, *Stages on Life's Way*, 479).

19. "*An objective uncertainty, held fast through appropriation with the most passionate inwardness, is the truth*, the highest truth there is for an *existing* person"; Kierkegaard, "Concluding Unscientific Postscript," in *Philosophical Fragments*, trans. Howard V. Hong and Edna H. Hong (Princeton, NJ: Princeton University Press, 1992), 1:203.

Chapter 12

1. Solzhenitsyn, *The Oak and the Calf*, trans. Harry Willets (New York: Harper and Row, 1979).

2. Leo Tolstoy, *War and Peace*, trans. Ann Dunnigan (New York: Signet, 1968), 1355.

3. Ibid., 1413.

4. Ibid., 978.

5. Solzhenitsyn employs the same device in his own short historical reflection, in which it is the February liberal revolution that is regarded as the decisive moment: "If one had to choose one fatal night in the history of Russia, if it was to be one of those in which in a few hours the whole fate of the country is condensed—several revolutions at once—it is likely to be that of the first to the second of March 1917"; see Aleksandr Solzhenitsyn, *Réflexions sur la revolution de Février*, trans. Nikita Struve (Paris: Fayard, 1995), 67.

6. Søren Kierkegaard, *Eighteen Upbuilding Discourses*, trans. Howard V. Hong and Edna H. Hong (Princeton, NJ: Princeton University Press, 1992), xv.

7. Both *Cancer Ward* and *In the First Circle* demonstrate the same technique.

8. Edward Ericson and Alexis Klimoff, *The Soul and Barbed Wire: An Introduction to Solzhenitsyn* (Wilmington, DE: Intercollegiate Studies Institute, 2008).

9. Aleksandr Solzhenitsyn, in *March 1917*, chap. 204. It is translated in *The Solzhenitsyn Reader*, ed. Edward Ericson and Daniel Mahoney (Wilmington, DE: Intercollegiate Studies Institute, 2006), 415–18.

10. A powerful example is the conclusion to one of the most luminous chapters of Aleksandr Solzhenitsyn, *The Gulag Archipelago*, Vol. 2, trans. Thomas P. Whitney (New York: Harper and Row, 1975), "The Ascent," in which Solzhenitsyn recounts his reawakening to the spiritual truth of existence. He concludes the rapturous meditation with the words "*Bless you, prison*, for having been in my life!" But he immediately follows with the counterbalancing: "(And from beyond the grave come replies: It is very well for you to say that—when you came out of it alive.)"

11. Aleksandr Solzhenitsyn, *Apricot Jam and Other Stories* (Berkeley, CA: Counterpoint, 2011).

12. Aleksandr Solzhenitsyn, *The Red Wheel*, Knot I, *August 1914*, trans. H. T. Willetts (New York: Farrar, Strauss and Giroux, 1989), 275.

13. Ibid., 275.

14. The deepest level of questioning around which *The Red Wheel* revolves is the one posed by Sergei Bulgakov, whom Solzhenitsyn quotes in his *Réflexions*: "Why, for what reason was Russia repudiated by God, condemned to agony and decay. Our sins were grave, but hardly enough to explain this unique historical destiny. Russia did not deserve this fate, it is like the lamb that carries the weight of all the sins of Europe. That is a mystery we must accept in faith" (117).

15. Solzhenitsyn, *Réflexions*, chap. 44.

Chapter 13

1. The same attainment of spiritual distance is suggested in the title of Liu Xiaobo's collection of dissident reflections, *No Enemies, No Hatred*, ed. Perry Link, Tienchi Martin Liao, and Liu Xia (Cambridge, MA: Belknap, 2012).

2. Solzhenitsyn, *The Gulag Archipelago*, trans. Thomas Whitney (New York: Harper and Row, 1975), pt. 4, chap. 1, "The Ascent," 2:606.

3. Aleksandr Solzhenitsyn, *The Red Wheel*, Knot I, *August 1914*, trans. H. T. Willetts (New York: Farrar, Strauss and Giroux, 1989), chap. 70, 655.

4. Ibid., chap. 65, 552.

5. Ibid., chap. 65, 582.

6. Ibid., chap. 69, 651.

7. Ibid., chap. 69, 646.

8. *Vekhi: Landmarks*, trans. Marshall Shatz and Judith Zimmerman (New York: Routledge, 2015).

9. This is reaffirmed in the second volume of *April 1917* when Sanya again encounters Varsonofiev: "I think that . . . the ordinary man can do nothing better than . . . carry out his duty. In whatever place he's in" (chap. 157). Vorotyntsev expresses the same conviction as he looks down from the Mogilov Ramparts and knows that all is lost. "And if victory cannot be ours," he reflects, "we must seek a worthy death" (chap. 186); Aleksandr Solzhenitsyn, *April 1917*, in *The Solzhenitsyn Reader*, ed. Eric Ericson (Wilmington, DE: Intercollegiate Studies Institute, 2006).

10. Aleksandr Solzhenitsyn, *November 1916*, trans. H. T. Willetts (New York: Farrar, Strauss and Giroux, 1999), chap. 5, 49–50.

11. Ibid., chap. 15, 170.

12. Ibid., chap. 17, 195.

13. Solzhenitsyn, *The Gulag Archipelago*, 2:611–12.

14. Solzhenitsyn, *November 1916*, chap. 75, 993.

15. Ibid., chap. 75, 1000.

16. This is a perspective on the modern totalitarian crisis, including Solzhenitsyn's emblematic response to it, that I have tried to present in David Walsh, *After Ideology* (San Francisco: HarperSanFrancisco, 1990).

Chapter 14

1. "The essential problem of our times, for Europe and for the world, is that although the fallacy of the communist economy has been recognized—so much so that former communists have unhesitatingly become economic liberals—the moral and religious question that it used to address has been almost totally repressed. The unresolved issue of Marxism lives on: the crumbling of man's original uncertainties about God, himself, and the universe. The decline of a moral conscience grounded in absolute values is still our problem today"; Joseph Ratzinger, "The Spiritual Roots of Europe: Yesterday, Today, and Tomorrow" (2004), in *Without Roots: The West, Relativism, Christianity, Islam*, trans. Michael Moore (New York: Basic, 2006), 73–74.

2. Joseph Ratzinger, "Retrieving the Tradition: Concerning the Notion of Person in Theology," *Communio* 17 (Fall 1990): 438–54 (German original, 1973).

3. John Paul II, *Centesimus Annus* (1991).

4. Jürgen Habermas and Joseph Ratzinger, *The Dialectics of Secularization: On Reason and Religion*, ed. Florian Schuller (San Francisco: Ignatius, 2006).

5. "Unfortunately, this instrument [natural law] has become blunt. Accordingly, I do not intend to appeal to it for support in this conversation. The idea of the natural law presupposed a concept of nature in which nature and reason overlap, since nature is itself rational. With the victory of the theory of evolution, this view of nature has capsized: nowadays we think that nature as such is not rational, even if there is rational behavior in nature" (ibid., 69–70).

6. James Schall, *The Regensburg Lecture* (Notre Dame, IN: St. Augustine's Press, 2007).

7. Benedict XVI, "Address of His Holiness," Meeting with the Members of the General Assembly of the United Nations Organization, April, 18, 2008, https://w2.vatican.va/content/benedict-xvi/en/speeches/2008/april/documents/hf_ben-xvi_spe_20080418_un-visit.html.

8. Benedict XVI, "The Listening Heart: Reflections on the Foundations of Law," Reichstag, Berlin, September 22, 2011, https://w2.vatican.va/content/benedict-xvi/en/speeches/2011/september/documents/hf_ben-xvi_spe_20110922_reichstag-berlin.html.

9. Joseph Cardinal Ratzinger, *Introduction to Christianity*, trans. J. R. Foster (San Francisco: Ignatius, 2004), 184.

10. See the famous study of Anders Nygren, *Agape and Eros*, trans. Philip Watson (Chicago: University of Chicago Press, 1982; Swedish original 1930–36).

11. Joseph Ratzinger, *Eschatology: Death and Eternal Life*, trans. Michael Waldstein and Aidan Nichols (Washington, DC: Catholic University of America Press, 1988; German original, 1977).

12. On this, see Jean-Luc Marion, *God without Being*, trans. Thomas A. Carlson (Chicago: University of Chicago Press, 1991), 95–102.

13. This is a thought that seems more poignant in light of his decision to resign the papacy. The decision is itself a recognition that mortal decline is not only inevitable, but a sure sign of our higher fulfillment. To make longevity the goal would be to mistake life for its transcendence.

14. "Remember particularly that you cannot be a judge of anyone. For no one can judge a criminal, until he recognizes that he is just such a criminal as the man standing before him, and that he more than all men is to blame for that crime"; Fyodor Dostoevsky, *The Brothers Karamazov*, trans. Constance Garnett (New York: Modern Library, 1950), 385.

15. The term derives, as far as I know, from the 1936 work of Jacques Maritain, *Integral Humanism*, trans. Joseph W. Evans (Notre Dame, IN: University of Notre Dame Press, 1973).

16. It is as if to underline the continuity of this idea with the deeper Catholic tradition that he quotes St. Thomas in a footnote to the effect that "the rationality of a part is contrary to the rationality of a person" (Aquinas, III *Sentences* d.5, q.3, a.2).

17. Most notably in *Dignitatis Humanae* (1965), the decree on religious liberty. For an account of the genesis of the document, see Piero Coda, "Religious Freedom and Dialogue: The Prophesy of *Dignitatis Humane*," in *The Human*

Voyage of Self-Discovery: Essays in Honour of Brendan Purcell, ed. Brendan Leahy and David Walsh (Dublin: Veritas, 2013), 284–300. The medieval origins of natural rights is well recounted in Brian Tierney, *The Idea of Natural Rights: Studies on Natural Rights, Natural Law, and Church Law 1150–1625* (Grand Rapids, MI: Eerdmans, 1997).

18. One thinks of *Gaudium et spes* (1965) with its characterization of modern atheism as different because it is a form of antitheism (par. 20). One can only revolt against a God in whom one still believes. The guiding intellectual influence on that document was Henri de Lubac, whose *Drama of Atheist Humanism* (1945) is one of the seminal treatments of the subject.

19. It is noteworthy that Benedict references an edition of Nietzsche that may have been in his possession since his student days. He alludes to a letter of Nietzsche to his sister published in *Werke in Drei Bänden* (Munich, 1954), 953ff.

Chapter 15

1. "The fact that every science as such, being the specific science it is, gains no access to its fundamental concepts and to what those concepts grasp, goes hand in hand with the fact that no science can assert something about itself with the help of its own scientific resources"; Martin Heidegger, *Nietzsche II: The Eternal Recurrence of the Same*, ed. and trans. David F. Krell (New York: Harper, 1987), 112.

2. Albert Einstein, *Ideas and Opinions*, trans. Sonja Bargmann (New York: Bonanza, 1954), 292.

3. Stephen Hawking and Leonard Mlodinow, *The Grand Design* (New York: Bantam, 2010).

4. Richard Dawkins, *The God Delusion* (Boston: Houghton Mifflin, 2006); Daniel Dennett, *Darwin's Dangerous Idea: Evolution and the Meanings of Life* (New York: Simon and Schuster, 1996).

5. "With me, the horrid doubt always arises whether the convictions of man's mind, which has been developed from the mind of the lower animals, are of any value or at all trustworthy. Would anyone trust in the convictions of a monkey's mind, if there are any convictions in such a mind?"; Charles Darwin, letter to W. Graham (1881), in *The Life and Letters of Charles Darwin*, ed. Francis Darwin (New York: Basic, 1959), 285. See the discussion in Brendan Purcell, *From Big Bang to Big Mystery: Human Origins in the Light of Creation and Evolution* (Hyde Park, NY: New City Press, 2012).

6. Thomas Nagel has argued forcefully for "a major conceptual revolution" that would address the inability of science to account for itself in a mindless universe. See Nagel, *Mind and Cosmos: Why the Materialist Neo-Darwinian Conception of Nature Is Almost Certainly False* (New York: Oxford University Press, 2012).

7. "All science . . . has at present the object of dissuading man from his former respect for himself, as if this had been nothing but a piece of bizarre conceit.

One might even say that its own pride, its own form of stoical ataraxy, consists in maintaining this hard won *self-contempt* of man as his ultimate and most serious claim to self-respect.... Is this really *to work against* the ascetic ideal?"; Friedrich Nietzsche, *Genealogy of Morals*, trans. Walter Kaufmann (New York: Vintage, 1967), sec. 25.

8. "A method of purification: to pray to God, not only in secret as far as men are concerned, but with the thought that God does not exist"; Simone Weil, *Gravity and Grace*, trans. Emma Crawford and Marion von der Ruhr (New York: Routledge, 2002), 20.

INDEX

abortion, as a right, 45
  and dehumanization, 86
  question of the person, 84
Abraham
  and Isaac, 227
  yielded to divine command, 230
Adams, Robert Merrihew, 109
Adorno, Theodor, 184, 283
Altanskaya, Zina (Zinaida), 264
apocalypse
  of the person, 2
  political, 137
  without apocalypse, 169, 219
Aquinas, Thomas, St., 182, 317
Aristotle, 93, 97, 149, 170, 174, 182, 189, 196, 209, 292, 308, 322
  analysis of existence, 202
  Metaphysics, 202, 204
art
  emanates from truth, 25, 238, 243
  and history, 254, 257, 265, 269
  transcendence, 184
artists, love their creations, 19
atheism, in name of God, 64
autonomy, 129

Bacon, Francis, 133
Barth, Karl, 112
beauty, prior to being, 209
being
  and hope, 317
  and naming, 149
  never revealed, 166
  only in man disclosed, 166, 218, 233
  opening of, 164
  prior to thinking, 154
  Sein and *Dasein*, 217
Benedict XVI (Joseph Ratzinger), 184
  Caritas in veritate, 279
  Deus caritas est, 274
  Lumen fidei, 284
  Regensburg Address, 271
  relation as primordial, 273
  Spe salvi, 276
  theological personalism, 270
Bergson, Henri, 141
Berlin, Isaiah, 40
Blumenberg, Hans, 144
Bodin, Jean, 34, 141
  Heptaplomeres, 104

Index

Brunner, Emil, 112
Buber, Martin, 17
Burke, Edmund, 65, 311

Camus, Albert, 187
Cassirer, Ernst, 153
Cervantes, Miguel de, 20
children, loved before they are
    known, 86
Christ
    death without dignity, 132
    encounter with the whole person, 287
    question to Peter, 23
Christianity
    in moral life, 190
    opening of the person, 98
    as revolution, 268
Coleridge, Thomas, 17–18
common good, 89
    of persons, 90
    possessing us, 97
    service to, not comprehended, 94
communication, possible and impossible, 221, 321
conciliarism, 126
consciousness, and the brain, 204, 298

Darwin, Charles, 296
Dawkins, Richard, 294
Dennett, Daniel, 294
Derrida, Jacques, 88, 139, 146, 149, 175
    différance, 59, 171, 221
    incapacity of language, 171
    and Kierkegaard, 220
    nothing outside text, 174
    religion without religion, 172
Descartes, René, 16, 24, 146, 195, 216
dignity, 81, 188
    cannot be lost, 132
    framework of rights, 124, 127
    as giving whole self, 134
    guarding inwardness, 128, 135
    and indignity, 129
    law must invoke, 127
    in rights resplendent, 136
    transcending status, 124
Dostoevsky, Fyodor, 100, 277, 279
    polyphonic novel, 246

economy, 129
    as human ecology, 281, 308
    market as social, 308
    web of hope, 304
Einstein, Albert, 292, 301
embryo, as gift of otherness, 86
epic, 244, 253
    and history, 255, 258, 259, 264
epistemology, and metaphysics, 147, 158
Ericson, Edward, 247
eros and *agápe*, 275
eschatology
    horizon of existence, 123, 176, 276
    of dignity, 133
    hope being, 277
    of the person, 88
evil, 267
existence as the person, 17, 61, 177

faith
    as certainty, 286
    as community, 289
    as heart knowledge, 132
    held by faith, 108, 284, 301
    paradox of, 216
    transcendence, 184
    as trust, 285
family
    human family, 281
    as real unity of persons, 95
fetus
    only known through inwardness, 85
    as purely other, 86
Finnis, John, 197, 203

freedom
  only perspective of thought, 240
  as paradox, 58
  structured by obligation, 315
  supererogatory, 184, 228
French Revolution, 237
friendship, 97

God
  contains his being, 89
  in every quest, 287
  as giving self away, 213
  guarantee of mutuality, 229
  horizon of thought, 15, 191, 216
  known as person, 16
  relationship as horizon of person, 226, 274
  we are outside of, 173
Goethe, on Kant, 16
good
  and evil before time, 100
  prior to being, 190, 209
Gregory, Eric, 103

Habermas, Jürgen, 107, 125, 270
Havel, Václav, 25–26, 55
Hawking, Stephen, 294, 302
Hayek, Friedrich, 42
Hegel, G. W. F., 61, 94, 96, 142, 143, 144, 145, 182, 193, 260, 309
  ideal within real, 313
  and Kierkegaard, 178
  on the person as transcendence, 15
  Philosophy of Right, 94
  turn toward existence, 159
Heidegger, Martin, 17, 106, 143, 146, 149, 163, 175, 182, 187, 191, 207, 215
  Being and Time, 164
  betrayal of own intuition, 166, 218
  centrality, 164
  failure of man or philosophy, 168
  "ontological difference," 165, 192

  points toward the person, 208
  thinking within being, 218
  Vom Ereignis (*Contributions to Philosophy*), 218
Herodotus, 257
Hindemith, Paul, 26
history
  events that constitute, not in history, 202, 252
  goal unreachable, 161
  horizon of existence, 145, 240, 255
  memorable, 258
  moral epiphanies, 247, 249, 265
  new beginning, 265
  opened through mutuality, 214
  perspective of action within, 242, 244, 250
  presupposes freedom, 56, 238, 240
  and providence, 261
  redemptive axis, 252, 262
  speaks for itself, 245, 259
  and truth, 238
Hobbes, Thomas
  and consent, 319
  and Leviathan, 70
  and modern self, 8–9
Hölderlin, Friedrich, 21
Homer, 258
hope
  can be forgotten, 309
  cannot lose, 323
  gift of being, 317, 320
  has reached goal, 303
  not optimism, 318
  principle and justification, 316
Horkheimer, Max, 184, 283
Husserl, Edmund, 148, 154

idealism, 158
identity, 206
individual
  exceeds universal, 221
  and God relationship, 216, 221

individual (*cont.*)
   and the person, 82, 232
   and the whole, 96, 307
   See also person
interiority, 196
   anchored in the transcendent, 210, 216, 228, 274
   of God, 229
I-Thou versus I-It, 24

Jaspers, Karl, 17, 215
John Paul II, 81, 90, 270
   Fides et ratio, 185, 271
Joyce, James, 19
judgment, 292
justice, enacted or constructed, 109

Kant, Immanuel, 61, 100, 109, 128, 129, 142, 146, 148, 154, 157, 207, 210, 228, 300
   Critique of Judgement, 147, 158
   Critique of Practical Reason, 116, 147
   Critique of Pure Reason, 147
   dignity of the person, 127, 158, 188, 283
   on duty as imprescriptible, 14, 108, 190
   Groundwork, 117
   and Kierkegaard, 177
   persons as ends-in-themselves, 35
   postulates, 15, 116, 147, 157, 187
   Religion Within the Boundaries of Reason Alone, 117
   room for faith, 120
Karamazov, Ivan, 183
Katkov, George, 257
Kelsen, Hans, 273
Kierkegaard, Søren, 22, 24, 55, 57, 67, 151, 210, 318
   author as text, 221, 227
   Either/Or, 222, 223
   establishes priority of the person, 152
   exemplar of modern philosophic revolution, 178, 215
   Fear and Trembling, 227
   first postmodern, 162
   Judge William and Seducer, 8, 222
   Stages on Life's Way, 223
   transacting eternal, 175
   Upbuilding Discourses, 226
Klimoff, Alexis, 247
Kuhn, Thomas, 297

law, acknowledges its insufficiency, 135
Lazhenitsyn, Sanya, 262
Lenin, Vladimir, 254, 263, 268
Levinas, Emmanuel, 17, 22, 85, 88, 150, 175
   face of the other, 219
   otherwise than being, 170
   priority of ethics to ontology, 169, 220
liberal democracy, 145
   capable of growth of soul, 47, 261
   Christian refraction of politics, 49, 98, 107
   conservative critique of, 30
   crisis as its condition, 73
   crisis of, 54, 65, 66, 92
   deepening mystery, 65, 73
   durability, 31
   founding as its work, 57, 68
   language of paradox, 99
   minimum consensus, 32
   pointing toward transcendent mystery, 50
   prior community, 319
   progressive critique of, 30
liberal principles
   as authoritative, 36, 114, 193
   dependence on spiritual traditions, 37, 261
   features, 48–51
   futility of justification, 40, 91
   inarticulate depth, 41
   liberty versus equality, 56

in Mill's evocation, 42
nightmare of instrumentalization, 76
notion of the person, 320
not metaphysical, 108
plural conceptions of good, 110
self-evidence, 54
stability and instability of, 39
and the term "liberal," 65
tied to moral universe, 43, 45
Lincoln, Abraham, 44, 56, 66, 69, 101
Locke, John, 96
  Essay Concerning Human Understanding, 53
  Letter on Toleration, 32
  On the Reasonableness of Christianity, 54
  Paraphrase and Notes on the Epistles of St. Paul, 54
  substance of person at stake, 10–11
  Two Treatises of Government, 53
Lonergan, Bernard, 197, 201, 203
love
  beyond reasons, 76, 96
  cannot lose, 229
  civilization of, 280
  as generative, 20
  as giving self, 60, 276
  life of persons, 274
  looks to eternal, 275
  opens community in time, 285
  as path to truth, 287, 288
  reality as, 285
luminosity, 74, 142, 144, 260, 279
  intentionality and, 165
  unfolding of existence, 171, 284

MacIntyre, Alasdair, 42
Maritain, Jacques, on "whole of wholes," 5, 68, 79f
  The Person and the Common Good, 81
marriage, 128, 176, 222, 229

Marx, Karl, 103, 306
  will to transform reality, 161
Mary, response through angel, 26, 279
metaphysics
  beyond metaphysics, 163
  condition of possibility, 210
  to ethics, 190, 223
  materialist paradigm, 297
  nonobjective, 149, 151
  and the person, 14, 222, 225
  of presence, 168
  of relation, 281
  return, 185
  yield to eschatology, 130, 278
metaxu, 197, 208
Mill, John Stuart, 40, 42
mind, and substance, 205
modernity
  legitimacy, 144
  negative assessment, 141
  philosophic revolution, 146, 156, 191
  as search for the self, 1
  spiritual aspiration, 219, 277
  tragic-comic, 142
morality
  action outside of time, 210
  provides time, 62
Mounier, Emmanuel, 81
myth, 160

Nagel, Thomas, 21, 24–25, 103
natural law, 271
Newman, John Henry, 18
Nietzsche, Friedrich, 56, 143, 148, 157, 269, 275, 301
  faith of, 163, 284
  and nihilism, 183, 185, 227
  seizing existence on the run, 163
  noumenon versus *phenomenon*, 158
nous
  and *logos*, 98, 189, 196
  and *peras*, 202
Nygren, Anders, 112

Oakeshott, Michael, 29, 40, 41, 42
  enterprise association versus enterprise association, 92
  nation-state as contradiction, 91
obligation
  more ancient than knowledge, 20
  prior to freedom, 314
ontology, primordiality, 148
other, the
  as irreducible, 88
  prior to name, 88
ousia, 185, 277

Parmenides, on thinking and being, 16, 217
participation
  condition of possibility of knowing, 204
  methexis, metalepsis, 200
Pascal, Blaise, 292
person, the
  acting person, 81, 174
  and being, 147
  beyond being, 21, 85, 130, 135, 206, 208, 219, 232, 316
  cannot be killed, 90, 131
  cannot name, 84, 150, 220
  dignity heightened, 35, 49, 282
  as ends-in-themselves, 18, 62, 280
  exceeds definition, 19, 131
  flash of transcendence, 22, 89, 112, 124, 176, 192, 212, 265, 279
  as gift, 60, 69, 89, 223, 280
  God relationship as core, 226, 231, 233
  growth of the soul, 46
  versus individual, 82
  multitude in one person, 10
  as *nous*, 2, 112
  only glimpsed, 21, 83
  paradox of freedom, 58, 62, 67
  as part able to conceive the whole, 3, 15, 34, 80, 214, 233
  as potency and act, 209, 317
  primacy of the person prior to theory, 6, 63
  prior to all that separates, 12, 115, 315
  prior to consciousness, 154
  prior to said, 17, 39, 59, 82
  related to as invisible, 131
  soul, 222, 223
  as substance, 205
  versus substance, 150, 273, 277
  as transcendental, 20, 68, 73
  transcending selves in covenant, 9, 96, 100, 222
  unconditional respect toward, 72, 85
  vocation of love, 290
  as wholes, 68, 223
  yes, as epiphany of, 26, 279
persona, 192
personalism
  incomplete development, 80
  inconclusive, 82
  and Kierkegaard, 225
  linguistic overhaul needed, 18, 20
  linguistic shift required, 83
Pfau, Thomas, 13, 16–18
philosophy
  in act, not in theory, 174
  with art and faith, 184
  assumes responsibility, 179
  becomes historical, 159
  collaborative, 182
  need to philosophize about, 157
  obligation of extending, 164
  reflection on being, 182
  response to crisis, 199
  and theology, 185
Pipes, Richard, 257
Plato, 22, 72, 149, 174, 185, 189, 197, 208, 210, 227, 278, 312, 317
  glimpse beyond knowledge, 207
political community
  carried within, 92, 93, 100
  eternal contract, 311
  historical existence, 310, 312, 316

as inward, 113
and love, 96
mutual self-giving, 99, 312, 313, 321
preserves hope, 318
prior to need and interest, 321
reciprocal, 96
spirit of hope apprehended, 310
political theory, 139
politics
    cannot await theory, 124, 192
    democracy as eschatological, 72, 75, 99
    founding community, 68, 101, 311
    gratuitous, 280, 290
    power of the powerless, 70
    priority of, 306
    shortsighted pragmatism, 70
    taking action, 307
    truth of economics, 309
primacy of the practical, 125
property, social recognition, 307
prosōpon versus *hypostasis*, 23, 212, 232

Rawls, John, 18, 25, 30, 42, 54
    A Brief Inquiry into the Meaning of Sin and Faith, 103
    crisis of faith, 105
    God as seal of personal, 115
    Justice as Fairness, 113
    "Justice as Fairness: Political Not Metaphysical," 108
    metaphysics of practice, 118
    personalism of, 109, 121
    persons, not nature, 112
    political constructivism, 109
    Political Liberalism, 111
    practical before theoretical, 120
    reasonable faith, 116, 118
    A Theory of Justice, 106
reason, secular, 103, 109, 271
    continuous with reality, 158, 217
    instrumental and substantive, 156, 282
    as practical reason, 213
    primacy of practical, 159, 190
    saved by revelation, 175
    transcendent imperative, 116
Reformation, 197
relation
    as community, 288
    intangibility of, 88
    as unconditioned, 85
    underpinned by faith, 286
religion
    liberty as basis of rights, 11
    and metaphysics, 227
repentance, 265
responsibility
    priority of the other, 87, 170
    responsible for, 87
    structures our relationship to reality, 20, 209, 260, 265
    unconditional, 229
    unique call of, 227
revelation
    as condition of time, 153
    as God, 231
    horizon of transcendence, 172
    of what cannot be revealed, 150
right
    cannot be subjective, 202
    priority of the person, 113, 122
    prior to good, 30, 43, 77, 108, 110
rights
    across generations, 75
    as authoritative intimations, 33, 59, 75
    beyond being, 12
    boundary of what can be thought, 46, 59, 80, 114, 125, 273
    cannot be alienated, 4, 126
    centrality of religious liberty, 272
    core of democratic idea, 74
    and dissidents, 76
    entailed within discourse, 125
    as infinity of the person, 84, 272
    inviolability, 66, 77, 90
    mutuality of, 5, 18, 113, 125

rights (*cont.*)
  resonance of Christian evocation, 34, 271
  rights-talk, 29, 43
  as spiritual arc, 8
  surpassed by language of person, 12
  vulnerability of, 39
  when under threat, 45
Rilke, Rainer Maria, 26
Rorty, Richard, 31, 41, 222
Rousseau, Jean-Jacques, 96
Russian Revolution, 237, 257, 259, 267

Saint-Exupéry, Antoine de, 19
Sakharov, Andrei, 55
Salgado, Sebastião, 19
Samsonov, Aleksandr, 250, 252, 253
Sartre, Jean-Paul, 174
Scheler, Max, 81, 112
  existence escapes reflection, 160
Schelling, F. W. J., 141
  aphorisms, 16
  primacy of existential disclosure, 161
Schleiermacher, Friedrich
  coined "personalism," 15
Schütz, Alfred, 149
science
  absolute assertion of probability, 295
  incapable of comprehending itself, 291
  as mind of God, 296
  mystery of its possibility, 293
  and scientism, 297
  as self-transcendence, 302
secular age
  impossible longing, 277
  as "postsecular," 271
self
  to become the infinite, 229
  cannot be known, 13, 206

Cartesian subject, 146, 195
  displaced by gaze of the other, 19, 170
  gained in self-giving, 223, 228
  giving self as unending, 89, 98
  sets itself aside, 211, 315
Socrates, 22, 197, 293
Solzhenitsyn, Aleksandr, 19
  Apricot Jam and Other Stories, 24
  August 1914, 250
  Gulag Archipelago, 248, 258
  juxtapositional form, 244, 247
  knots, 245, 250
  "Matryona's House," 70
  November 1916, 263
  The Red Wheel, 237, 244, 257, 265
Spaemann, Robert, 18
St. Ambrose, 277
St. Augustine
  first existentialist, 173
  interior turn, 23, 58, 60, 83
Stolypin, Pyotr, 254, 260
St. Paul, conflict in will, 23
Strauss, Leo, 197, 199, 203
  Natural Right and History, 200
subject, 205
  must be a person, 212
  not a thing, 211, 225
  and subjectivism, 197
  transcends itself, 210
suffering, 132

technology
  defense of the person, 282
  and disclosure of being, 156
  and mastery, 155
  no longer reigning, 165
teleology, 231
thinking
  as *anamnesis*, 208
  and being, 148, 197, 207
  cannot contain itself, 89
  as freedom, 187
  within hope, 322

insignificance of, 295
neither subjective nor objective, 299
saved from answers and liberated to questions, 64
about thinking, 196, 197, 292
thinking lays hold of itself in, 204
as transcendent perspective, 210, 294, 300
Thucydides, 257
Tierney, Brian
  The Idea of Natural Rights, 126
Tinder, Glenn, 30, 139
Tocqueville, Alexis de, 40, 41, 46, 55, 76
  on enlargement of heart, 93
toleration, 104
Tolstoy, Leo, 237, 243, 262
  elevation of fate, 240
  War and Peace, 239
transcendent
  as horizon, 190
  makes subjectivity possible, 213
  as transcendent, 191, 284
transparence, 187
  of being as person, 207
truth
  deeper than lie, 207, 265
  and ideology, 254
  limit of thinking, 186
  as movement of faith, 159, 284, 286

prior to being, 209
prior to experience, 150, 152, 201
and subjectivism, 200

universal humanity, 141
UN Universal Declaration, 127, 272

Vico, Giambattista, 141
Vitoria, Francisco de, 126
Voegelin, Eric, 139, 188, 197, 199, 203, 206, 208
  "Debate and Existence," 201
  The Ecumenic Age, 142
  experience, 153
  The History of Political Ideas, 142, 153
  In Search of Order, 141, 142, 153
  intentionality and luminosity, 148
  The New Science of Politics, 200
  priority of the person to consciousness, 154
  "reality-experience-symbol," 149
  "Reason: The Classic Experience," 201
  theoretical contribution, 145
Vorotyntsev, Georgi, 247, 253, 264

Weber, Max, 139, 187
Whitman, Walt, 18
William of Ockham, 126
Wittgenstein, Ludwig, 48, 204
Wojtyla, Karol, 18

DAVID WALSH
is professor of politics at the Catholic University of America. He is the author and editor of a number of books, including *Politics of the Person as the Politics of Being* (University of Notre Dame Press, 2015).